PROFILE
000
STUDIO LOUD in SCHOOL

"It's pizza! It's burning! It's the toaster oven! It's *saba* (mackerel)! It's *mizutaki* (water-simmered stew)! It's the hot pot! It's the mushroom special! It's humming through the nose! It's shrimp & crab *shonen*! It's *musse*! It's *Studio Loud in Schooooool!*"

–Kazushi Hagiwara, 1989

Volume 4

STORY & ART by: Kazushi Hagiwara

English Adaptation	Fred Burke
Translator	Kaori Kawakubo Inoue
Touch-up & Lettering	Susan Daigle-Leach
Cover Design & Graphics	Yuki Ameda
Layout	Sean Lee & Walden Wong
Senior Editor	Jason Thompson
Managing Editor	Annette Roman
Senior V.P. of Editorial	Hyoe Narita
Director of Licensing & Acquisitions	Rika Inouye
V.P. of Marketing	Liza Coppola
Senior V.P. of Sales & Marketing	Rick Bauer
V.P. of Strategic Development	Yumi Hoashi
Publisher	Seiji Horibuchi

Kazushi Hagiwara's bilingual webpage: **http://www01.vaio.ne.jp/BASTA/**

This graphic novel contains the last one-third of the monthly comic BASTARD!! #10, as well as #11-13 in their entirety.

Printed in Canada.

Published by
VIZ, LLC
P.O. Box 77010
San Francisco, CA
94107

www.viz.com

VIZ

Volume 4

暗黒の破壊神 バスタード
BASTARD!!
Heavy Metal Dark Fantasy

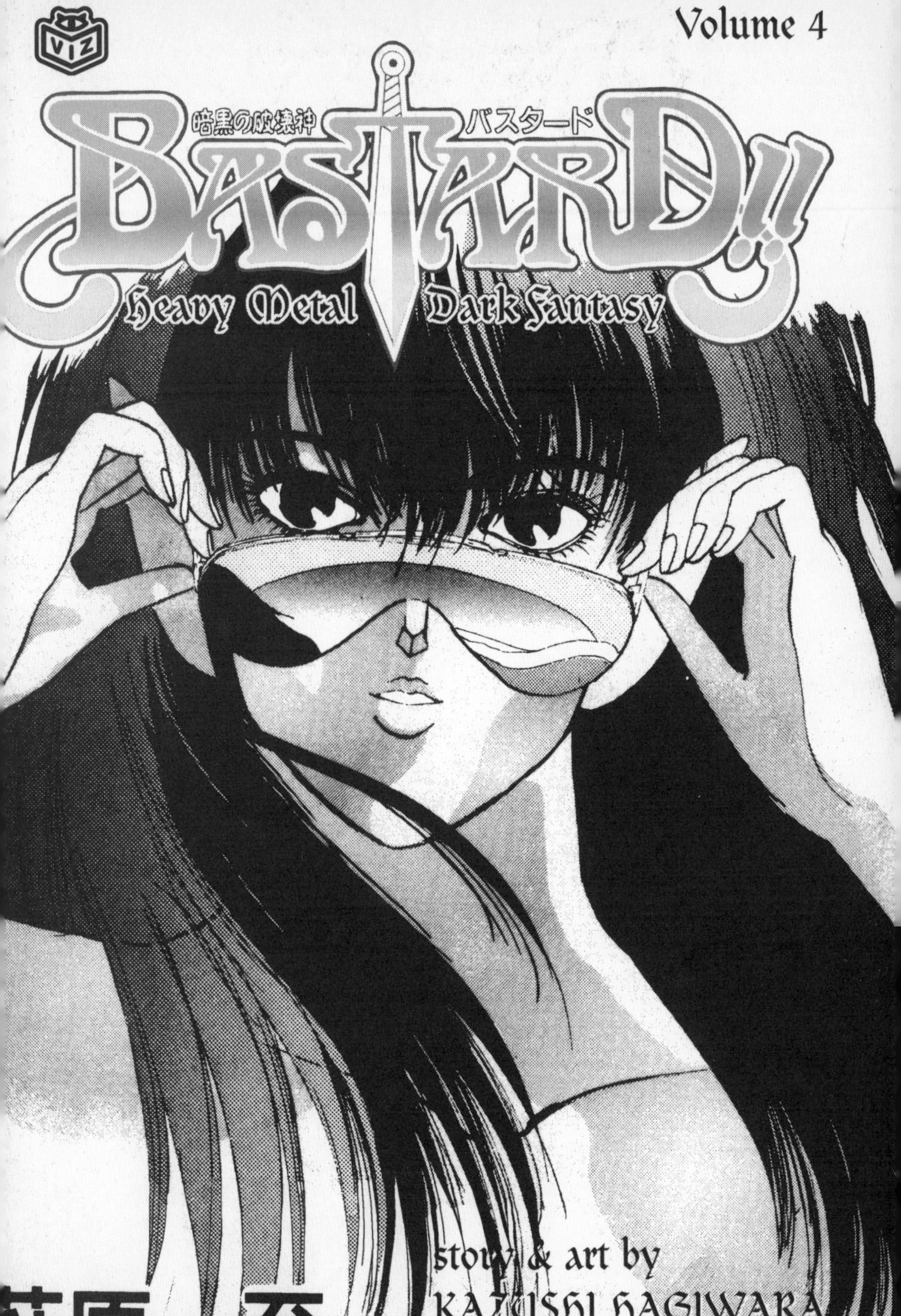

story & art by

萩原一至

KAZUSHI HAGIWARA

Besieged by the dark armies of the so-called Four Divine Kings, the desperate defenders of Metallicana turned to a legend that a virgin's kiss might awaken Dark Schneider, an ancient wizard sealed within the body of a 14-year-old boy. Awakened by the kiss of the boy's adopted sister Tia Noto Yoko, the evil Dark Schneider turned out to be little better than the invaders—they're his own former cohorts!—but agrees to help Metallicana out of loyalty to Yoko. When Dark Schneider convinces one of the invaders, Ninja Master Gara, to defect to his side, the remaining Divine Kings fear that Arshes Nei, D.S.'s former lover, will be next. To prove her loyalty, Nei agrees to undergo the "Blue Nail Curse of the Accused"...forcing her to kill D.S. or be turned into a toad!

The CAST

Dark Schneider
Class: *Wizard* • **Race:** *Human*
Age: *About 400* • **Alignment:** *Chaotic Evil (with neutral tendencies)*
A mighty magic user, lecherous and cruel, also known as the "lord of the fiery explosion" or "D.S." for short. Some say he is as old as the world itself. Fifteen years ago, in his last attempt at world domination, he was killed by the legendary Dragon Knight and his soul was bound in the body of an infant.

Ninja Master Gara
Class: *Fighter/Ninja* • **Race:** *Human*
Age: *Unknown* • **Alignment:** *Neutral*
A defector from the Four Divine Kings, he now hangs out with Dark Schneider again, just like old times. A master of many esoteric techniques, Gara leads an army of 2,000 ninja, and also possesses the Murasame Blade, the Sword of Mystery.

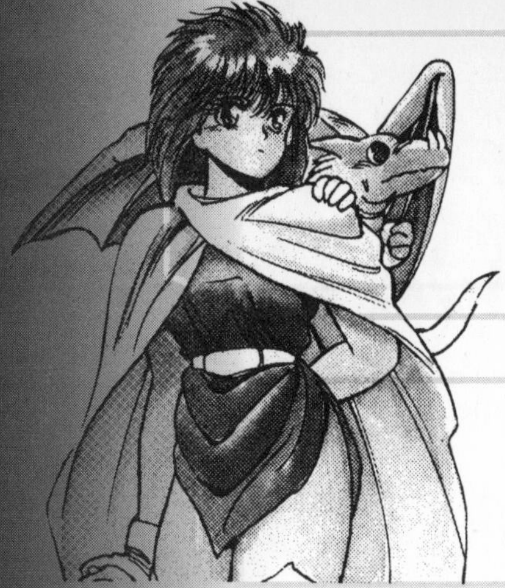

Tia Noto Yoko

Class: *Cleric (White Magic)*
Race: *Human* • **Age:** *15*
Alignment: *Lawful Good*
Daughter of Geo Noto Soto, high priest of Metallicana, whose magic bound D.S. in her step-brother Lucien's body. She still thinks of D.S. as her little brother.

Lars

Class: *Fighter* • **Race:** *Dragon*
Age: *Unknown* • **Alignment:** *Neutral Good*
A baby dragon (off-white in color) with the ability to speak telepathically to Dark Schneider. They seem to have some mysterious connection.

Sean Ari

Class: *Wizard* • **Race:** *Human*
Age: *About 18* • **Alignment:** *Neutral*
One of Arshes Nei's three sorcerer generals. A young adept in talismanic magic, she is able to summon monsters using magic *o-fuda* (spells written on slips of paper). She was sent by Arshes Nei to kill Dark Schneider, but fell in love with him instead.

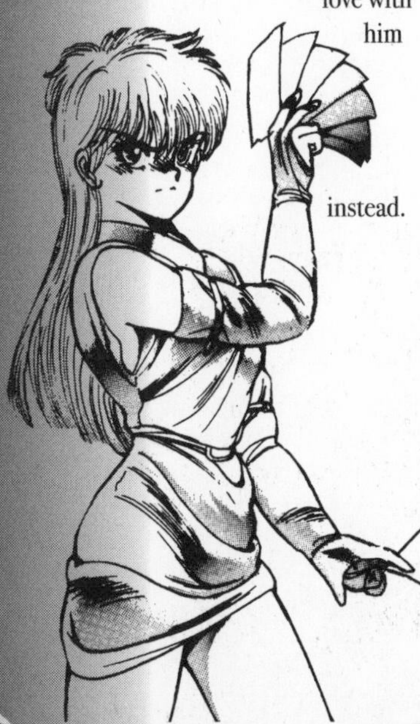

Arshes Nei

Class: *Fighter/Wizard*
Race: *Half-Dark Elf*
Age: *About 117*
Alignment: *Lawful Evil*
One of the Four Divine Kings, this half-elf spellcaster commands a regiment of the Dark Rebel Armies. Over 100 years ago, when she was an orphan, D.S. took her in and raised her as his daughter. (Note: D.S.'s definition of "father-daughter relationships" may not match most people's.)

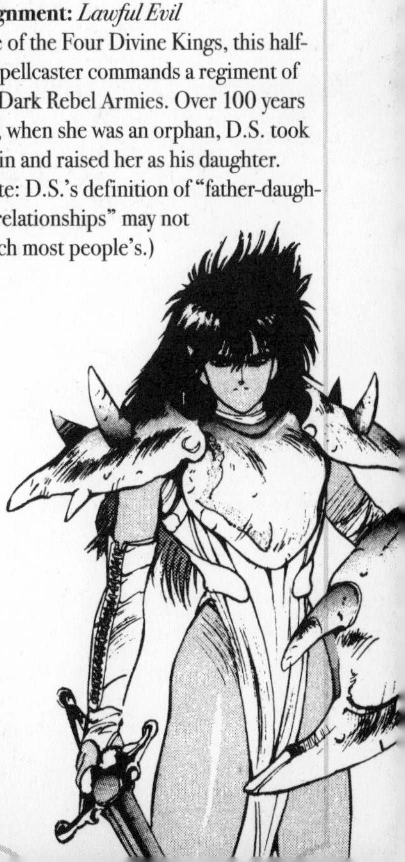

Volume 4

PART 1: THE DARK REBEL ARMIES

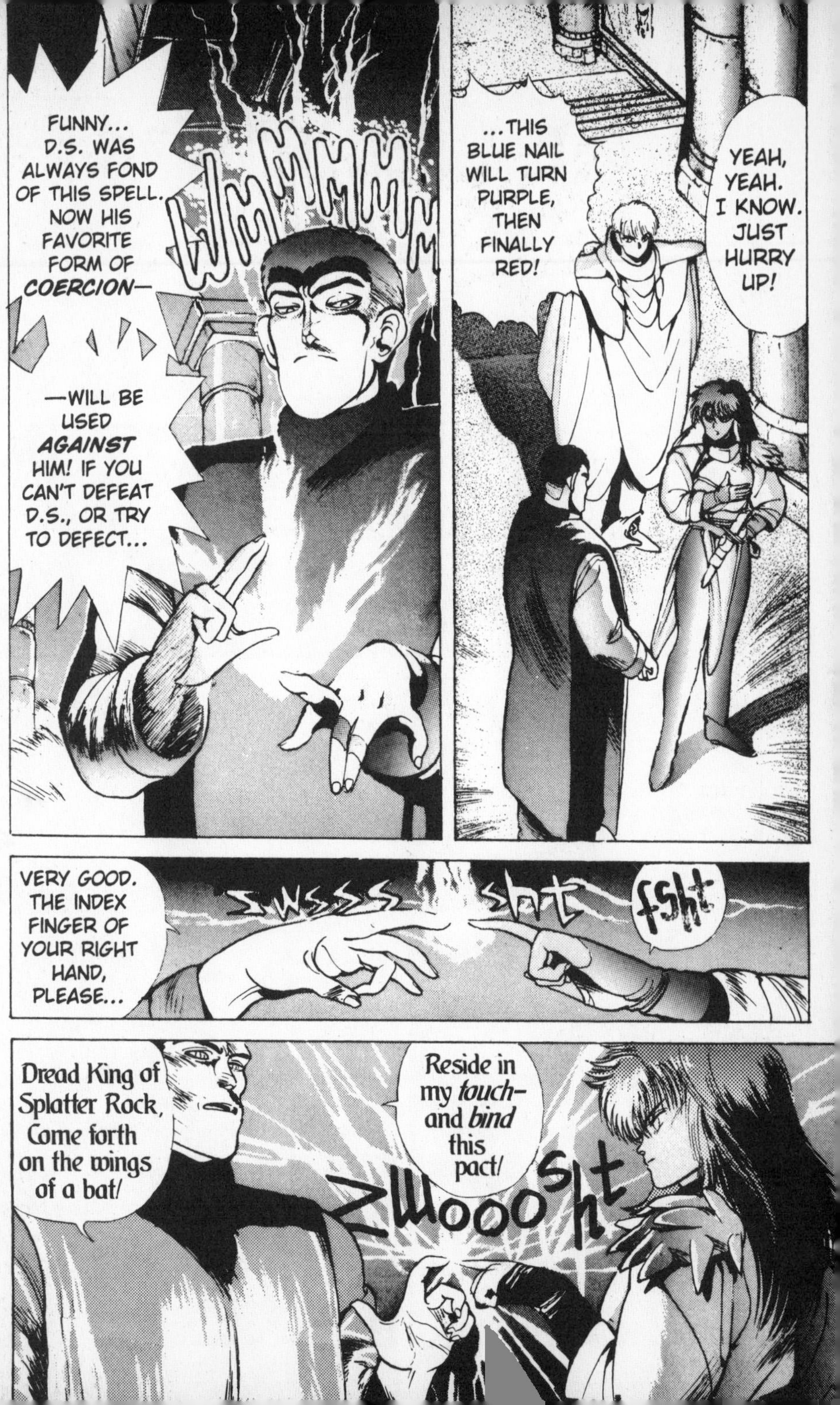
FUNNY... D.S. WAS ALWAYS FOND OF THIS SPELL. NOW HIS FAVORITE FORM OF *COERCION*—
—WILL BE USED *AGAINST* HIM! IF YOU CAN'T DEFEAT D.S., OR TRY TO DEFECT...
...THIS BLUE NAIL WILL TURN PURPLE, THEN FINALLY RED!
YEAH, YEAH. I KNOW. JUST HURRY UP!
VERY GOOD. THE INDEX FINGER OF YOUR RIGHT HAND, PLEASE...
fsht
Dread King of Splatter Rock, Come forth on the wings of a bat!
Reside in my *touch*—and *bind* this pact!
ZWOOOSHT

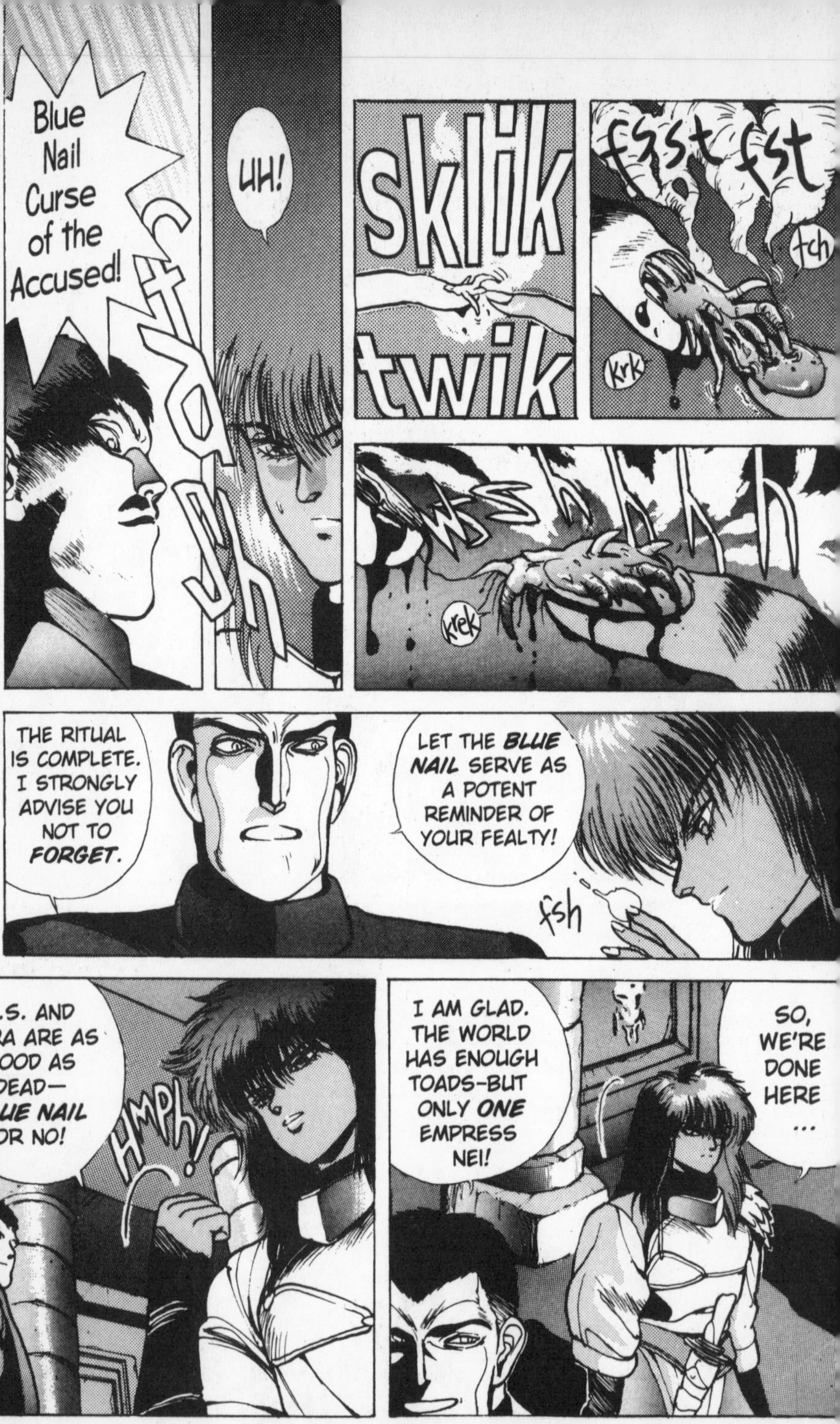
Blue Nail Curse of the Accused!
UH!
sklik
twik
fsst fst
tch
krk
krek
THE RITUAL IS COMPLETE. I STRONGLY ADVISE YOU NOT TO FORGET.
LET THE BLUE NAIL SERVE AS A POTENT REMINDER OF YOUR FEALTY!
fsh
D.S. AND GARA ARE AS GOOD AS DEAD— BLUE NAIL OR NO!
HMPH!
I AM GLAD. THE WORLD HAS ENOUGH TOADS–BUT ONLY ONE EMPRESS NEI!
SO, WE'RE DONE HERE ...

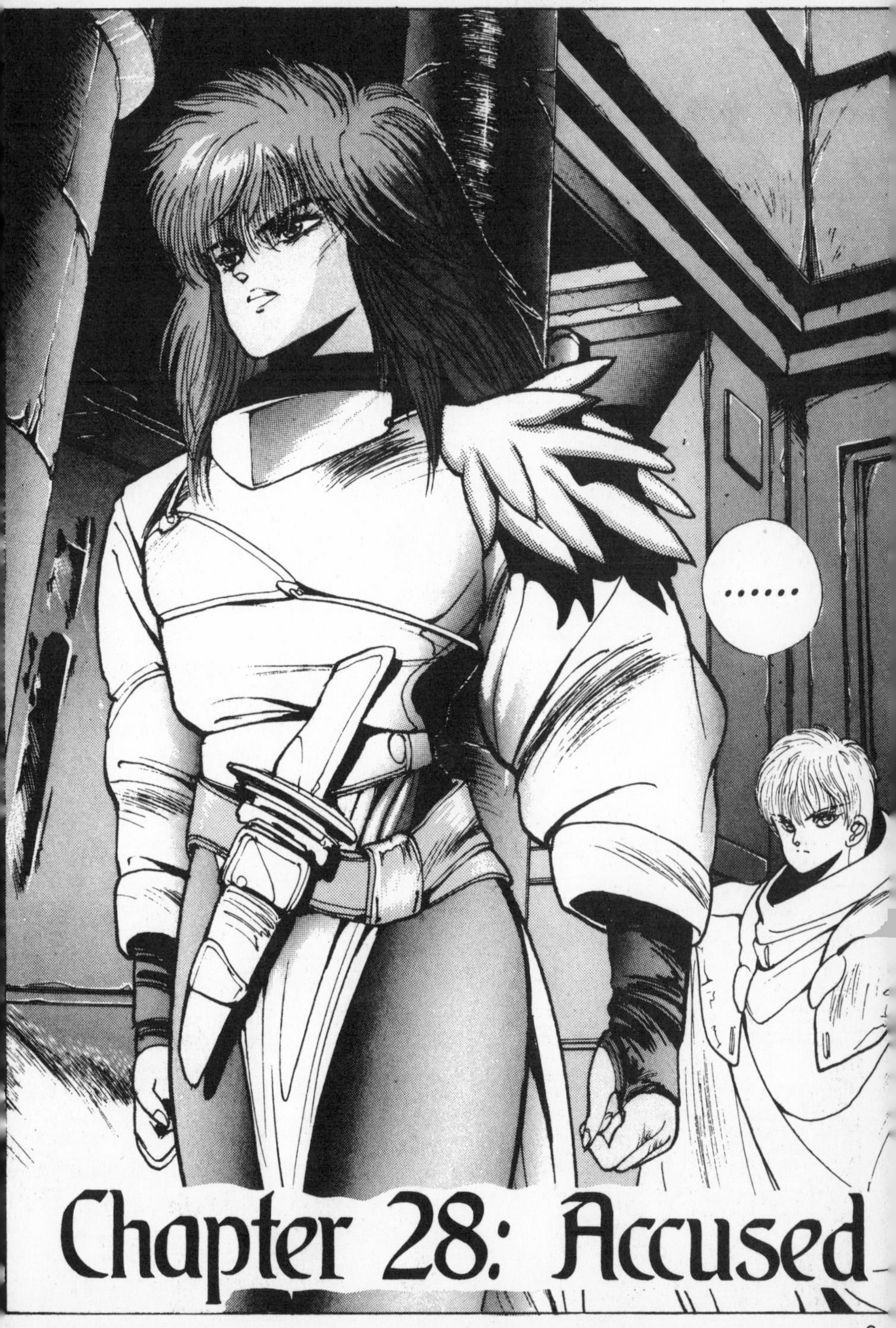
......
Chapter 28: Accused

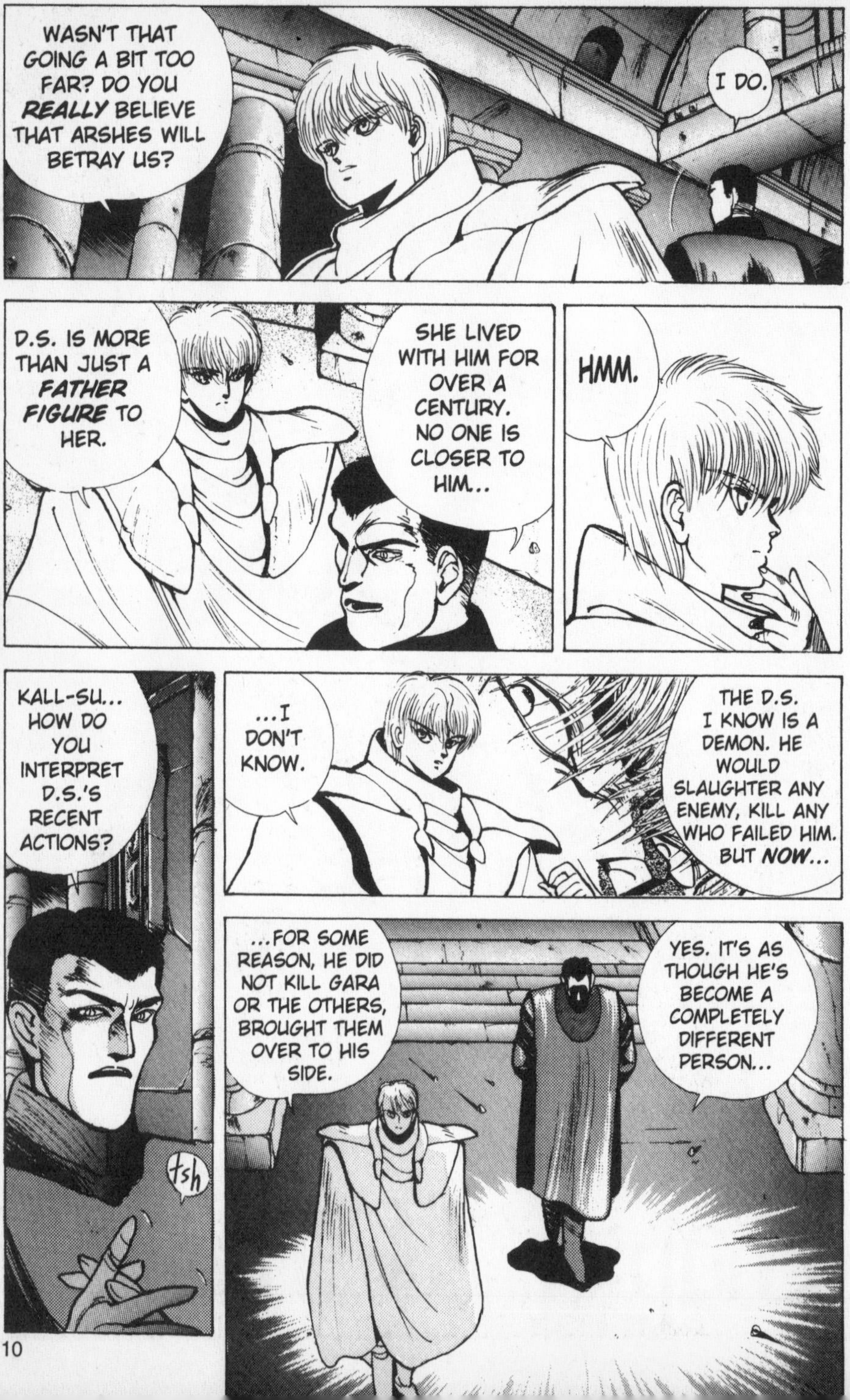
WASN'T THAT GOING A BIT TOO FAR? DO YOU REALLY BELIEVE THAT ARSHES WILL BETRAY US?
I DO.
D.S. IS MORE THAN JUST A FATHER FIGURE TO HER.
SHE LIVED WITH HIM FOR OVER A CENTURY. NO ONE IS CLOSER TO HIM...
HMM.
KALL-SU... HOW DO YOU INTERPRET D.S.'S RECENT ACTIONS?
...I DON'T KNOW.
THE D.S. I KNOW IS A DEMON. HE WOULD SLAUGHTER ANY ENEMY, KILL ANY WHO FAILED HIM. BUT NOW...
tsh
...FOR SOME REASON, HE DID NOT KILL GARA OR THE OTHERS, BROUGHT THEM OVER TO HIS SIDE.
YES. IT'S AS THOUGH HE'S BECOME A COMPLETELY DIFFERENT PERSON...

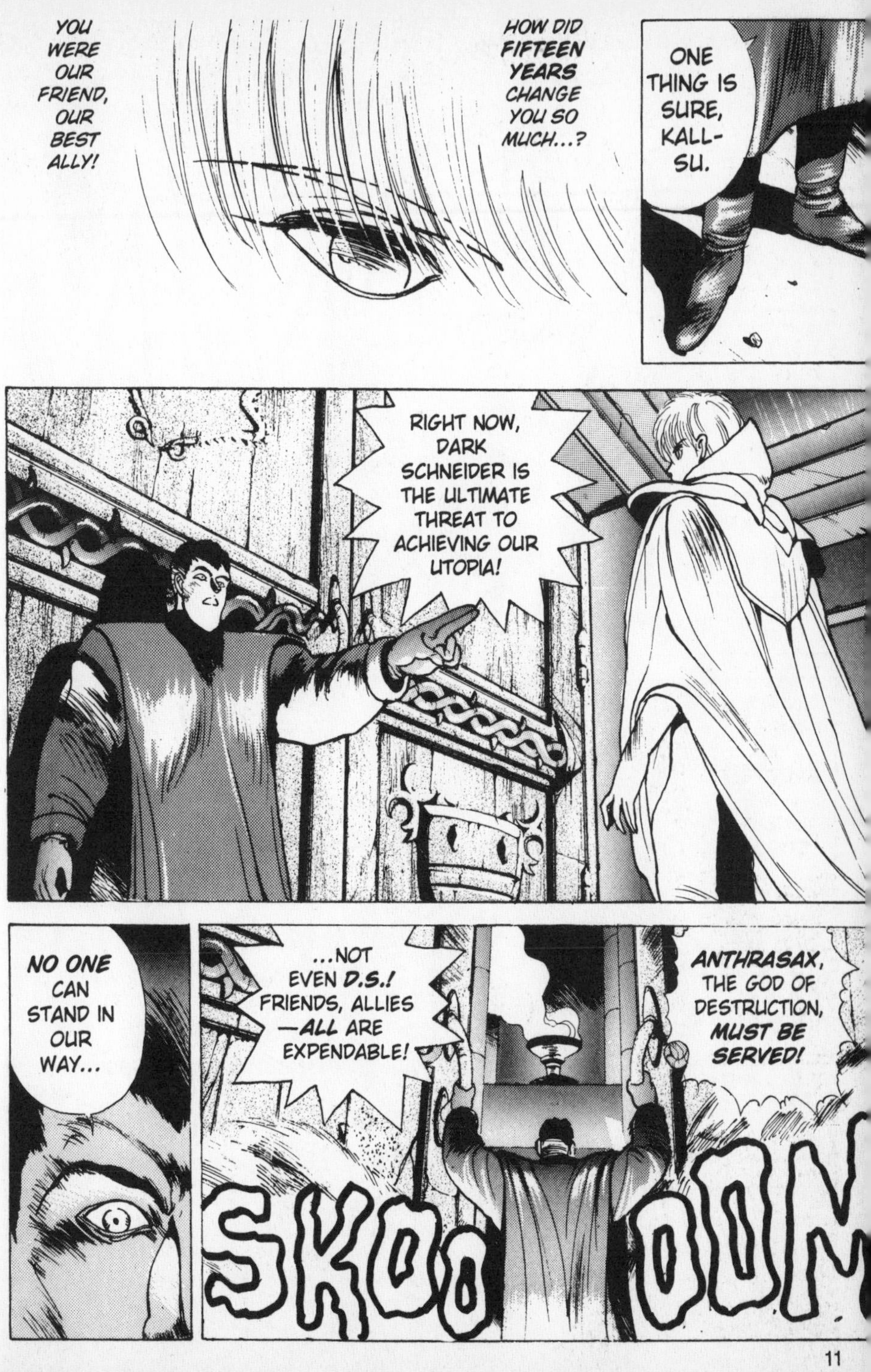
YOU WERE OUR FRIEND, OUR BEST ALLY!
HOW DID FIFTEEN YEARS CHANGE YOU SO MUCH...?
ONE THING IS SURE, KALL-SU.
RIGHT NOW, DARK SCHNEIDER IS THE ULTIMATE THREAT TO ACHIEVING OUR UTOPIA!
NO ONE CAN STAND IN OUR WAY...
...NOT EVEN D.S.! FRIENDS, ALLIES —ALL ARE EXPENDABLE!
ANTHRASAX, THE GOD OF DESTRUCTION, MUST BE SERVED!
SKOOOOM

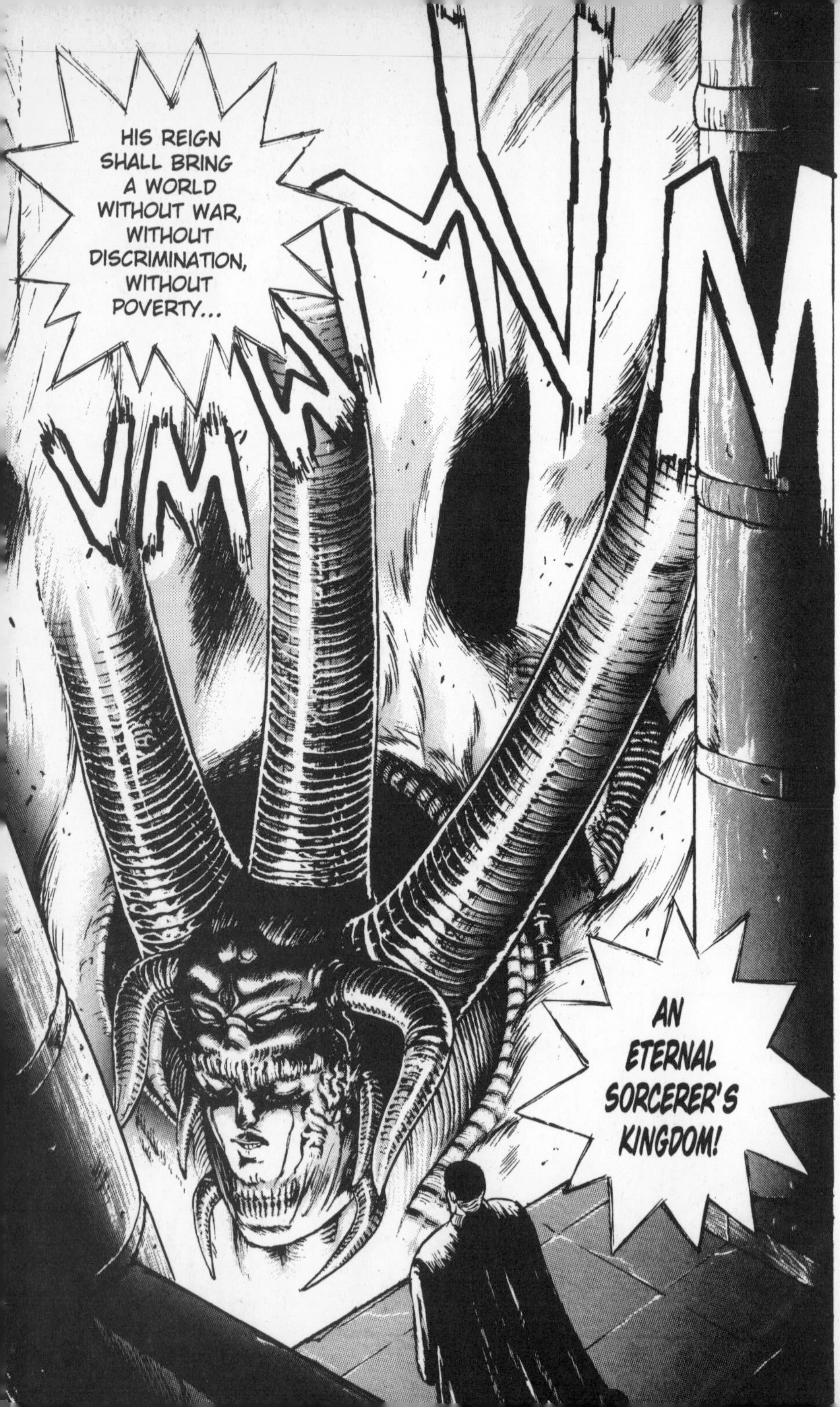
HIS REIGN SHALL BRING A WORLD WITHOUT WAR, WITHOUT DISCRIMINATION, WITHOUT POVERTY...
AN ETERNAL SORCERER'S KINGDOM!

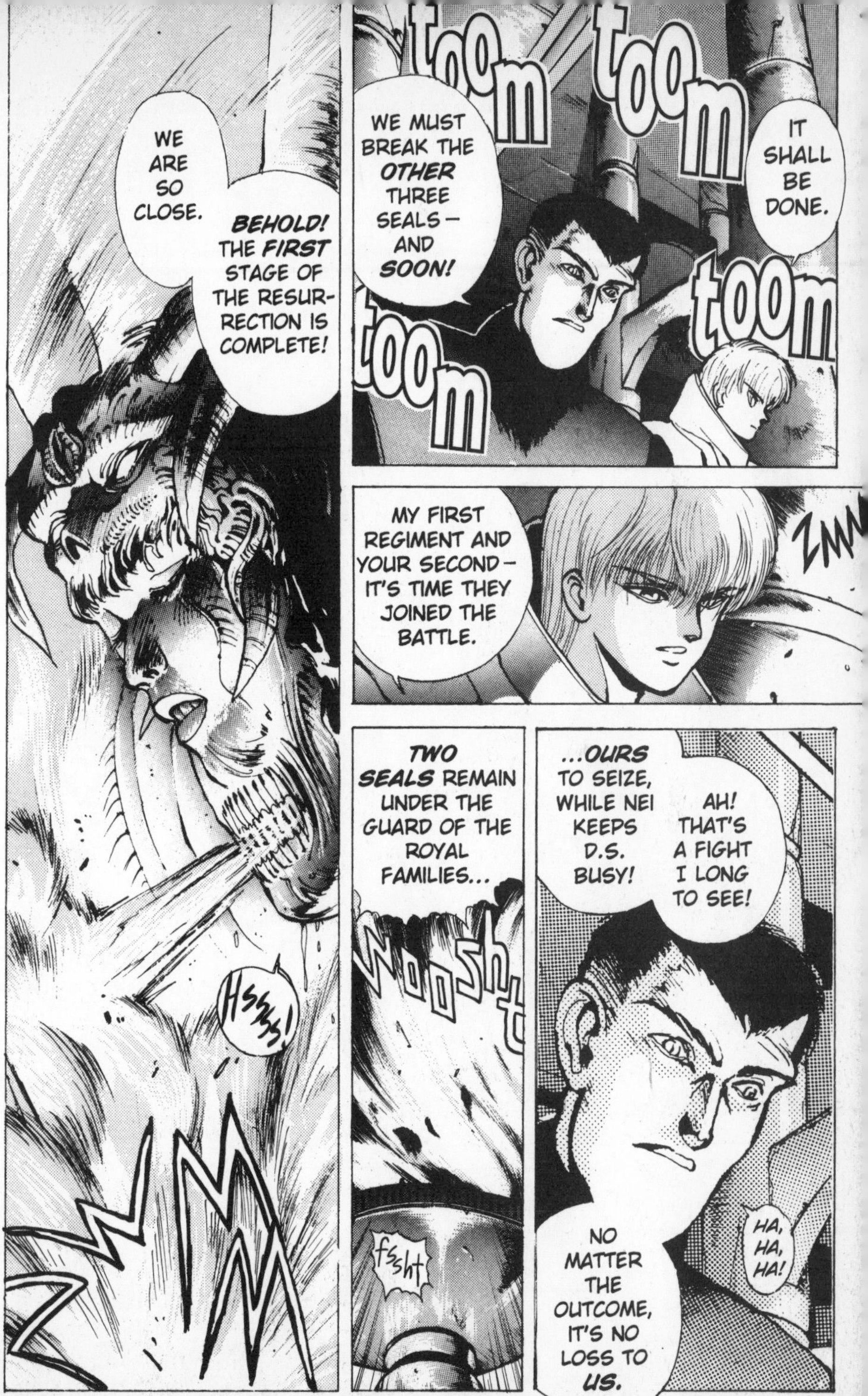
WE ARE SO CLOSE.
BEHOLD! THE FIRST STAGE OF THE RESURRECTION IS COMPLETE!
HSSSS!
TOOM TOOM
WE MUST BREAK THE OTHER THREE SEALS—AND SOON!
IT SHALL BE DONE.
TOOM TOOM
MY FIRST REGIMENT AND YOUR SECOND—IT'S TIME THEY JOINED THE BATTLE.
TWO SEALS REMAIN UNDER THE GUARD OF THE ROYAL FAMILIES...
WOOSHT
FSSHT
...OURS TO SEIZE, WHILE NEI KEEPS D.S. BUSY!
AH! THAT'S A FIGHT I LONG TO SEE!
NO MATTER THE OUTCOME, IT'S NO LOSS TO US.
HA, HA, HA!

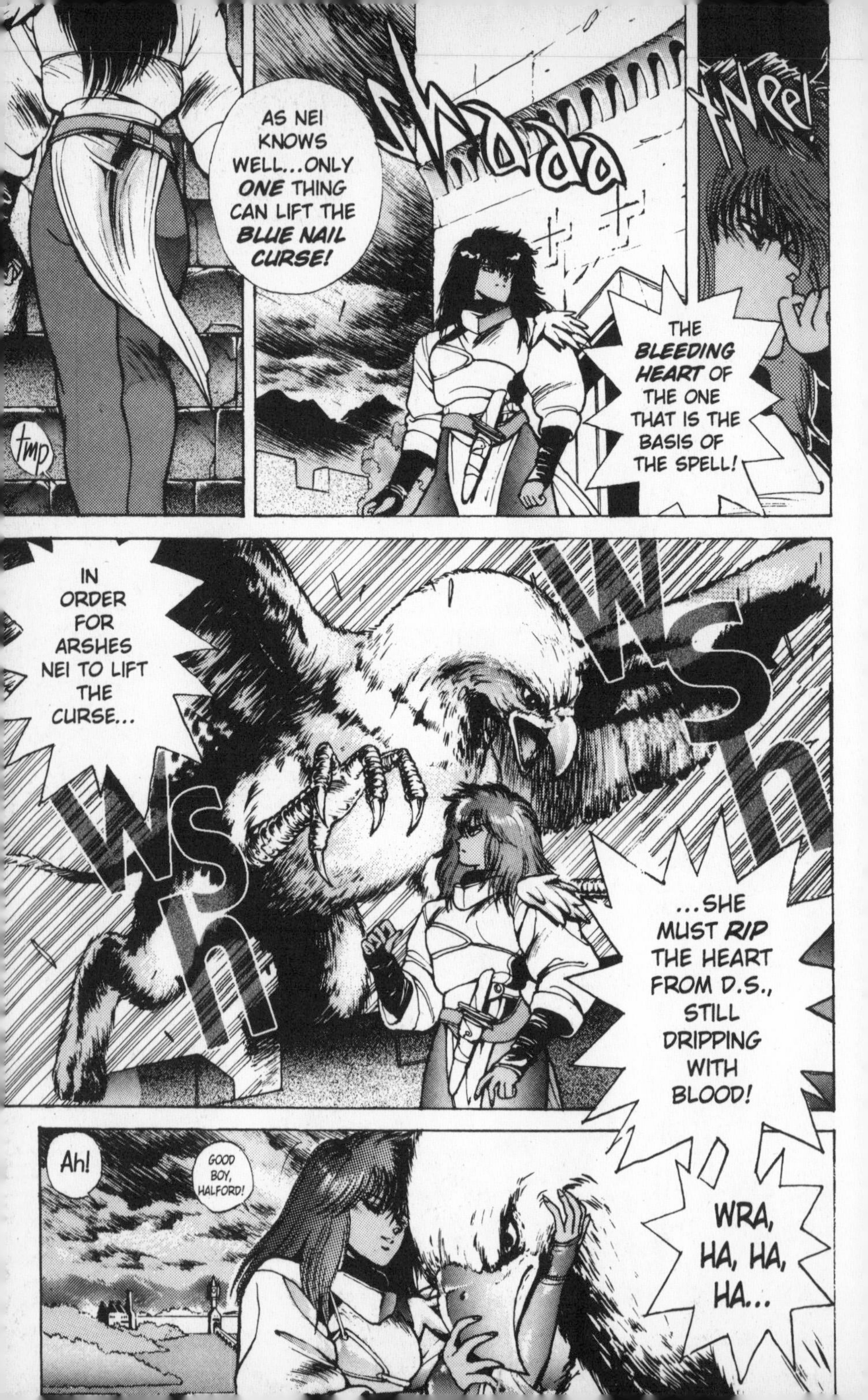
tmp
AS NEI KNOWS WELL...ONLY ONE THING CAN LIFT THE BLUE NAIL CURSE!
THE BLEEDING HEART OF THE ONE THAT IS THE BASIS OF THE SPELL!
IN ORDER FOR ARSHES NEI TO LIFT THE CURSE...
...SHE MUST RIP THE HEART FROM D.S., STILL DRIPPING WITH BLOOD!
Ah!
GOOD BOY, HALFORD!
WRA, HA, HA, HA...

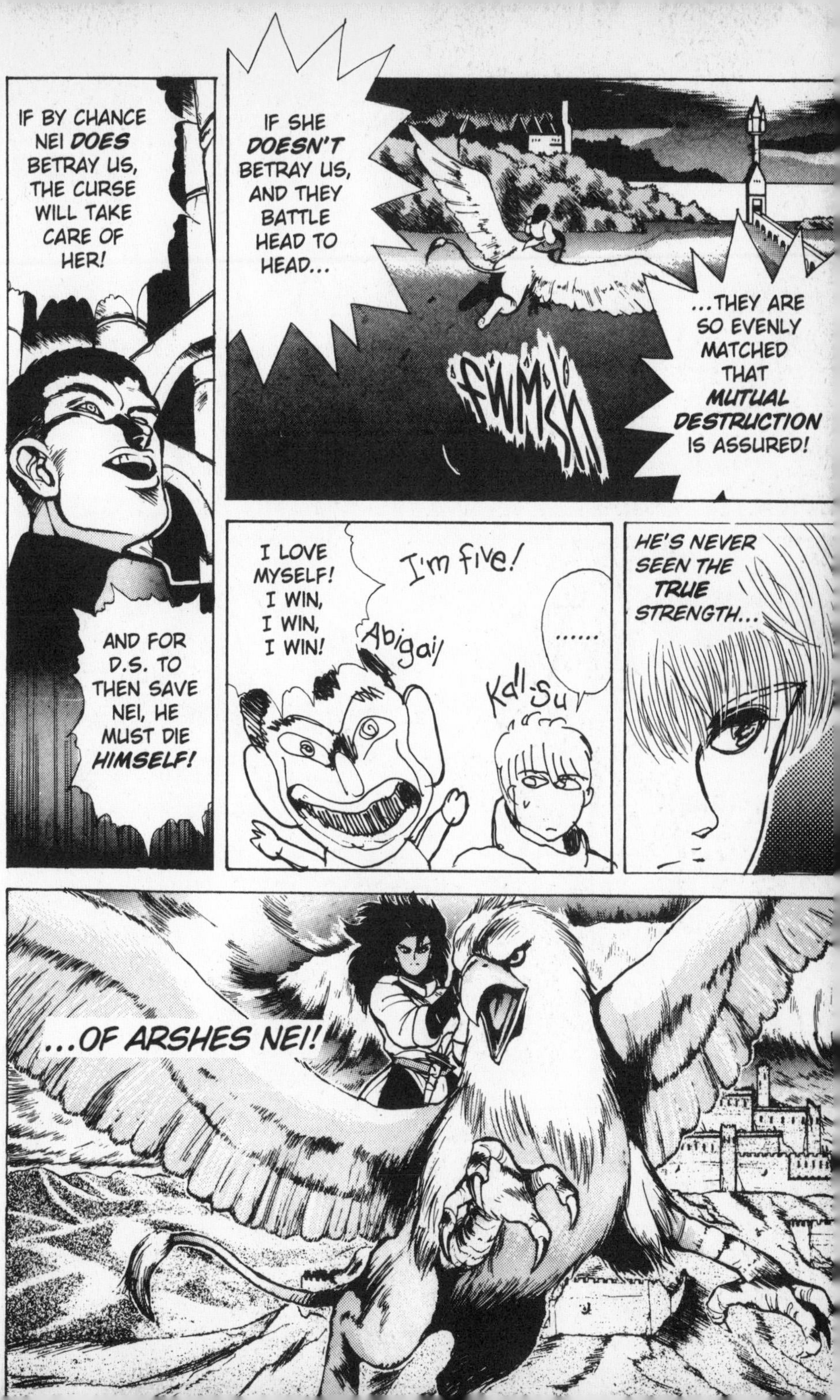
IF BY CHANCE NEI DOES BETRAY US, THE CURSE WILL TAKE CARE OF HER!
AND FOR D.S. TO THEN SAVE NEI, HE MUST DIE HIMSELF!
IF SHE DOESN'T BETRAY US, AND THEY BATTLE HEAD TO HEAD...
FWMSH
...THEY ARE SO EVENLY MATCHED THAT MUTUAL DESTRUCTION IS ASSURED!
I LOVE MYSELF! I WIN, I WIN, I WIN!
I'm five!
Abigail
......
Kall-Su
HE'S NEVER SEEN THE TRUE STRENGTH...
...OF ARSHES NEI!

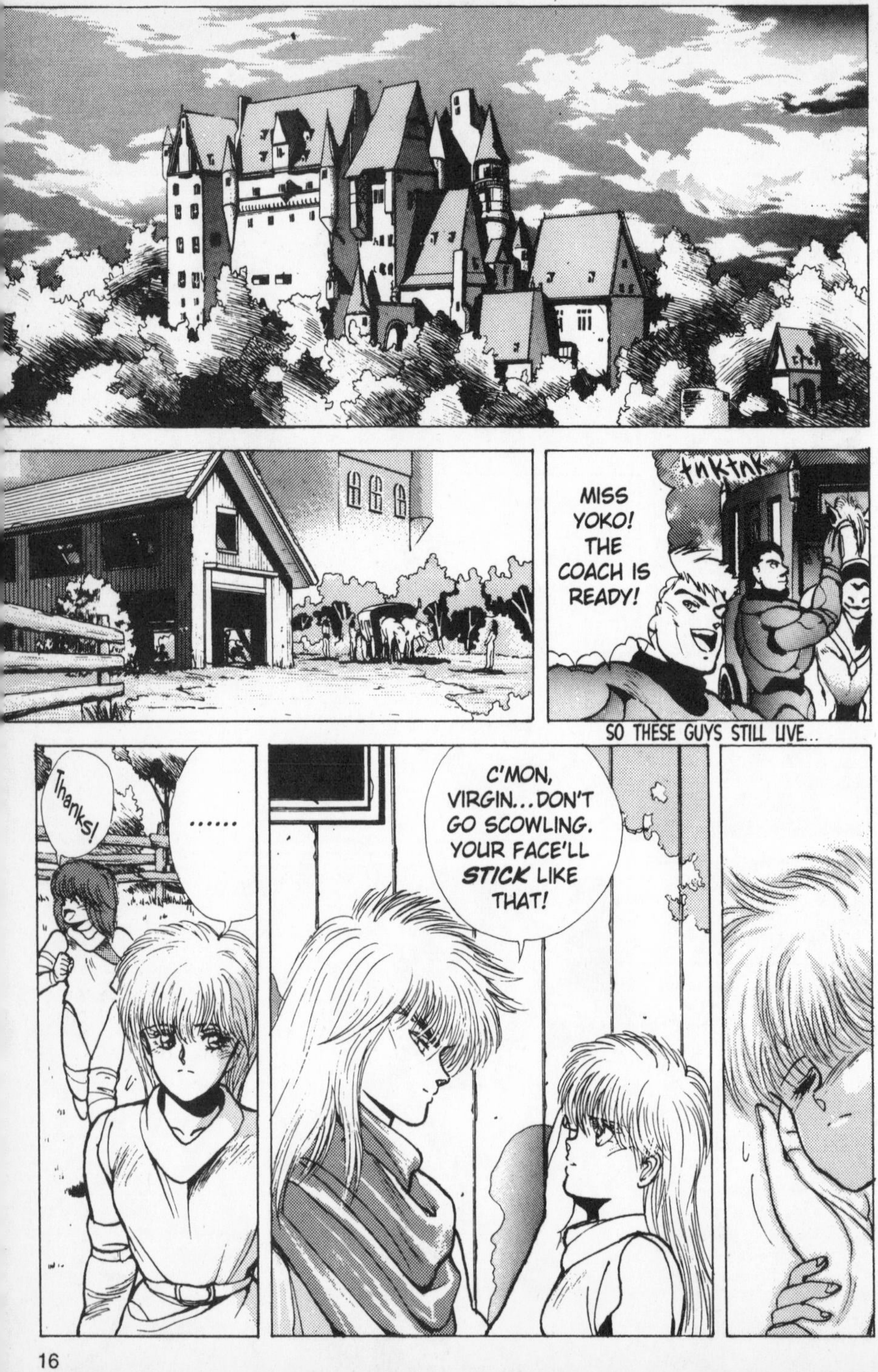
tnktnk
MISS YOKO! THE COACH IS READY!
SO THESE GUYS STILL LIVE...
Thanks!
......
C'MON, VIRGIN...DON'T GO SCOWLING. YOUR FACE'LL STICK LIKE THAT!

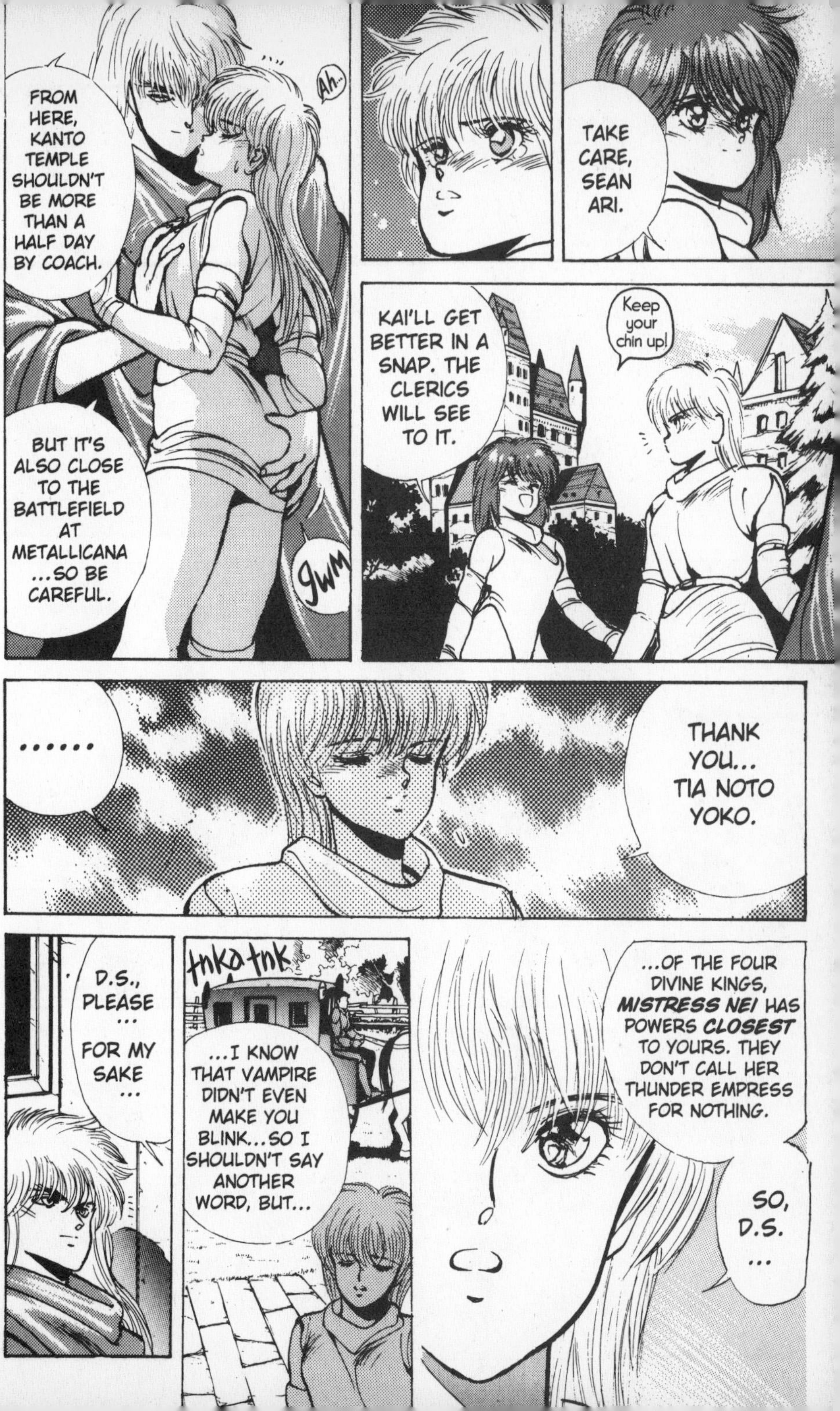
FROM HERE, KANTO TEMPLE SHOULDN'T BE MORE THAN A HALF DAY BY COACH.
Ah...
BUT IT'S ALSO CLOSE TO THE BATTLEFIELD AT METALLICANA ...SO BE CAREFUL.
GWM
TAKE CARE, SEAN ARI.
KAI'LL GET BETTER IN A SNAP. THE CLERICS WILL SEE TO IT.
Keep your chin up!
......
THANK YOU... TIA NOTO YOKO.
D.S., PLEASE ... FOR MY SAKE ...
tnka tnk
...I KNOW THAT VAMPIRE DIDN'T EVEN MAKE YOU BLINK...SO I SHOULDN'T SAY ANOTHER WORD, BUT...
...OF THE FOUR DIVINE KINGS, ***MISTRESS NEI*** HAS POWERS ***CLOSEST*** TO YOURS. THEY DON'T CALL HER THUNDER EMPRESS FOR NOTHING.
SO, D.S. ...

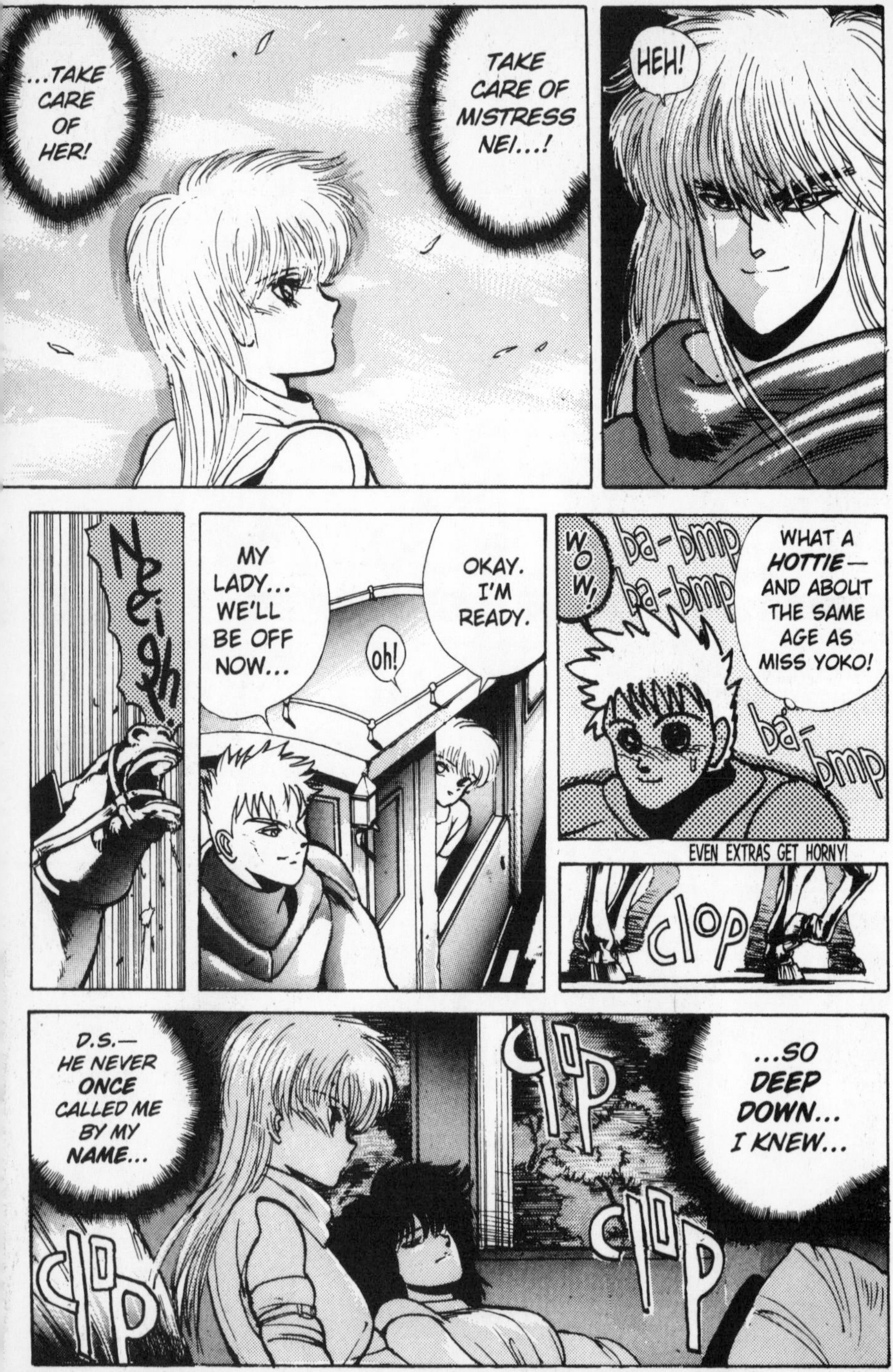
...TAKE CARE OF HER!
TAKE CARE OF MISTRESS NEI...!
HEH!
Neigh!
MY LADY... WE'LL BE OFF NOW...
OKAY. I'M READY.
oh!
WOW!
ba-bmp ba-bmp
WHAT A *HOTTIE*—AND ABOUT THE SAME AGE AS MISS YOKO!
ba-bmp
EVEN EXTRAS GET HORNY!
clop
D.S.—HE NEVER **ONCE** CALLED ME BY MY **NAME**...
clop
clop
clop
...SO **DEEP DOWN**... I KNEW...

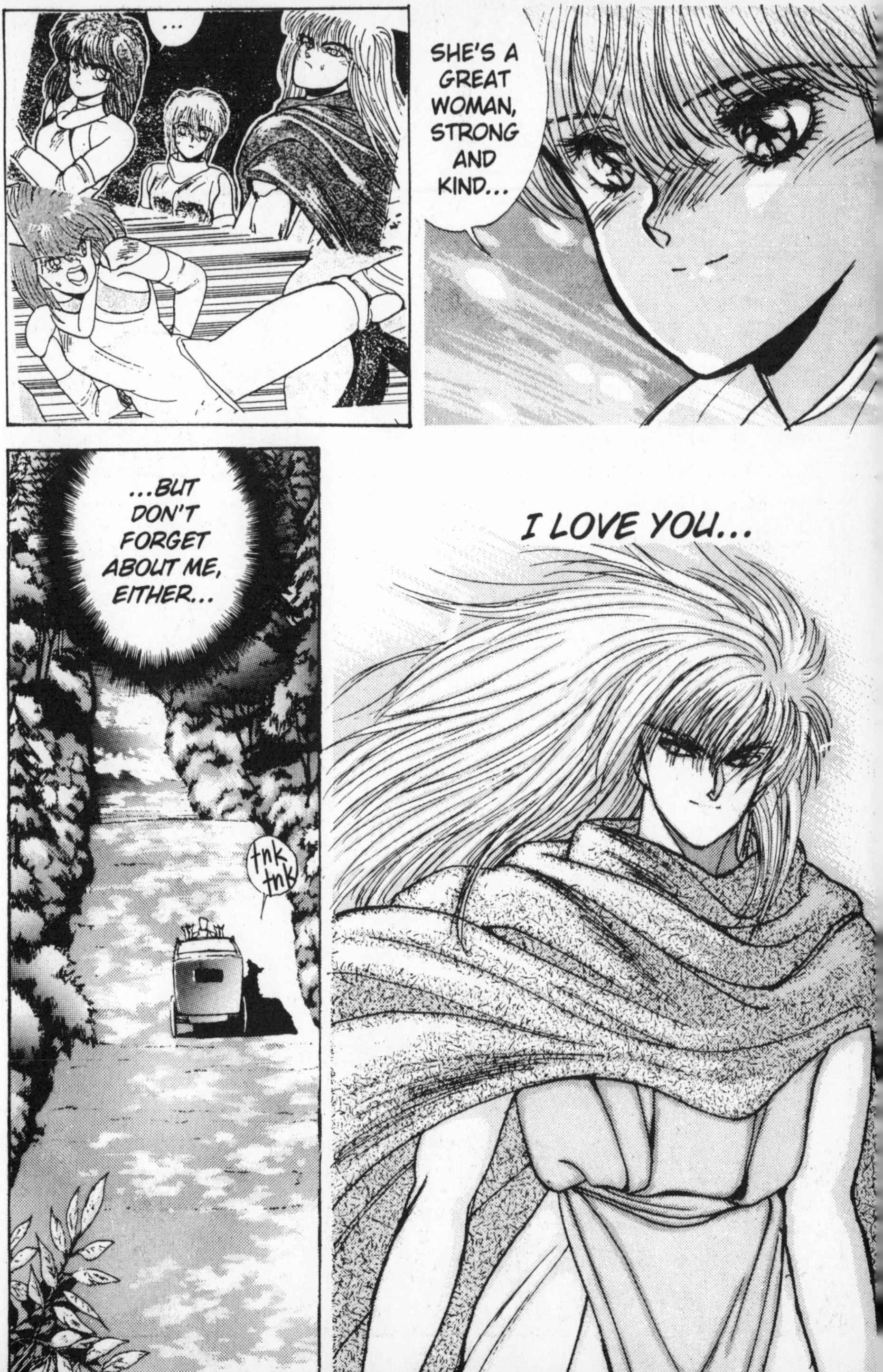
...
SHE'S A GREAT WOMAN, STRONG AND KIND...
...BUT DON'T FORGET ABOUT ME, EITHER...
tnk tnk
I LOVE YOU...

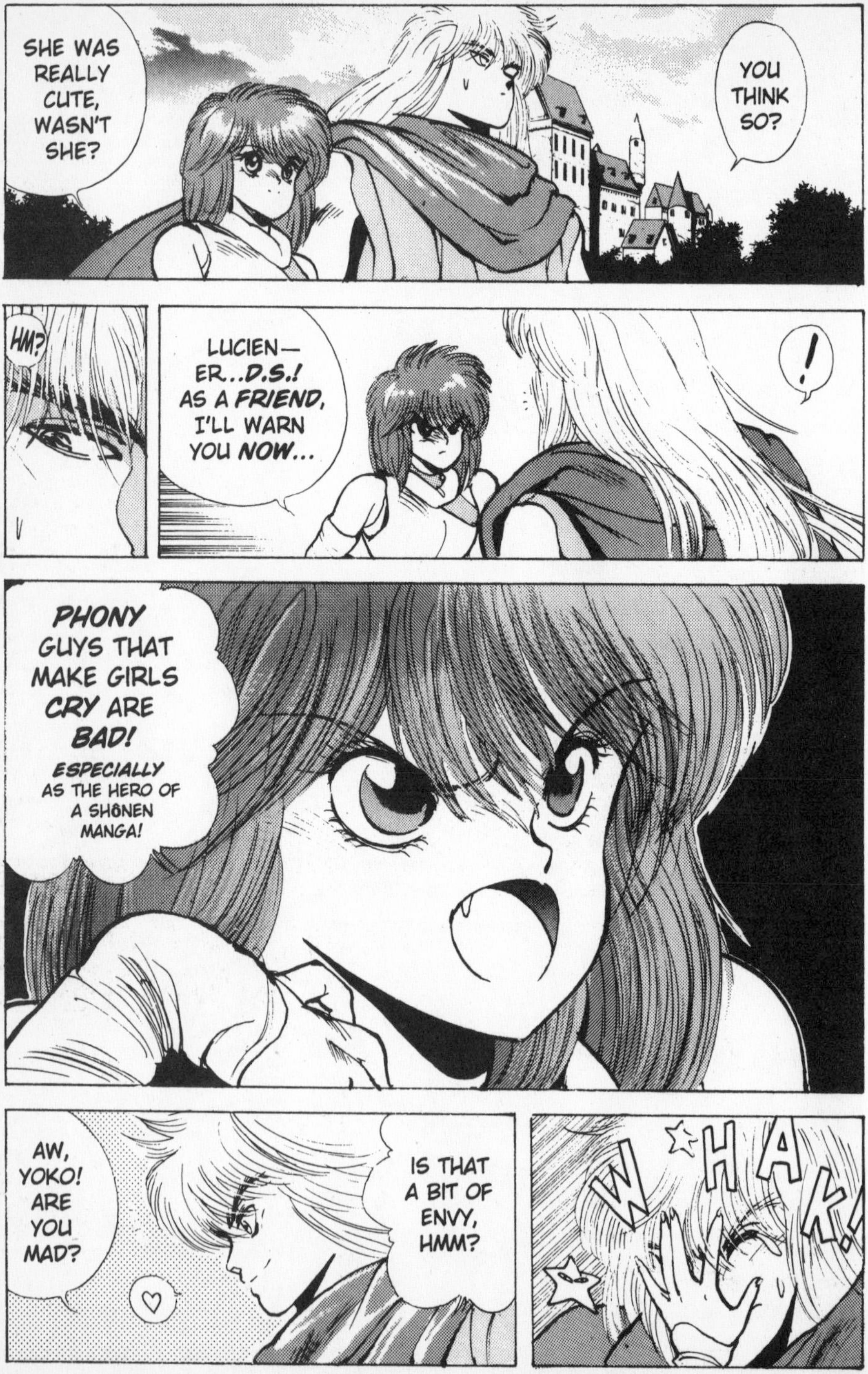
SHE WAS REALLY CUTE, WASN'T SHE?
YOU THINK SO?
HM?
LUCIEN— ER...D.S.! AS A FRIEND, I'LL WARN YOU NOW...
!
PHONY GUYS THAT MAKE GIRLS CRY ARE BAD!
ESPECIALLY AS THE HERO OF A SHŌNEN MANGA!
AW, YOKO! ARE YOU MAD?
IS THAT A BIT OF ENVY, HMM?
♡
WHAK!

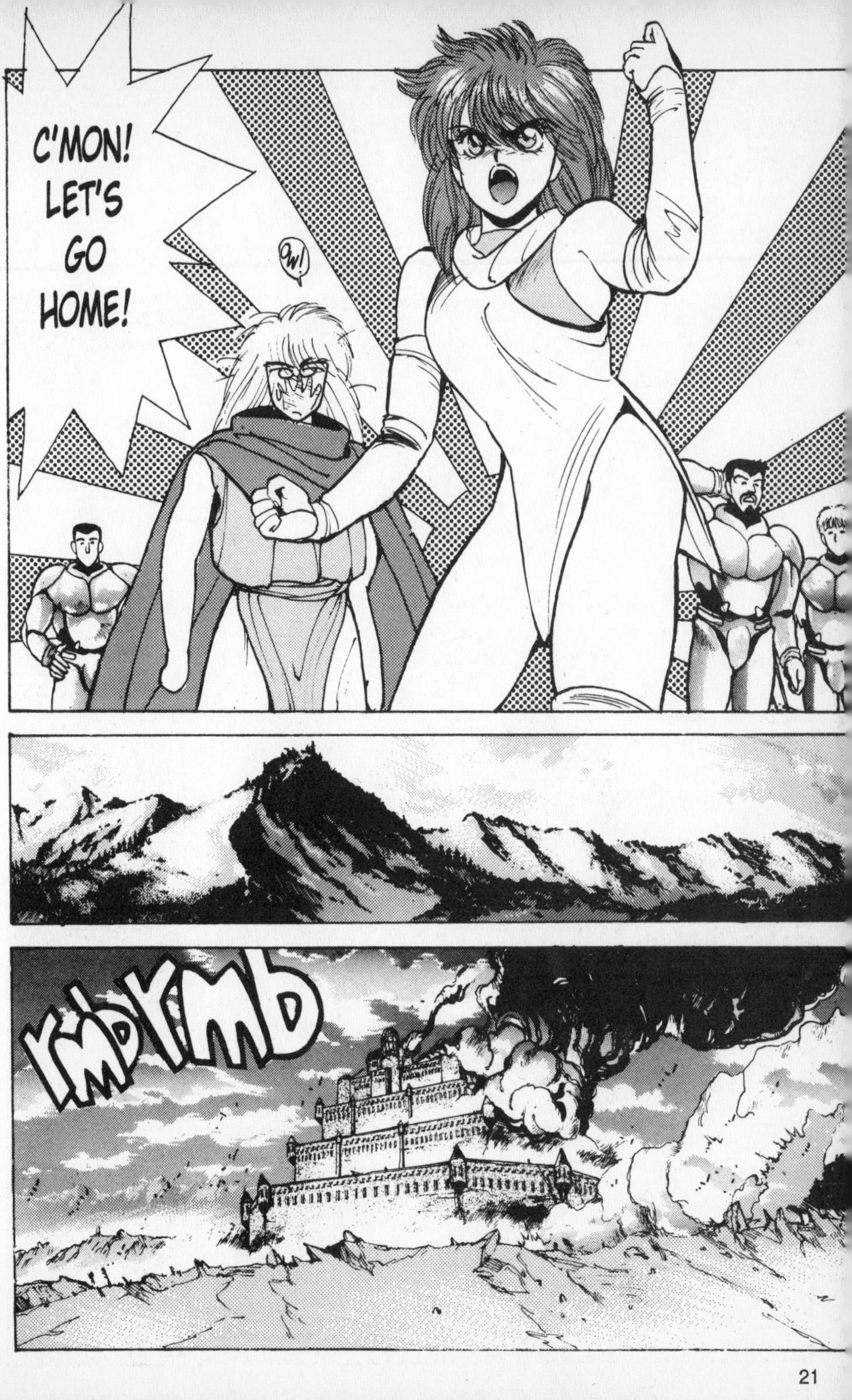
C'MON! LET'S GO HOME!
OW!
RMBRMB

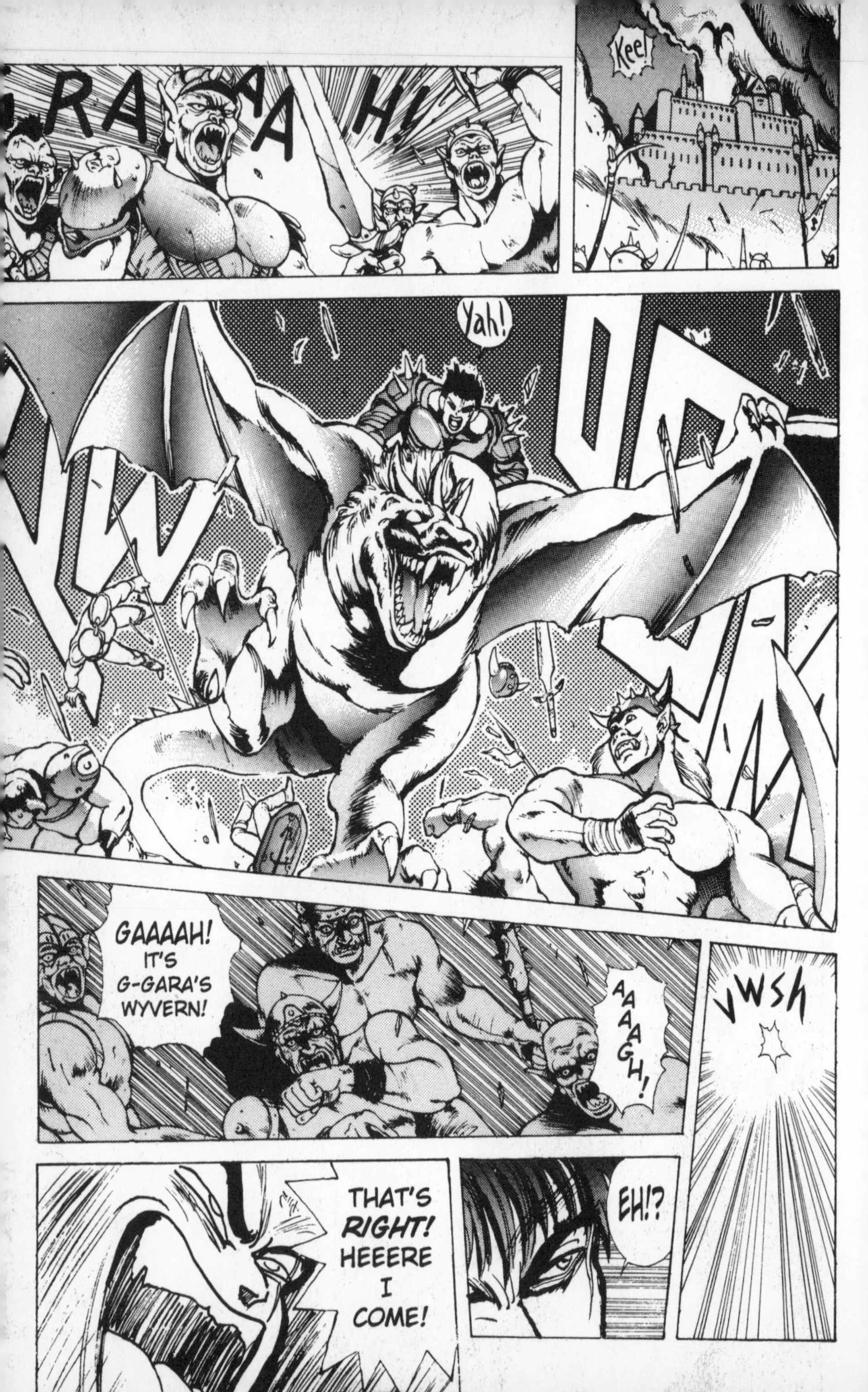
RAAAAH!
Kee!
Yah!
GAAAAH! IT'S G-GARA'S WYVERN!
AAAAGH!
VWSH
THAT'S ***RIGHT!*** HEEERE I COME!
EH!?

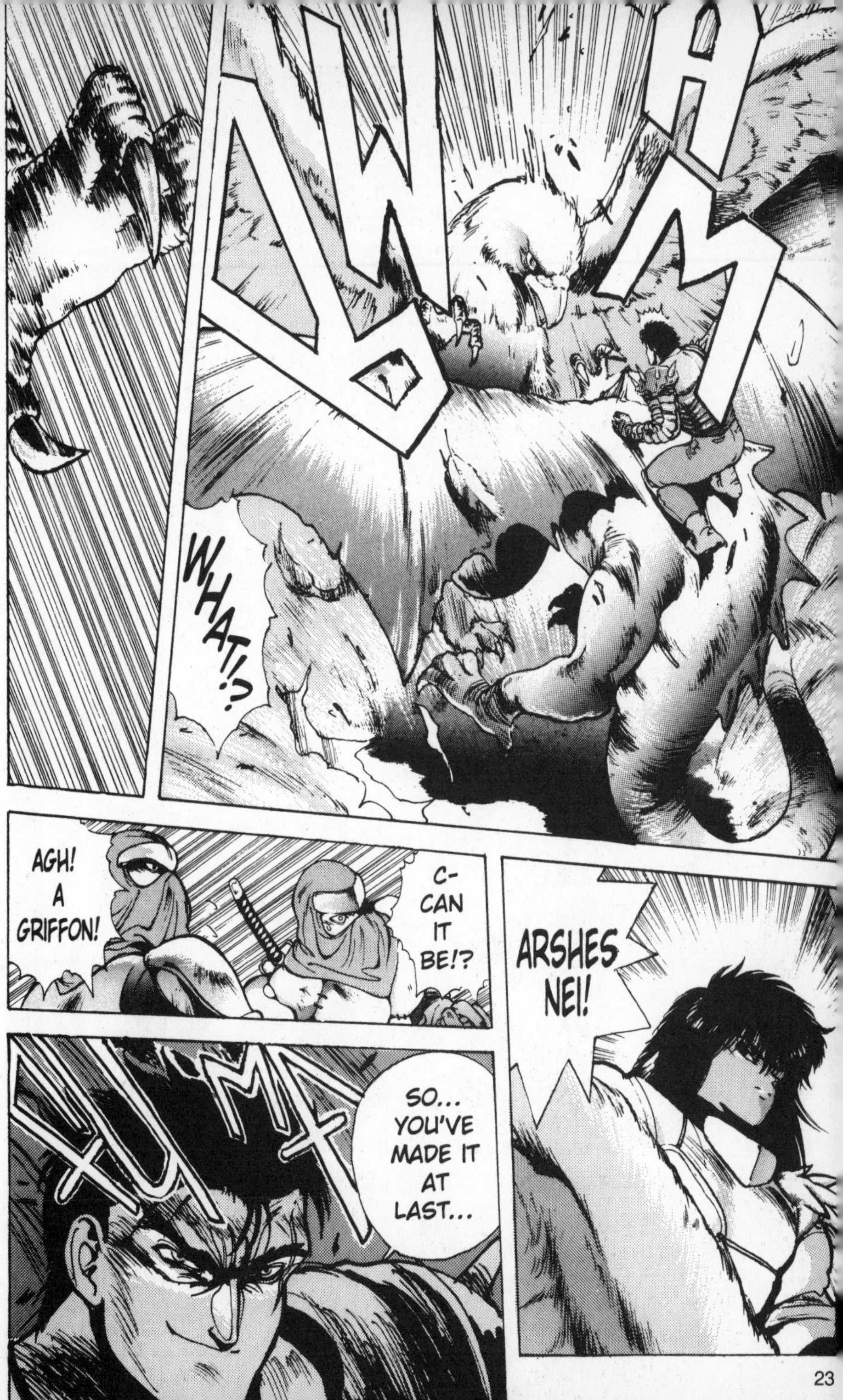
WHAT!?
AGH! A GRIFFON!
C-CAN IT BE!?
ARSHES NEI!
SO... YOU'VE MADE IT AT LAST...

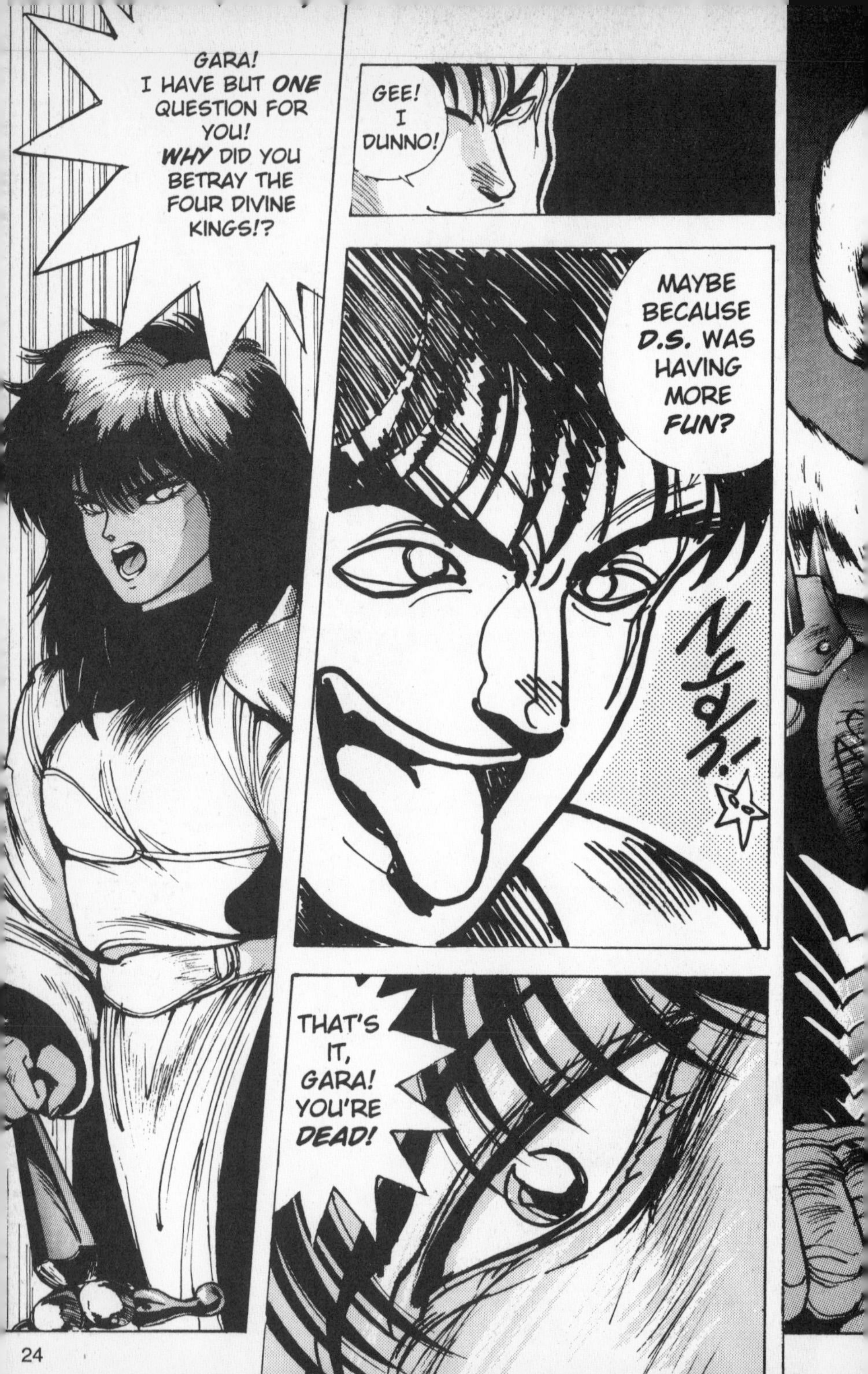
GARA! I HAVE BUT ONE QUESTION FOR YOU! WHY DID YOU BETRAY THE FOUR DIVINE KINGS!?
GEE! I DUNNO!
MAYBE BECAUSE D.S. WAS HAVING MORE FUN?
Nyah!
THAT'S IT, GARA! YOU'RE DEAD!

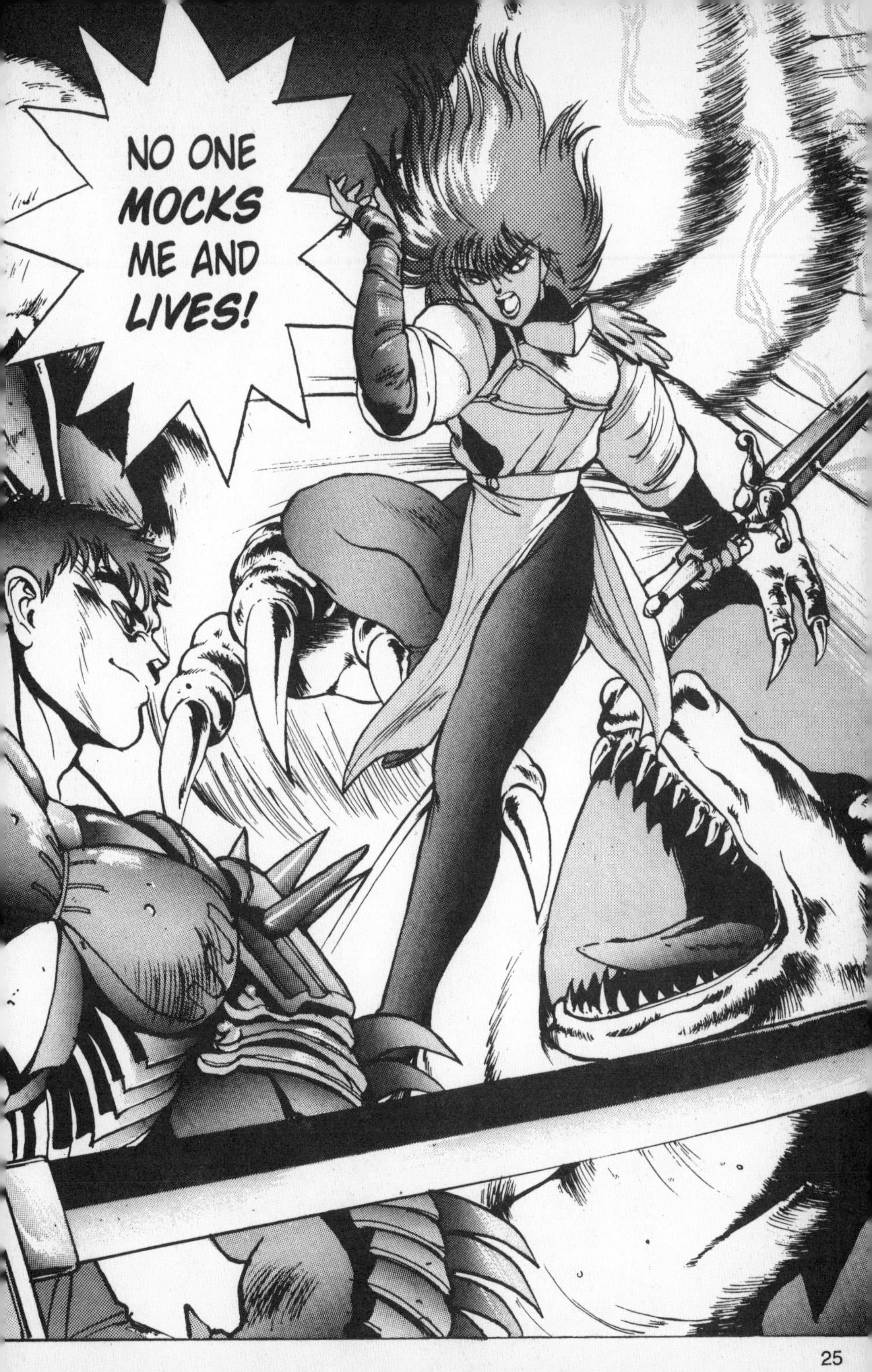
NO ONE MOCKS ME AND LIVES!

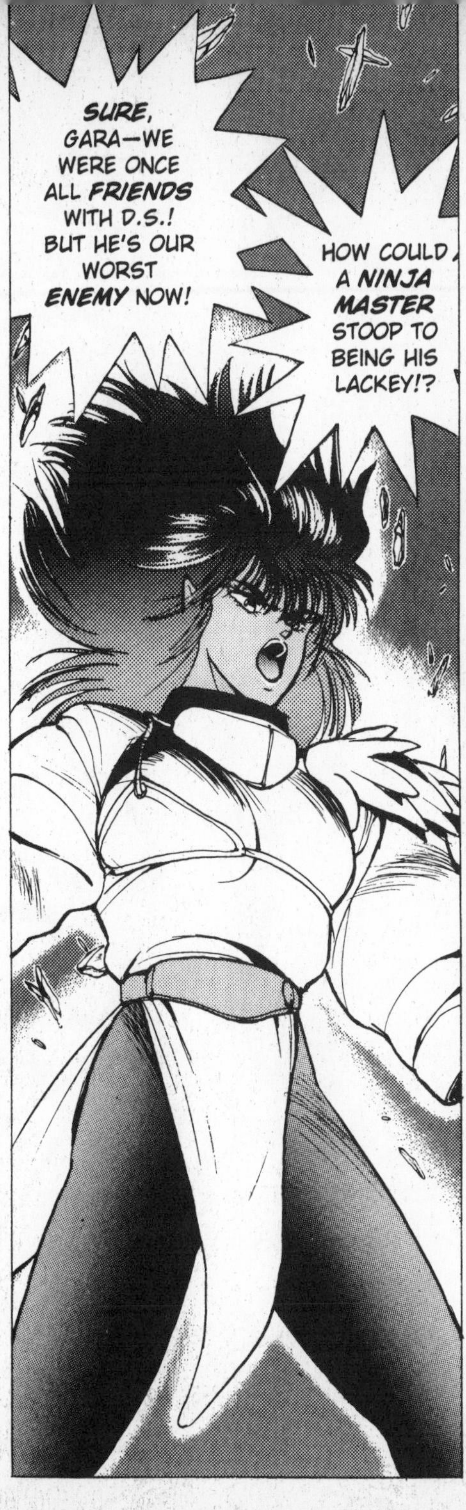
SURE, GARA—WE WERE ONCE ALL FRIENDS WITH D.S.! BUT HE'S OUR WORST ENEMY NOW!
HOW COULD A NINJA MASTER STOOP TO BEING HIS LACKEY!?
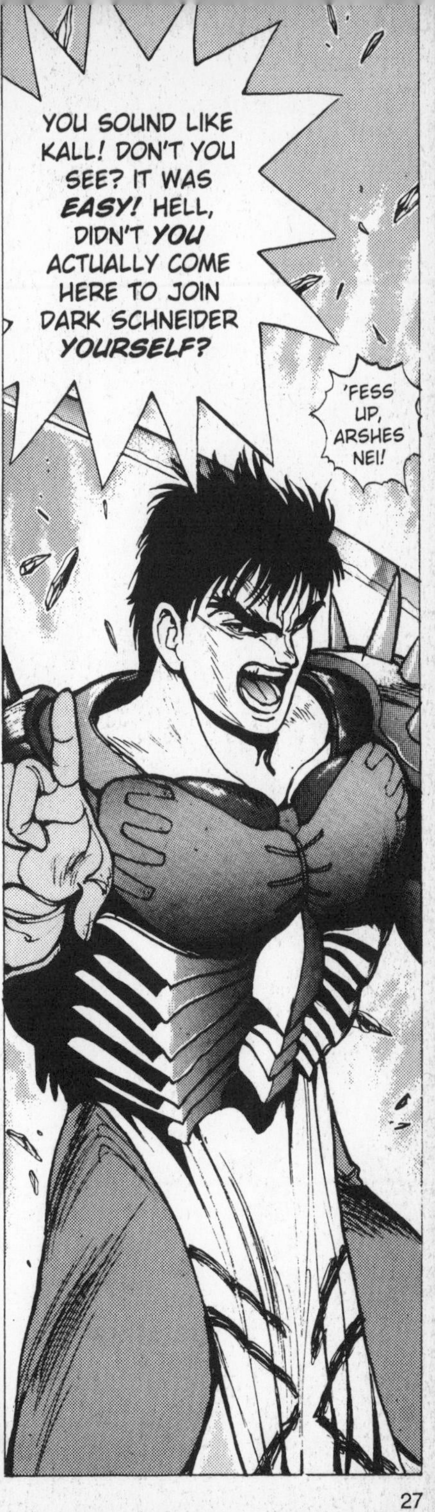
YOU SOUND LIKE KALL! DON'T YOU SEE? IT WAS EASY! HELL, DIDN'T YOU ACTUALLY COME HERE TO JOIN DARK SCHNEIDER YOURSELF?
'FESS UP, ARSHES NEI!

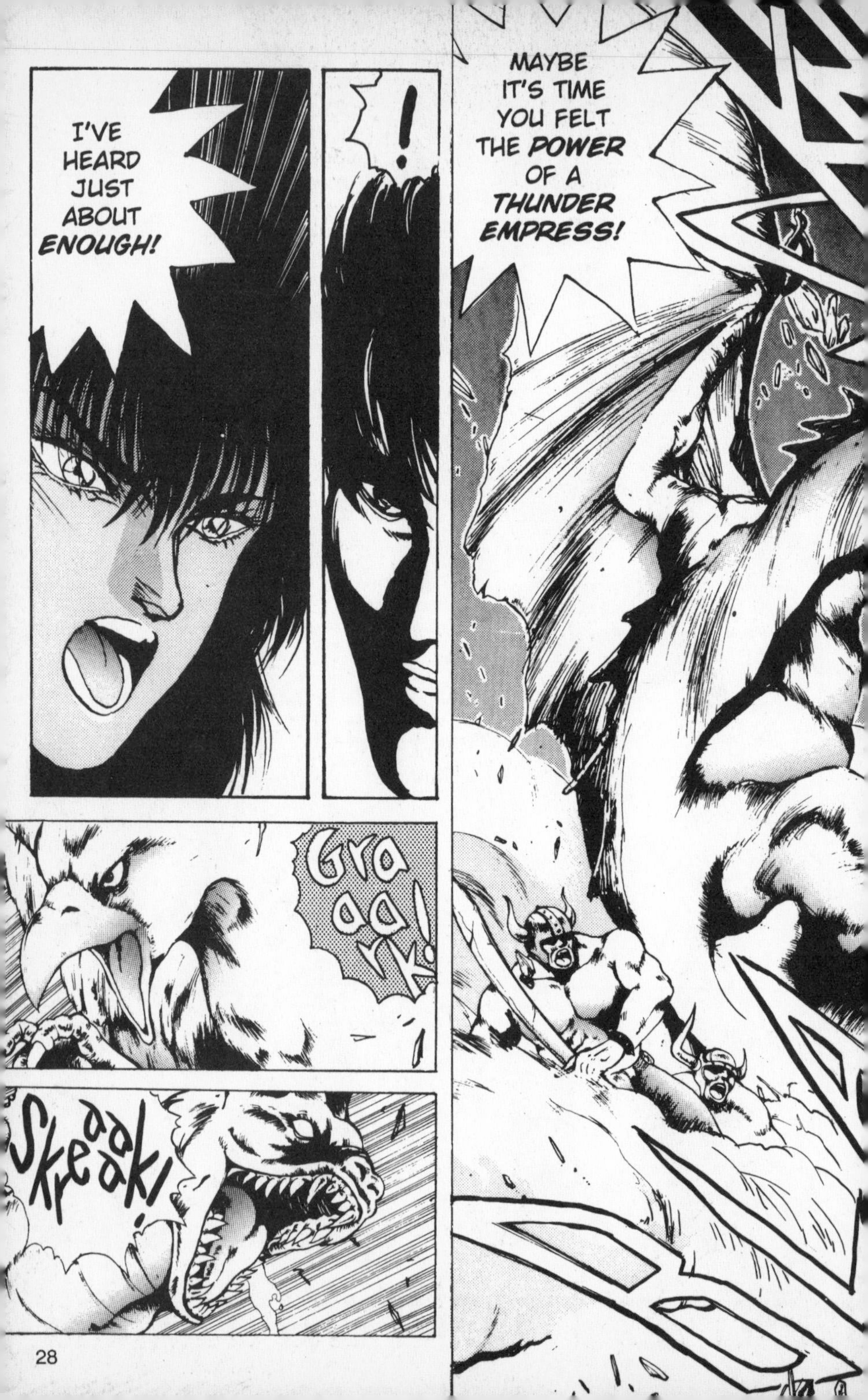
I'VE HEARD JUST ABOUT *ENOUGH!*
!
Graaark!
Skreaak!
MAYBE IT'S TIME YOU FELT THE *POWER* OF A *THUNDER EMPRESS!*

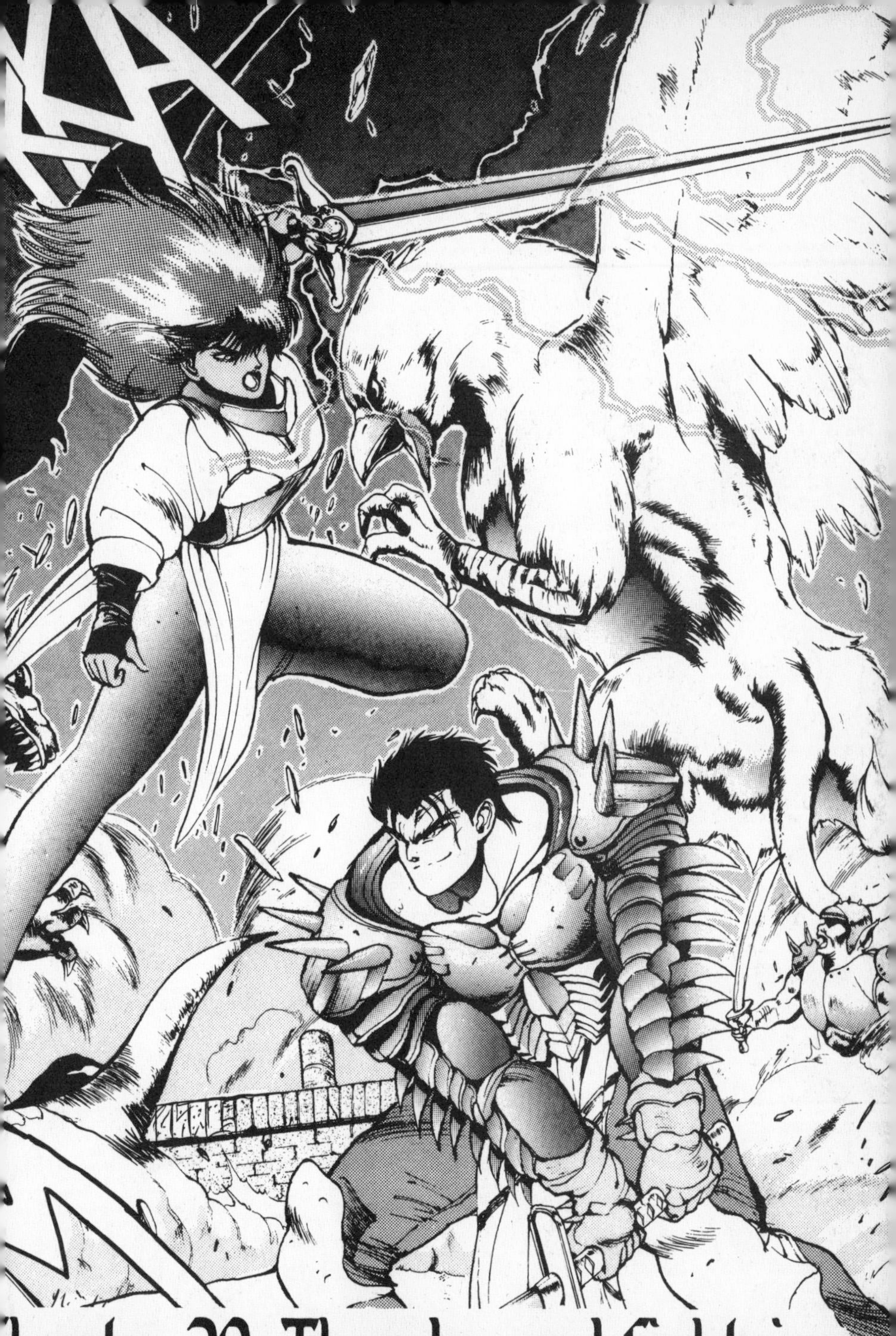

Chapter 29: Thunder and Lightning

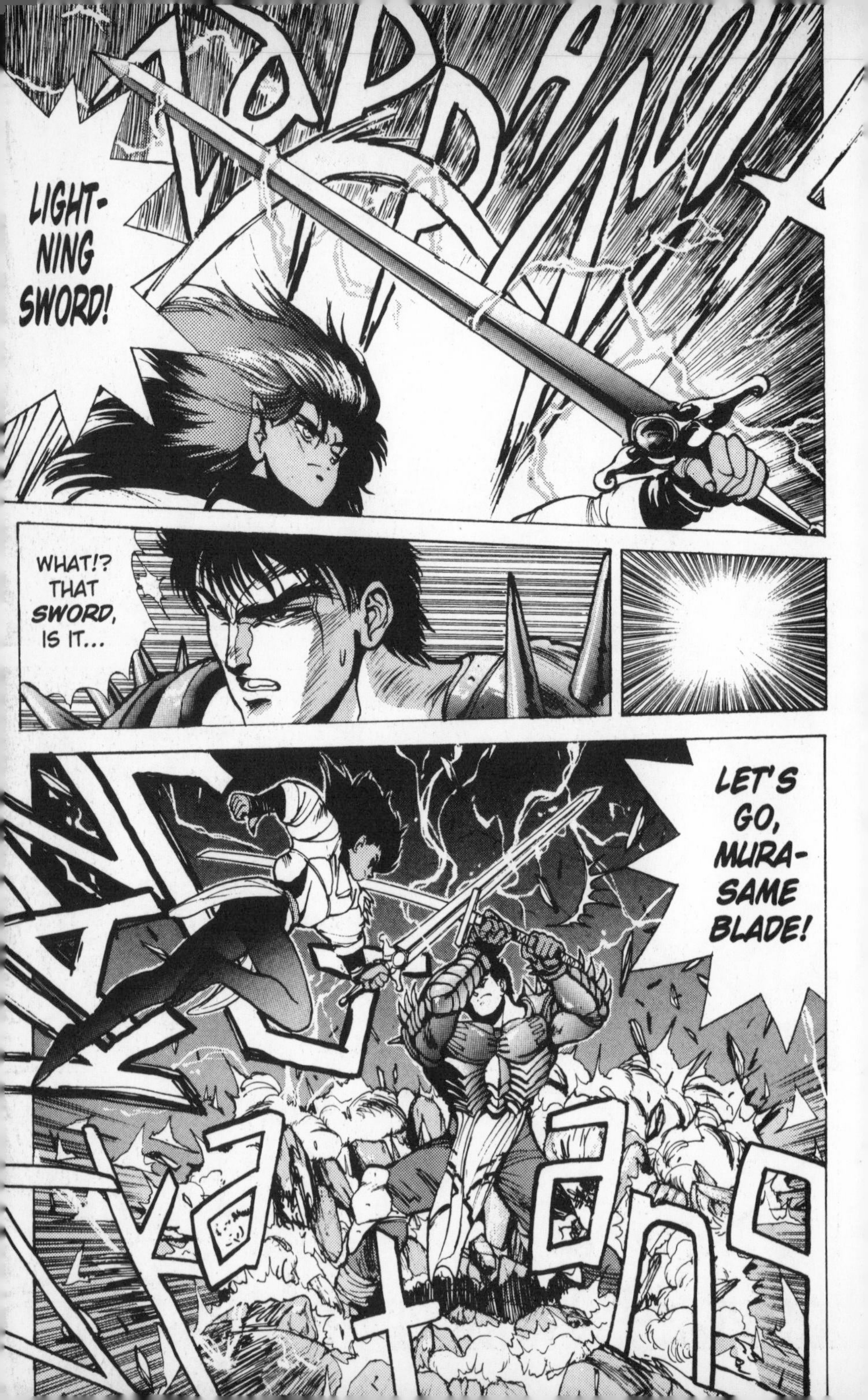
LIGHT-NING SWORD!
WHAT!? THAT SWORD, IS IT...
LET'S GO, MURA-SAME BLADE!

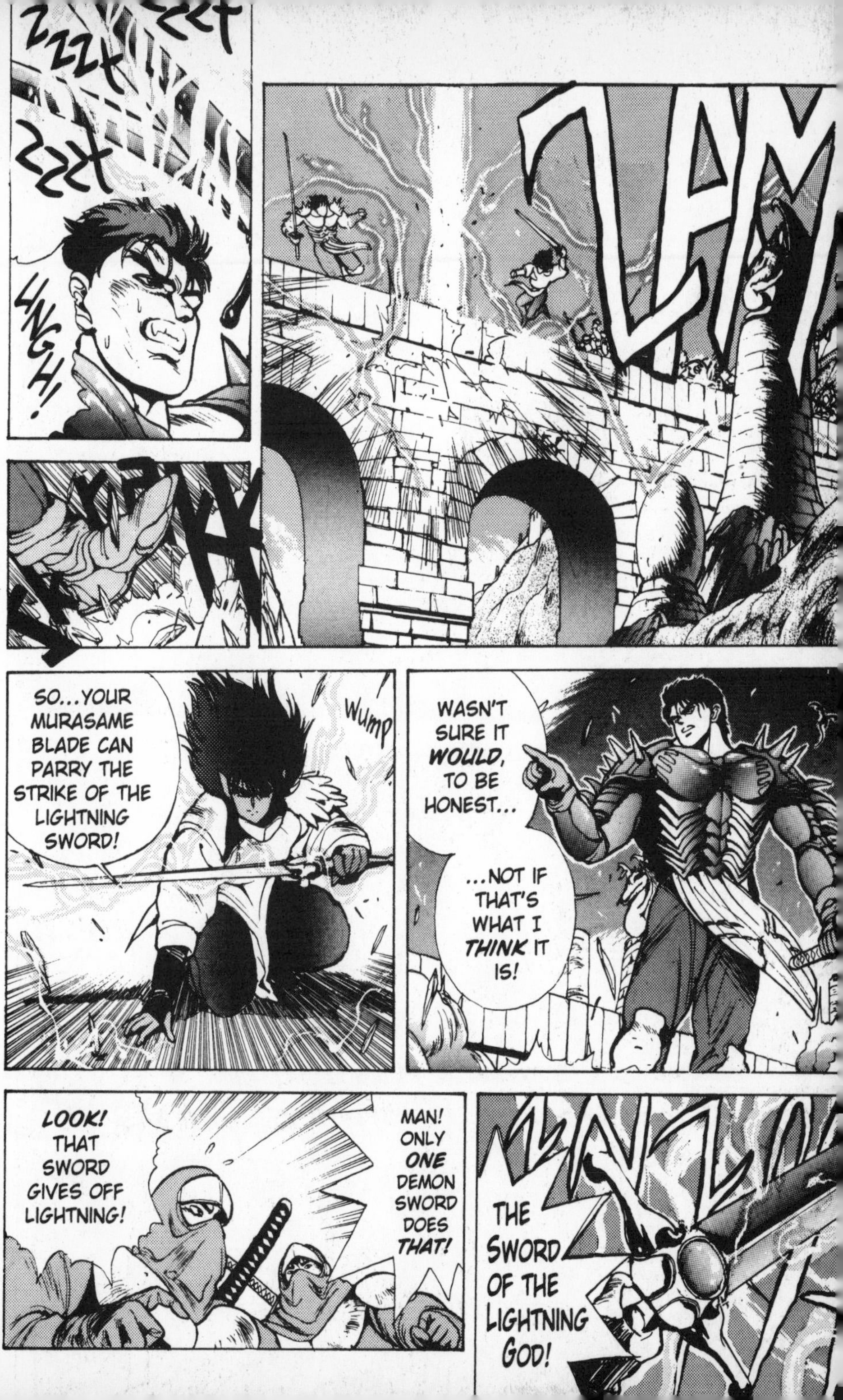
UNGH!
SO...YOUR MURASAME BLADE CAN PARRY THE STRIKE OF THE LIGHTNING SWORD!
Wump
WASN'T SURE IT WOULD, TO BE HONEST...
...NOT IF THAT'S WHAT I THINK IT IS!
LOOK! THAT SWORD GIVES OFF LIGHTNING!
MAN! ONLY ONE DEMON SWORD DOES THAT!
THE SWORD OF THE LIGHTNING GOD!

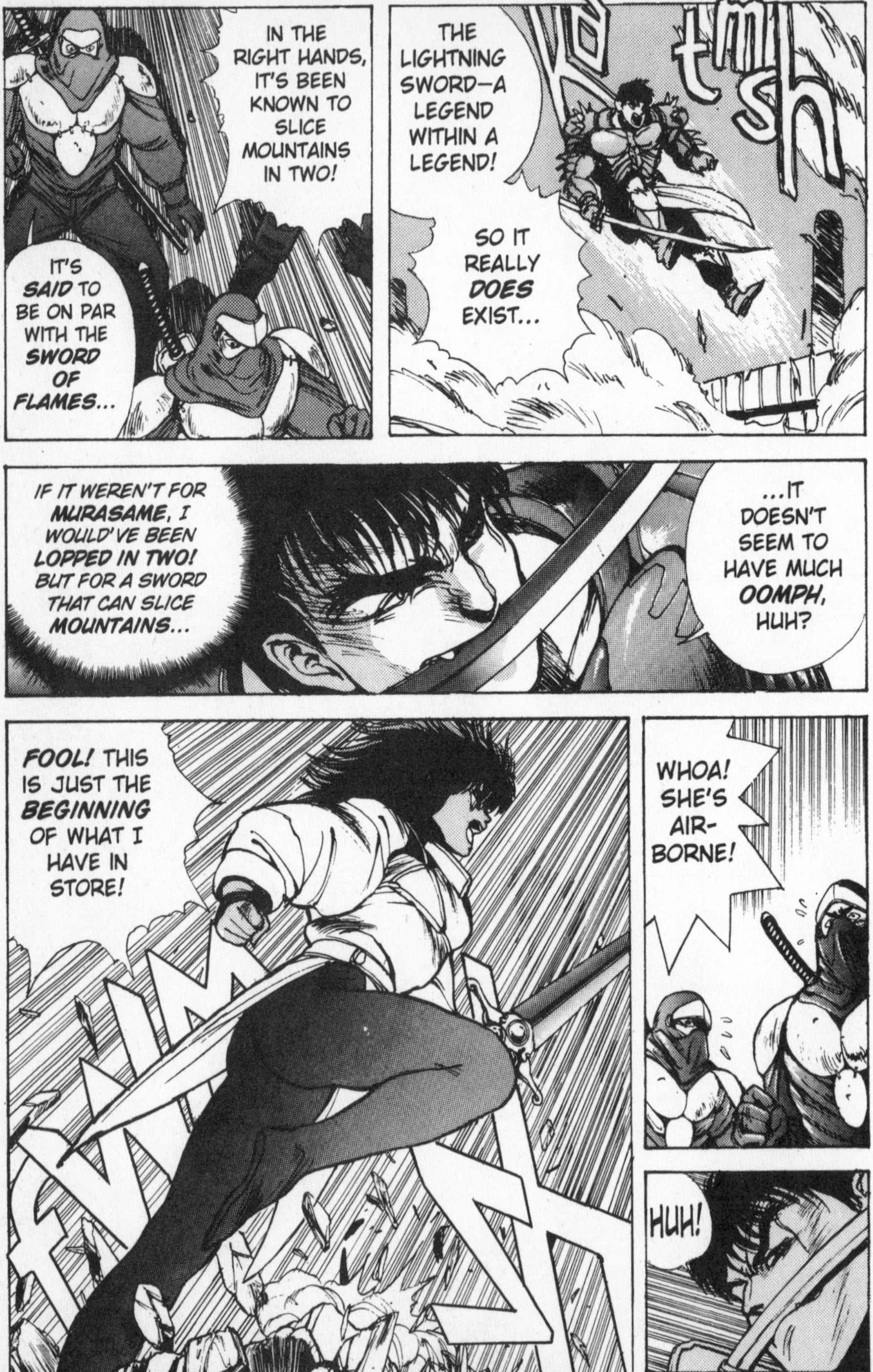
IN THE RIGHT HANDS, IT'S BEEN KNOWN TO SLICE MOUNTAINS IN TWO!
IT'S SAID TO BE ON PAR WITH THE SWORD OF FLAMES...
THE LIGHTNING SWORD—A LEGEND WITHIN A LEGEND!
SO IT REALLY DOES EXIST...
IF IT WEREN'T FOR MURASAME, I WOULD'VE BEEN LOPPED IN TWO! BUT FOR A SWORD THAT CAN SLICE MOUNTAINS...
...IT DOESN'T SEEM TO HAVE MUCH OOMPH, HUH?
FOOL! THIS IS JUST THE BEGINNING OF WHAT I HAVE IN STORE!
WHOA! SHE'S AIR-BORNE!
HUH!

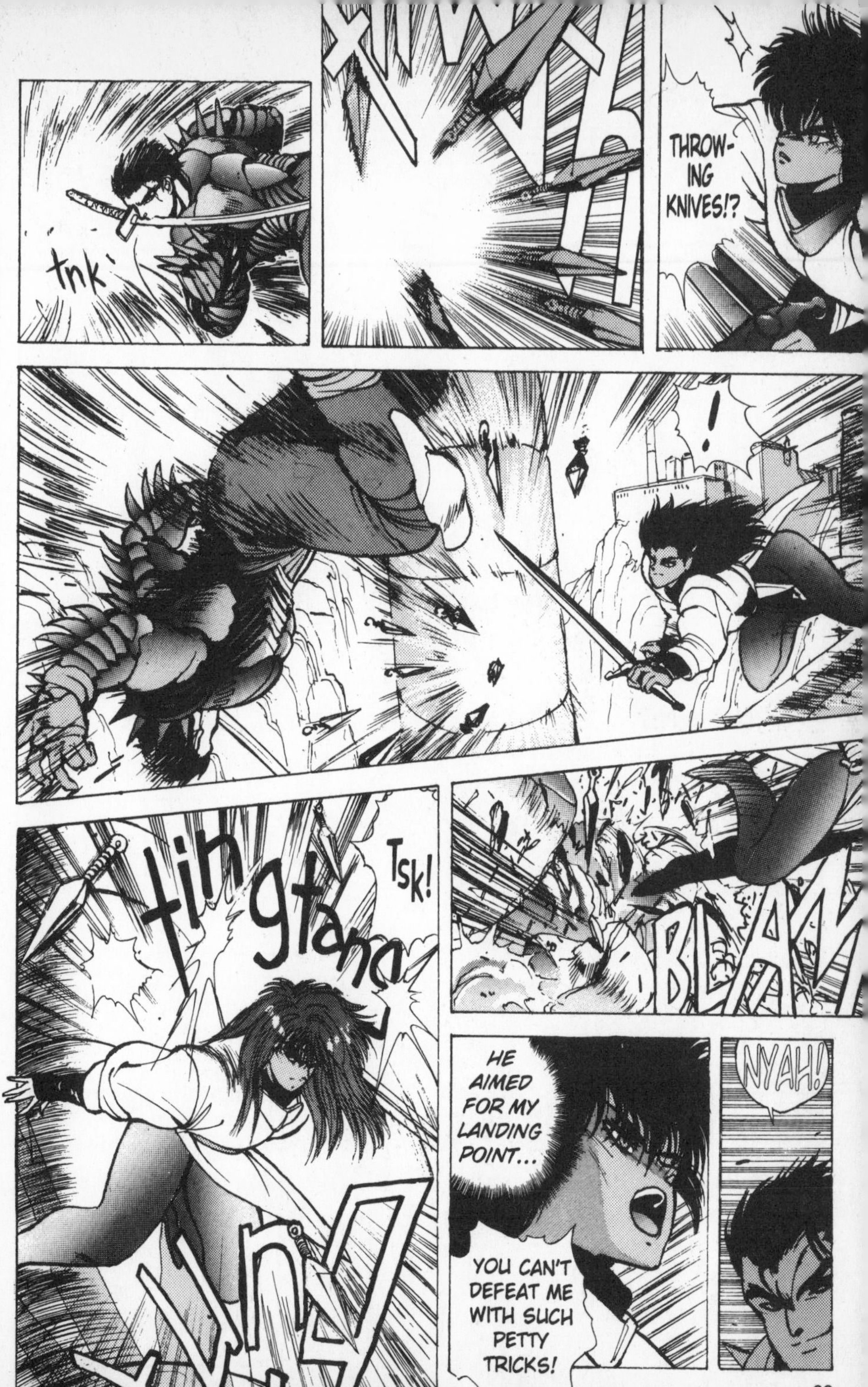
tnk
THROW-ING KNIVES!?
!
tin
gtang
TSK!
BLAM
HE AIMED FOR MY LANDING POINT...
YOU CAN'T DEFEAT ME WITH SUCH PETTY TRICKS!
NYAH!

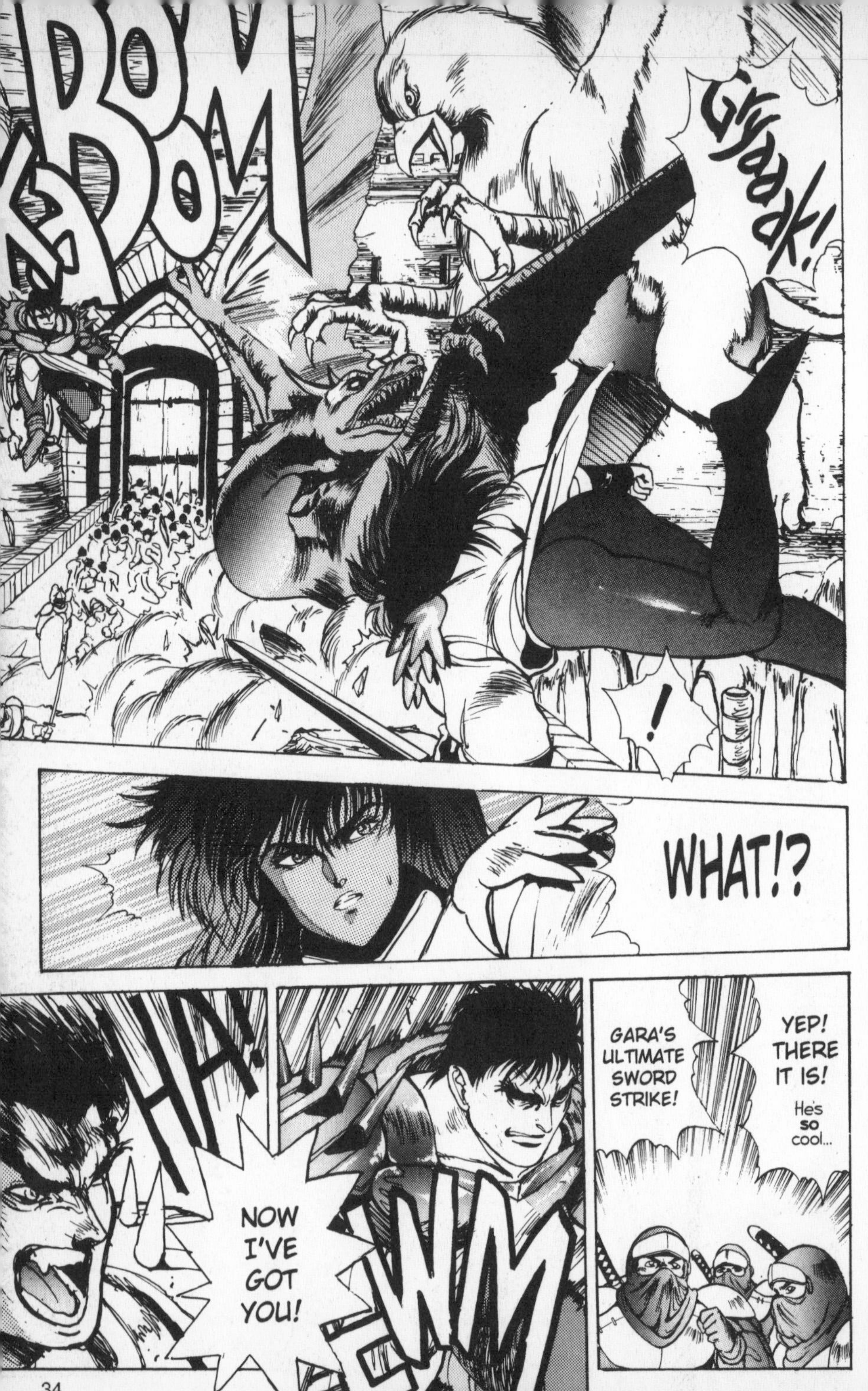
Gryaaak!
!
WHAT!?
HA!
NOW I'VE GOT YOU!
GARA'S ULTIMATE SWORD STRIKE!
YEP! THERE IT IS!
He's so cool...

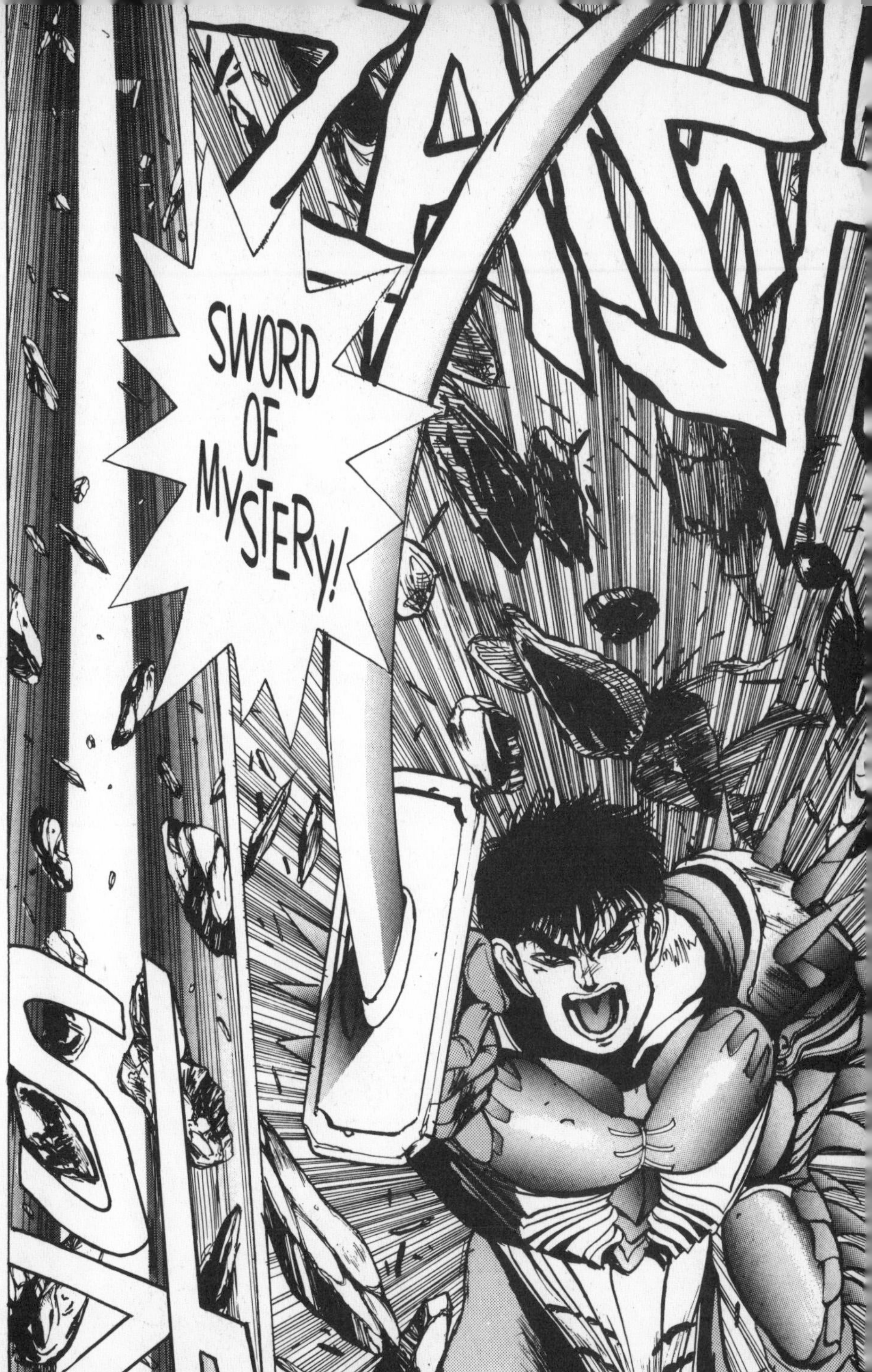
SWORD OF MYSTERY!

YEAH! SPLIT IN TWO! WHAT A NINJA!

SUCH **STRATEGY**— TIMING HIS ATTACK BASED ON THE GRIFFIN AND WYVERN...!

THAT WAS TOO EASY... BUT I **FELT** THE STRIKE.

WHA!?

FOOSH

AN ILLUSION? DAMN HER!

blrsh

TSK!

WSh

GRARRK!

SKREAK!

36

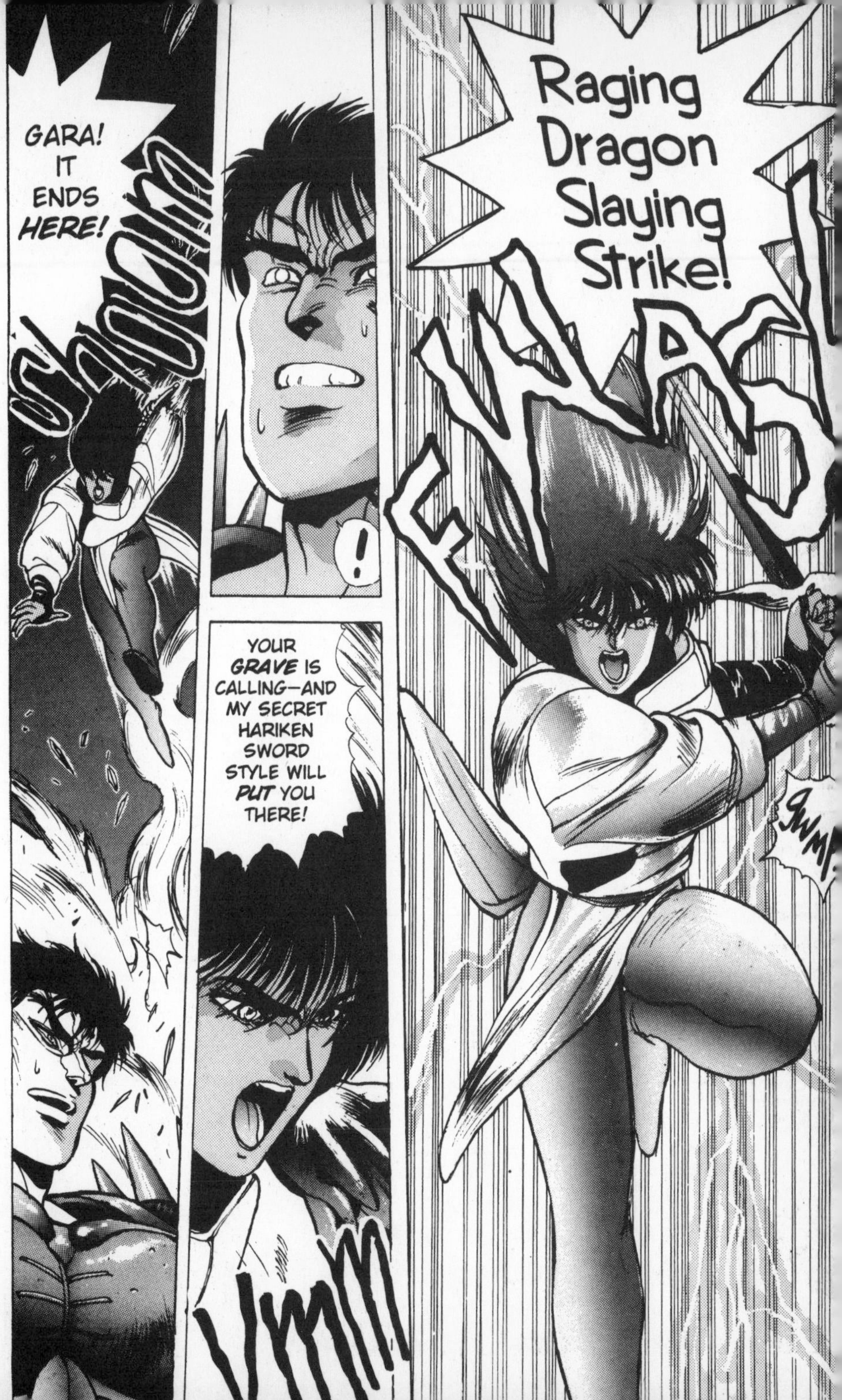
GARA! IT ENDS HERE!
!
YOUR GRAVE IS CALLING—AND MY SECRET HARIKEN SWORD STYLE WILL PUT YOU THERE!
Raging Dragon Slaying Strike!

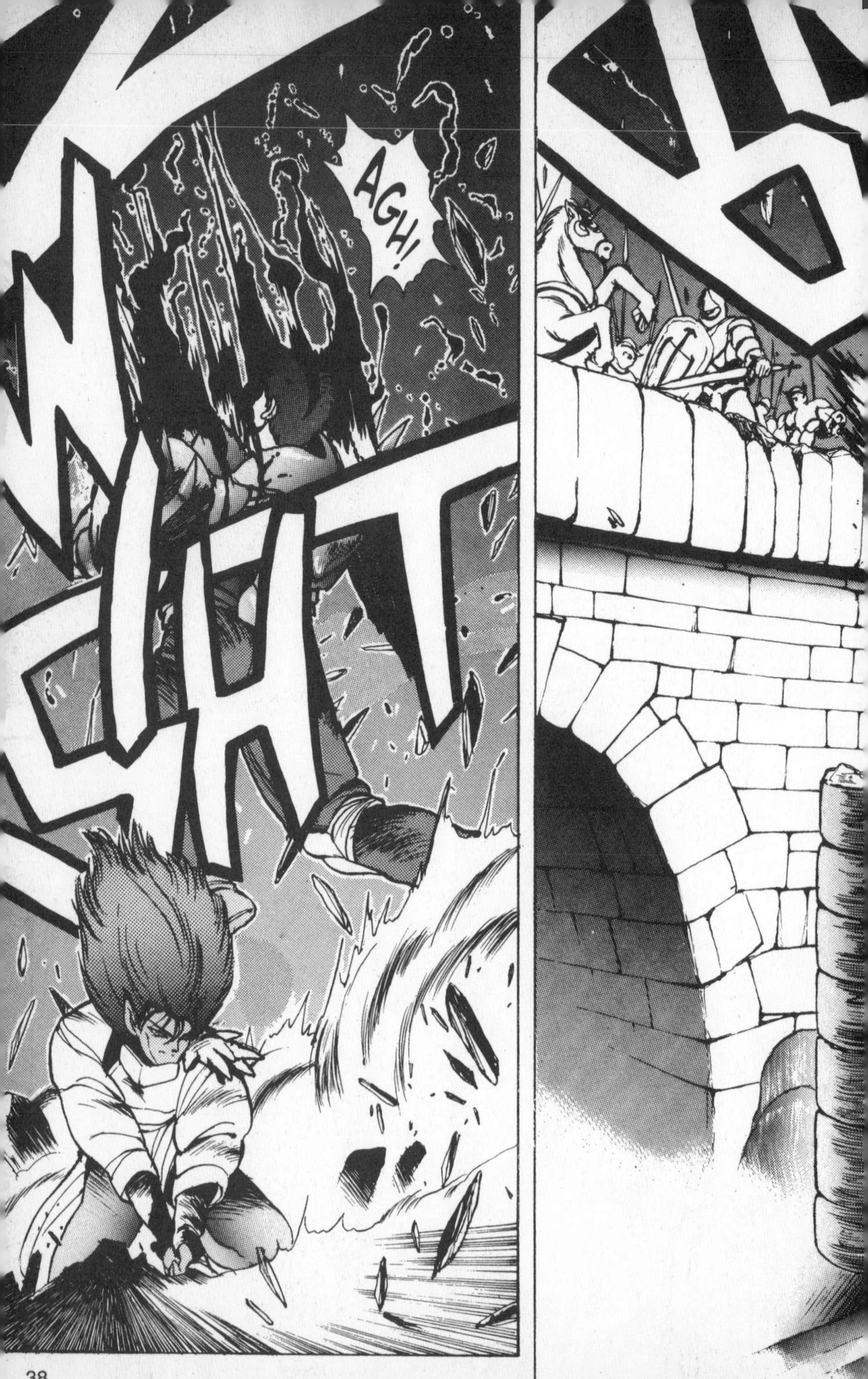
AGH!

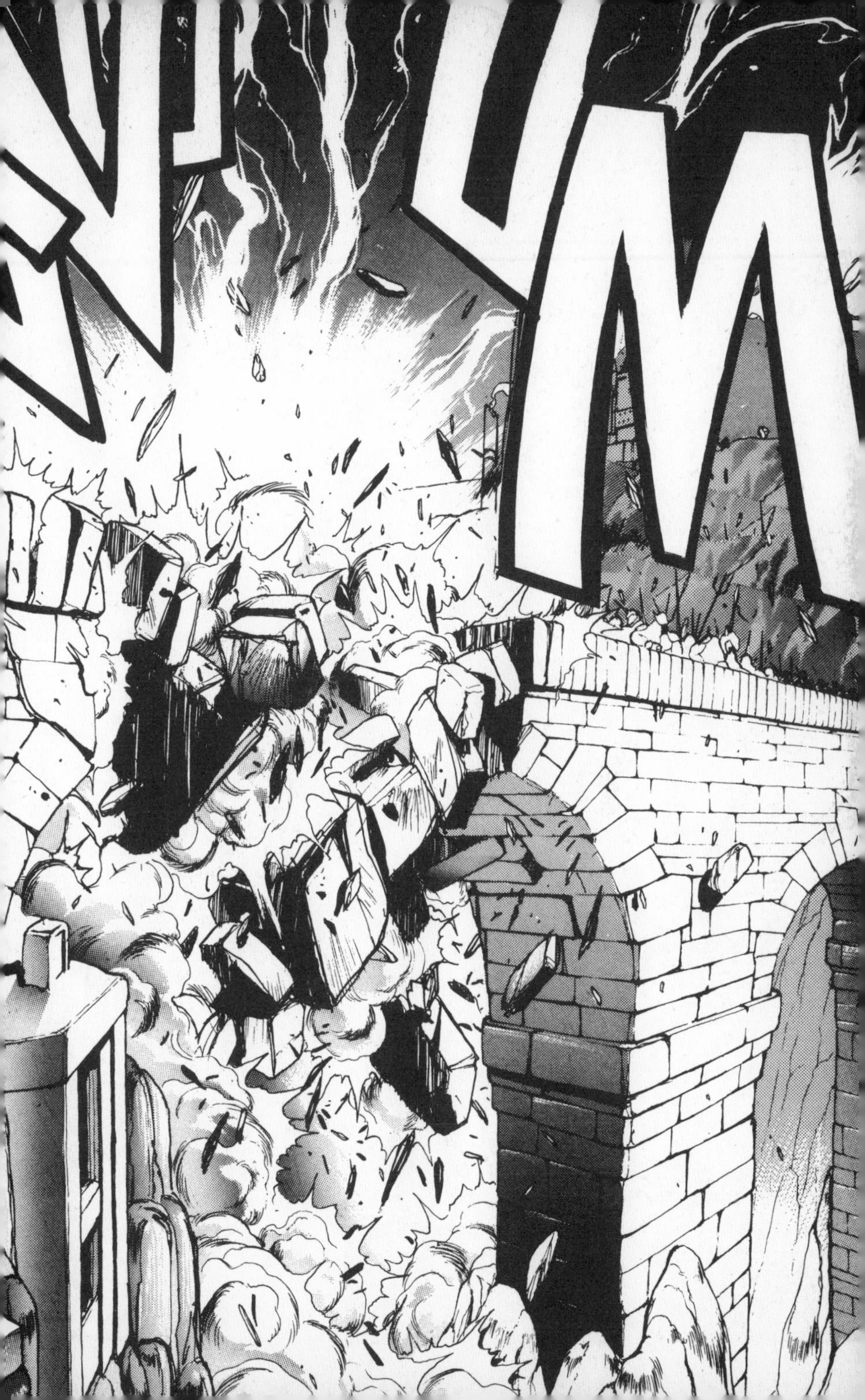

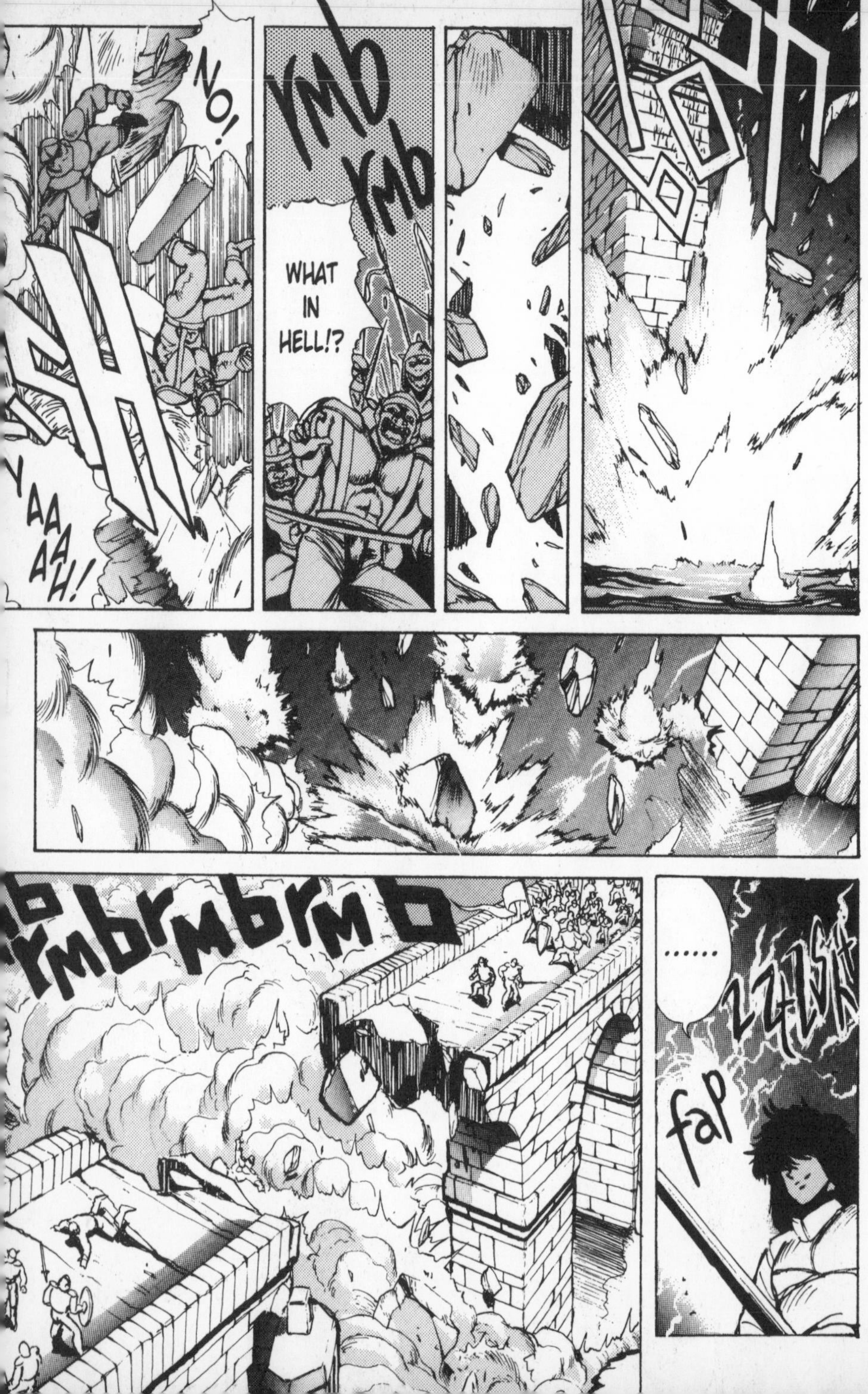
NO!
YAAAAAH!
WHAT IN HELL!?
......
fap

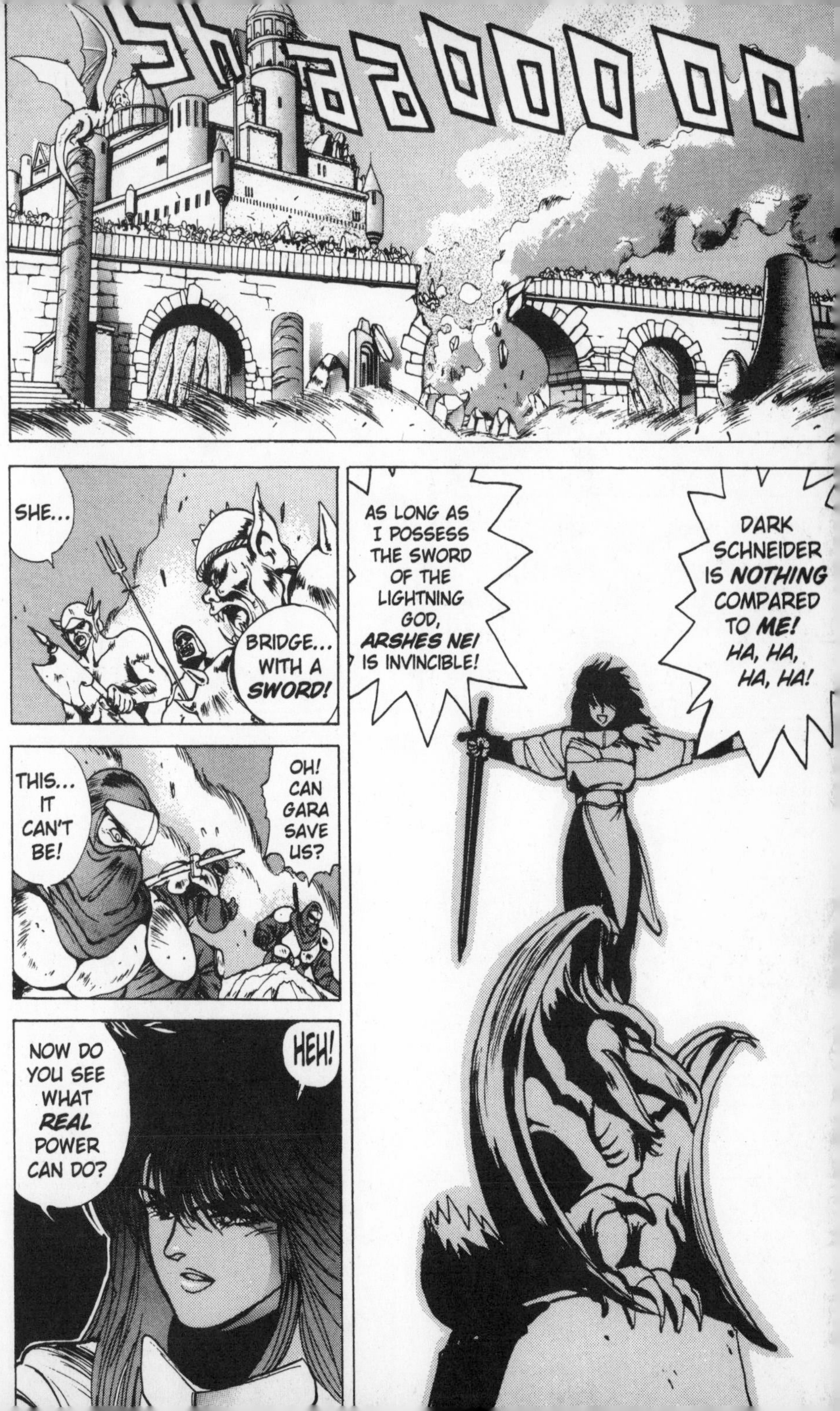

SHE...
BRIDGE... WITH A SWORD!
THIS... IT CAN'T BE!
OH! CAN GARA SAVE US?
NOW DO YOU SEE WHAT REAL POWER CAN DO?
HEH!
AS LONG AS I POSSESS THE SWORD OF THE LIGHTNING GOD, ARSHES NEI IS INVINCIBLE!
DARK SCHNEIDER IS NOTHING COMPARED TO ME! HA, HA, HA, HA!

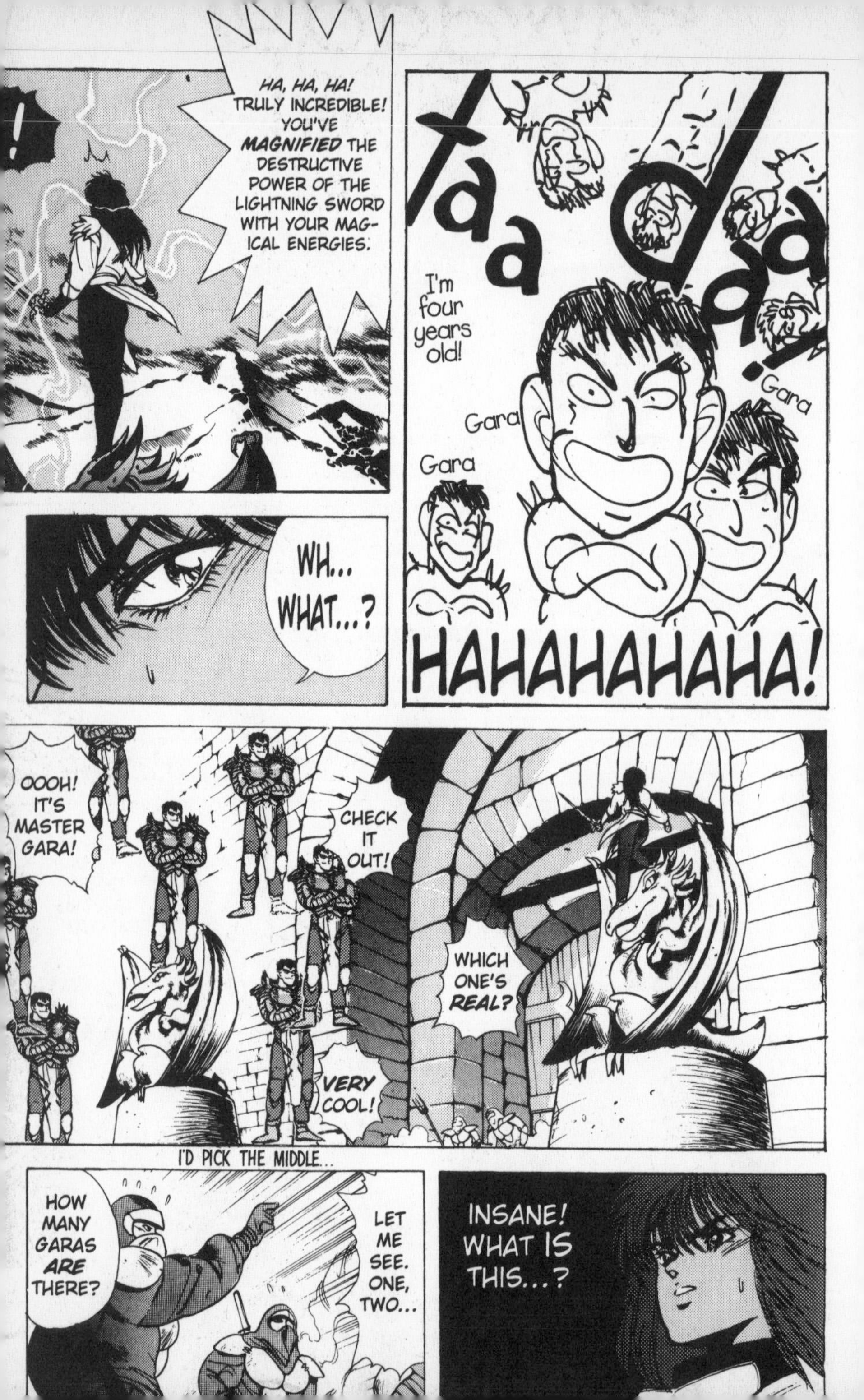
!
HA, HA, HA! TRULY INCREDIBLE! YOU'VE MAGNIFIED THE DESTRUCTIVE POWER OF THE LIGHTNING SWORD WITH YOUR MAGICAL ENERGIES.
WH... WHAT...?
Ta da!
I'm four years old!
Gara
Gara
Gara
HAHAHAHAHA!
OOOH! IT'S MASTER GARA!
CHECK IT OUT!
VERY COOL!
WHICH ONE'S REAL?
I'D PICK THE MIDDLE...
HOW MANY GARAS ARE THERE?
LET ME SEE. ONE, TWO...
INSANE! WHAT IS THIS...?

ZWOOOP!

Ninja Art of the Seven Body Split!

HA, HA, HA! ALL YOU DID WAS CUT DOWN ONE OF MY MIRROR IMAGES! DIDN'T YOU NOTICE?

WHERE DID YOU LEARN SUCH A STRANGE ART...?

NONE OF YOUR BEESWAX! WE'VE BOTH CHANGED, OKAY? LOOK AT YOU—HOW'D YOU BECOME SUCH A COLD-HEARTED BITCH?

sktch

YOU WERE *BASICALLY* D.S.'S LOVER. I'D HAVE *THOUGHT* YOU'D BE ON HIS SIDE, *BUT*...

YOW! ZMMMMM MMM zolt zzzap

AWWW! NOT THE INTROSPECTIVE TYPE, I SUPPOSE. OH, WELL—IF WE *MUST* GET SERIOUS...

BAM

Here we go!

MASTER GARA THREW AWAY HIS ARMOR!

WHAT!?

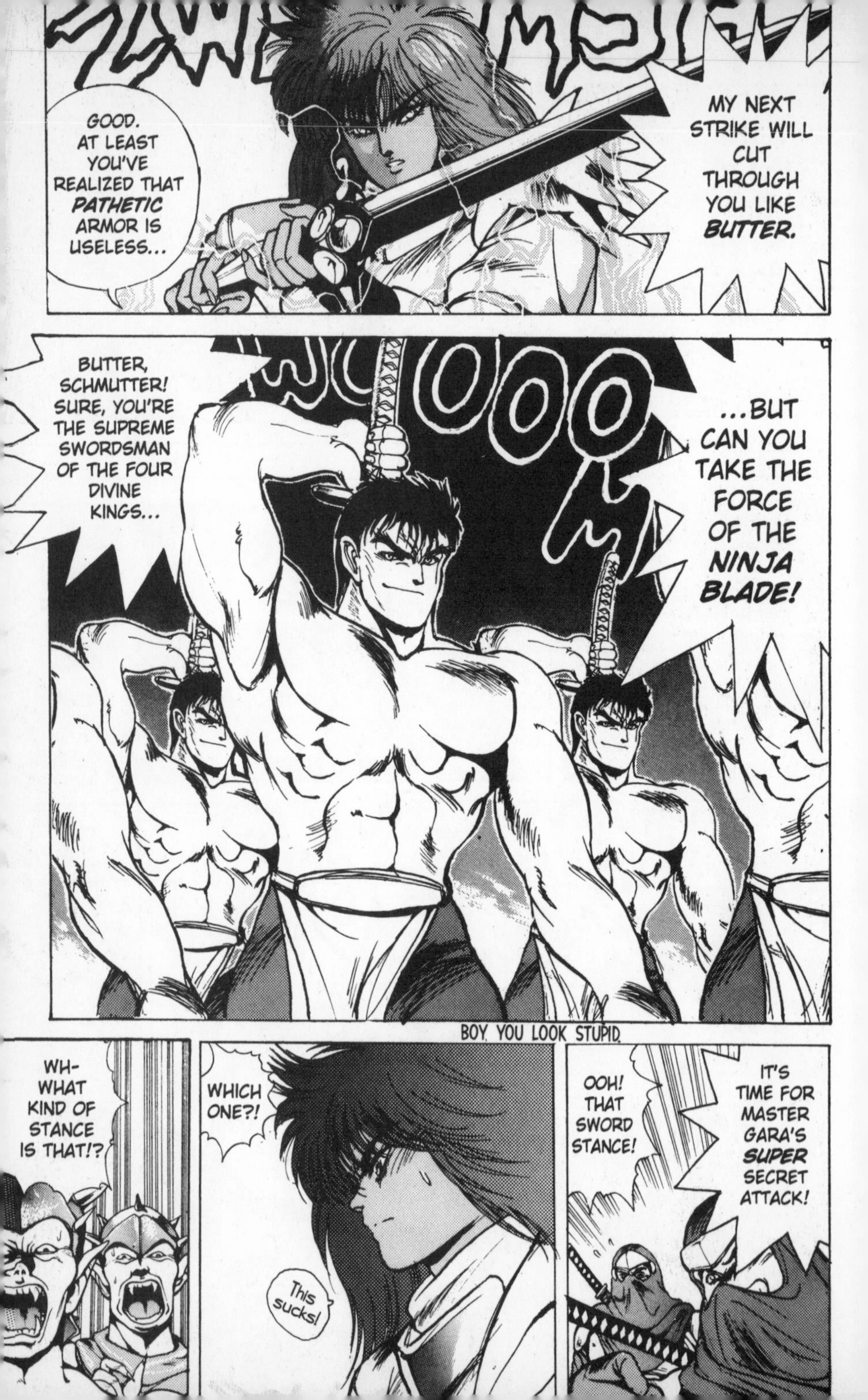

GOOD. AT LEAST YOU'VE REALIZED THAT PATHETIC ARMOR IS USELESS...
MY NEXT STRIKE WILL CUT THROUGH YOU LIKE BUTTER.
BUTTER, SCHMUTTER! SURE, YOU'RE THE SUPREME SWORDSMAN OF THE FOUR DIVINE KINGS...
...BUT CAN YOU TAKE THE FORCE OF THE NINJA BLADE!
BOY, YOU LOOK STUPID.
WH-WHAT KIND OF STANCE IS THAT!?
WHICH ONE?!
This sucks!
OOH! THAT SWORD STANCE!
IT'S TIME FOR MASTER GARA'S SUPER SECRET ATTACK!

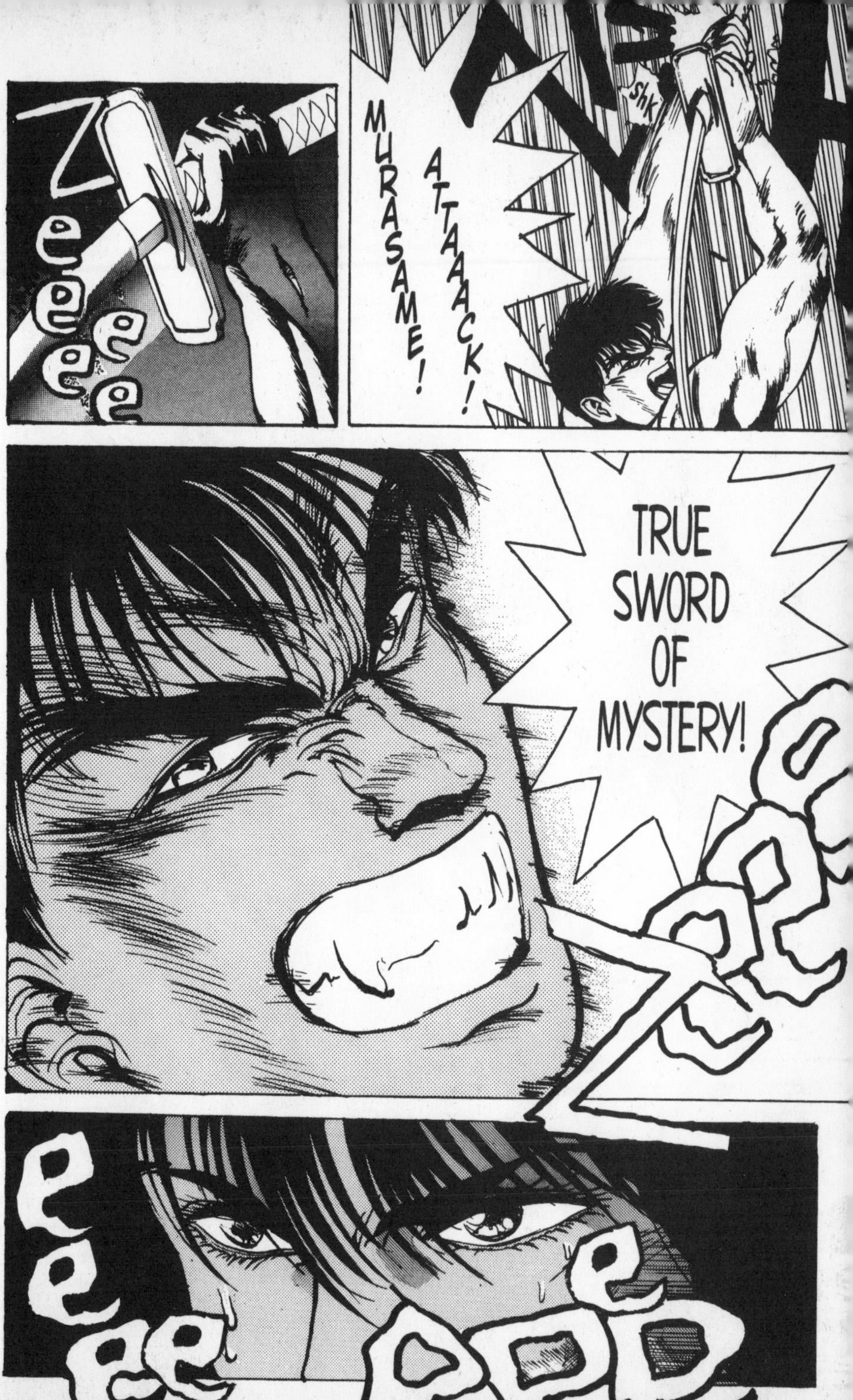
MURASAME!
ATTAAACK!
Shk
TRUE SWORD OF MYSTERY!

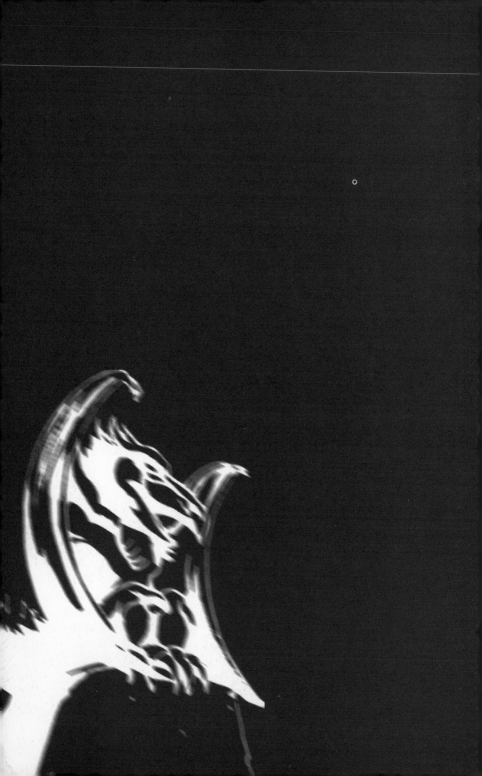

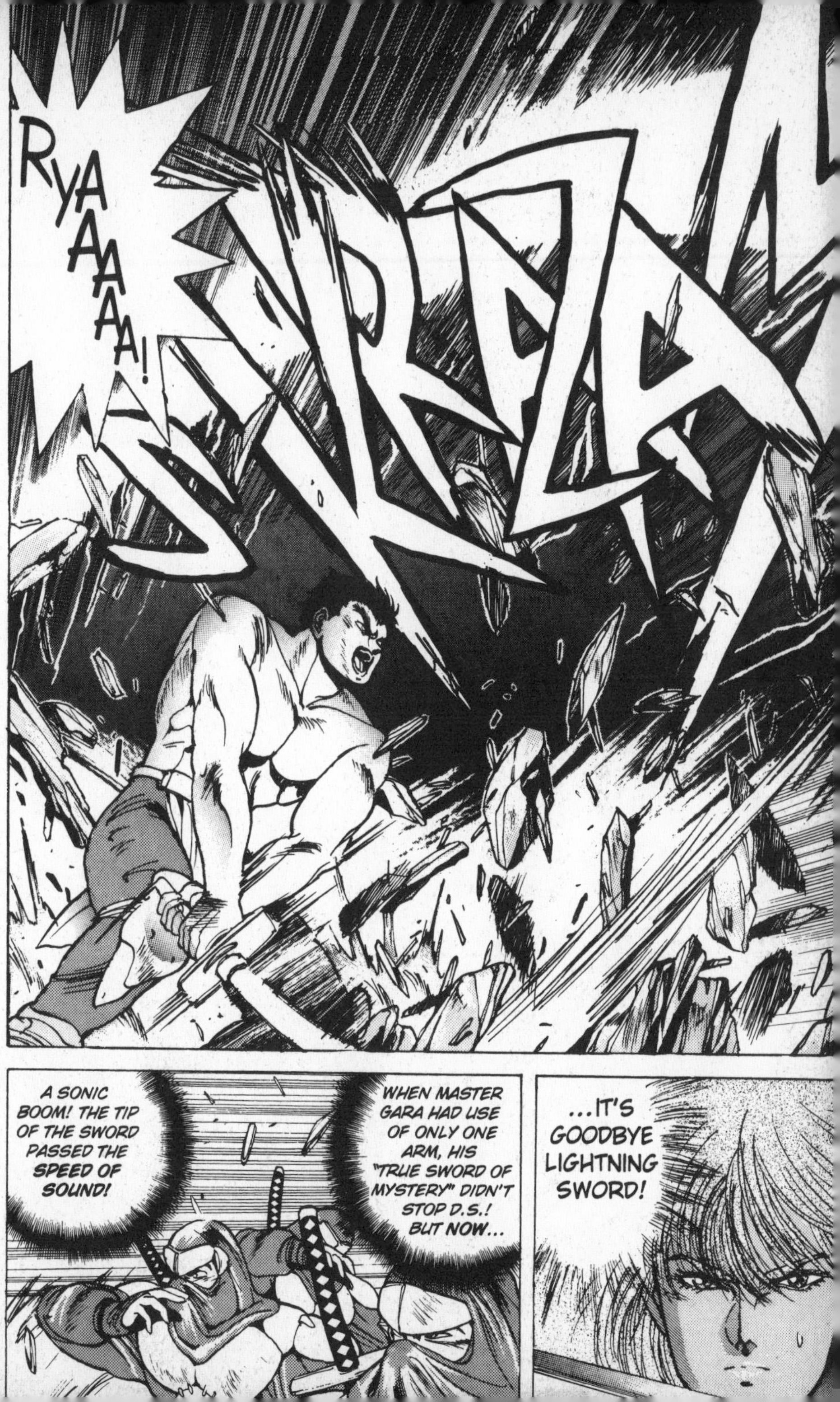
RYAAAAAA!
A SONIC BOOM! THE TIP OF THE SWORD PASSED THE SPEED OF SOUND!
WHEN MASTER GARA HAD USE OF ONLY ONE ARM, HIS "TRUE SWORD OF MYSTERY" DIDN'T STOP D.S.! BUT NOW...
...IT'S GOODBYE LIGHTNING SWORD!

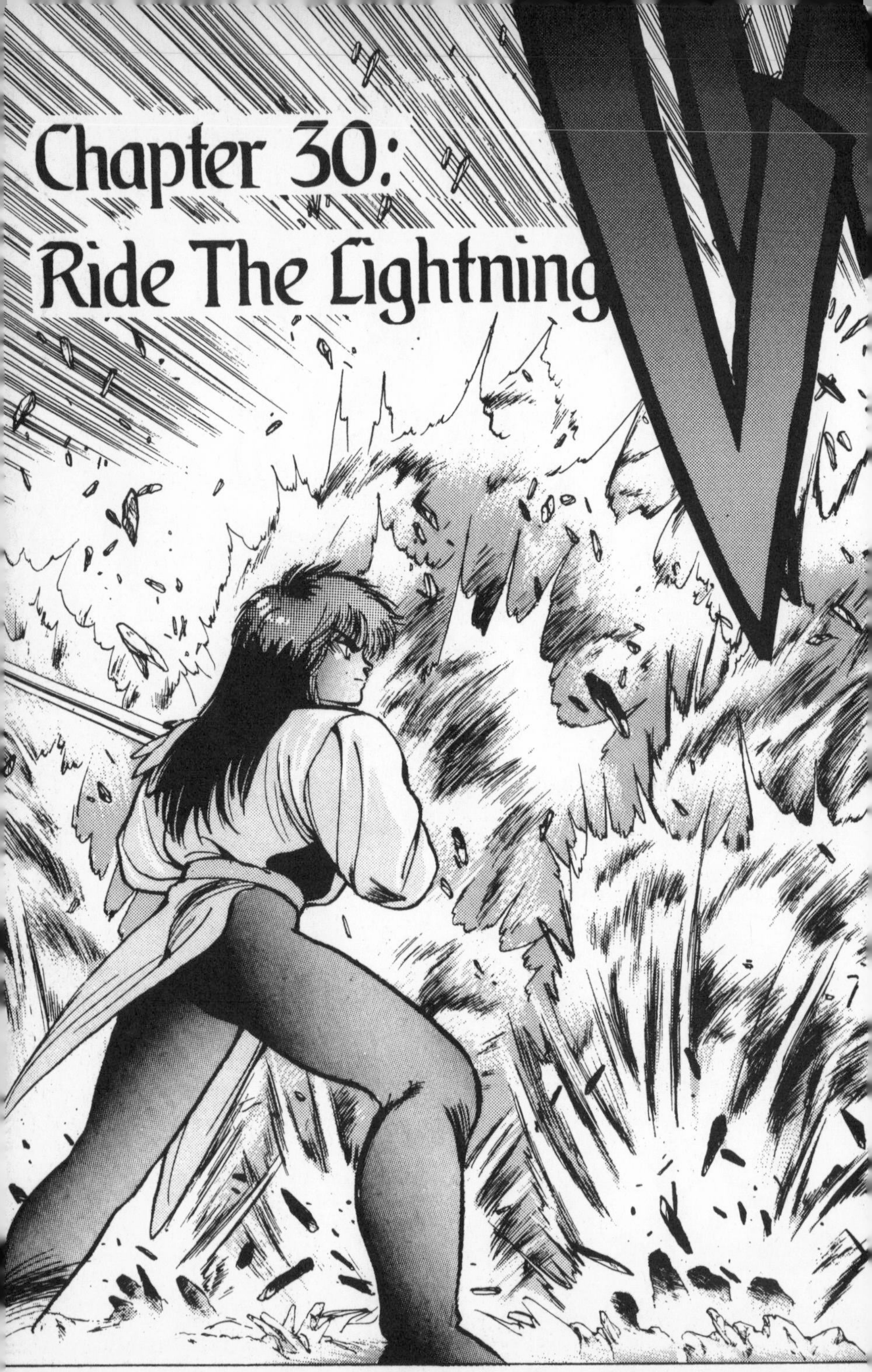
Chapter 30:
Ride The Lightning

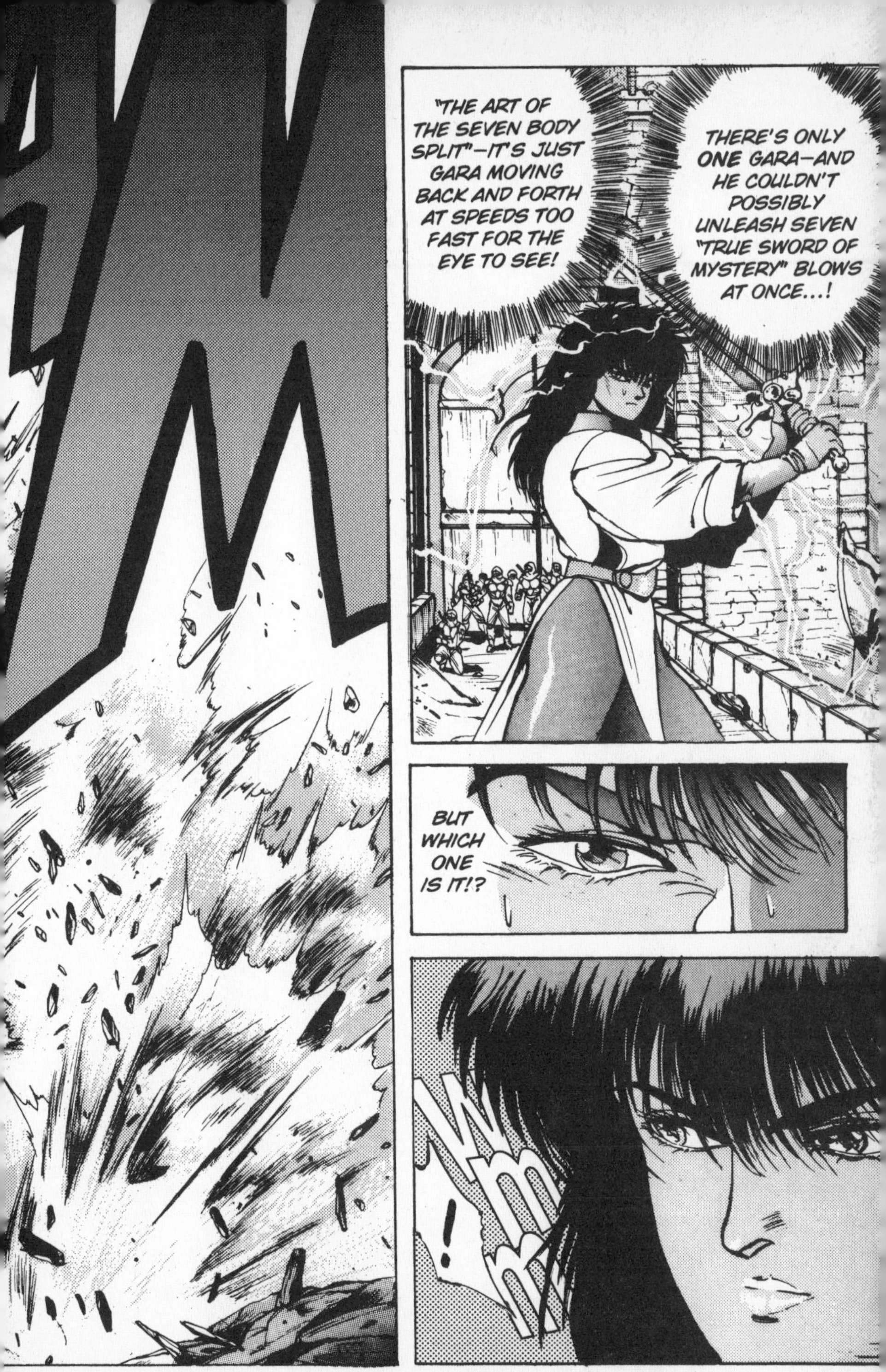
"THE ART OF THE SEVEN BODY SPLIT"—IT'S JUST GARA MOVING BACK AND FORTH AT SPEEDS TOO FAST FOR THE EYE TO SEE!
THERE'S ONLY ONE GARA—AND HE COULDN'T POSSIBLY UNLEASH SEVEN "TRUE SWORD OF MYSTERY" BLOWS AT ONCE...!
BUT WHICH ONE IS IT!?
!

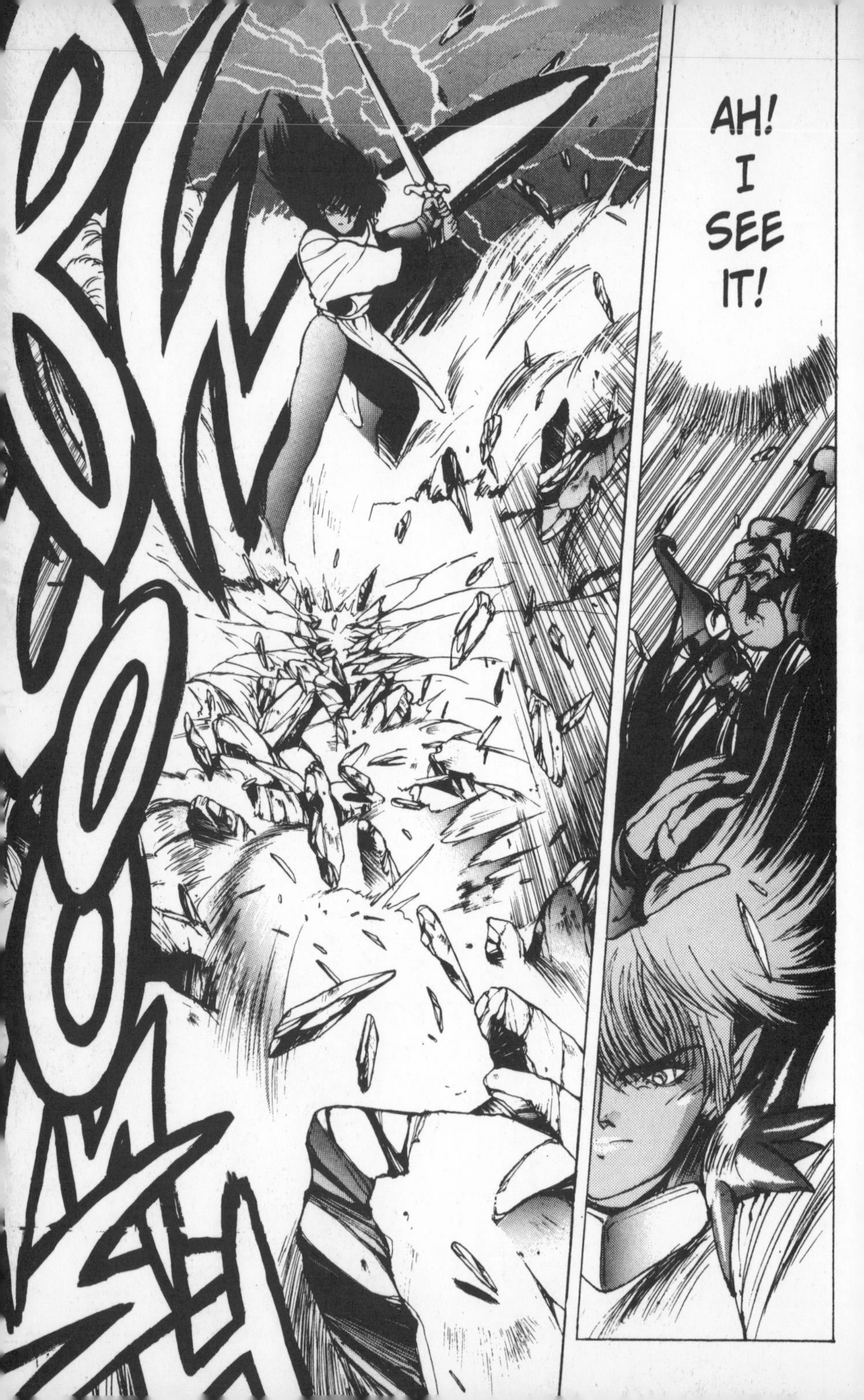
AH!
I
SEE
IT!

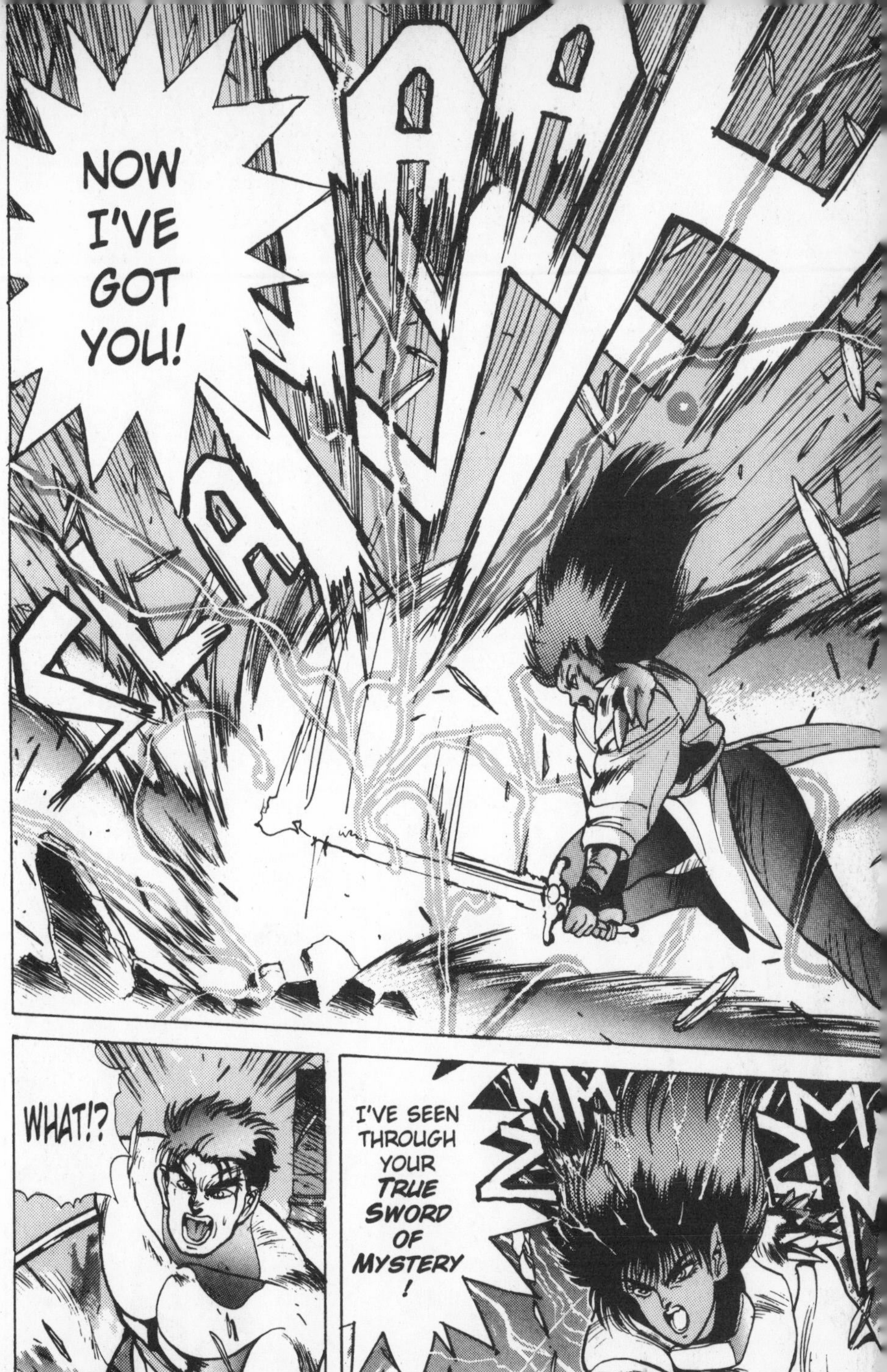
NOW I'VE GOT YOU!
WHAT!?
I'VE SEEN THROUGH YOUR *TRUE SWORD OF MYSTERY*!

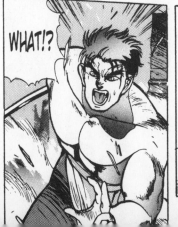

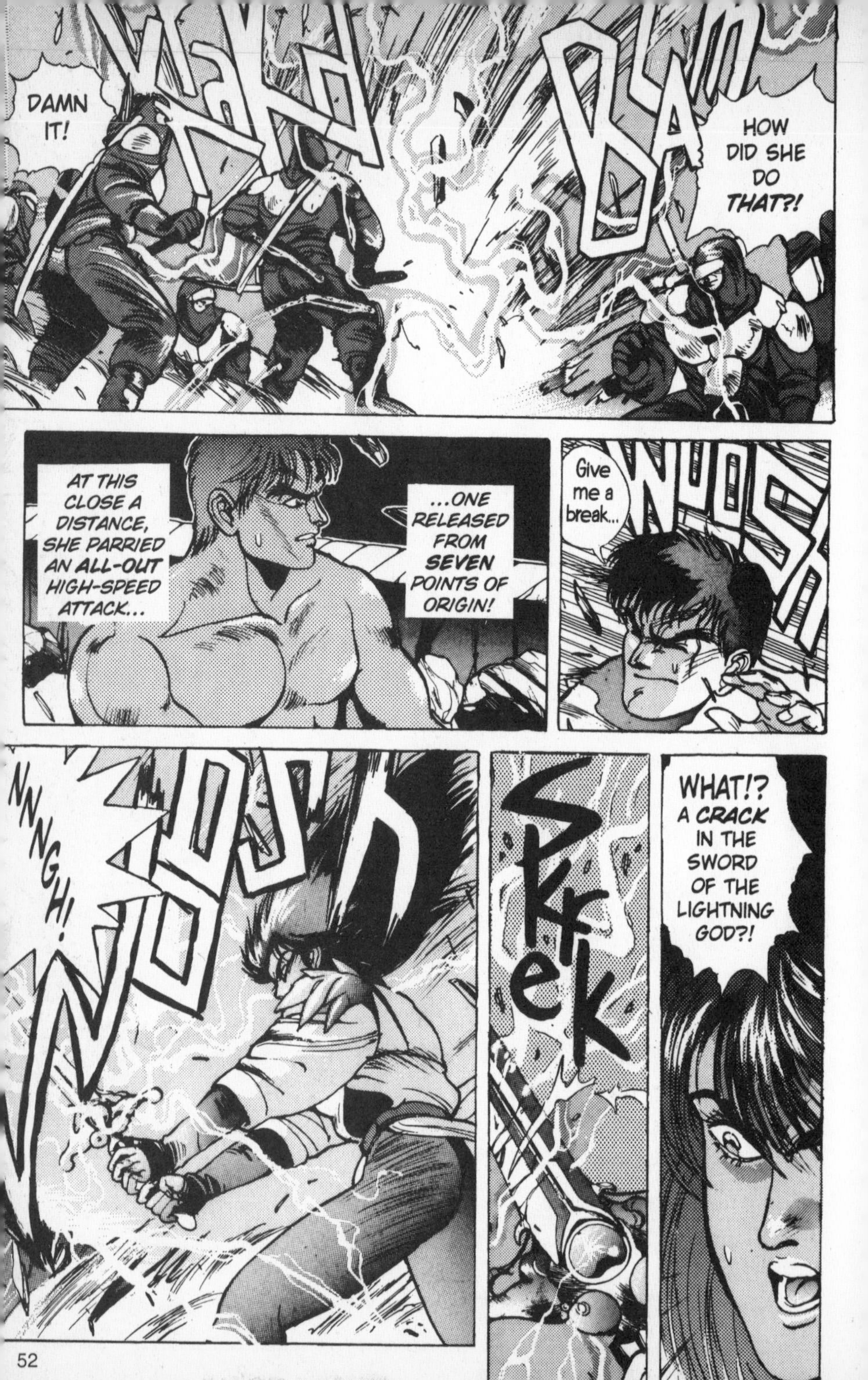
DAMN IT!
HOW DID SHE DO *THAT?!*
AT THIS CLOSE A DISTANCE, SHE PARRIED AN **ALL-OUT** HIGH-SPEED ATTACK...
...ONE RELEASED FROM **SEVEN** POINTS OF ORIGIN!
Give me a break...
NNNGH!
WHAT!? A ***CRACK*** IN THE SWORD OF THE LIGHTNING GOD?!

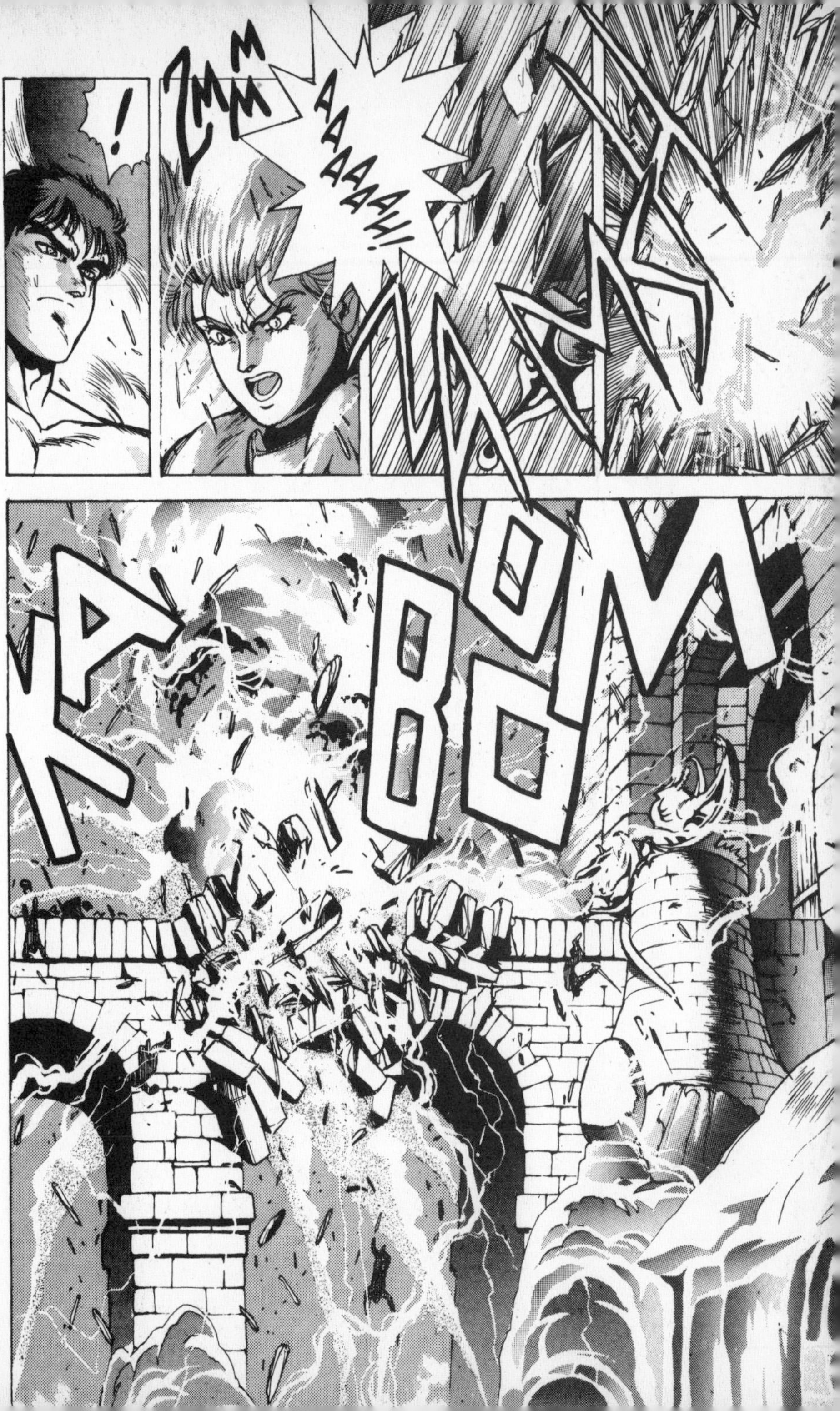

!
ZMMMM
AAAAAAAH!!
KA BOOM

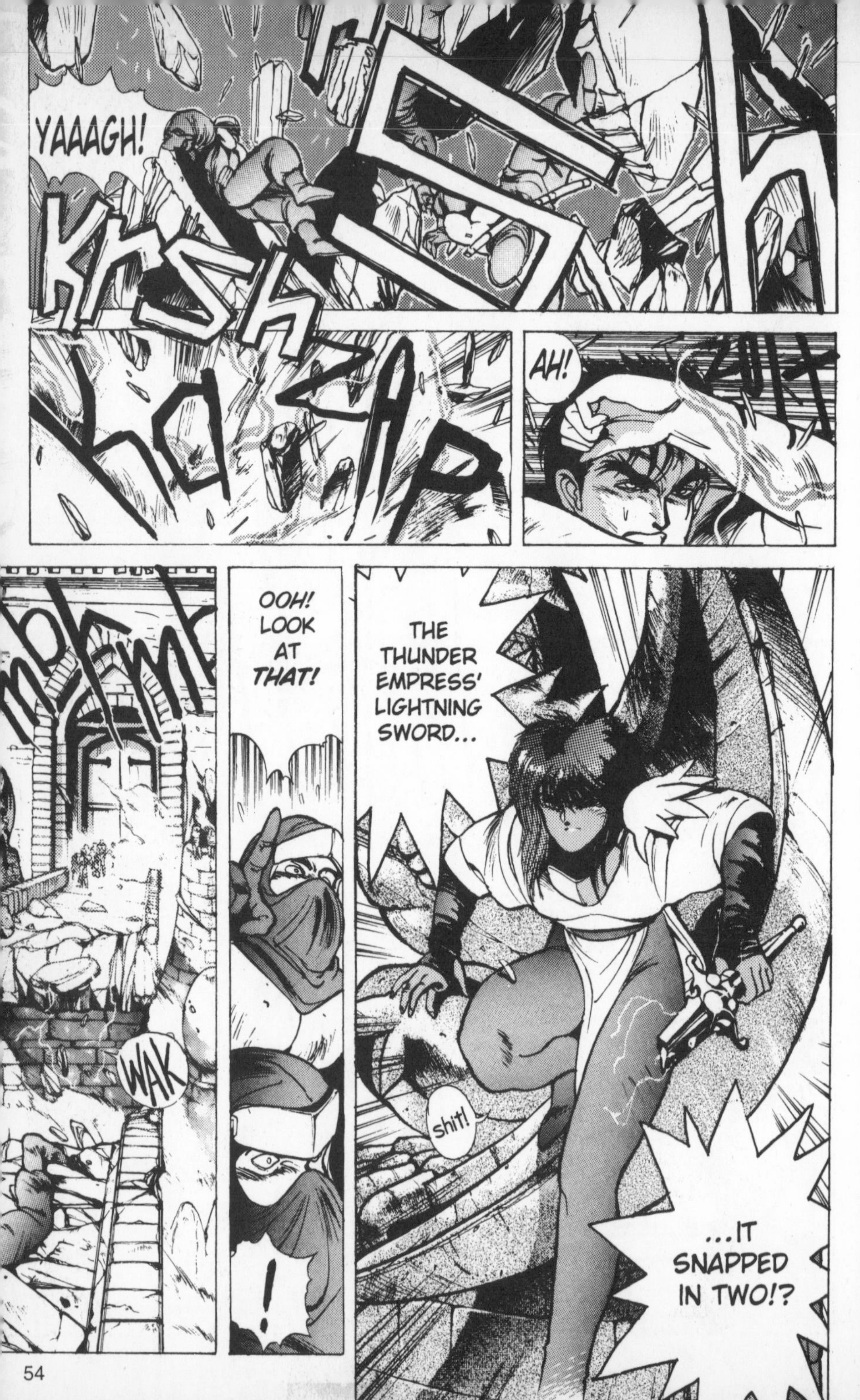
YAAAGH!
KRASH
KAZAP
AH!
WAK
OOH! LOOK AT THAT!
!
THE THUNDER EMPRESS' LIGHTNING SWORD...
shit!
...IT SNAPPED IN TWO!?

THIS JUST CAN'T BE!

THE TRUE SWORD OF MYSTERY... WHAT A FEARSOME BLADE!

HA HA HA HA HA HA

WITH YOUR SWORD BROKEN, YOU CAN'T FIGHT ANYMORE!

HA, HA, HA! BUT DON'T WORRY—YOU'RE AN IMPORTANT WOMAN TO D.S.. HE WON'T KILL YOU!

SO IT'S *MY* WIN, RIGHT, NEI?

YEAAAAAH!

Oooooh!

MASTER GARA'S NINJA FORCE OF 2000 BEAT THE THIRD REGI-MENT—20,000 STRONG!

WH... WHY...?

NNGH... H-HOW COULD MISTRESS NEI LOSE TO H...

Yaaay!

...TSK.

Yeeeha!

HO, HO! WE *DID* IT! WE DID IT, PRIN-CESS SHEILA!

NINJA MASTER GARA HAS DEFEATED THE ENEMY!

Woo hoo

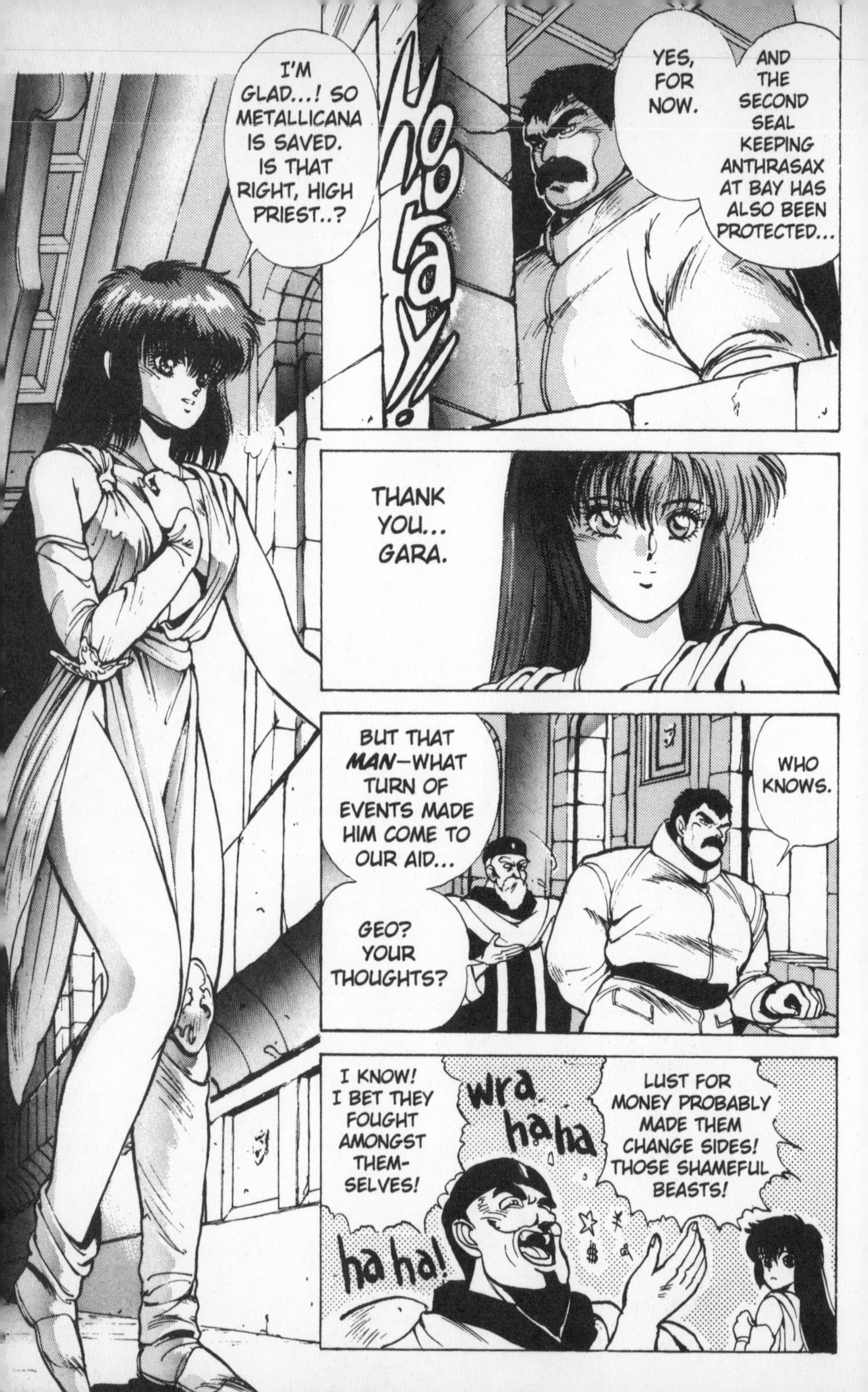
I'M GLAD...! SO METALLICANA IS SAVED. IS THAT RIGHT, HIGH PRIEST..?
Hooray!
YES, FOR NOW.
AND THE SECOND SEAL KEEPING ANTHRASAX AT BAY HAS ALSO BEEN PROTECTED...
THANK YOU... GARA.
BUT THAT MAN—WHAT TURN OF EVENTS MADE HIM COME TO OUR AID...
GEO? YOUR THOUGHTS?
WHO KNOWS.
I KNOW! I BET THEY FOUGHT AMONGST THEM-SELVES!
wra haha
LUST FOR MONEY PROBABLY MADE THEM CHANGE SIDES! THOSE SHAMEFUL BEASTS!
ha ha!

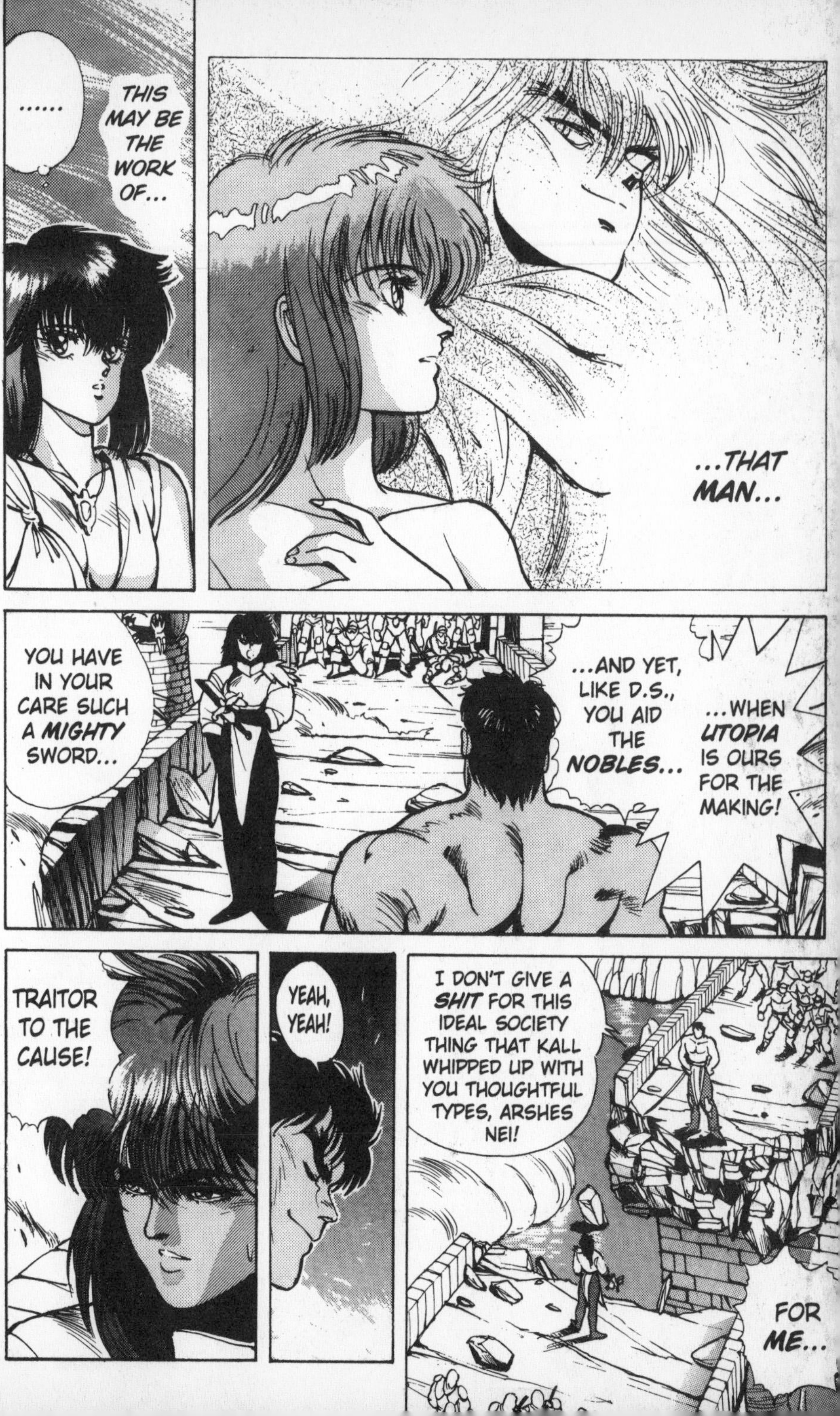
......
THIS MAY BE THE WORK OF...
...THAT MAN...
YOU HAVE IN YOUR CARE SUCH A MIGHTY SWORD...
...AND YET, LIKE D.S., YOU AID THE NOBLES...
...WHEN UTOPIA IS OURS FOR THE MAKING!
TRAITOR TO THE CAUSE!
YEAH, YEAH!
I DON'T GIVE A SHIT FOR THIS IDEAL SOCIETY THING THAT KALL WHIPPED UP WITH YOU THOUGHTFUL TYPES, ARSHES NEI!
FOR ME...

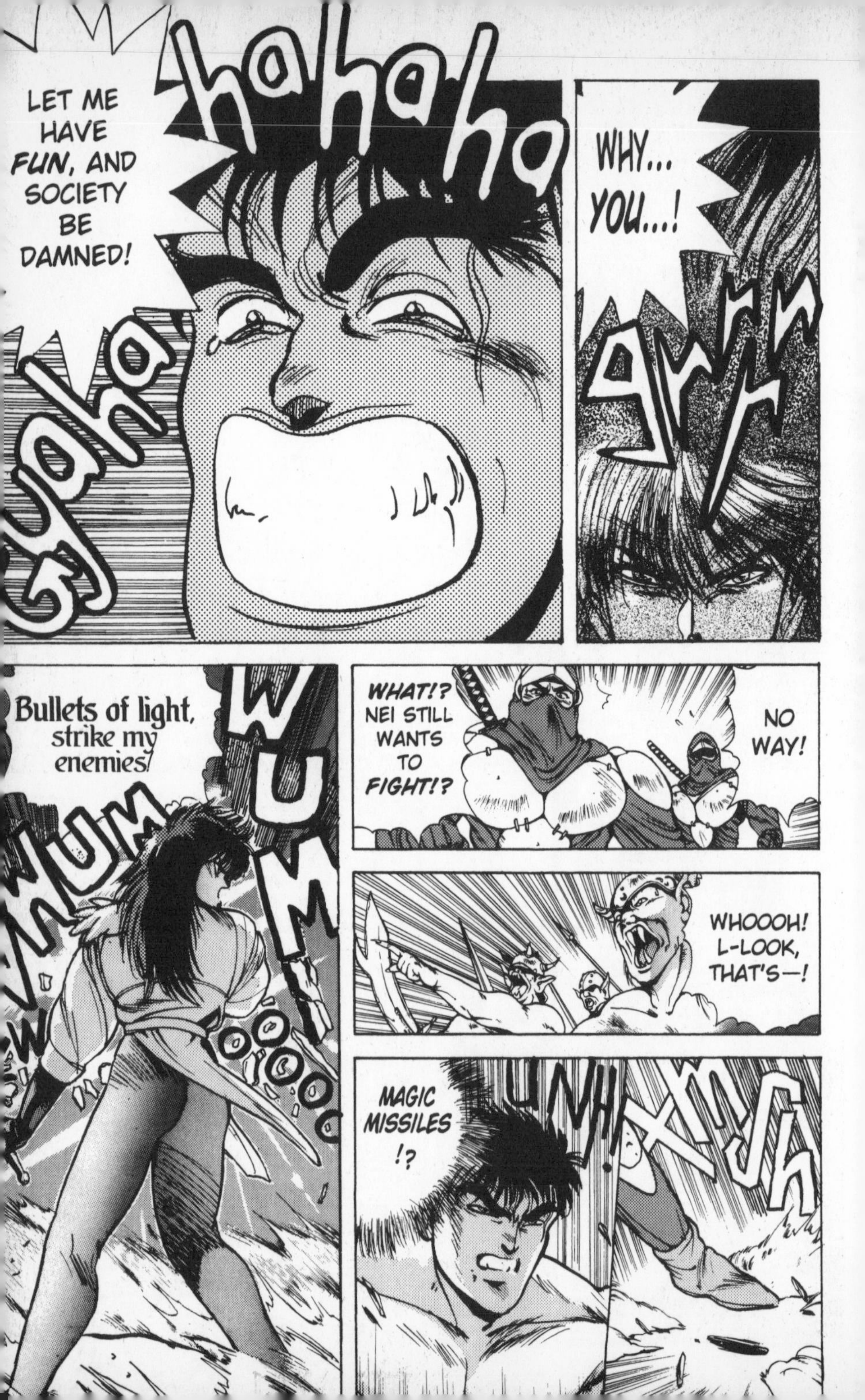
LET ME HAVE FUN, AND SOCIETY BE DAMNED!
hahahaha
Gyaha
WHY... YOU...!
grrrr
Bullets of light, strike my enemies!
WUM WUM WUM
WHOOOOO
WHAT!? NEI STILL WANTS TO FIGHT!?
NO WAY!
WHOOOH! L-LOOK, THAT'S—!
MAGIC MISSILES !?
UNH!
XHASH

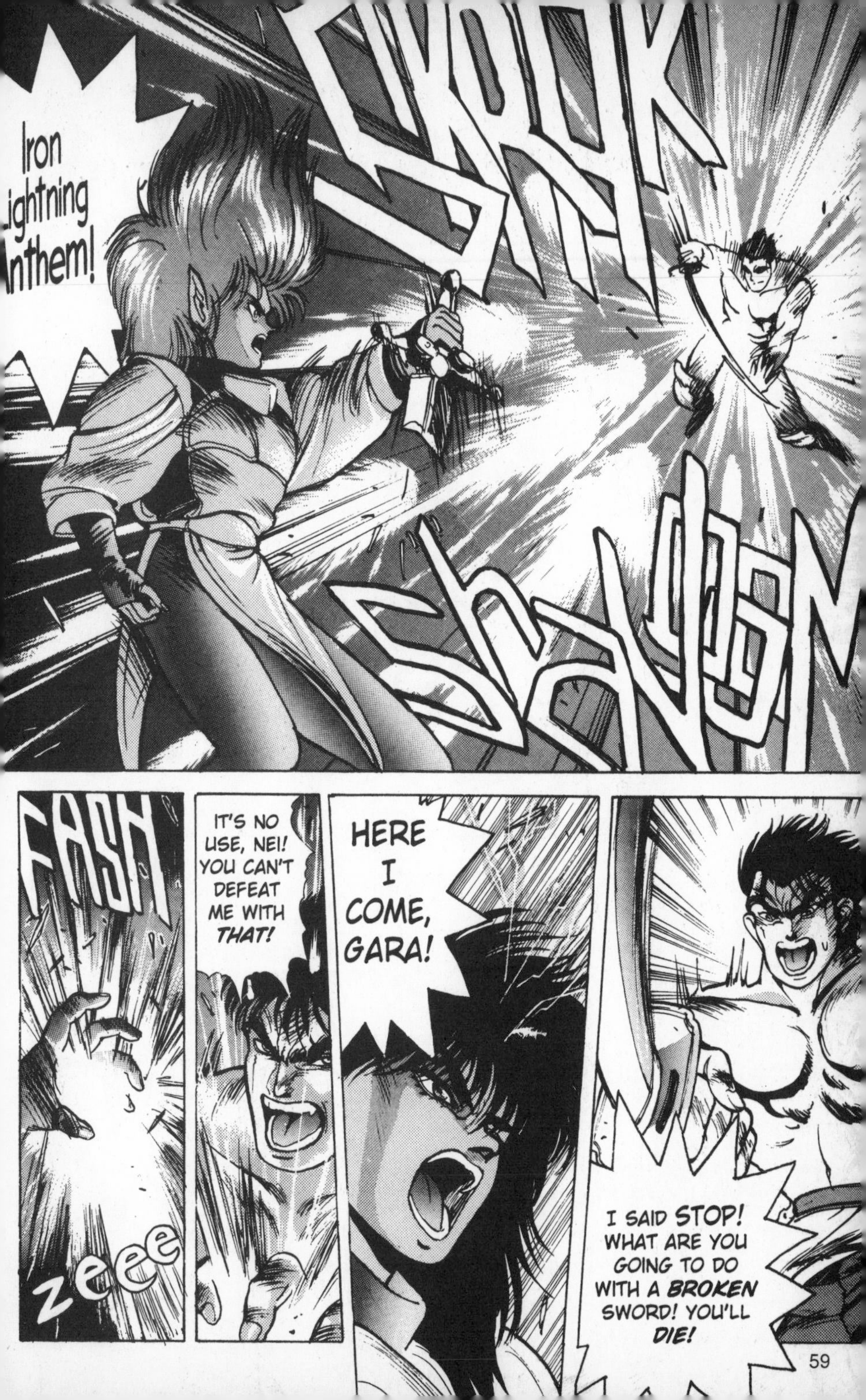
Iron Lightning Anthem!
FASH
zeee
IT'S NO USE, NEI! YOU CAN'T DEFEAT ME WITH THAT!
HERE I COME, GARA!
I SAID STOP! WHAT ARE YOU GOING TO DO WITH A BROKEN SWORD! YOU'LL DIE!

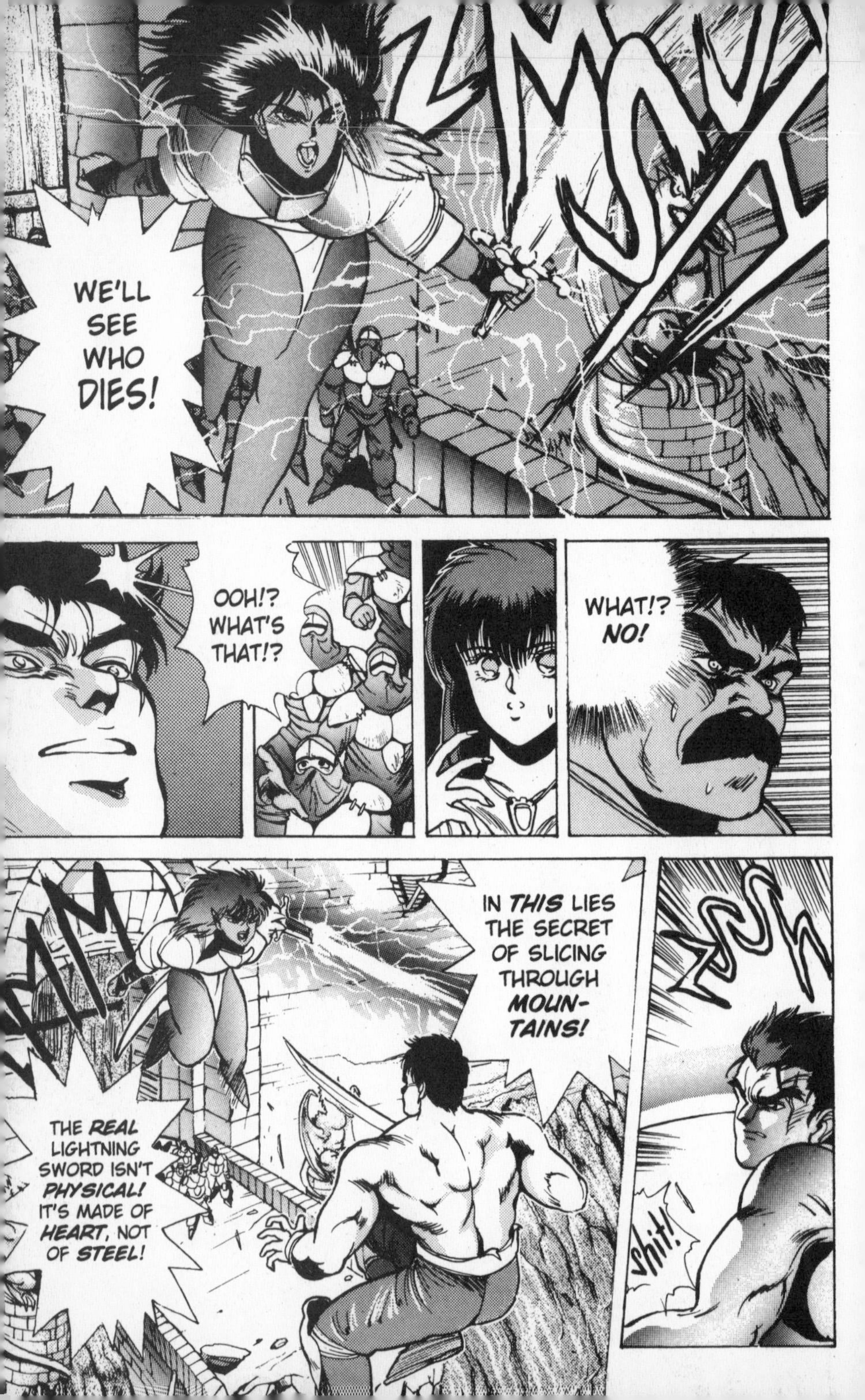
WE'LL SEE WHO DIES!
OOH!? WHAT'S THAT!?
WHAT!? NO!
IN THIS LIES THE SECRET OF SLICING THROUGH MOUN-TAINS!
THE REAL LIGHTNING SWORD ISN'T PHYSICAL! IT'S MADE OF HEART, NOT OF STEEL!
shit!

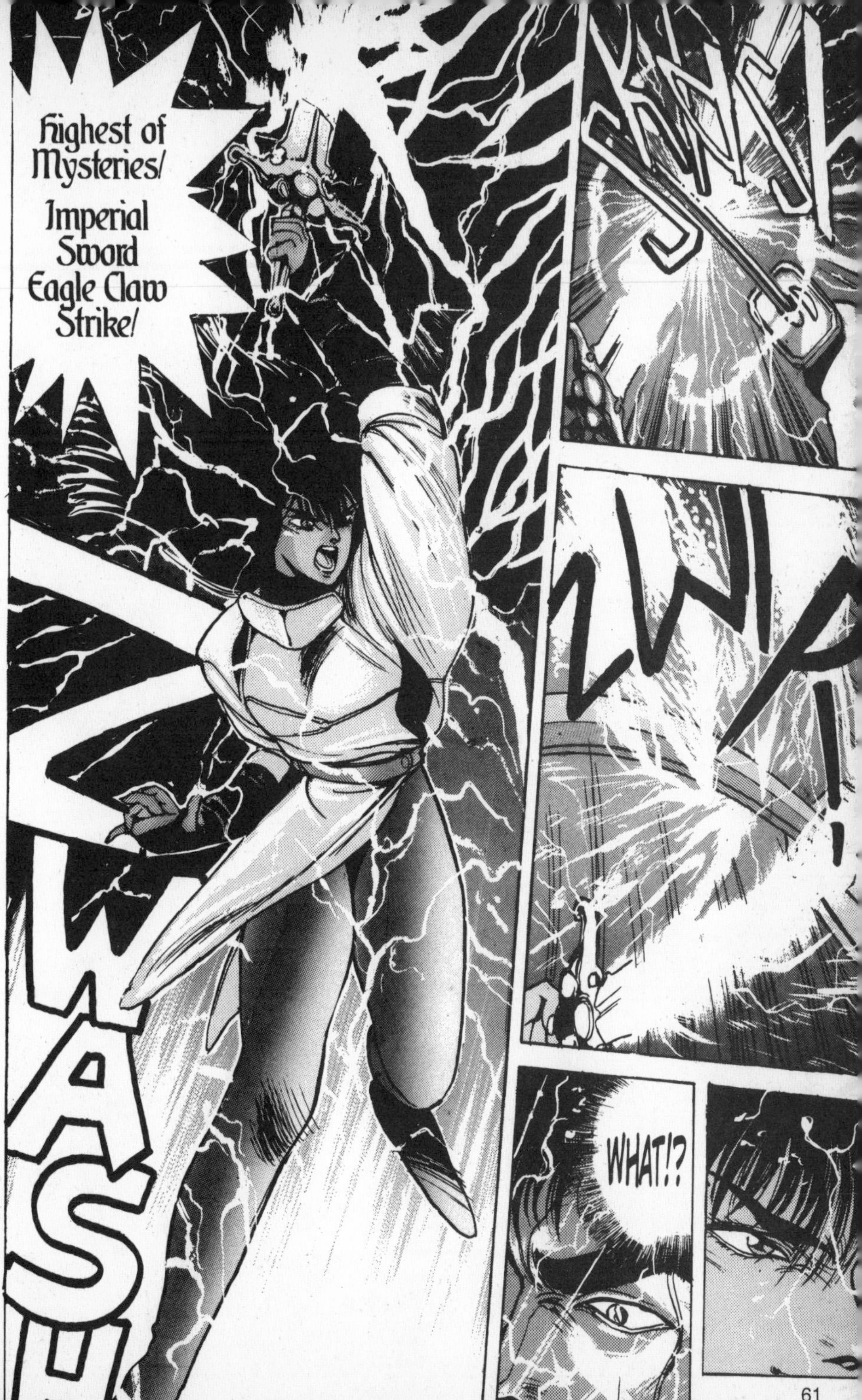
Highest of Mysteries!
Imperial Sword Eagle Claw Strike!
WASH
ZWIP!
WHAT!?

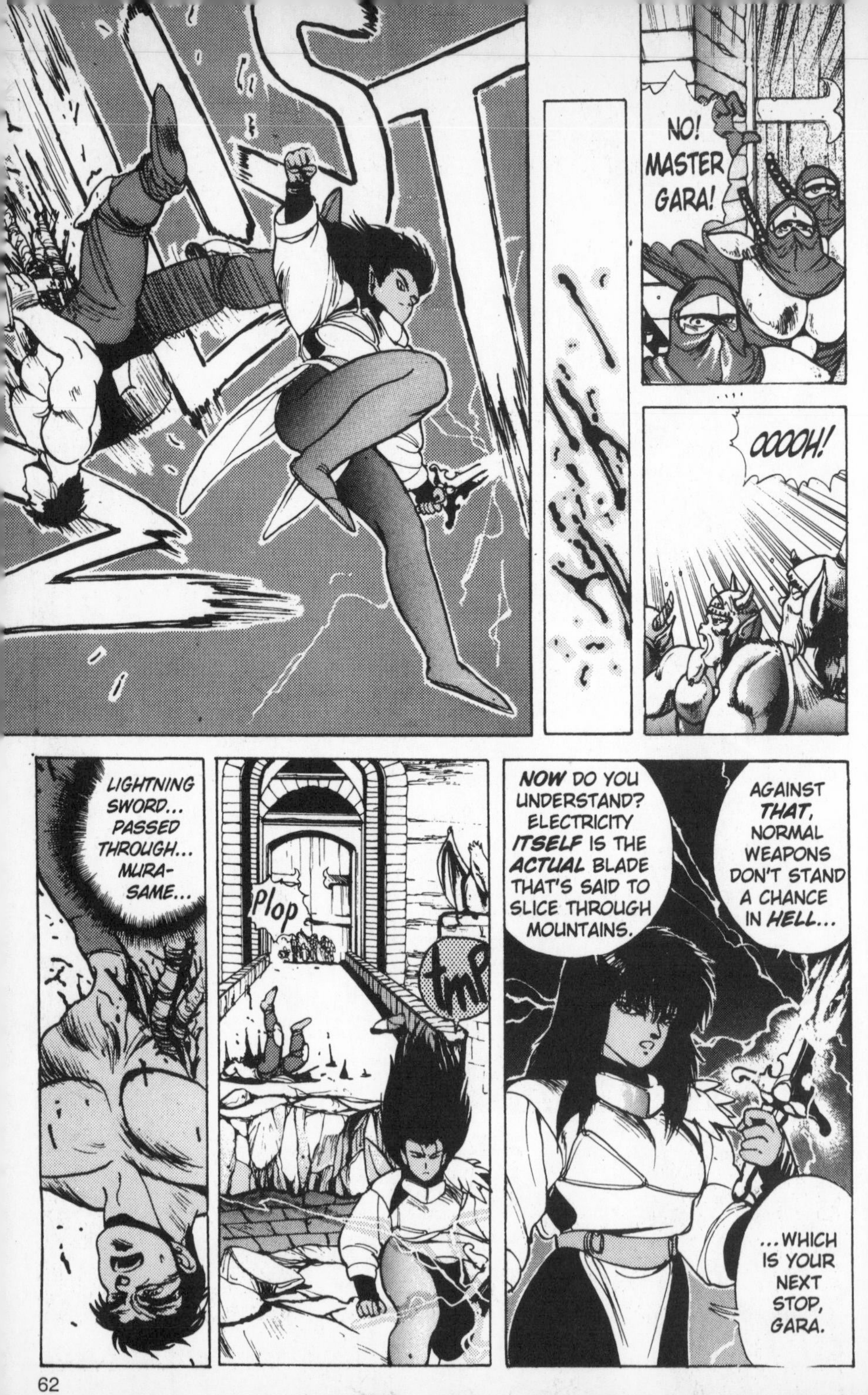

NO! MASTER GARA!
OOOOH!
LIGHTNING SWORD... PASSED THROUGH... MURA-SAME...
Plop
tmp
NOW DO YOU UNDERSTAND? ELECTRICITY ITSELF IS THE ACTUAL BLADE THAT'S SAID TO SLICE THROUGH MOUNTAINS.
AGAINST THAT, NORMAL WEAPONS DON'T STAND A CHANCE IN HELL...
...WHICH IS YOUR NEXT STOP, GARA.

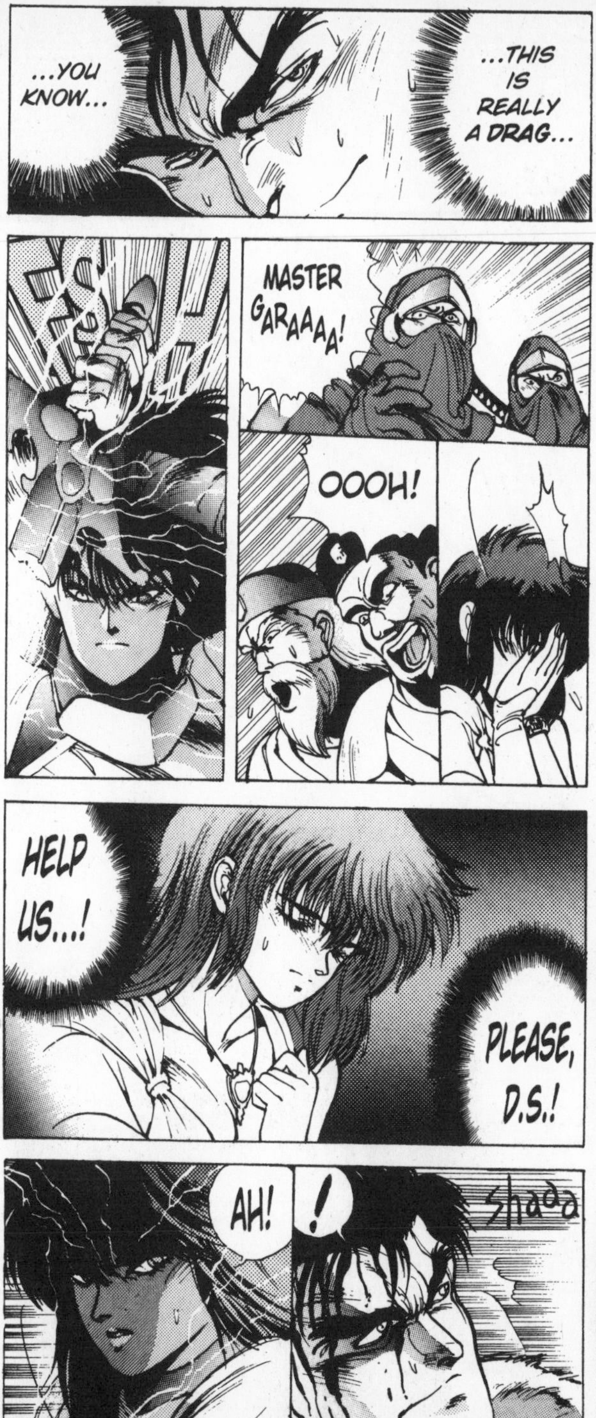
...YOU KNOW...
...THIS IS REALLY A DRAG...
MASTER GARAAAAA!
OOOH!
HELP US...!
PLEASE, D.S.!
AH!
!
shada

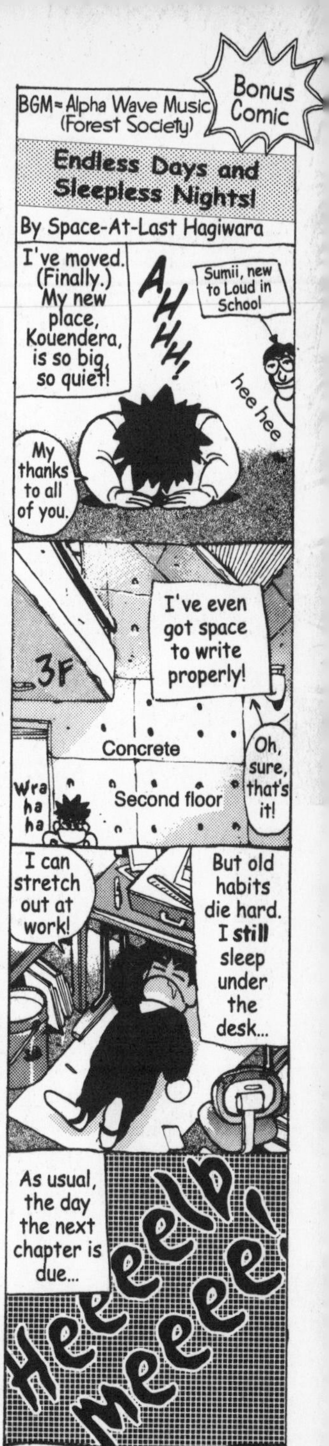
Bonus Comic
BGM = Alpha Wave Music (Forest Society)
Endless Days and Sleepless Nights!
By Space-At-Last Hagiwara
I've moved. (Finally.) My new place, Kouendera, is so big, so quiet!
AHHH!
Sumii, new to Loud in School
hee hee
My thanks to all of you.
I've even got space to write properly!
3F
Concrete
Second floor
Wra ha ha
Oh, sure, that's it!
I can stretch out at work!
But old habits die hard. I still sleep under the desk...
As usual, the day the next chapter is due...
Heeeelp meeeee!
"Just bury this guy!" - Evil Editor Takahashi

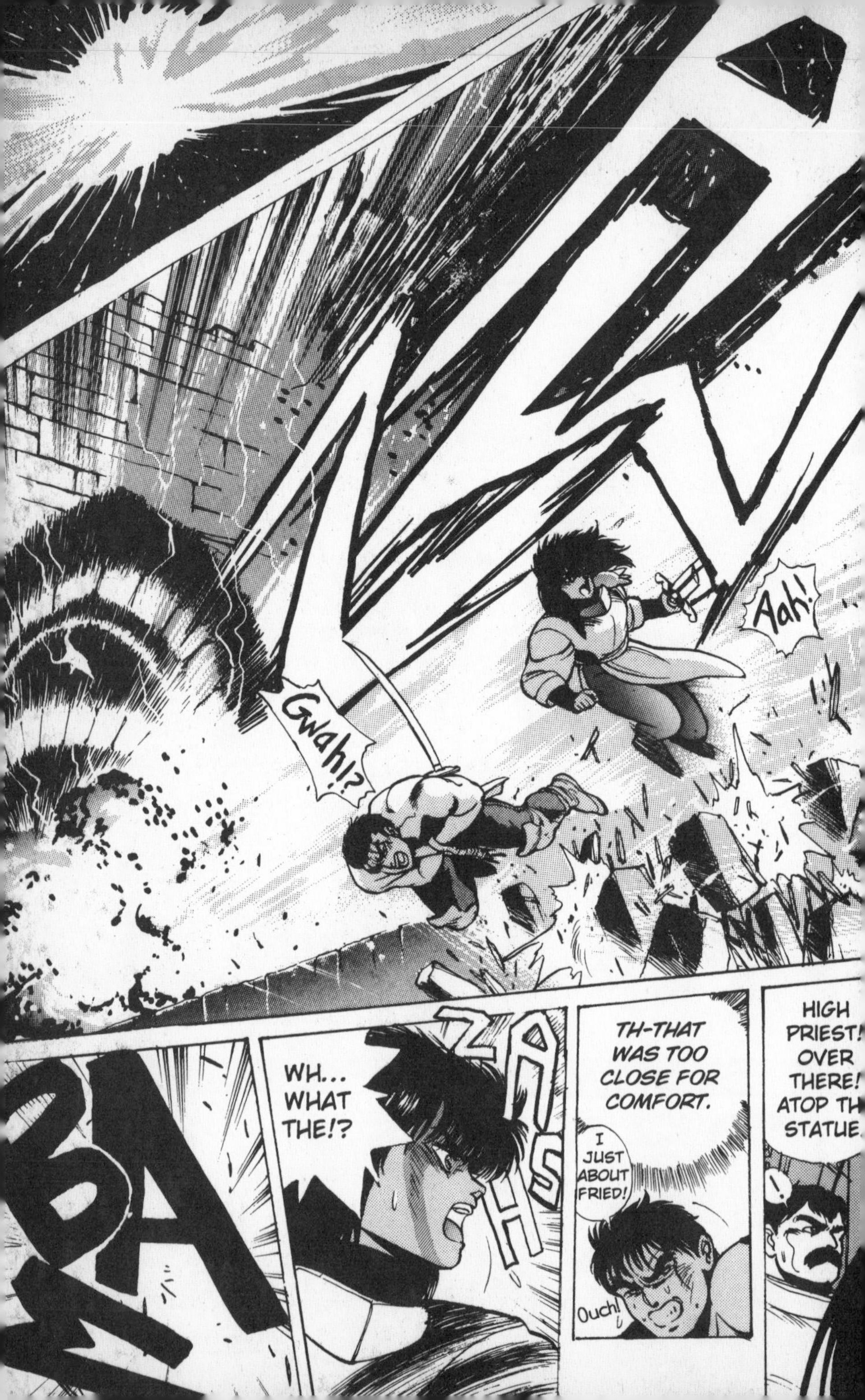
Gwah!?
Aah!
BA
WH... WHAT THE!?
TH-THAT WAS TOO CLOSE FOR COMFORT.
I JUST ABOUT FRIED!
Ouch!
HIGH PRIEST! OVER THERE! ATOP TH STATUE

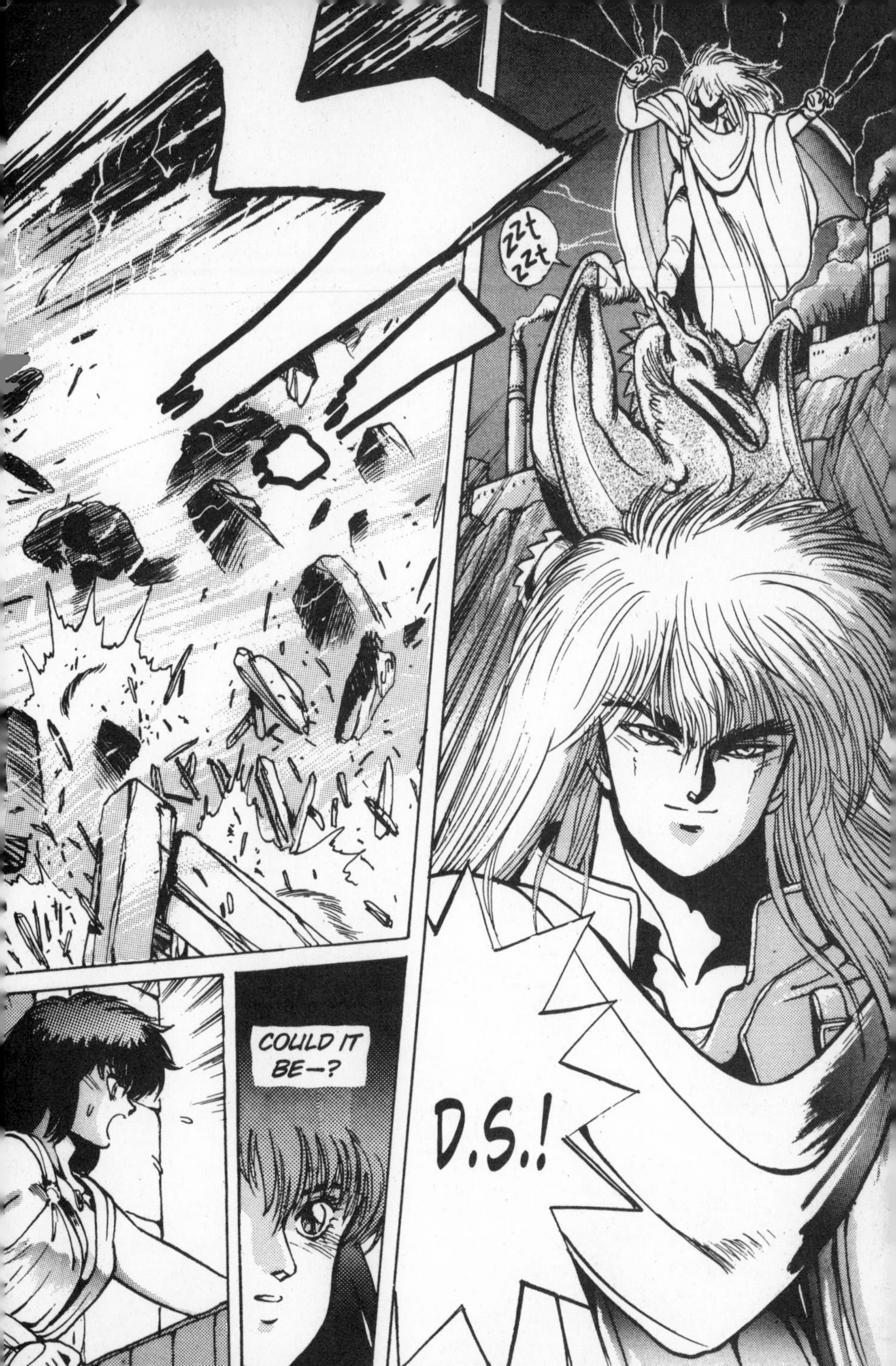

zzt zzt
COULD IT BE--?
D.S.!

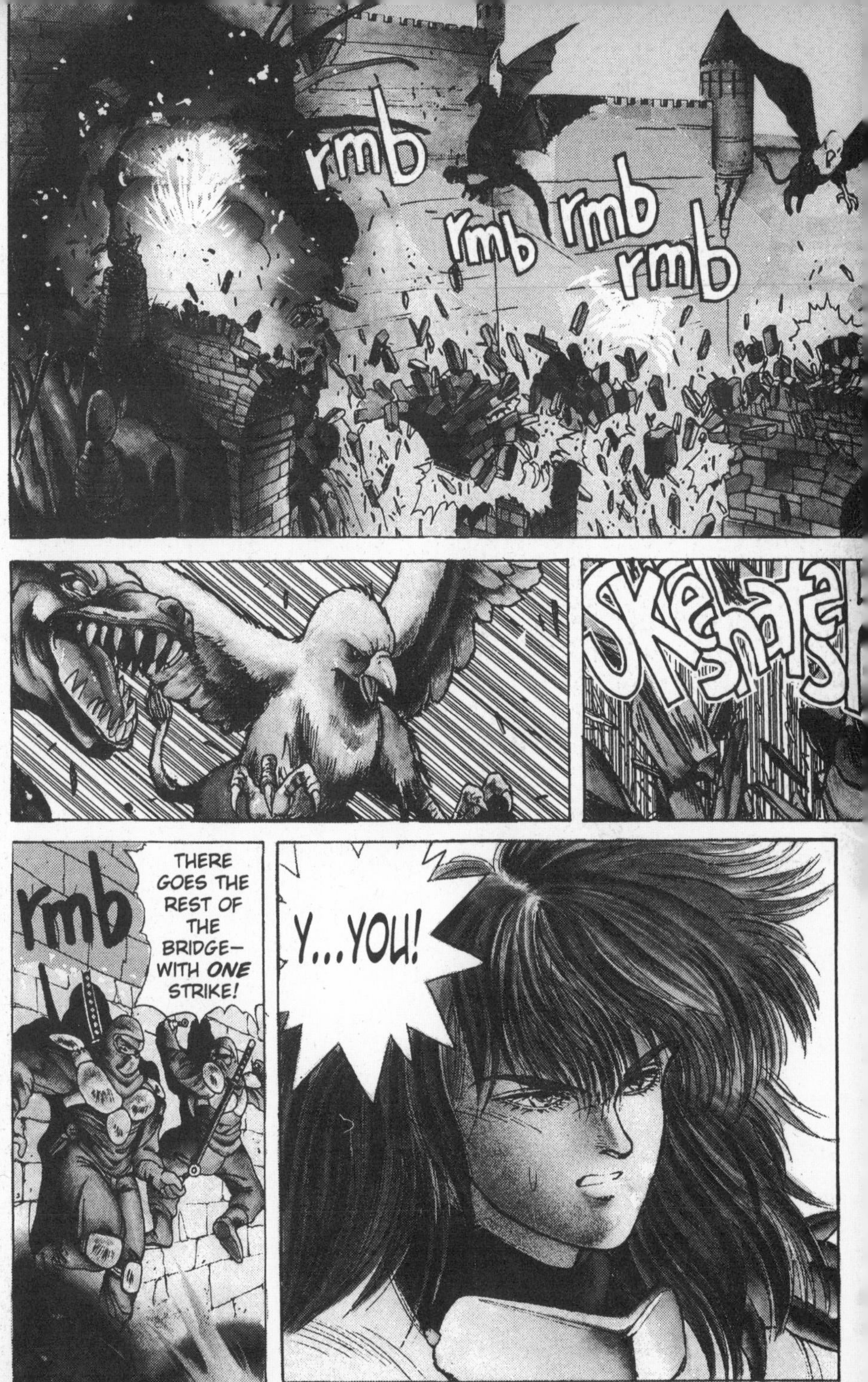
rmb
rmb rmb
rmb
rmb
THERE GOES THE REST OF THE BRIDGE— WITH *ONE* STRIKE!
Y...YOU!

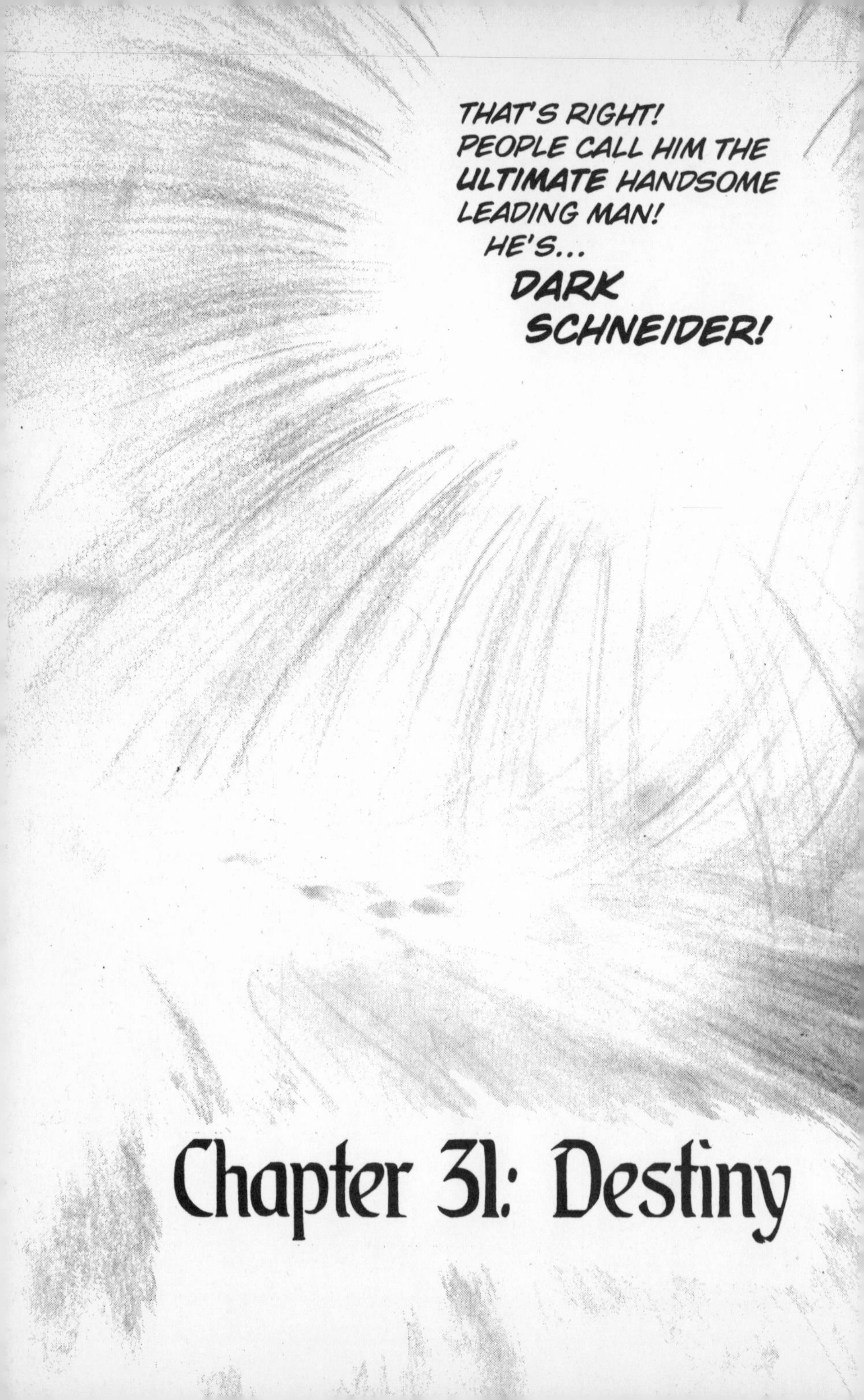
THAT'S RIGHT! PEOPLE CALL HIM THE ULTIMATE HANDSOME LEADING MAN!
HE'S...
DARK SCHNEIDER!

Chapter 31: Destiny

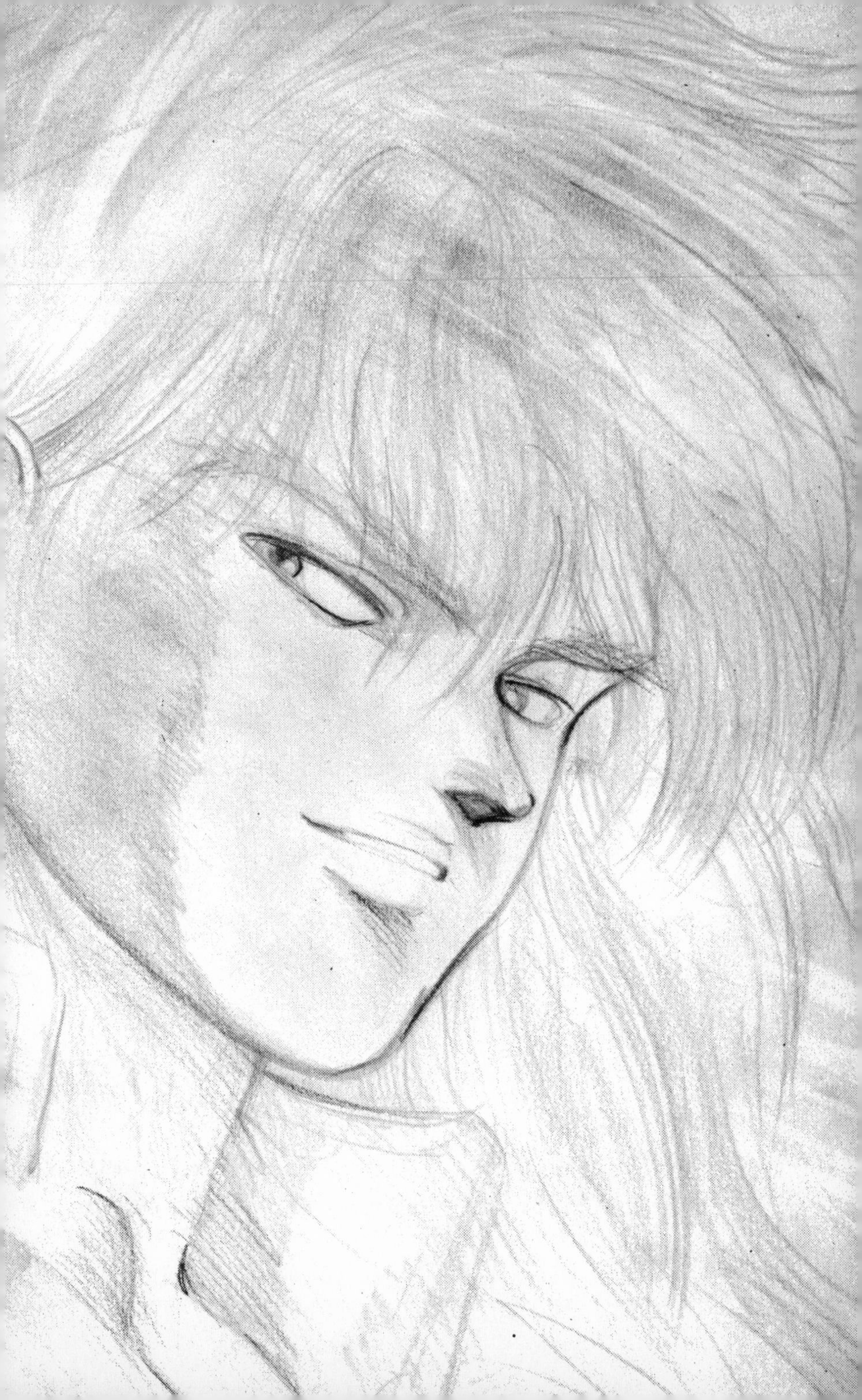

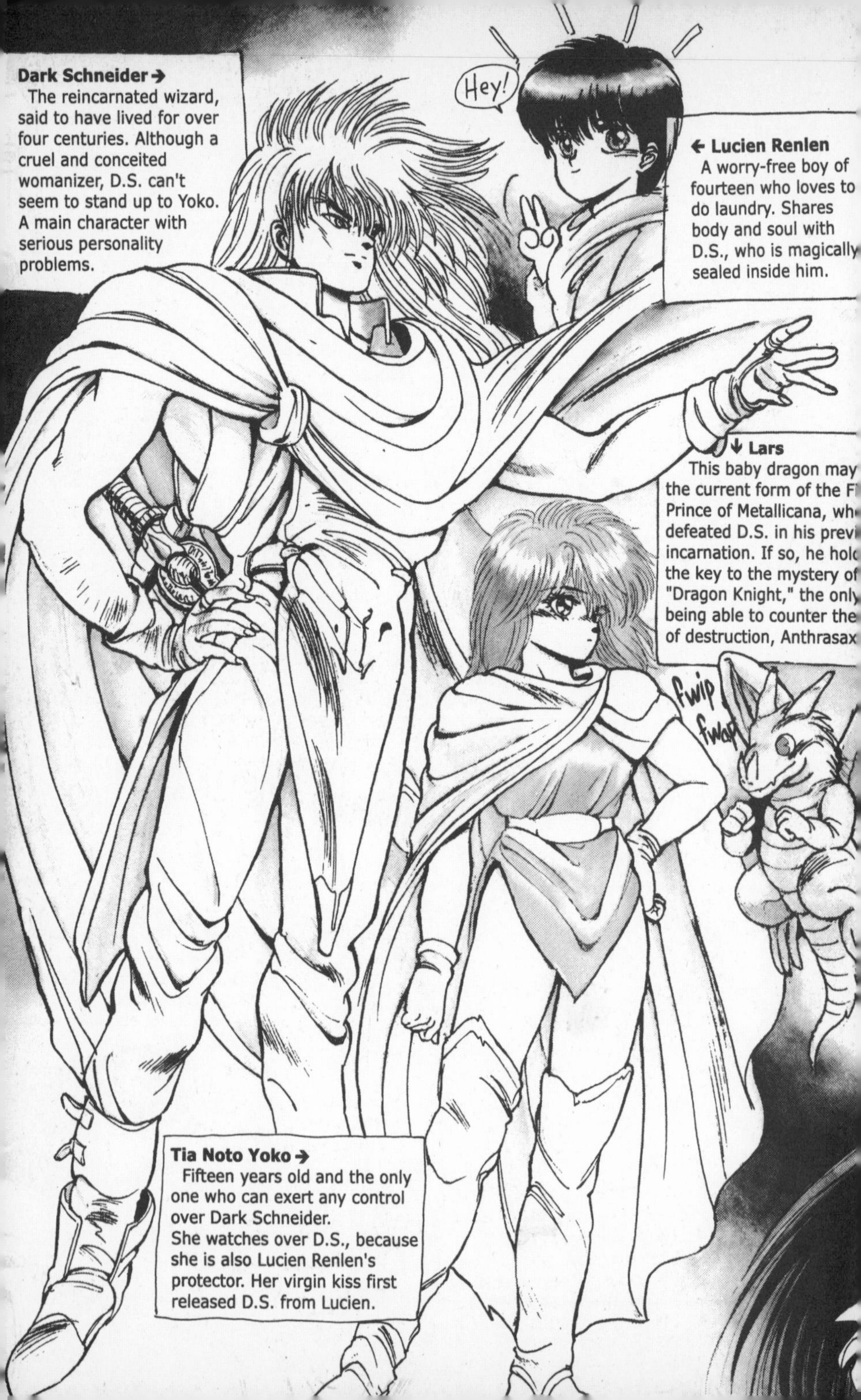
Dark Schneider →
The reincarnated wizard, said to have lived for over four centuries. Although a cruel and conceited womanizer, D.S. can't seem to stand up to Yoko. A main character with serious personality problems.
Hey!
← Lucien Renlen
A worry-free boy of fourteen who loves to do laundry. Shares body and soul with D.S., who is magically sealed inside him.
↓ Lars
This baby dragon may the current form of the F Prince of Metallicana, wh defeated D.S. in his previ incarnation. If so, he hold the key to the mystery of "Dragon Knight," the only being able to counter the of destruction, Anthrasax
fwip fwap
Tia Noto Yoko →
Fifteen years old and the only one who can exert any control over Dark Schneider.
She watches over D.S., because she is also Lucien Renlen's protector. Her virgin kiss first released D.S. from Lucien.

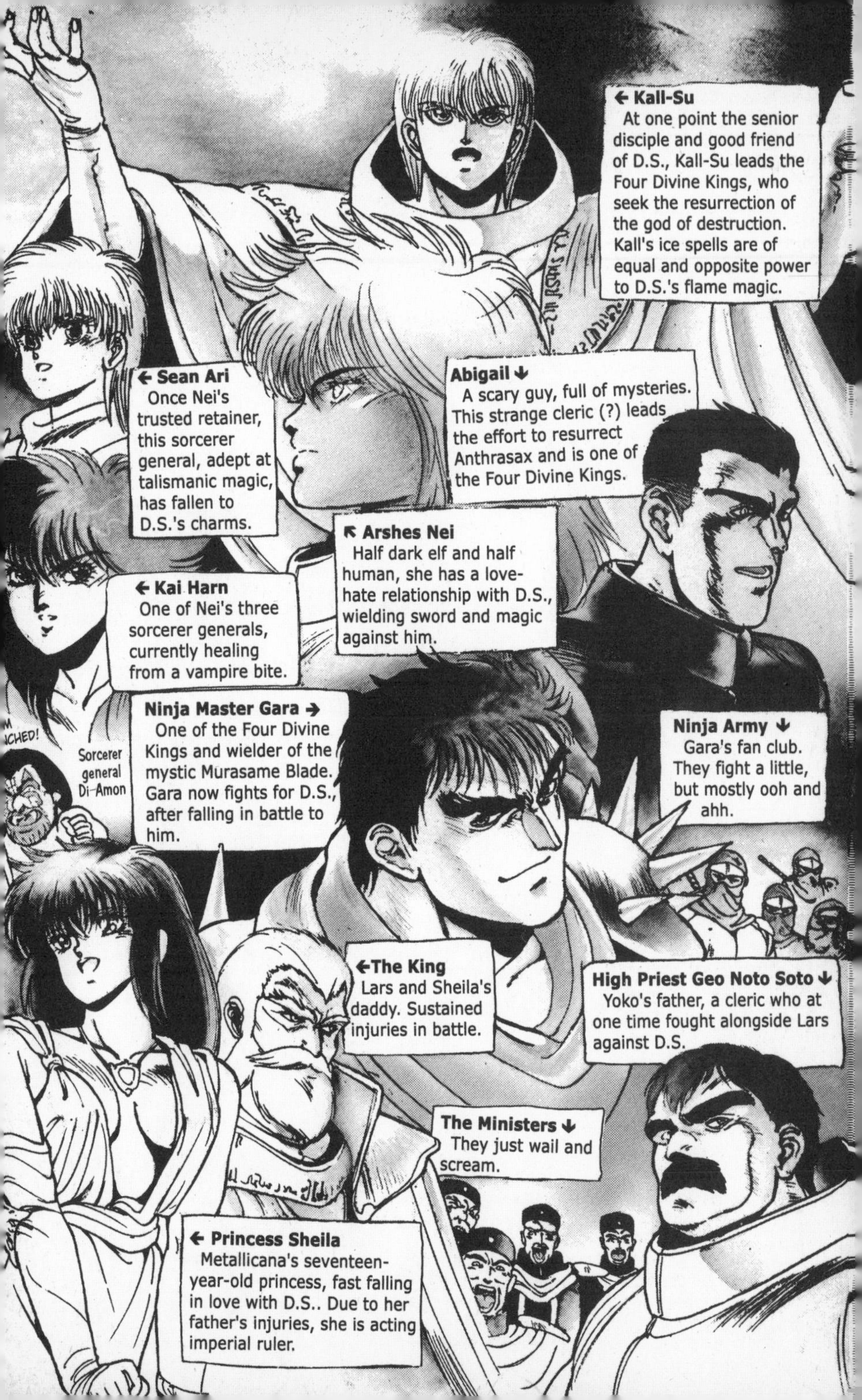
← Kall-Su
At one point the senior disciple and good friend of D.S., Kall-Su leads the Four Divine Kings, who seek the resurrection of the god of destruction. Kall's ice spells are of equal and opposite power to D.S.'s flame magic.
← Sean Ari
Once Nei's trusted retainer, this sorcerer general, adept at talismanic magic, has fallen to D.S.'s charms.
Abigail ↓
A scary guy, full of mysteries. This strange cleric (?) leads the effort to resurrect Anthrasax and is one of the Four Divine Kings.
↖ Arshes Nei
Half dark elf and half human, she has a love-hate relationship with D.S., wielding sword and magic against him.
← Kai Harn
One of Nei's three sorcerer generals, currently healing from a vampire bite.
Ninja Master Gara →
One of the Four Divine Kings and wielder of the mystic Murasame Blade. Gara now fights for D.S., after falling in battle to him.
Sorcerer general Di-Amon
Ninja Army ↓
Gara's fan club. They fight a little, but mostly ooh and ahh.
←The King
Lars and Sheila's daddy. Sustained injuries in battle.
High Priest Geo Noto Soto ↓
Yoko's father, a cleric who at one time fought alongside Lars against D.S.
The Ministers ↓
They just wail and scream.
← Princess Sheila
Metallicana's seventeen-year-old princess, fast falling in love with D.S.. Due to her father's injuries, she is acting imperial ruler.

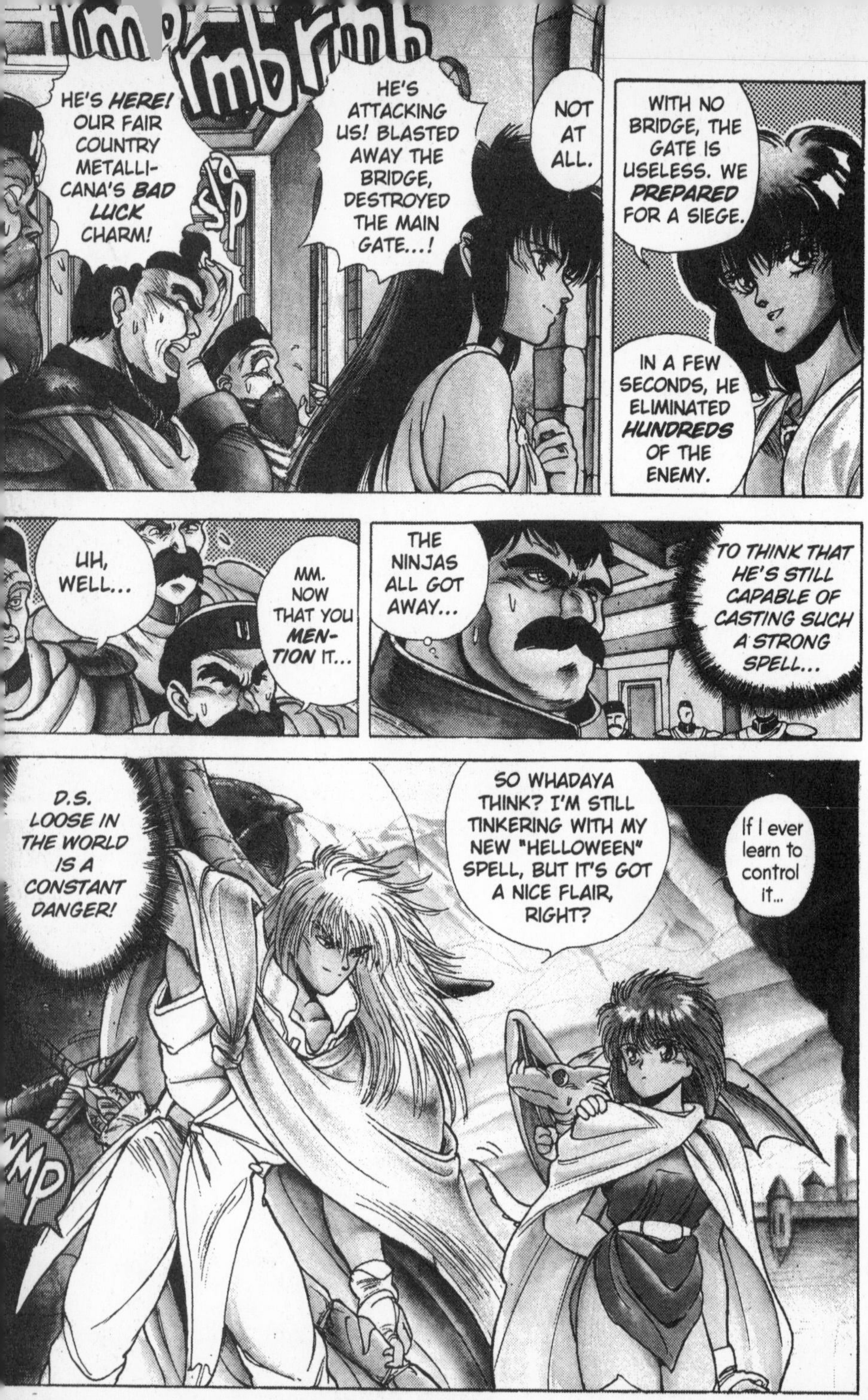
HE'S HERE! OUR FAIR COUNTRY METALLI-CANA'S BAD LUCK CHARM!
HE'S ATTACKING US! BLASTED AWAY THE BRIDGE, DESTROYED THE MAIN GATE...!
NOT AT ALL.
WITH NO BRIDGE, THE GATE IS USELESS. WE PREPARED FOR A SIEGE.
IN A FEW SECONDS, HE ELIMINATED HUNDREDS OF THE ENEMY.
UH, WELL...
MM. NOW THAT YOU MEN-TION IT...
THE NINJAS ALL GOT AWAY...
TO THINK THAT HE'S STILL CAPABLE OF CASTING SUCH A STRONG SPELL...
D.S. LOOSE IN THE WORLD IS A CONSTANT DANGER!
SO WHADAYA THINK? I'M STILL TINKERING WITH MY NEW "HELLOWEEN" SPELL, BUT IT'S GOT A NICE FLAIR, RIGHT?
If I ever learn to control it...

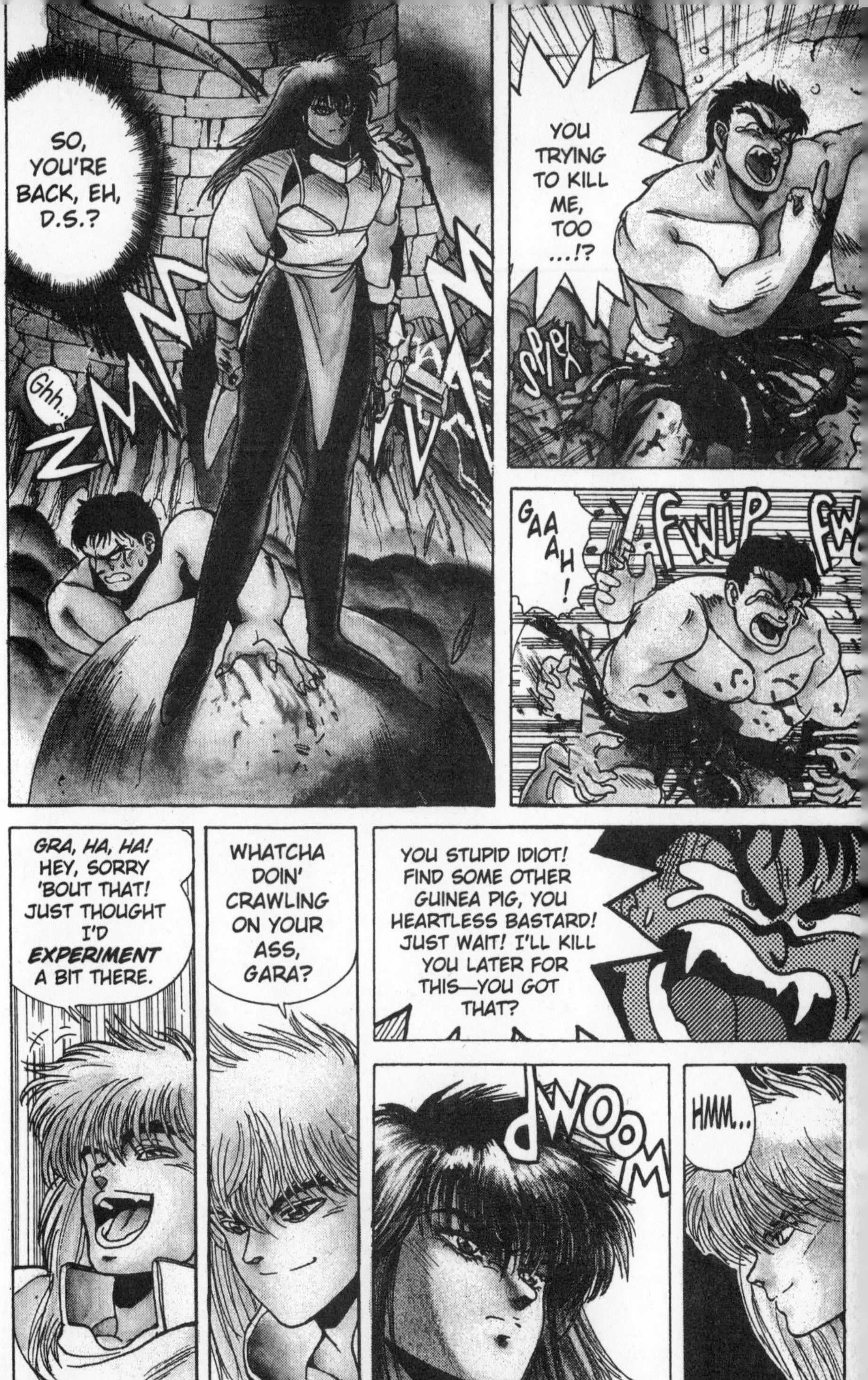
SO, YOU'RE BACK, EH, D.S.?
Ghh...
YOU TRYING TO KILL ME, TOO ...!?
SPLEX
GAAAH!
FWIP
GRA, HA, HA! HEY, SORRY 'BOUT THAT! JUST THOUGHT I'D *EXPERIMENT* A BIT THERE.
WHATCHA DOIN' CRAWLING ON YOUR ASS, GARA?
YOU STUPID IDIOT! FIND SOME OTHER GUINEA PIG, YOU HEARTLESS BASTARD! JUST WAIT! I'LL KILL YOU LATER FOR THIS—YOU GOT THAT?
HMM...

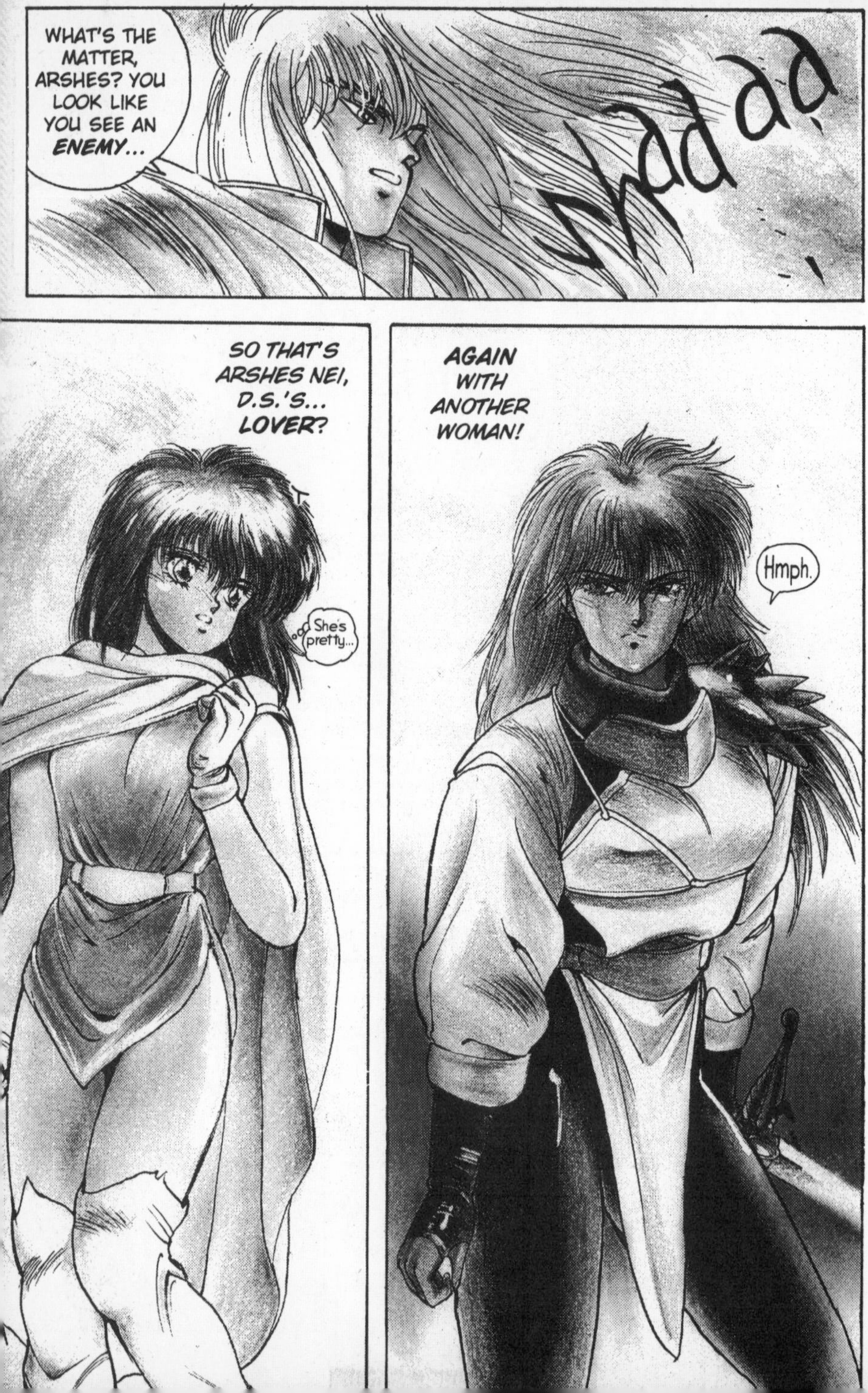
WHAT'S THE MATTER, ARSHES? YOU LOOK LIKE YOU SEE AN **ENEMY...**
SO THAT'S ARSHES NEI, D.S.'S... **LOVER?**
She's pretty...
AGAIN WITH ANOTHER WOMAN!
Hmph.

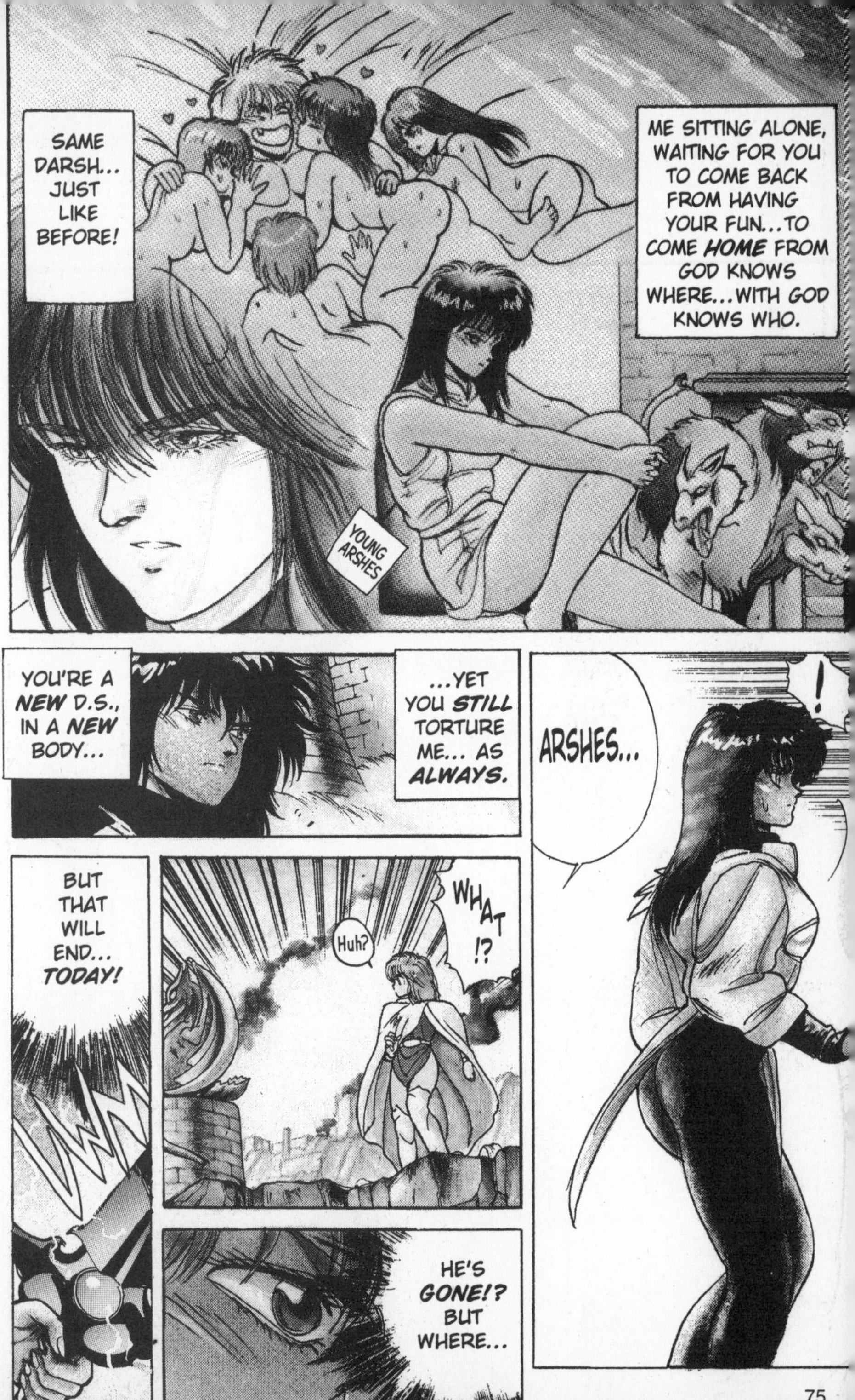
SAME DARSH... JUST LIKE BEFORE!
ME SITTING ALONE, WAITING FOR YOU TO COME BACK FROM HAVING YOUR FUN...TO COME HOME FROM GOD KNOWS WHERE...WITH GOD KNOWS WHO.
YOUNG ARSHES
YOU'RE A NEW D.S., IN A NEW BODY...
...YET YOU STILL TORTURE ME... AS ALWAYS.
BUT THAT WILL END... TODAY!
Huh?
WHAT !?
HE'S GONE!? BUT WHERE...
!
ARSHES...

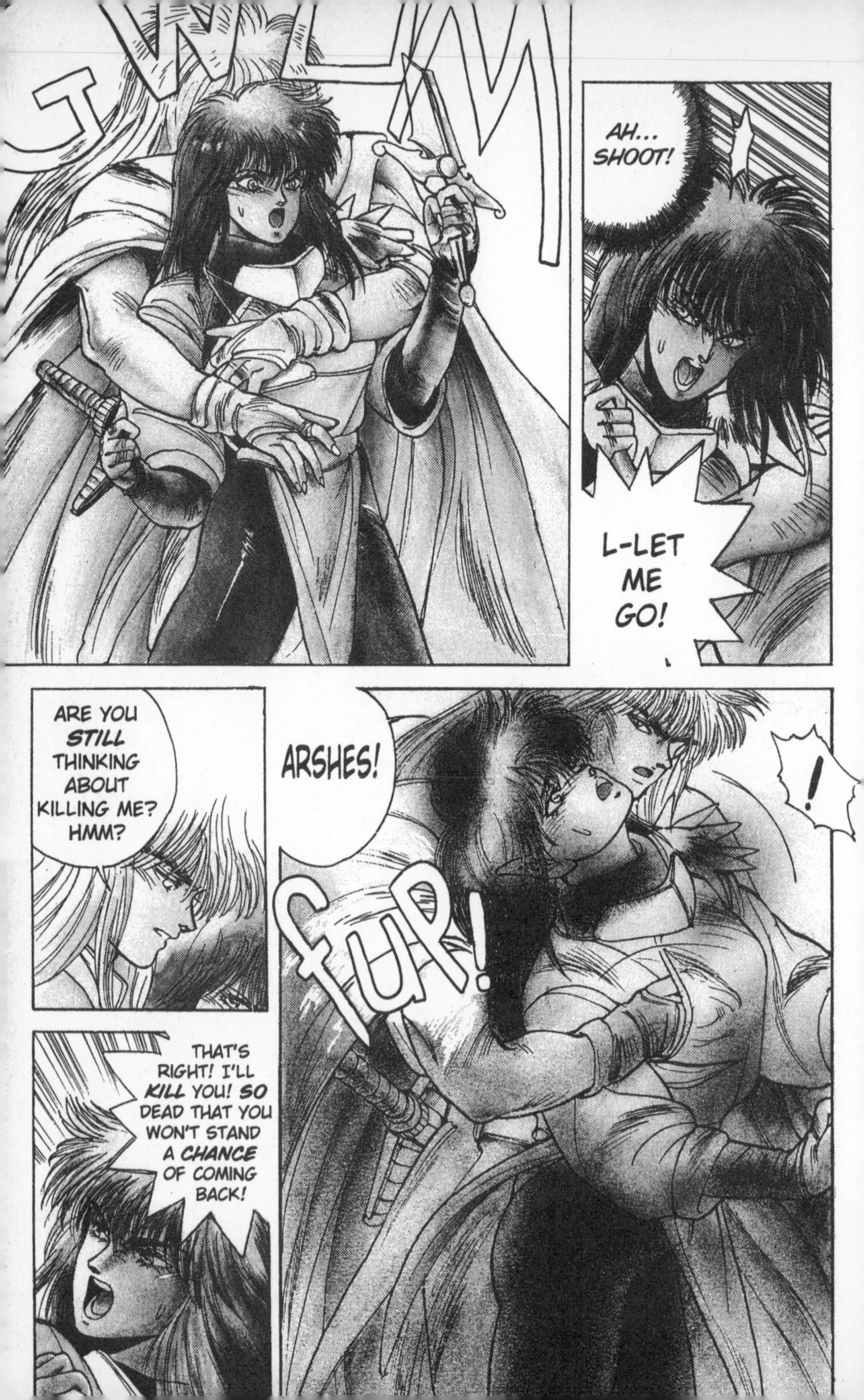
AH... SHOOT!
L-LET ME GO!
ARE YOU **STILL** THINKING ABOUT KILLING ME? HMM?
THAT'S RIGHT! I'LL **KILL** YOU! **SO** DEAD THAT YOU WON'T STAND A **CHANCE** OF COMING BACK!
ARSHES!
!
FUP!

WHY **SAY** SUCH THINGS AGAINST YOUR FATHER?

DIDN'T I RAISE YOU BETTER THAN THAT?

YOU KNOW THAT I LOVE YOU, ARSHES...

nibble

YES?

OH! I...

aaah

N... NO... NO...

FEELS GOOD, HUH? WHO **ELSE** KNOWS ALL YOUR **FAVORITE** SPOTS?

Heh!

PoK PoK

ST...OP ...AH ...AH!

Nnh...

UNNH... AM I... AM I GOING TO **DIE**...?

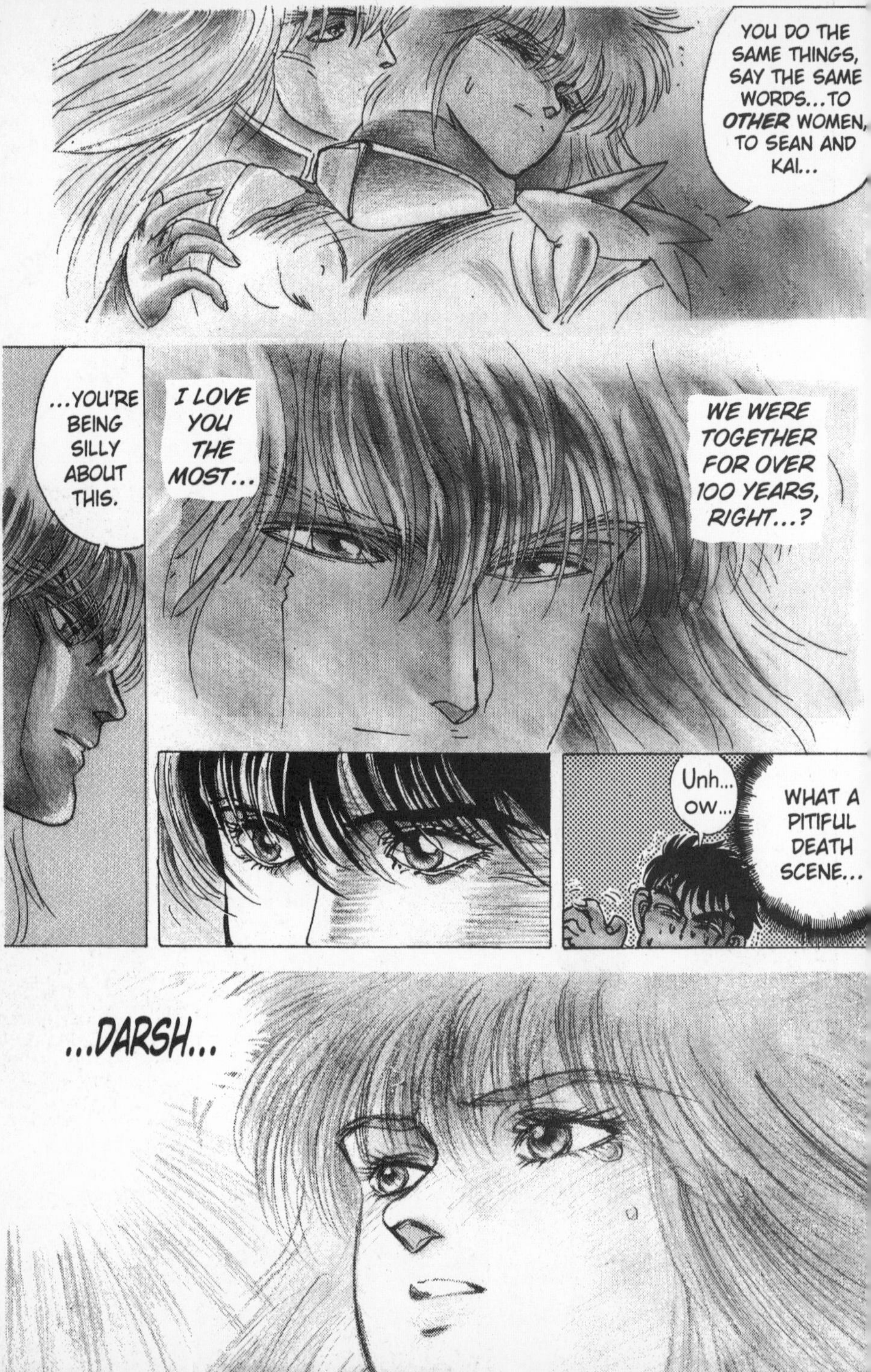
YOU DO THE SAME THINGS, SAY THE SAME WORDS...TO OTHER WOMEN, TO SEAN AND KAI...
...YOU'RE BEING SILLY ABOUT THIS.
I LOVE YOU THE MOST...
WE WERE TOGETHER FOR OVER 100 YEARS, RIGHT...?
Unh... ow...
WHAT A PITIFUL DEATH SCENE...
...DARSH...

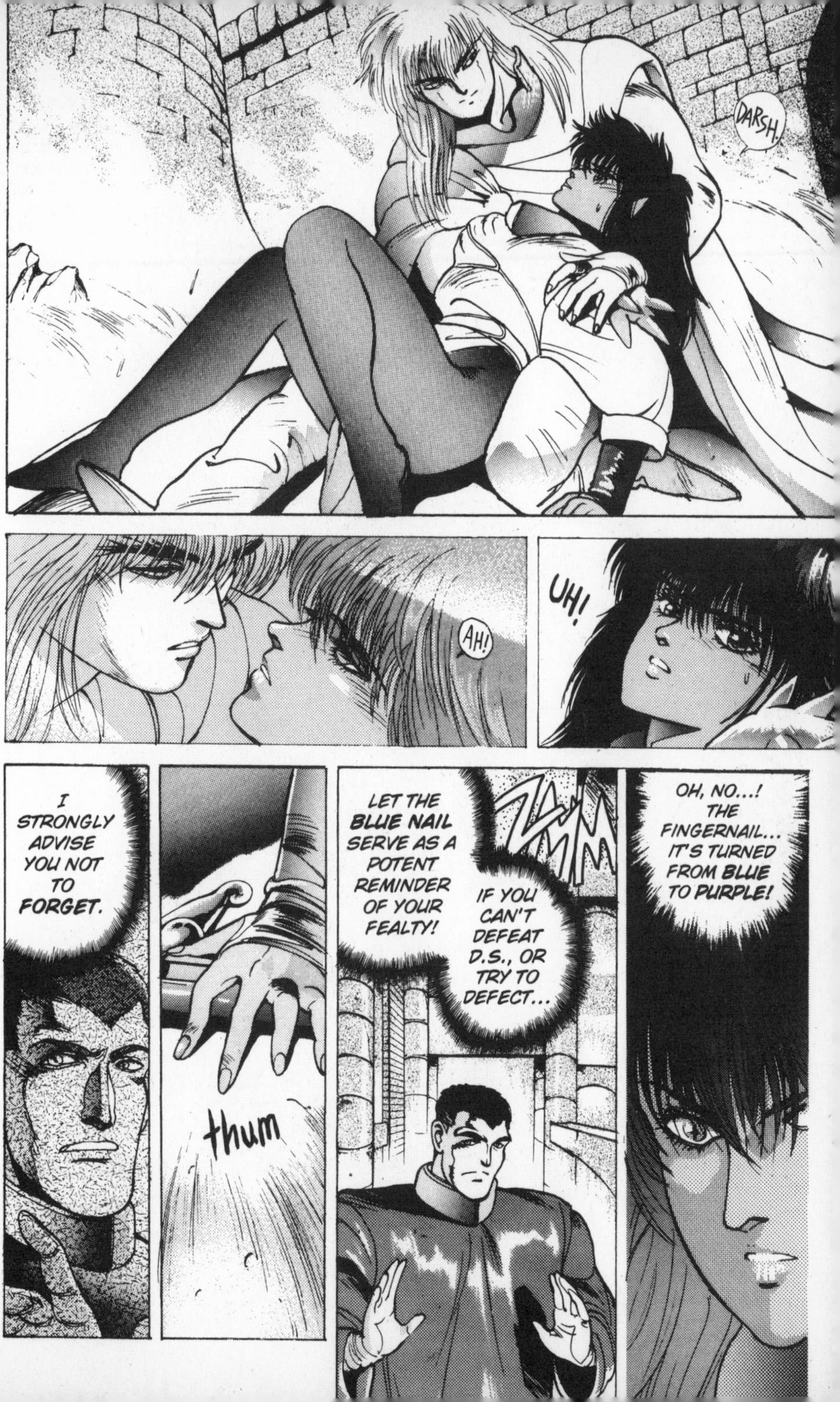
DARSH.
AH!
UH!
I STRONGLY ADVISE YOU NOT TO FORGET.
thum
LET THE BLUE NAIL SERVE AS A POTENT REMINDER OF YOUR FEALTY!
IF YOU CAN'T DEFEAT D.S., OR TRY TO DEFECT...
OH, NO...! THE FINGERNAIL... IT'S TURNED FROM BLUE TO PURPLE!

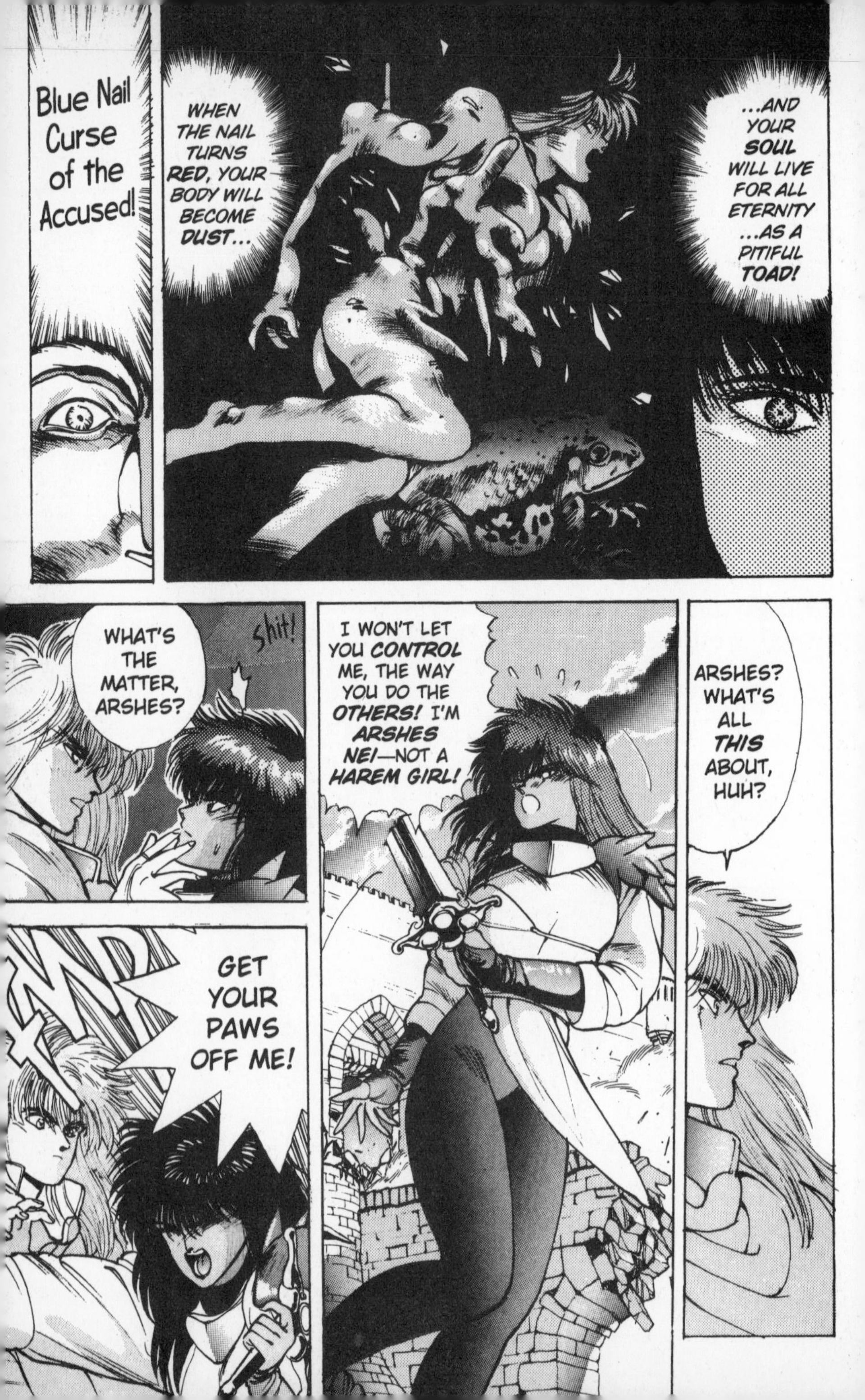

Blue Nail Curse of the Accused!
WHEN THE NAIL TURNS RED, YOUR BODY WILL BECOME DUST...
...AND YOUR SOUL WILL LIVE FOR ALL ETERNITY ...AS A PITIFUL TOAD!
WHAT'S THE MATTER, ARSHES?
Shit!
I WON'T LET YOU CONTROL ME, THE WAY YOU DO THE OTHERS! I'M ARSHES NEI—NOT A HAREM GIRL!
ARSHES? WHAT'S ALL THIS ABOUT, HUH?
GET YOUR PAWS OFF ME!

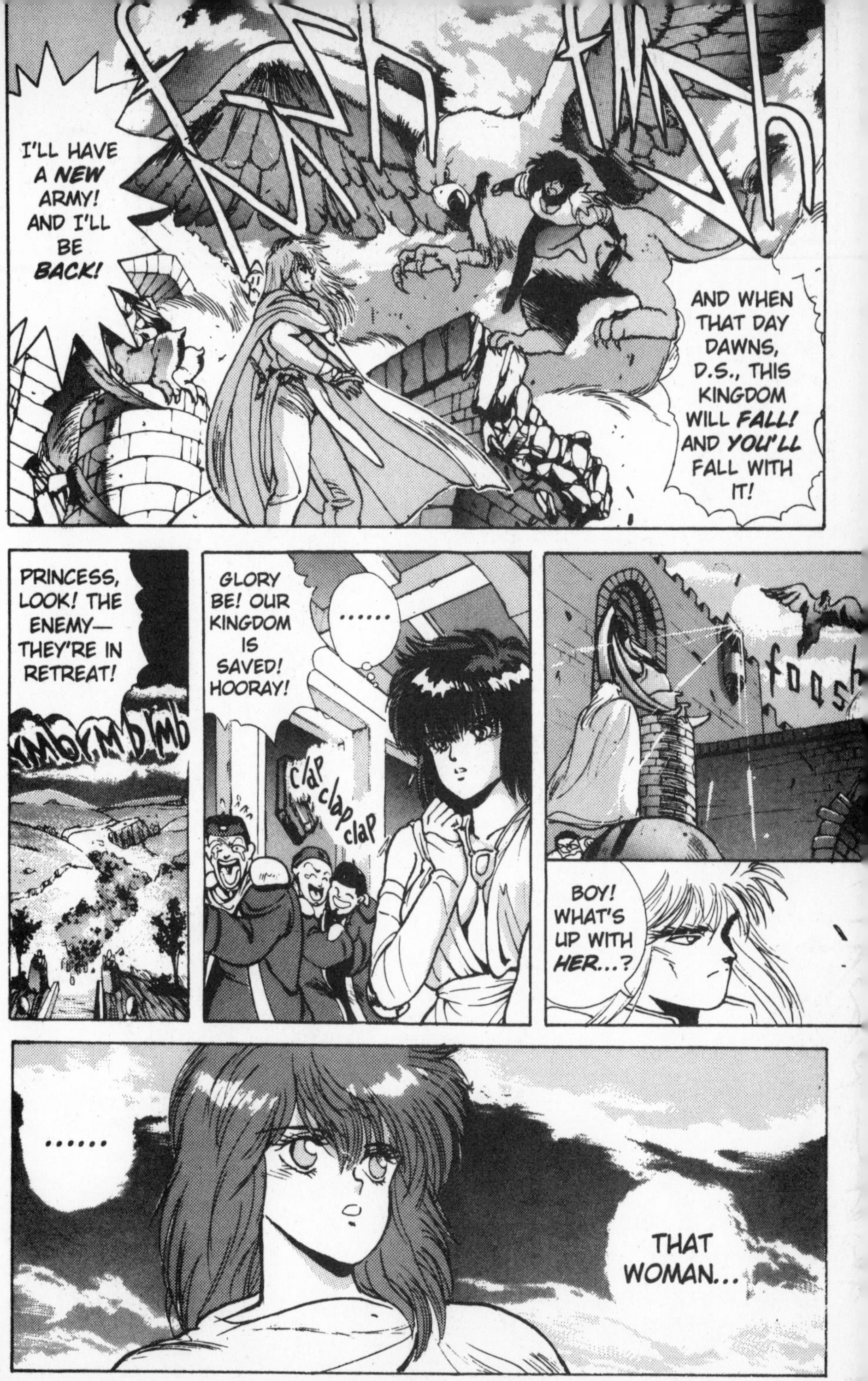
I'LL HAVE A NEW ARMY! AND I'LL BE BACK!
AND WHEN THAT DAY DAWNS, D.S., THIS KINGDOM WILL FALL! AND YOU'LL FALL WITH IT!
PRINCESS, LOOK! THE ENEMY— THEY'RE IN RETREAT!
GLORY BE! OUR KINGDOM IS SAVED! HOORAY!
......
clap clap clap
BOY! WHAT'S UP WITH HER...?
......
THAT WOMAN...

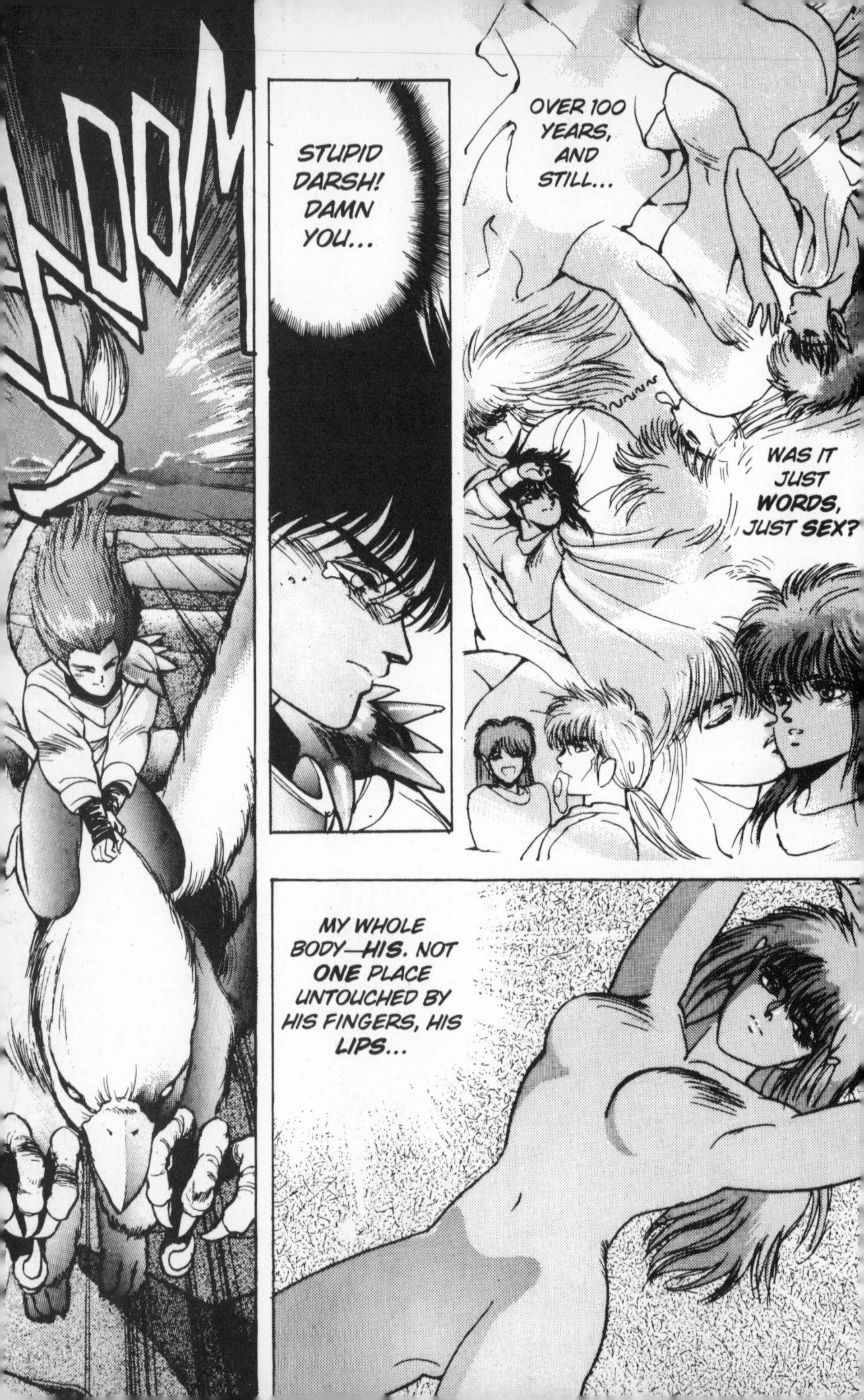
STUPID DARSH! DAMN YOU...
OVER 100 YEARS, AND STILL...
WAS IT JUST WORDS, JUST SEX?
MY WHOLE BODY—HIS. NOT ONE PLACE UNTOUCHED BY HIS FINGERS, HIS LIPS...

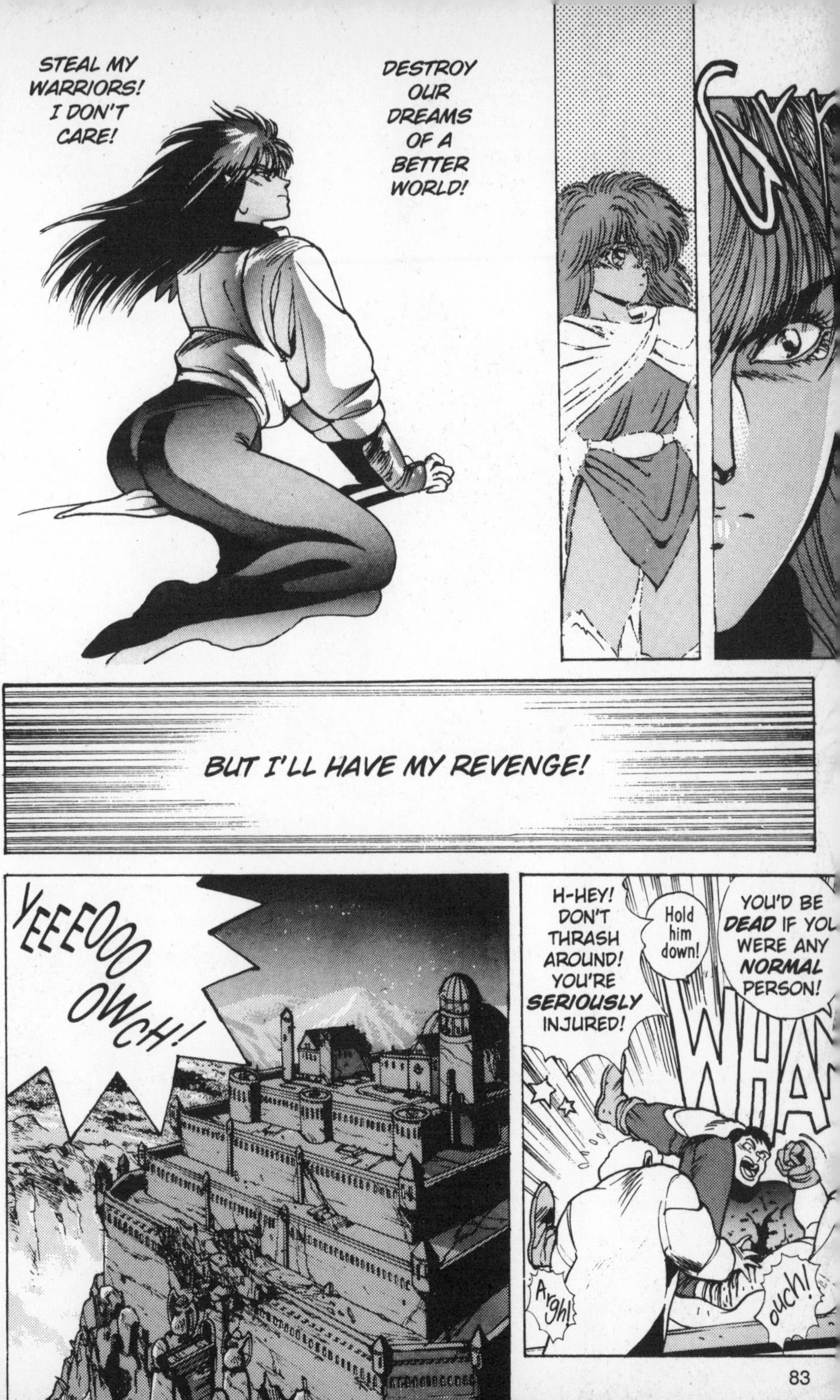
STEAL MY WARRIORS! I DON'T CARE!
DESTROY OUR DREAMS OF A BETTER WORLD!
BUT I'LL HAVE MY REVENGE!
YEEEOOO OWCH!
H-HEY! DON'T THRASH AROUND! YOU'RE SERIOUSLY INJURED!
Hold him down!
YOU'D BE DEAD IF YOU WERE ANY NORMAL PERSON!
Argh!
ouch!

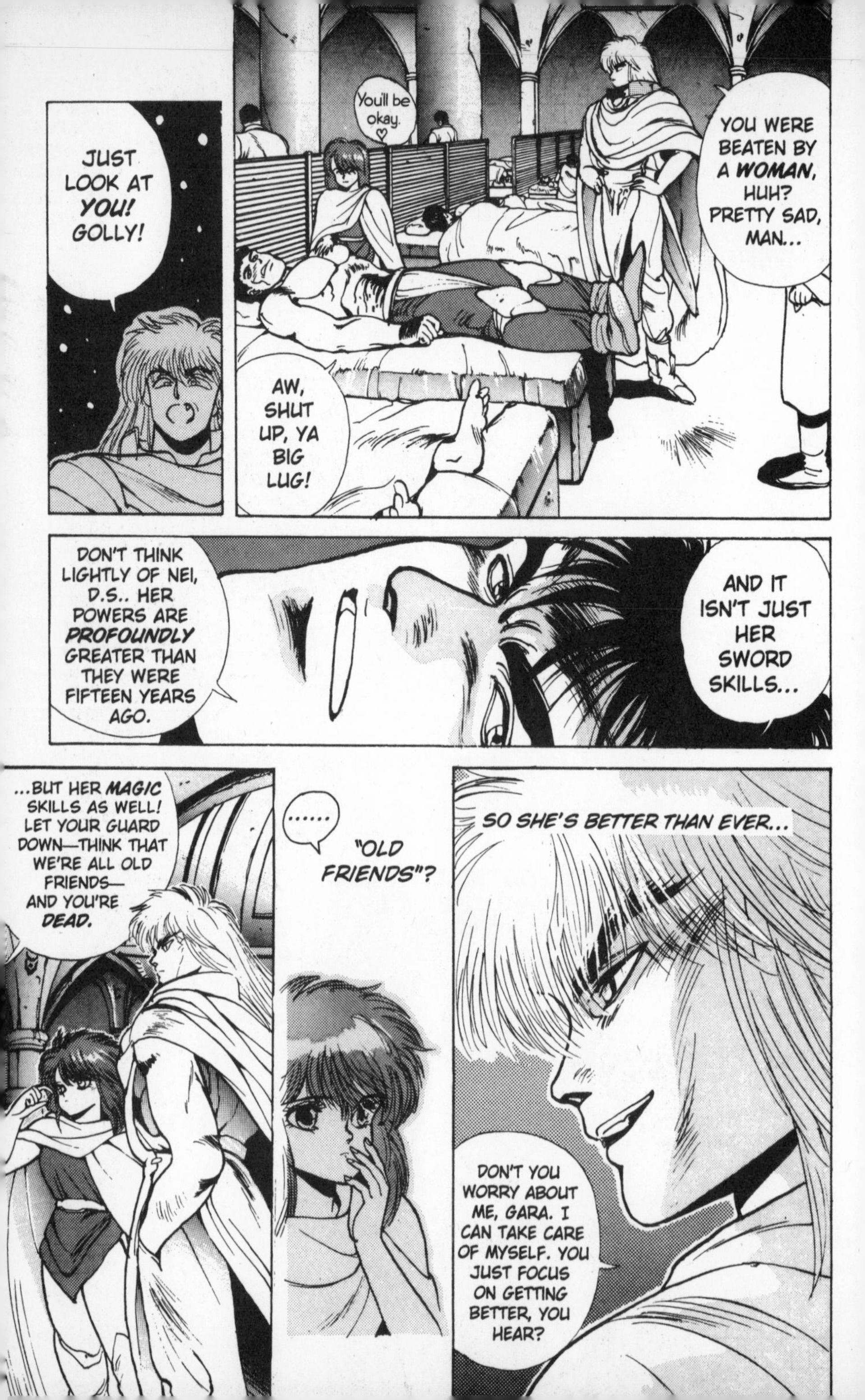
JUST LOOK AT *YOU!* GOLLY!
You'll be okay. ♡
YOU WERE BEATEN BY A ***WOMAN***, HUH? PRETTY SAD, MAN...
AW, SHUT UP, YA BIG LUG!
DON'T THINK LIGHTLY OF NEI, D.S.. HER POWERS ARE ***PROFOUNDLY*** GREATER THAN THEY WERE FIFTEEN YEARS AGO.
AND IT ISN'T JUST HER SWORD SKILLS...
...BUT HER ***MAGIC*** SKILLS AS WELL! LET YOUR GUARD DOWN—THINK THAT WE'RE ALL OLD FRIENDS—AND YOU'RE ***DEAD.***
......
"OLD FRIENDS"?
SO SHE'S BETTER THAN EVER...
DON'T YOU WORRY ABOUT ME, GARA. I CAN TAKE CARE OF MYSELF. YOU JUST FOCUS ON GETTING BETTER, YOU HEAR?

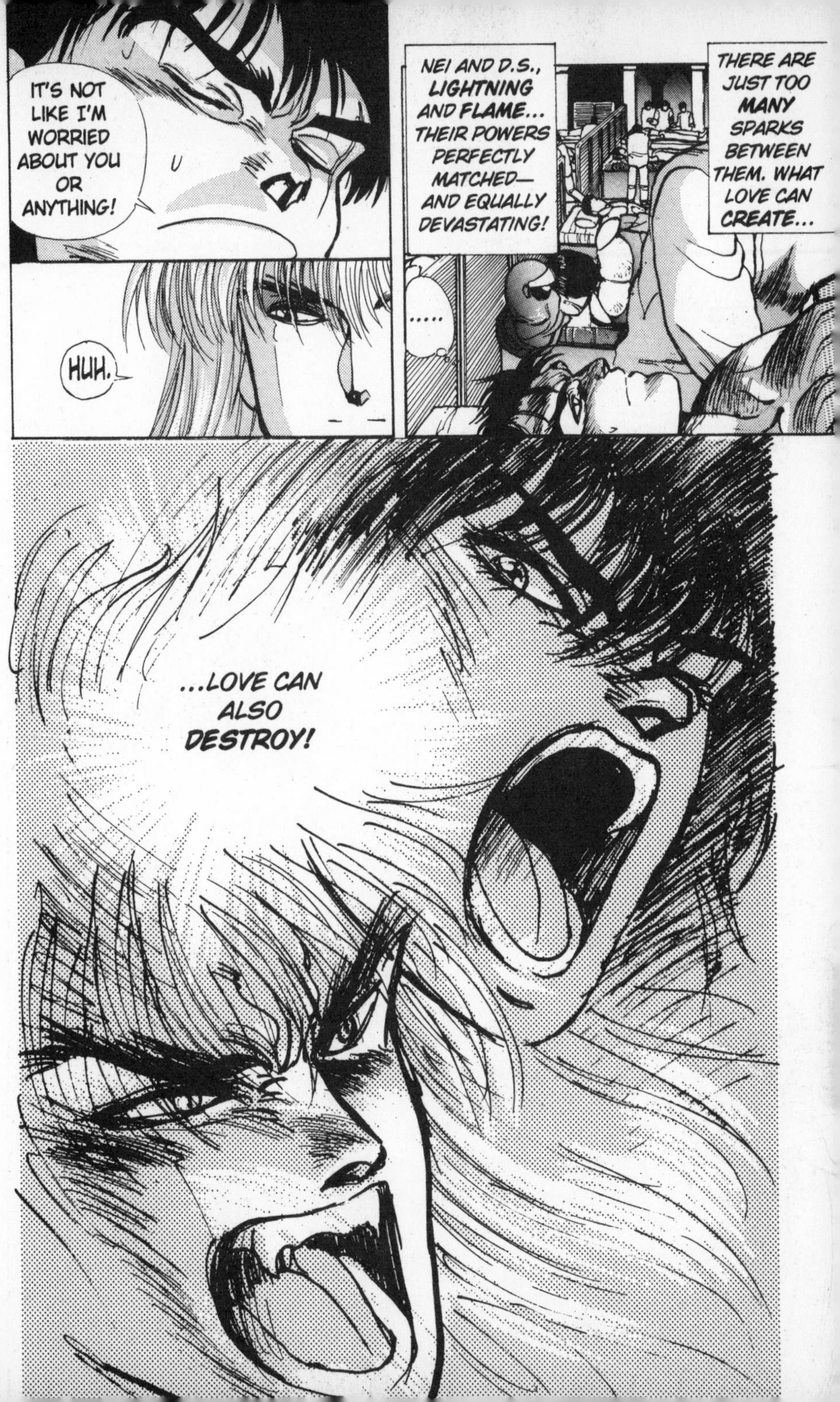
IT'S NOT LIKE I'M WORRIED ABOUT YOU OR ANYTHING!
HUH.
NEI AND D.S., **LIGHTNING** AND **FLAME**... THEIR POWERS PERFECTLY MATCHED—AND EQUALLY DEVASTATING!
.....
THERE ARE JUST TOO **MANY** SPARKS BETWEEN THEM. WHAT LOVE CAN **CREATE**...
...LOVE CAN ALSO **DESTROY!**

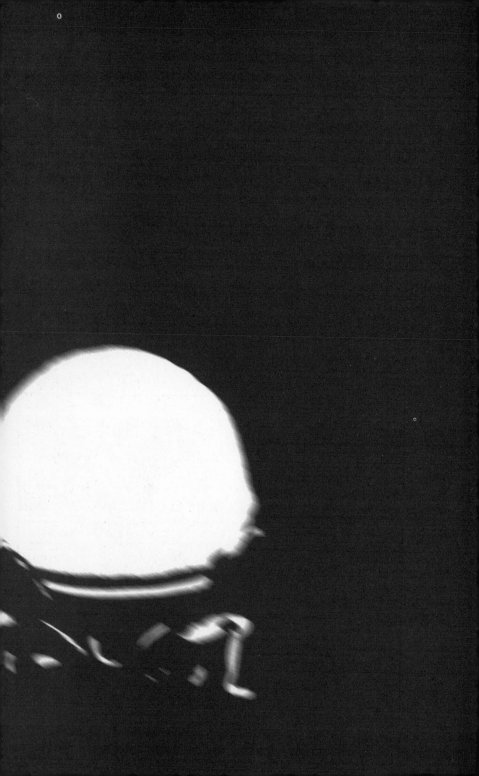

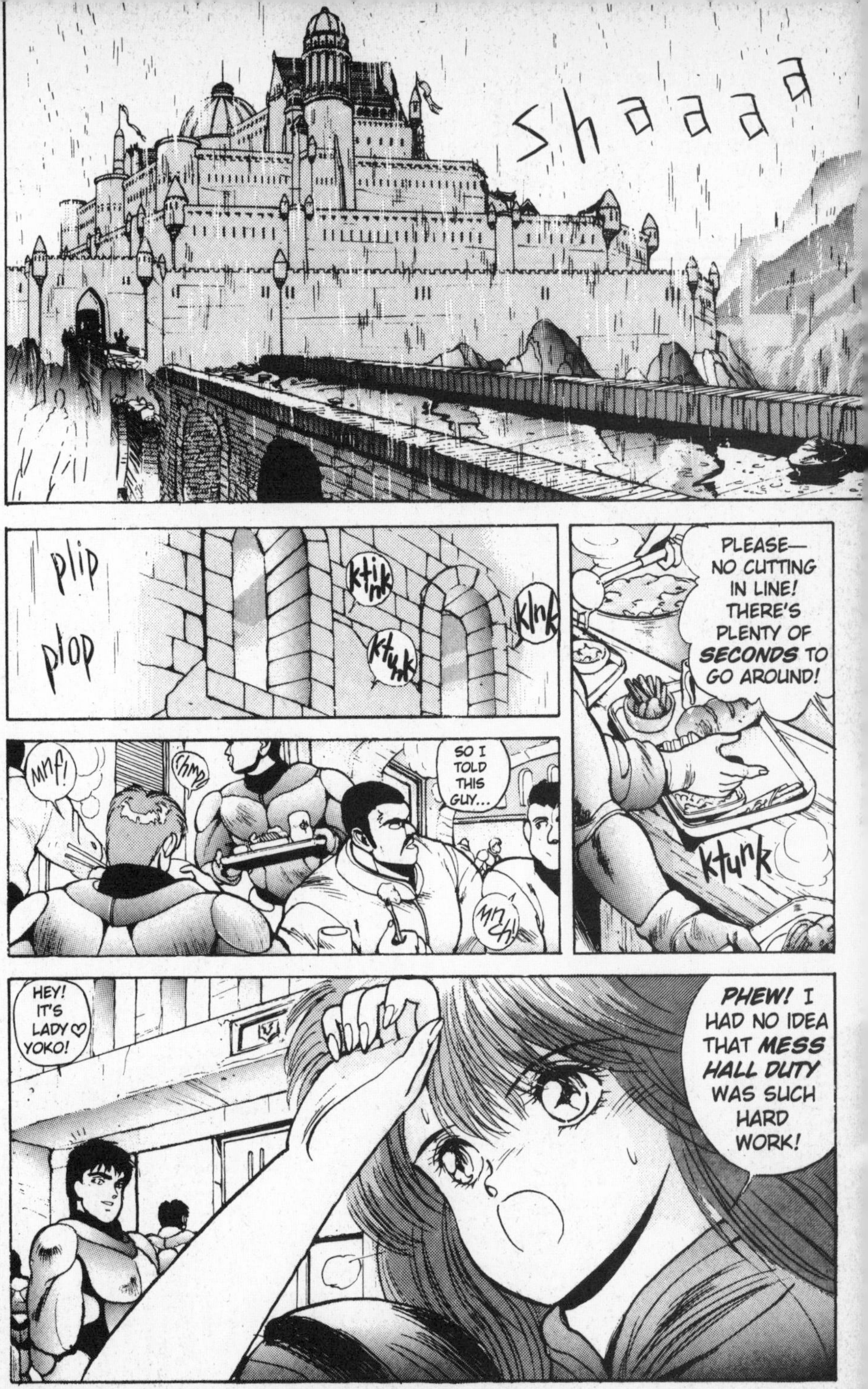
Shaaaaa
plip
plop
ktink
klink
ktunk
mnf!
chmp
SO I TOLD THIS GUY...
mnch!
PLEASE—NO CUTTING IN LINE! THERE'S PLENTY OF SECONDS TO GO AROUND!
ktunk
HEY! IT'S LADY♡ YOKO!
PHEW! I HAD NO IDEA THAT MESS HALL DUTY WAS SUCH HARD WORK!

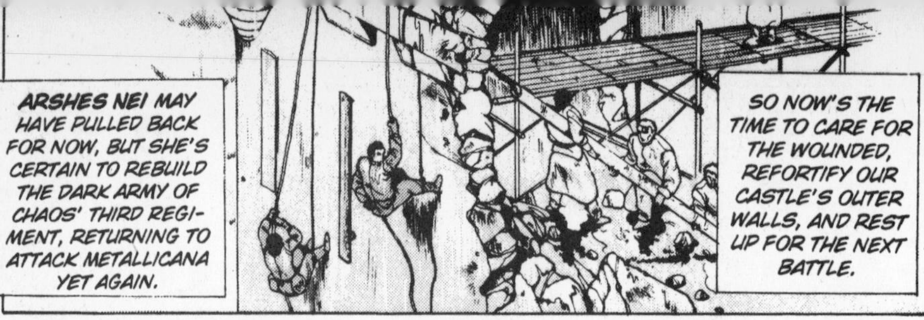
ARSHES NEI MAY HAVE PULLED BACK FOR NOW, BUT SHE'S CERTAIN TO REBUILD THE DARK ARMY OF CHAOS' THIRD REGIMENT, RETURNING TO ATTACK METALLICANA YET AGAIN.
SO NOW'S THE TIME TO CARE FOR THE WOUNDED, REFORTIFY OUR CASTLE'S OUTER WALLS, AND REST UP FOR THE NEXT BATTLE.
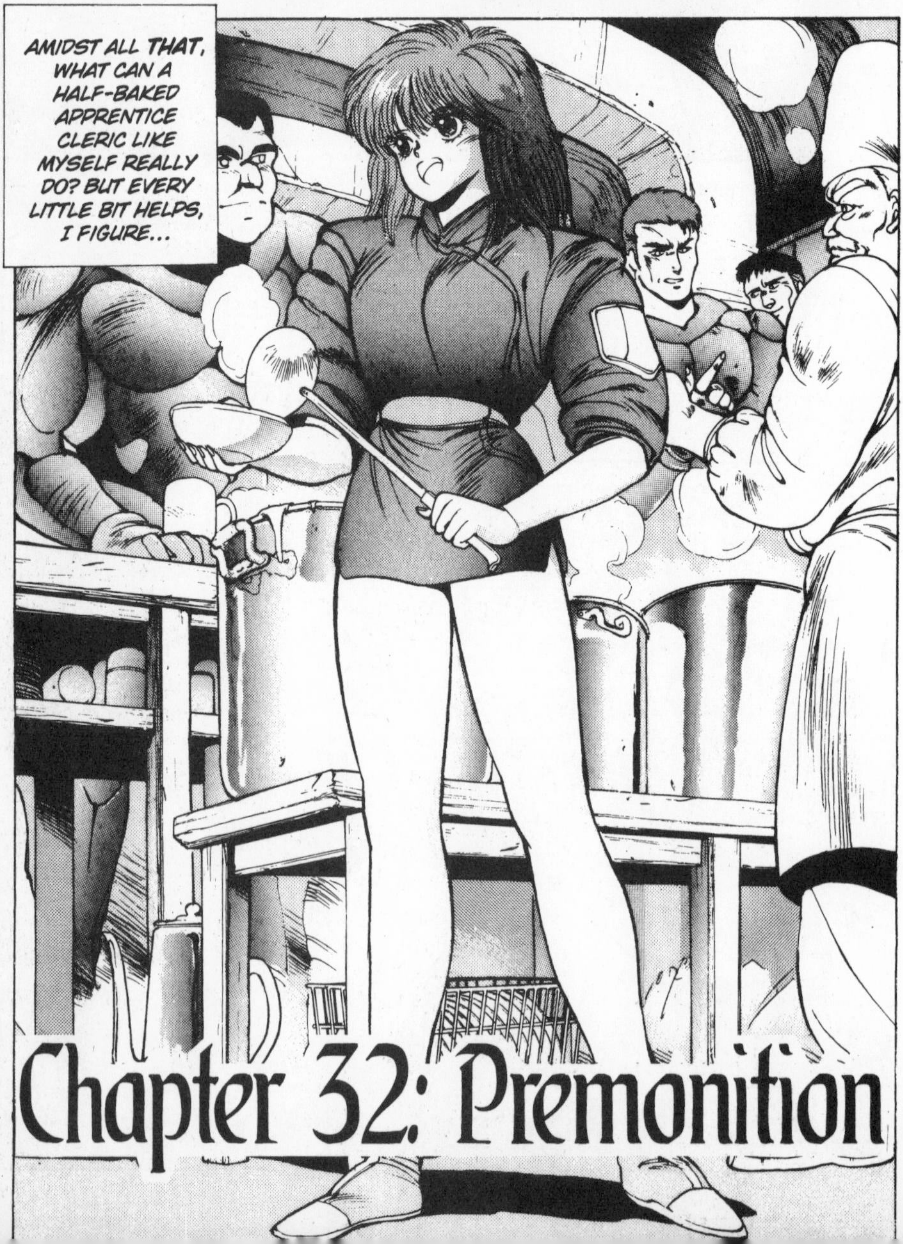
AMIDST ALL THAT, WHAT CAN A HALF-BAKED APPRENTICE CLERIC LIKE MYSELF REALLY DO? BUT EVERY LITTLE BIT HELPS, I FIGURE...

Chapter 32: Premonition

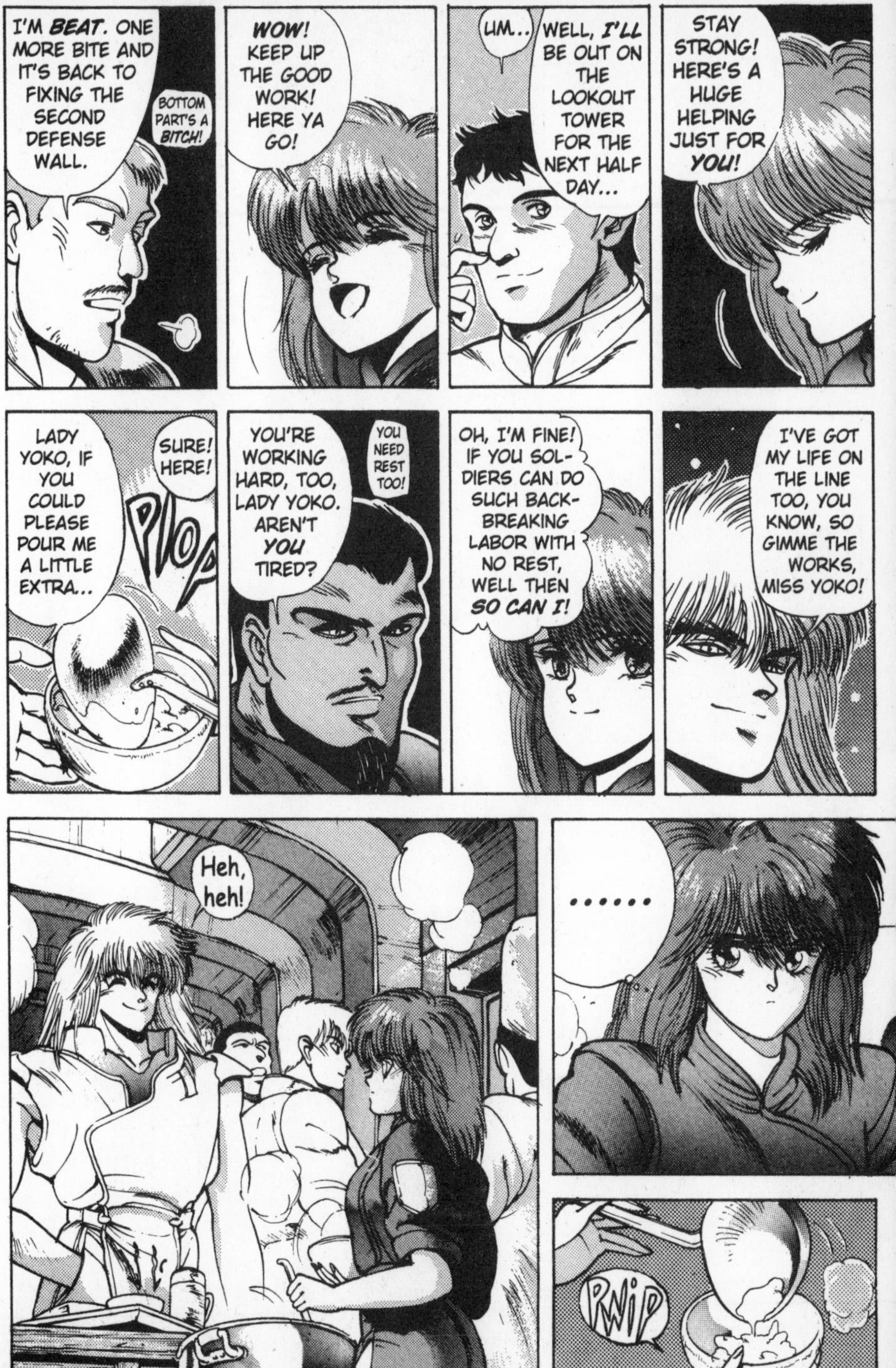
I'M BEAT. ONE MORE BITE AND IT'S BACK TO FIXING THE SECOND DEFENSE WALL.
BOTTOM PART'S A BITCH!
WOW! KEEP UP THE GOOD WORK! HERE YA GO!
UM...
WELL, I'LL BE OUT ON THE LOOKOUT TOWER FOR THE NEXT HALF DAY...
STAY STRONG! HERE'S A HUGE HELPING JUST FOR YOU!
LADY YOKO, IF YOU COULD PLEASE POUR ME A LITTLE EXTRA...
SURE! HERE!
PLOP
YOU'RE WORKING HARD, TOO, LADY YOKO. AREN'T YOU TIRED?
YOU NEED REST TOO!
OH, I'M FINE! IF YOU SOLDIERS CAN DO SUCH BACK-BREAKING LABOR WITH NO REST, WELL THEN SO CAN I!
I'VE GOT MY LIFE ON THE LINE TOO, YOU KNOW, SO GIMME THE WORKS, MISS YOKO!
Heh, heh!
......
PWIP

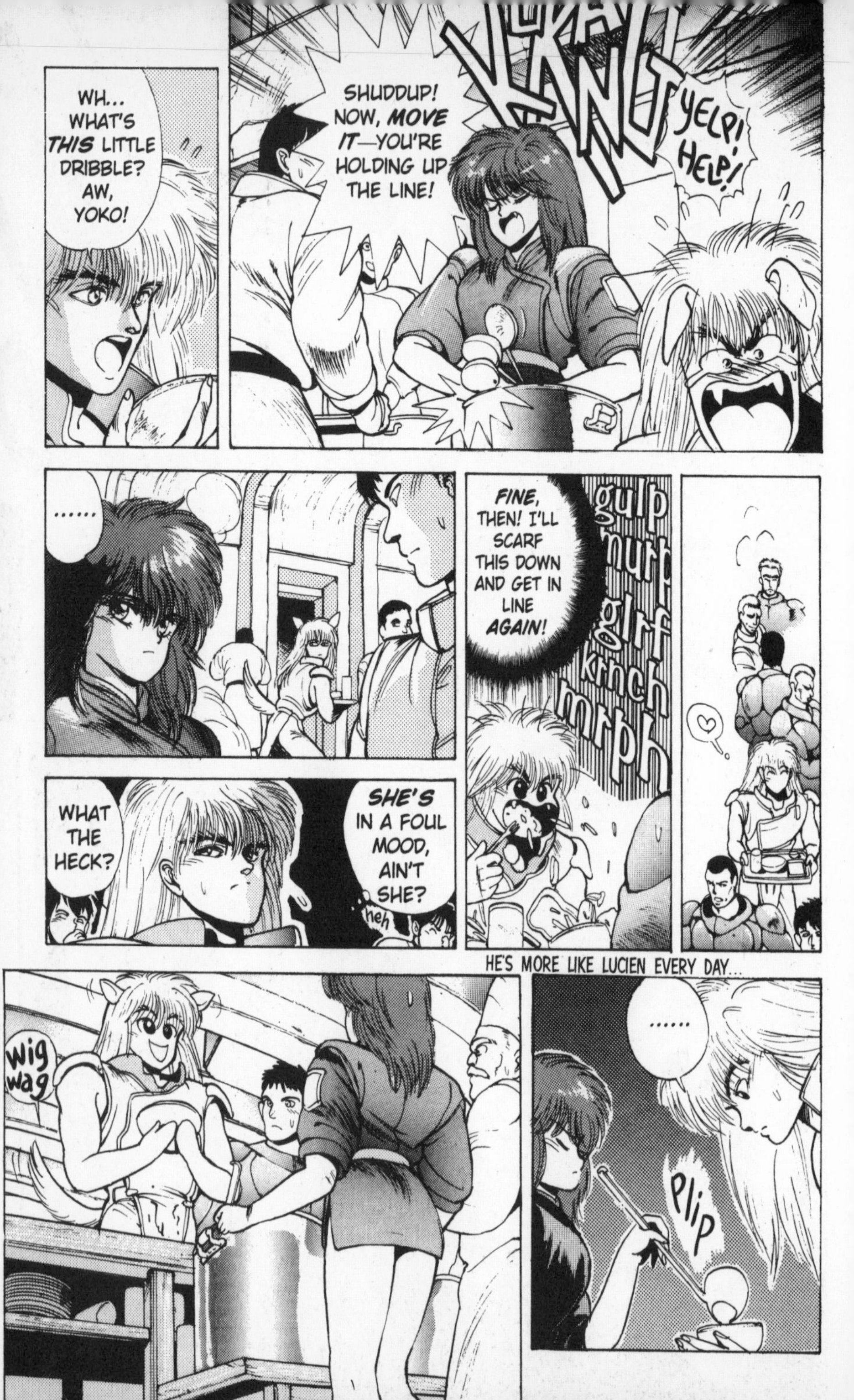
WH... WHAT'S THIS LITTLE DRIBBLE? AW, YOKO!
SHUDDUP! NOW, MOVE IT—YOU'RE HOLDING UP THE LINE!
YANK
YELP! HELP!
......
FINE, THEN! I'LL SCARF THIS DOWN AND GET IN LINE AGAIN!
gulp
murp
glrf
krnch
mrph
WHAT THE HECK?
SHE'S IN A FOUL MOOD, AIN'T SHE?
heh
HE'S MORE LIKE LUCIEN EVERY DAY...
wig wag
......
plip

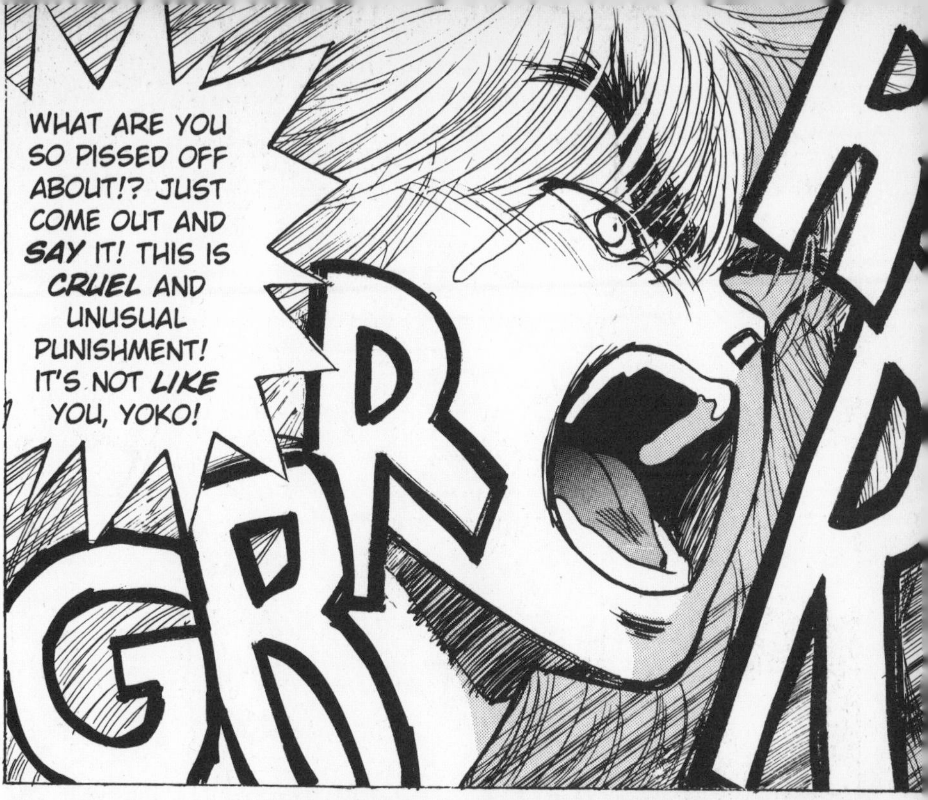
WHAT ARE YOU SO PISSED OFF ABOUT!? JUST COME OUT AND ***SAY*** IT! THIS IS ***CRUEL*** AND UNUSUAL PUNISHMENT! IT'S NOT ***LIKE*** YOU, YOKO!
GRR

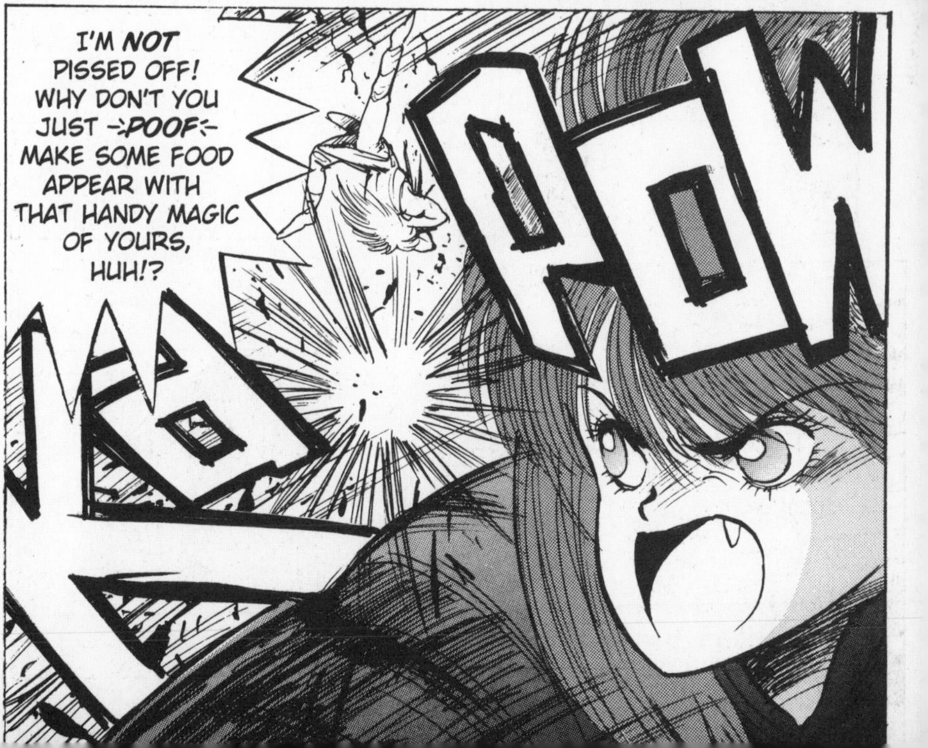
I'M ***NOT*** PISSED OFF! WHY DON'T YOU JUST ⇢***POOF***⇠ MAKE SOME FOOD APPEAR WITH THAT HANDY MAGIC OF YOURS, HUH!?
POW

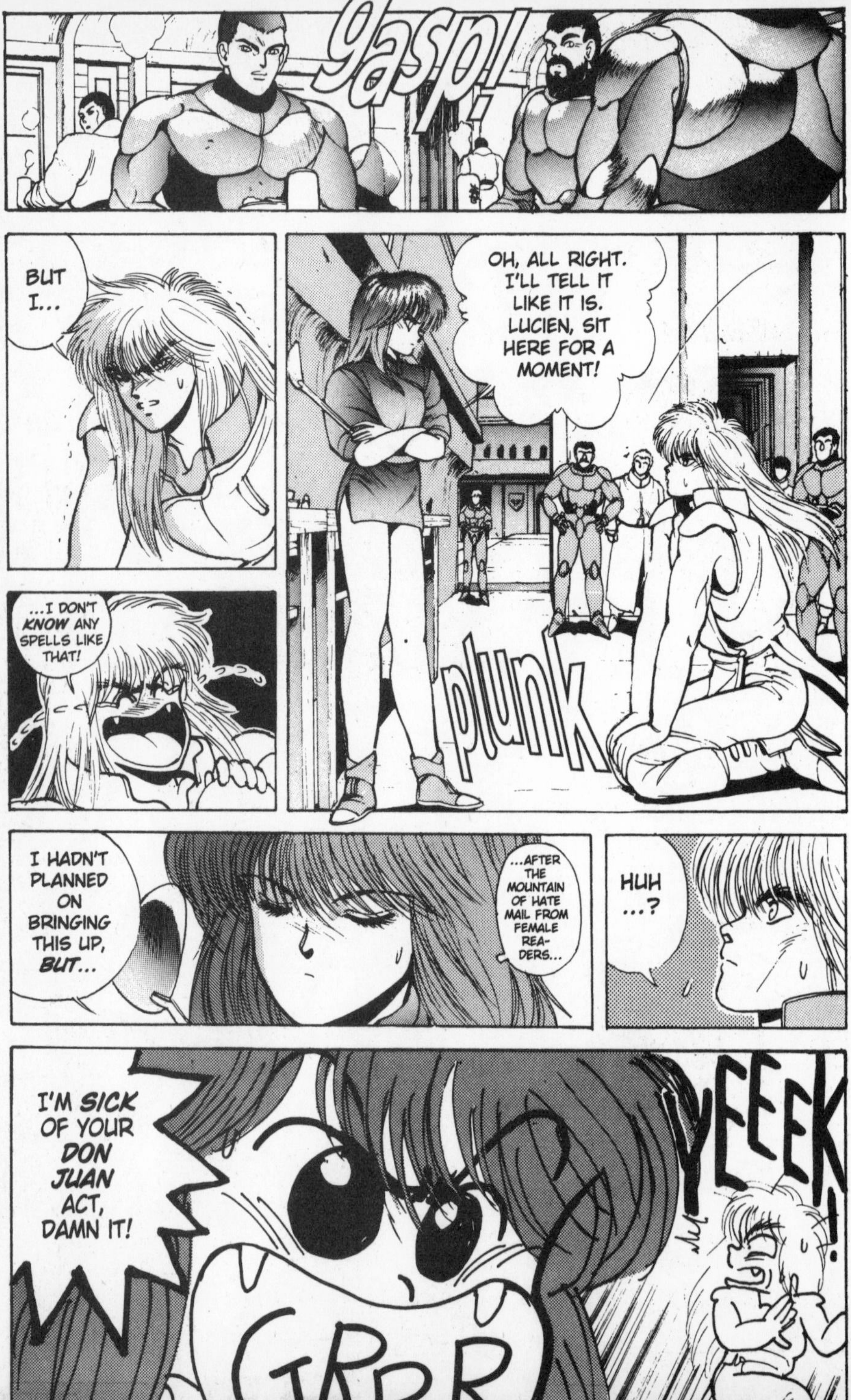
gasp!
BUT I...
OH, ALL RIGHT. I'LL TELL IT LIKE IT IS. LUCIEN, SIT HERE FOR A MOMENT!
...I DON'T *KNOW* ANY SPELLS LIKE THAT!
plunk
I HADN'T PLANNED ON BRINGING THIS UP, *BUT*...
...AFTER THE MOUNTAIN OF HATE MAIL FROM FEMALE READERS...
HUH ...?
I'M *SICK* OF YOUR *DON JUAN* ACT, DAMN IT!
YEEK!
GRRR

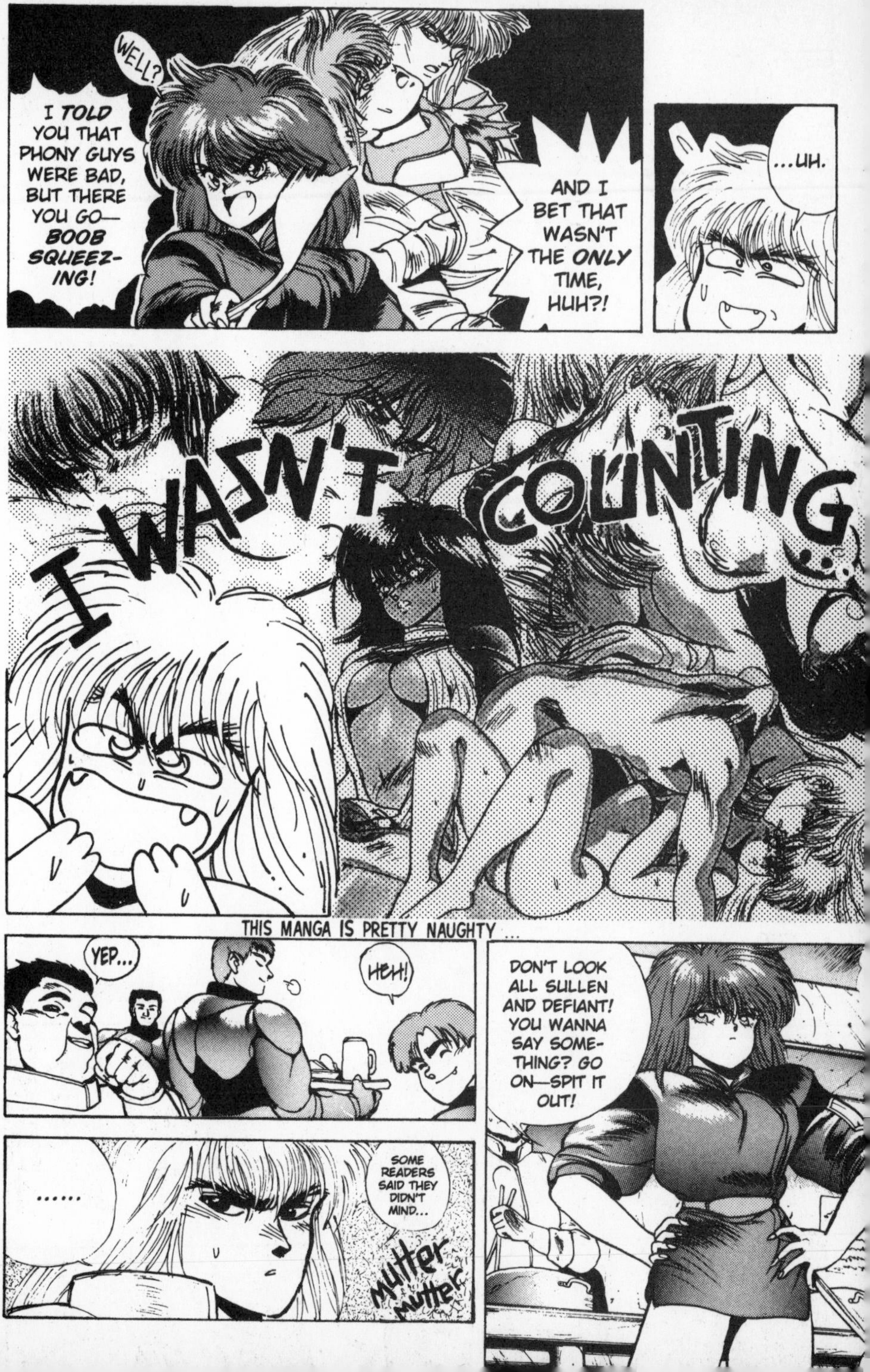
WELL?
I TOLD YOU THAT PHONY GUYS WERE BAD, BUT THERE YOU GO— BOOB SQUEEZ-ING!
AND I BET THAT WASN'T THE ONLY TIME, HUH?!
...UH.
I WASN'T COUNTING
THIS MANGA IS PRETTY NAUGHTY ...
YEP...
HEH!
DON'T LOOK ALL SULLEN AND DEFIANT! YOU WANNA SAY SOME-THING? GO ON—SPIT IT OUT!
......
SOME READERS SAID THEY DIDN'T MIND...
mutter mutter

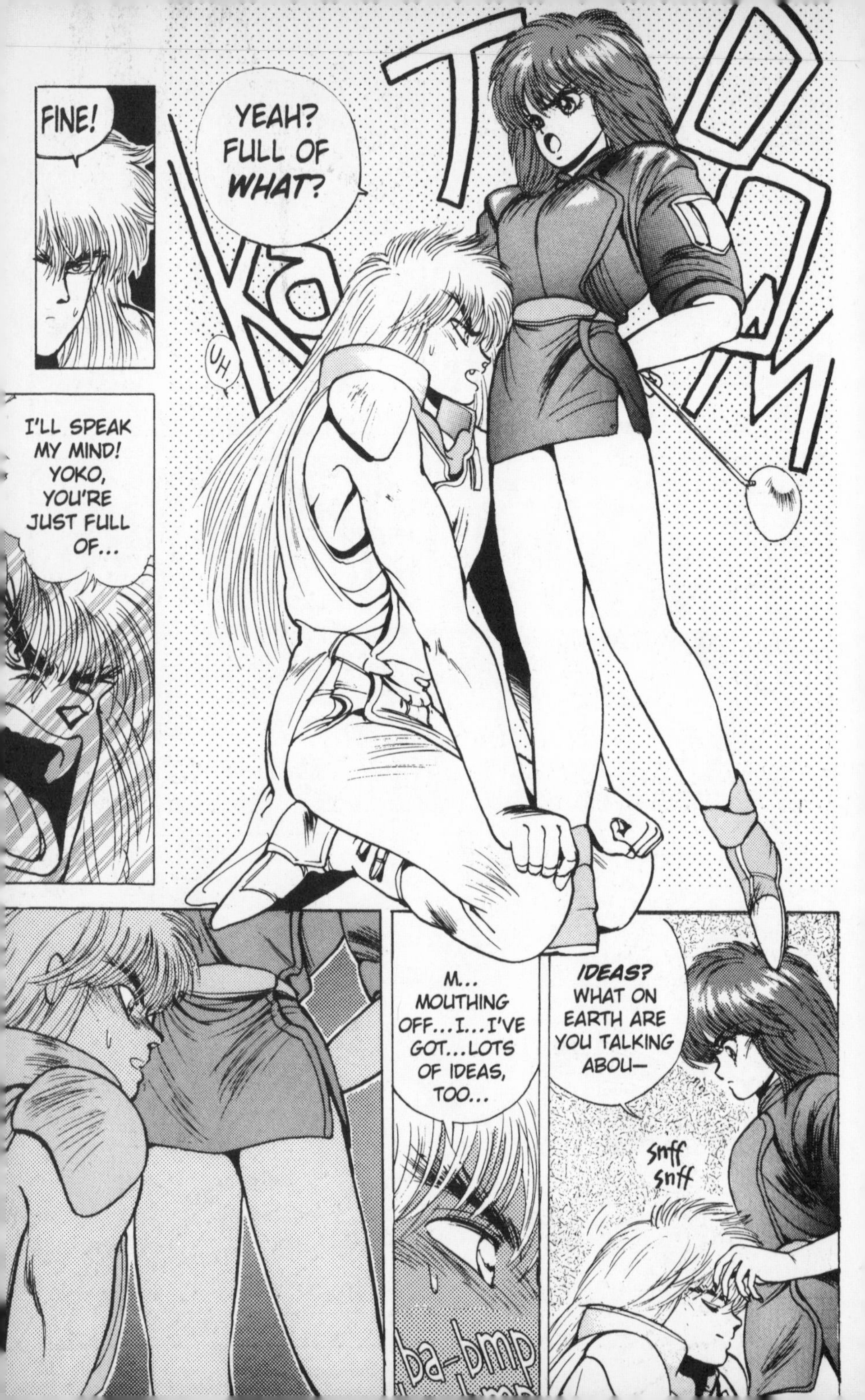
FINE!
I'LL SPEAK MY MIND! YOKO, YOU'RE JUST FULL OF...
YEAH? FULL OF *WHAT?*
UH.
M... MOUTHING OFF...I...I'VE GOT...LOTS OF IDEAS, TOO...
ba-bmp
IDEAS? WHAT ON EARTH ARE YOU TALKING ABOU—
snff snff

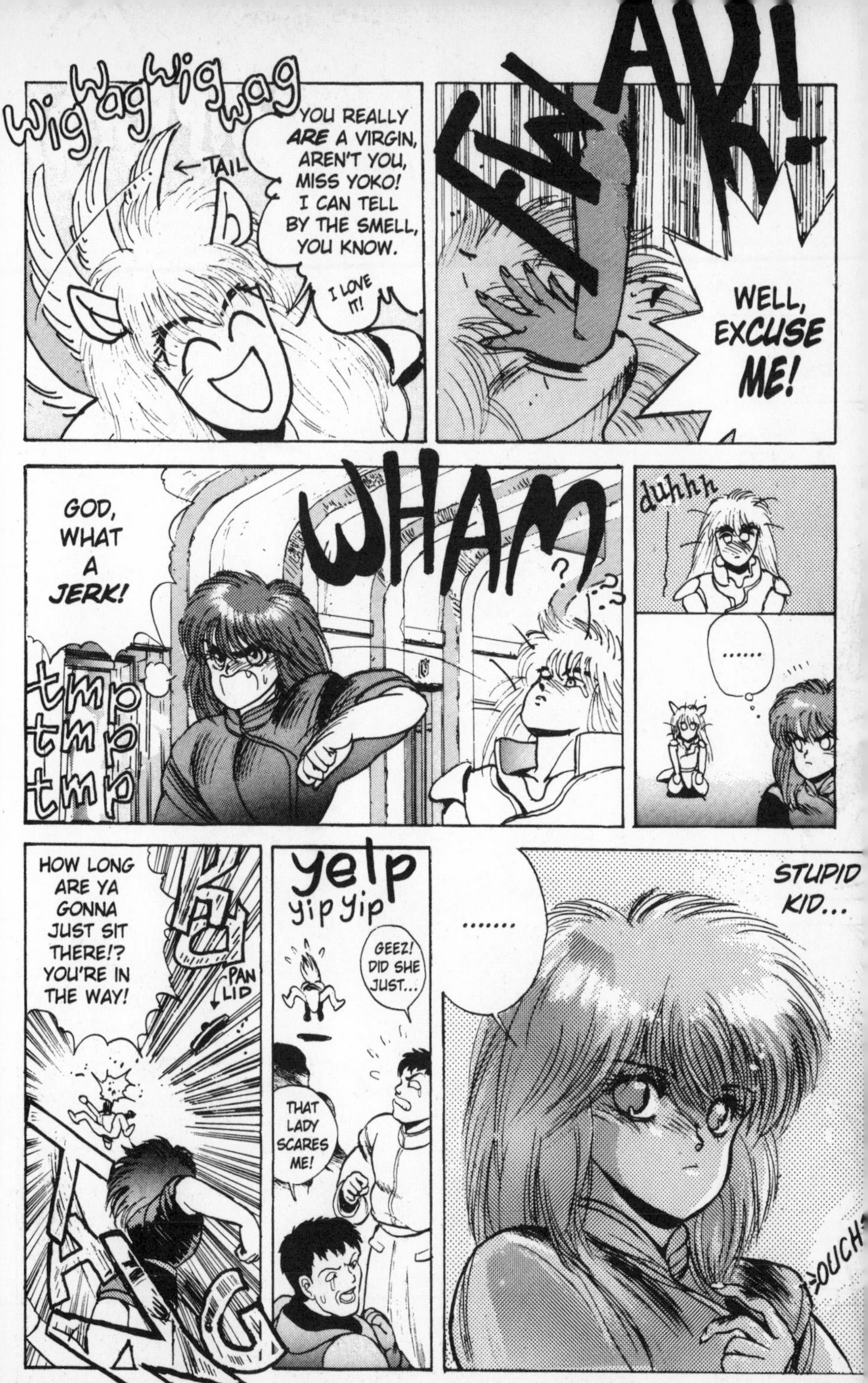

Wig wag wig wag
YOU REALLY ARE A VIRGIN, AREN'T YOU, MISS YOKO! I CAN TELL BY THE SMELL, YOU KNOW.
← TAIL
I LOVE IT!
WELL, EXCUSE ME!
GOD, WHAT A JERK!
WHAM
tmp tmp tmp
duhhh
......
HOW LONG ARE YA GONNA JUST SIT THERE!? YOU'RE IN THE WAY!
PAN LID
yelp
yip yip
GEEZ! DID SHE JUST...
THAT LADY SCARES ME!
....
STUPID KID...
OUCH

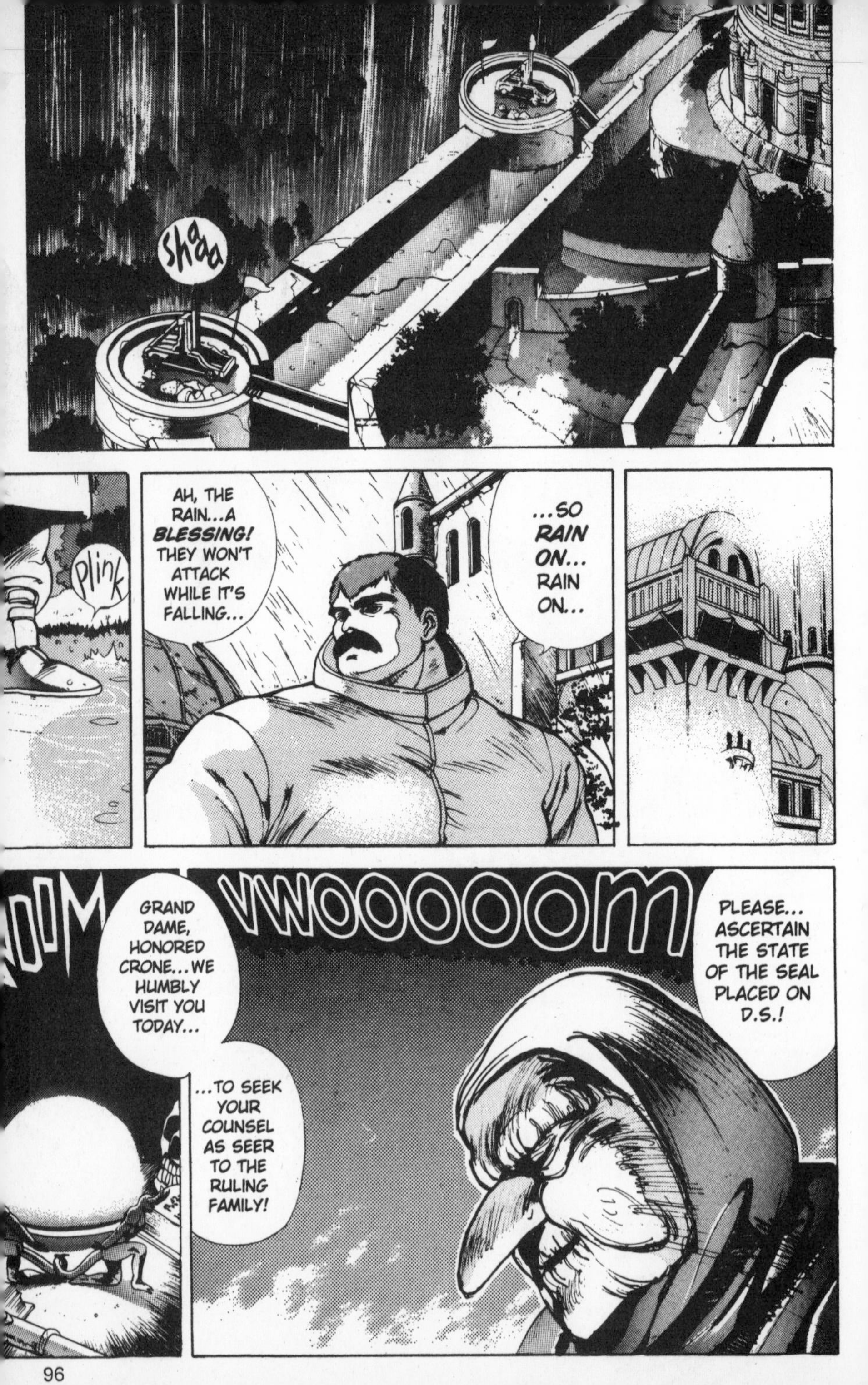

Shaaa
plink
AH, THE RAIN...A **BLESSING!** THEY WON'T ATTACK WHILE IT'S FALLING...
...SO **RAIN ON...** RAIN ON...
VWOOOOOM
GRAND DAME, HONORED CRONE...WE HUMBLY VISIT YOU TODAY...
...TO SEEK YOUR COUNSEL AS SEER TO THE RULING FAMILY!
PLEASE... ASCERTAIN THE STATE OF THE SEAL PLACED ON D.S.!

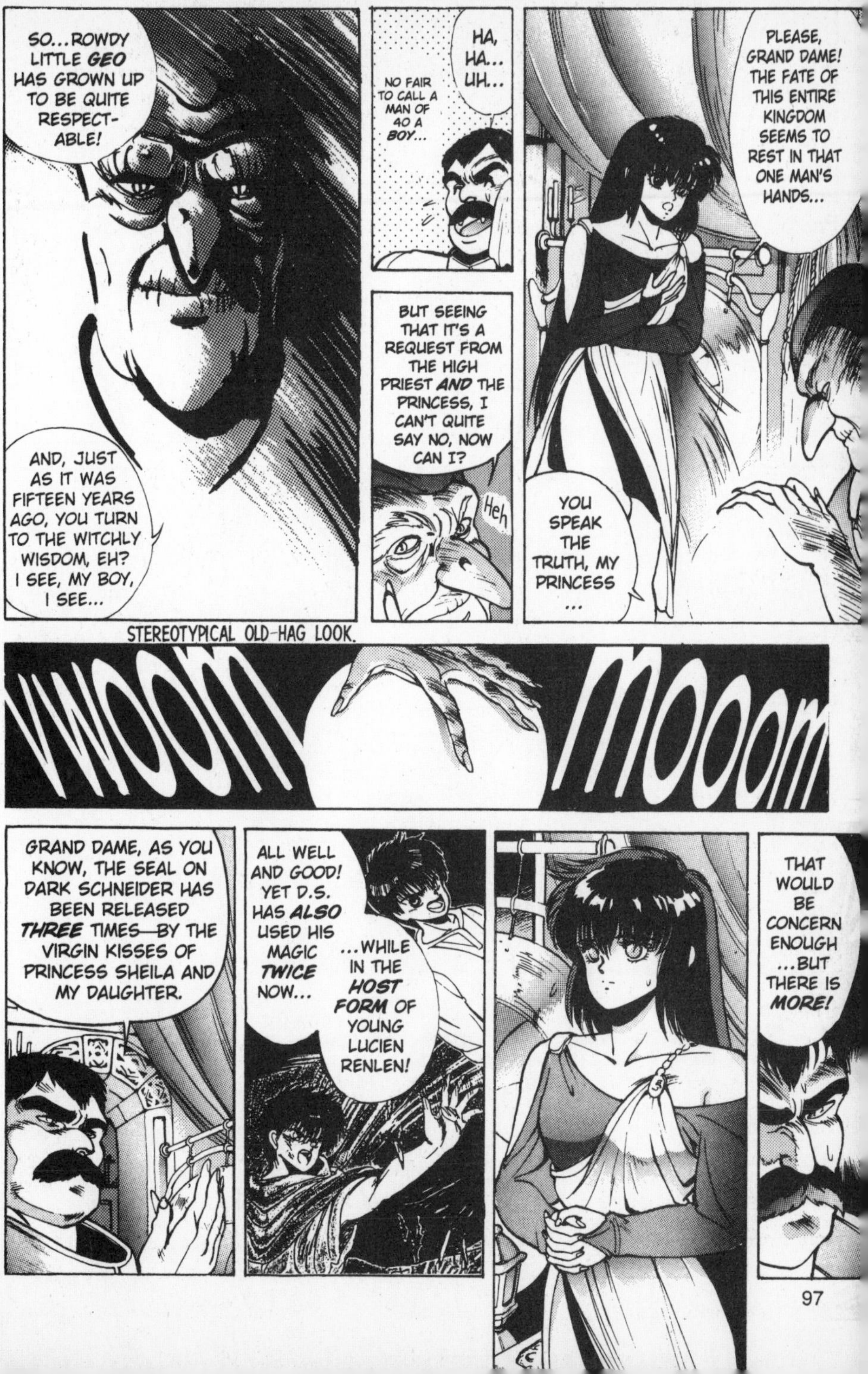
SO...ROWDY LITTLE GEO HAS GROWN UP TO BE QUITE RESPECT-ABLE!
AND, JUST AS IT WAS FIFTEEN YEARS AGO, YOU TURN TO THE WITCHLY WISDOM, EH? I SEE, MY BOY, I SEE...
STEREOTYPICAL OLD-HAG LOOK.
HA, HA... UH...
NO FAIR TO CALL A MAN OF 40 A BOY...
BUT SEEING THAT IT'S A REQUEST FROM THE HIGH PRIEST AND THE PRINCESS, I CAN'T QUITE SAY NO, NOW CAN I?
Heh
PLEASE, GRAND DAME! THE FATE OF THIS ENTIRE KINGDOM SEEMS TO REST IN THAT ONE MAN'S HANDS...
YOU SPEAK THE TRUTH, MY PRINCESS ...
VWOOM
MOOOM
GRAND DAME, AS YOU KNOW, THE SEAL ON DARK SCHNEIDER HAS BEEN RELEASED THREE TIMES—BY THE VIRGIN KISSES OF PRINCESS SHEILA AND MY DAUGHTER.
ALL WELL AND GOOD! YET D.S. HAS ALSO USED HIS MAGIC TWICE NOW...
...WHILE IN THE HOST FORM OF YOUNG LUCIEN RENLEN!
THAT WOULD BE CONCERN ENOUGH ...BUT THERE IS MORE!

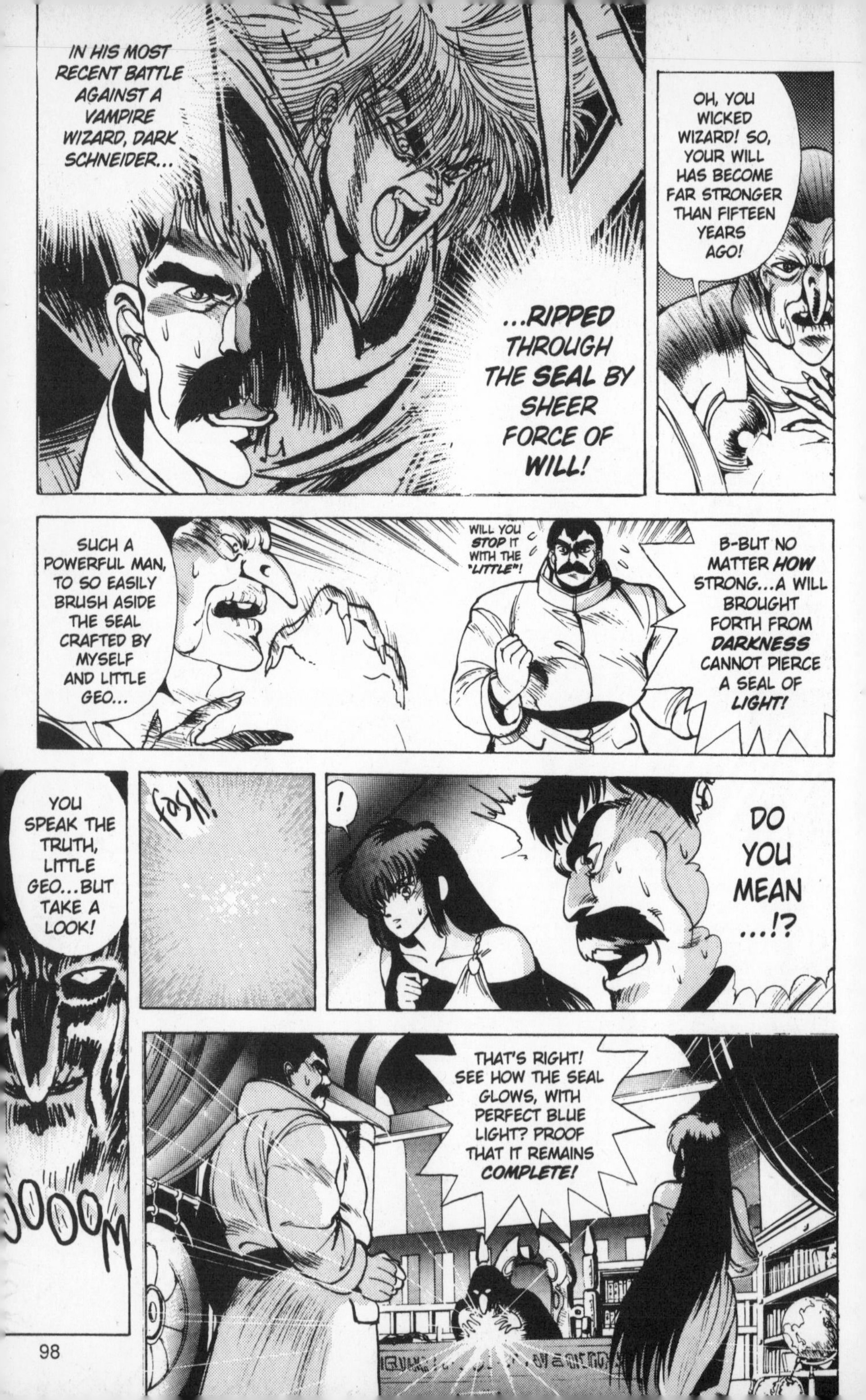
IN HIS MOST RECENT BATTLE AGAINST A VAMPIRE WIZARD, DARK SCHNEIDER...
...RIPPED THROUGH THE SEAL BY SHEER FORCE OF WILL!
OH, YOU WICKED WIZARD! SO, YOUR WILL HAS BECOME FAR STRONGER THAN FIFTEEN YEARS AGO!
SUCH A POWERFUL MAN, TO SO EASILY BRUSH ASIDE THE SEAL CRAFTED BY MYSELF AND LITTLE GEO...
WILL YOU STOP IT WITH THE "LITTLE"!
B-BUT NO MATTER HOW STRONG...A WILL BROUGHT FORTH FROM DARKNESS CANNOT PIERCE A SEAL OF LIGHT!
YOU SPEAK THE TRUTH, LITTLE GEO...BUT TAKE A LOOK!
OOOOM
fosh!
!
DO YOU MEAN ...!?
THAT'S RIGHT! SEE HOW THE SEAL GLOWS, WITH PERFECT BLUE LIGHT? PROOF THAT IT REMAINS COMPLETE!

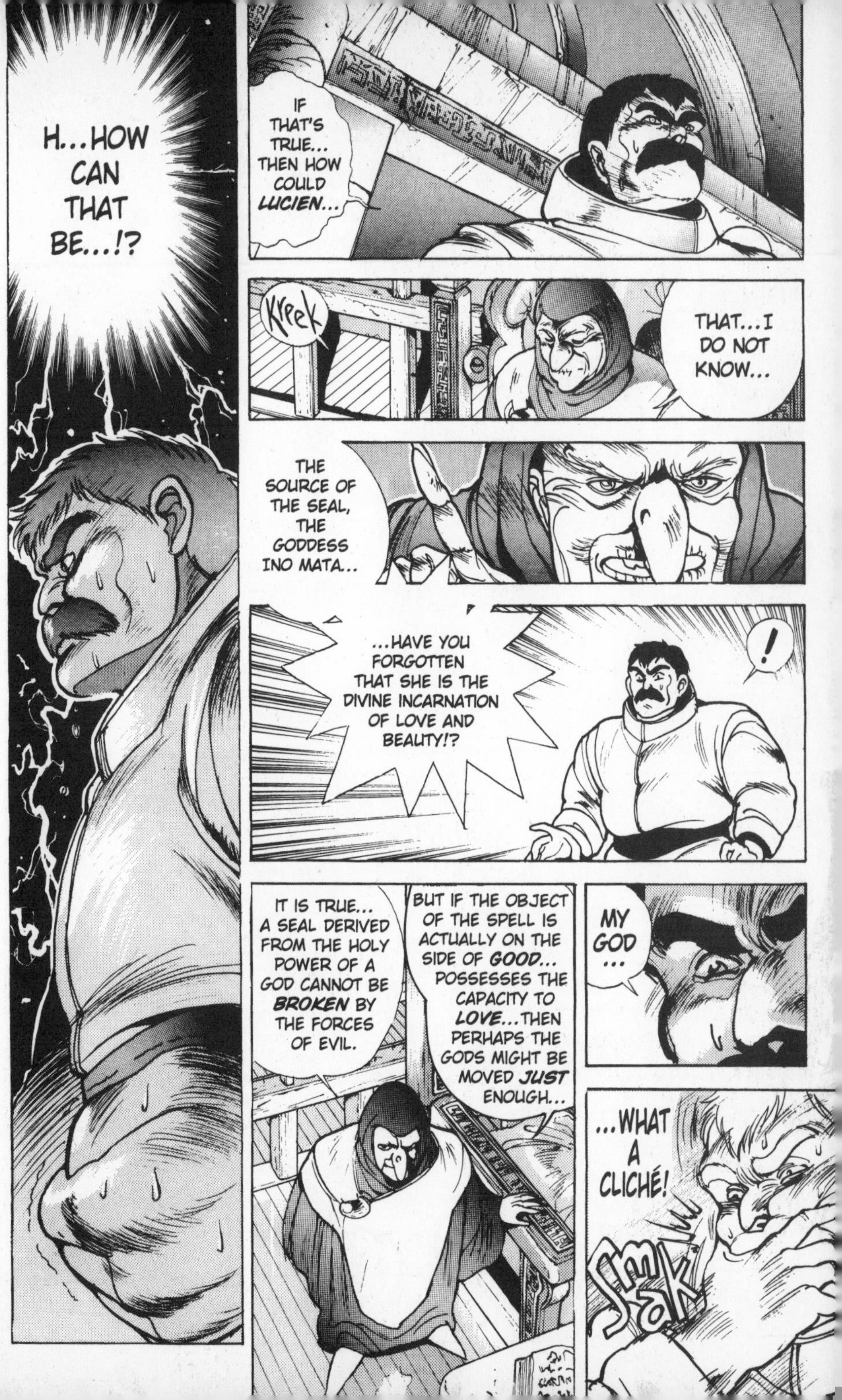
H...HOW CAN THAT BE...!?
IF THAT'S TRUE... THEN HOW COULD LUCIEN...
Kreek
THAT...I DO NOT KNOW...
THE SOURCE OF THE SEAL, THE GODDESS INO MATA...
...HAVE YOU FORGOTTEN THAT SHE IS THE DIVINE INCARNATION OF LOVE AND BEAUTY!?
!
IT IS TRUE... A SEAL DERIVED FROM THE HOLY POWER OF A GOD CANNOT BE BROKEN BY THE FORCES OF EVIL.
BUT IF THE OBJECT OF THE SPELL IS ACTUALLY ON THE SIDE OF GOOD... POSSESSES THE CAPACITY TO LOVE...THEN PERHAPS THE GODS MIGHT BE MOVED JUST ENOUGH...
MY GOD ...
...WHAT A CLICHÉ!
SMOK

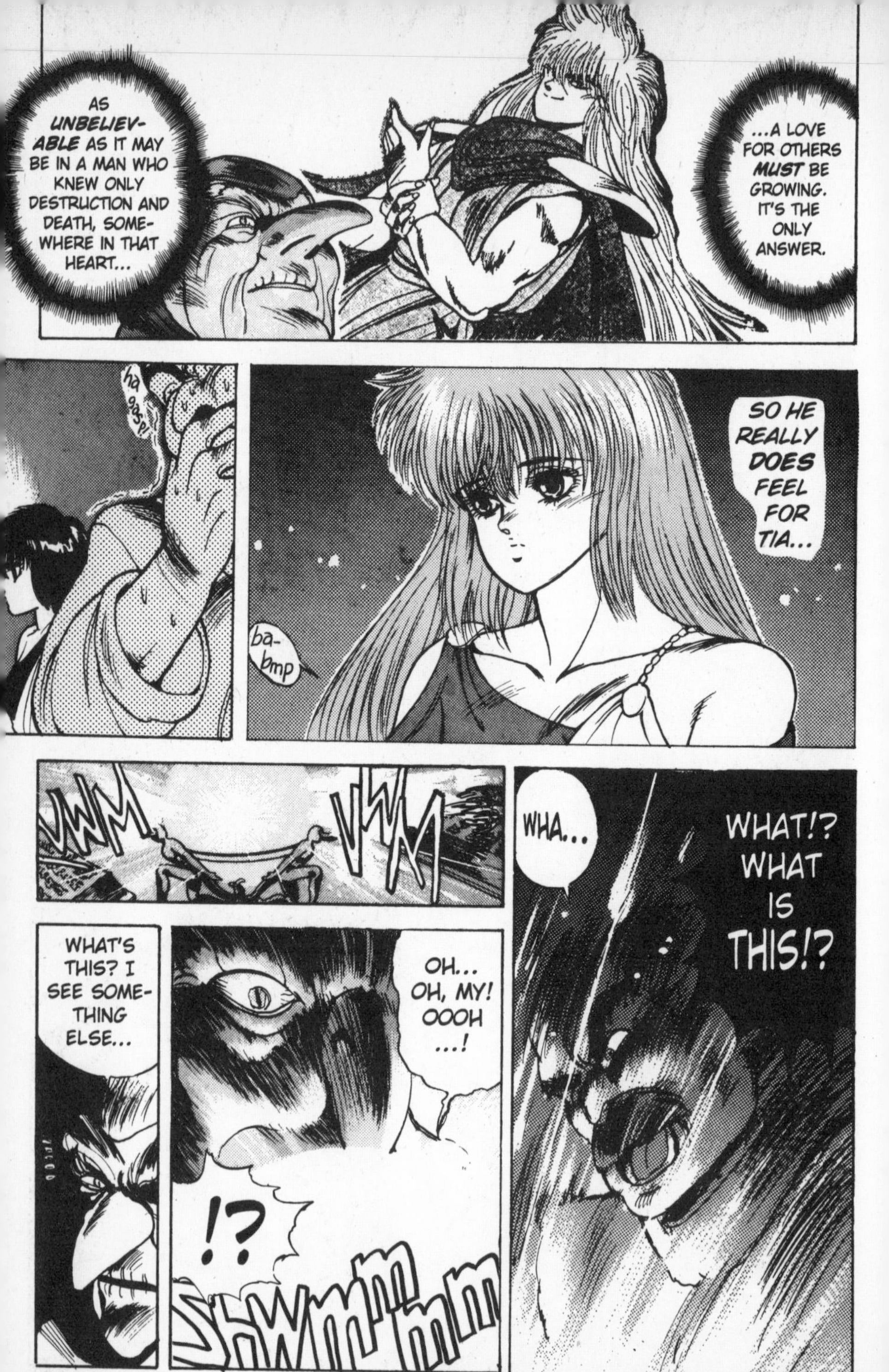
AS UNBELIEVABLE AS IT MAY BE IN A MAN WHO KNEW ONLY DESTRUCTION AND DEATH, SOMEWHERE IN THAT HEART...
...A LOVE FOR OTHERS MUST BE GROWING. IT'S THE ONLY ANSWER.
ha gasp!
SO HE REALLY DOES FEEL FOR TIA...
ba-bmp
WWM
VWM
WHAT'S THIS? I SEE SOMETHING ELSE...
OH... OH, MY! OOOH ...!
!?
SHWMMMM
WHA...
WHAT!? WHAT IS THIS!?

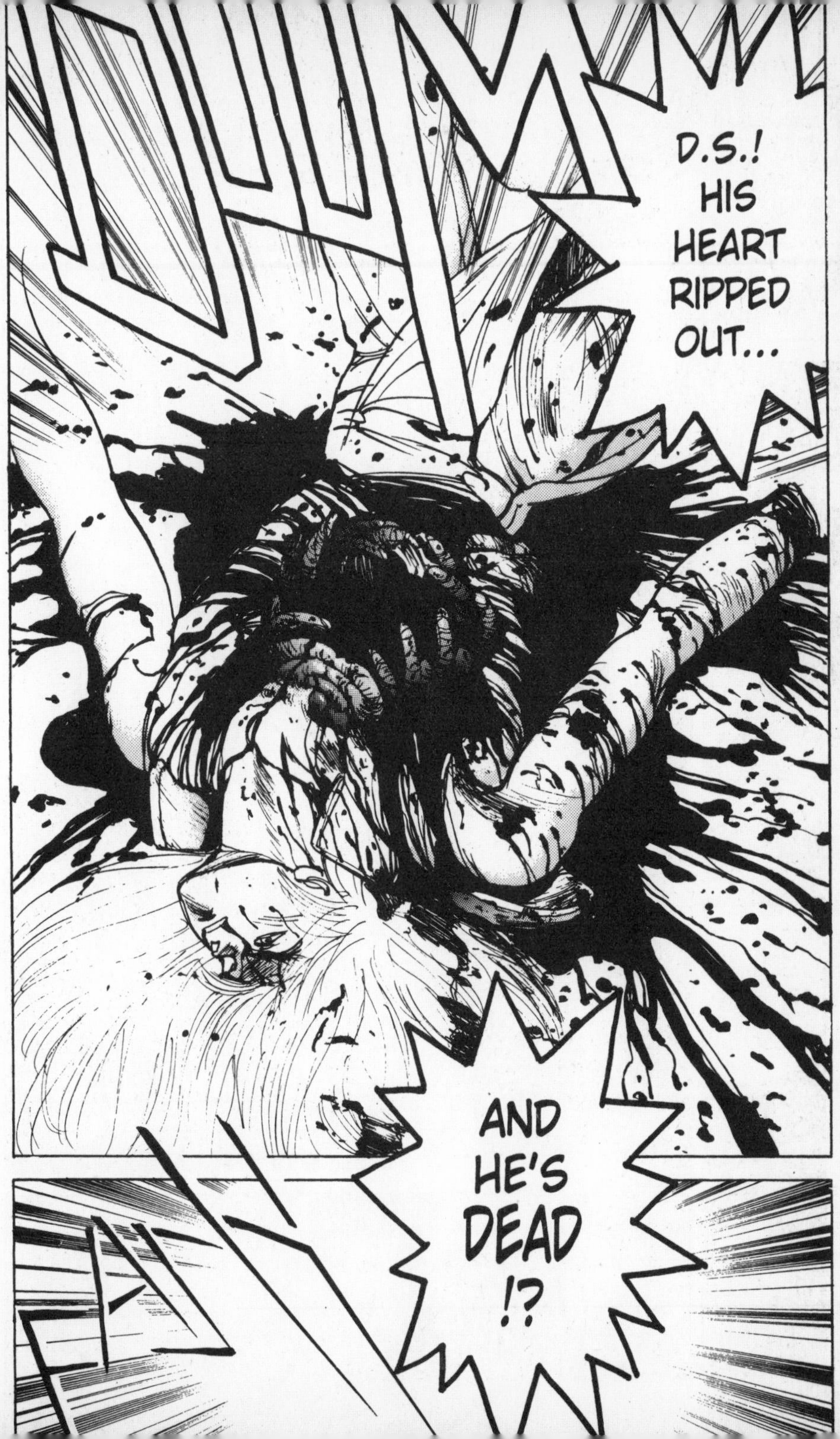
D.S.! HIS HEART RIPPED OUT...
AND HE'S DEAD !?

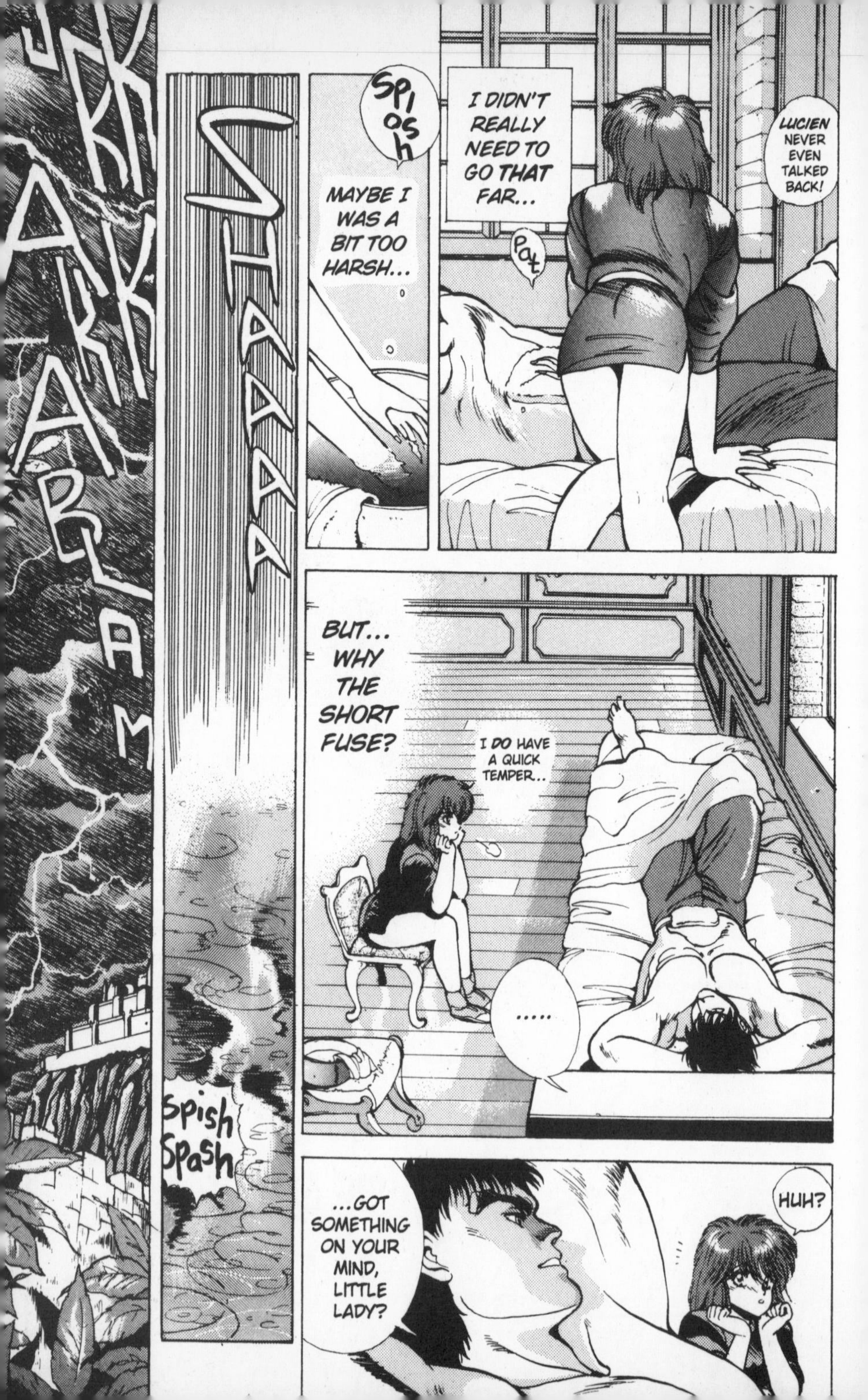
BLAM
SHAAAAAA
Spish Spash
Spi osh
MAYBE I WAS A BIT TOO HARSH...
I DIDN'T REALLY NEED TO GO THAT FAR...
Pat
LUCIEN NEVER EVEN TALKED BACK!
BUT... WHY THE SHORT FUSE?
I DO HAVE A QUICK TEMPER...
.....
...GOT SOMETHING ON YOUR MIND, LITTLE LADY?
HUH?

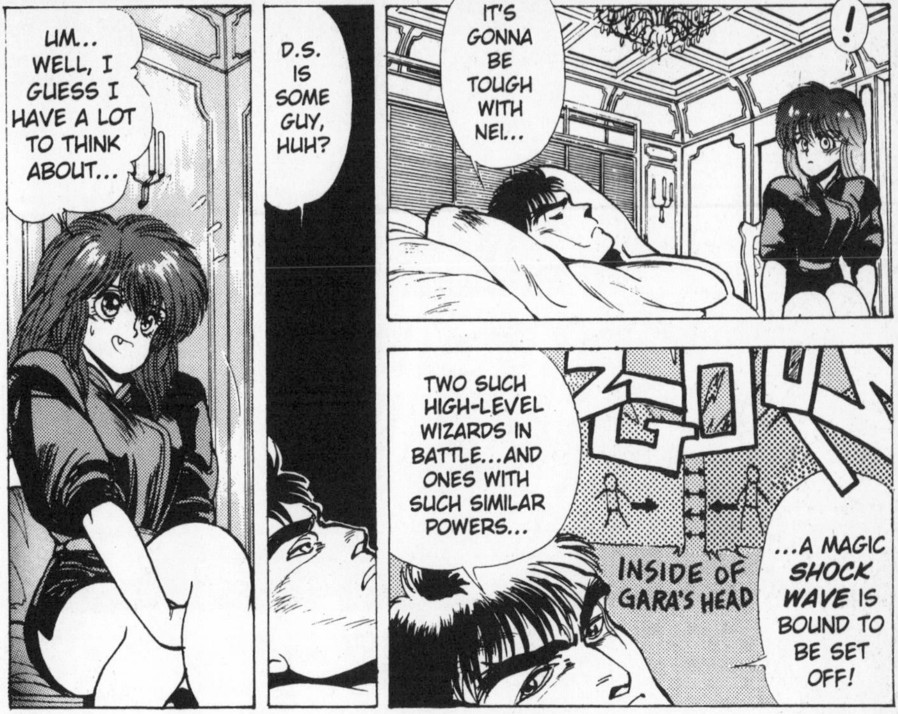
UM... WELL, I GUESS I HAVE A LOT TO THINK ABOUT...
D.S. IS SOME GUY, HUH?
IT'S GONNA BE TOUGH WITH NEI...
!
TWO SUCH HIGH-LEVEL WIZARDS IN BATTLE...AND ONES WITH SUCH SIMILAR POWERS...
INSIDE OF GARA'S HEAD
...A MAGIC *SHOCK WAVE* IS BOUND TO BE SET OFF!

SEAN ARI is very popular

People's tastes vary a lot, but many say they like how straightforward she is. Thanks!

Her motto of "a bond deeper than blood" shows a great strength of character.

(↙)

(↗)

She's in her teens... She was probably a war orphan, raised by Arshes Nei alongside Kai Harn. Bet that's where she learned the Secret Arts of the Ancients.

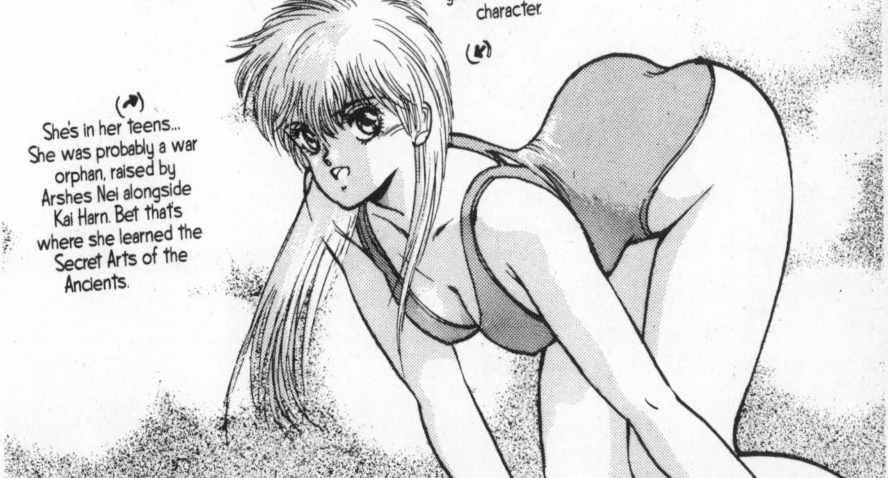

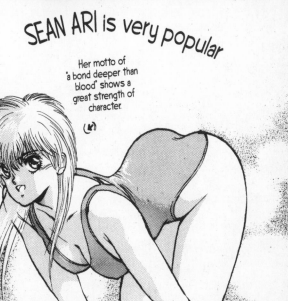

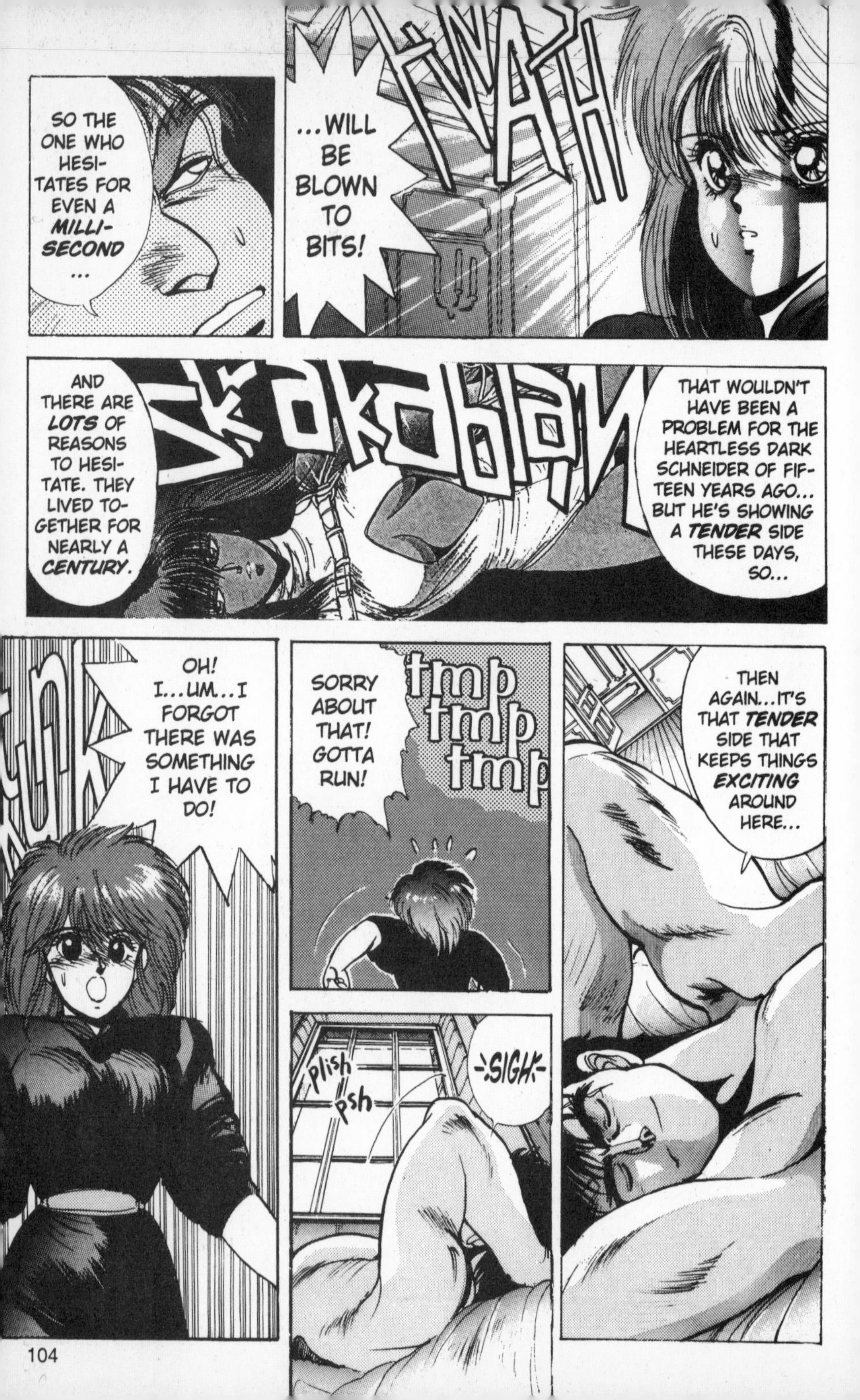
SO THE ONE WHO HESITATES FOR EVEN A MILLISECOND ...
...WILL BE BLOWN TO BITS!
AND THERE ARE LOTS OF REASONS TO HESITATE. THEY LIVED TOGETHER FOR NEARLY A CENTURY.
THAT WOULDN'T HAVE BEEN A PROBLEM FOR THE HEARTLESS DARK SCHNEIDER OF FIFTEEN YEARS AGO... BUT HE'S SHOWING A TENDER SIDE THESE DAYS, SO...
OH! I...UM...I FORGOT THERE WAS SOMETHING I HAVE TO DO!
SORRY ABOUT THAT! GOTTA RUN!
tmp tmp tmp
plish psh
-SIGH-
THEN AGAIN...IT'S THAT TENDER SIDE THAT KEEPS THINGS EXCITING AROUND HERE...

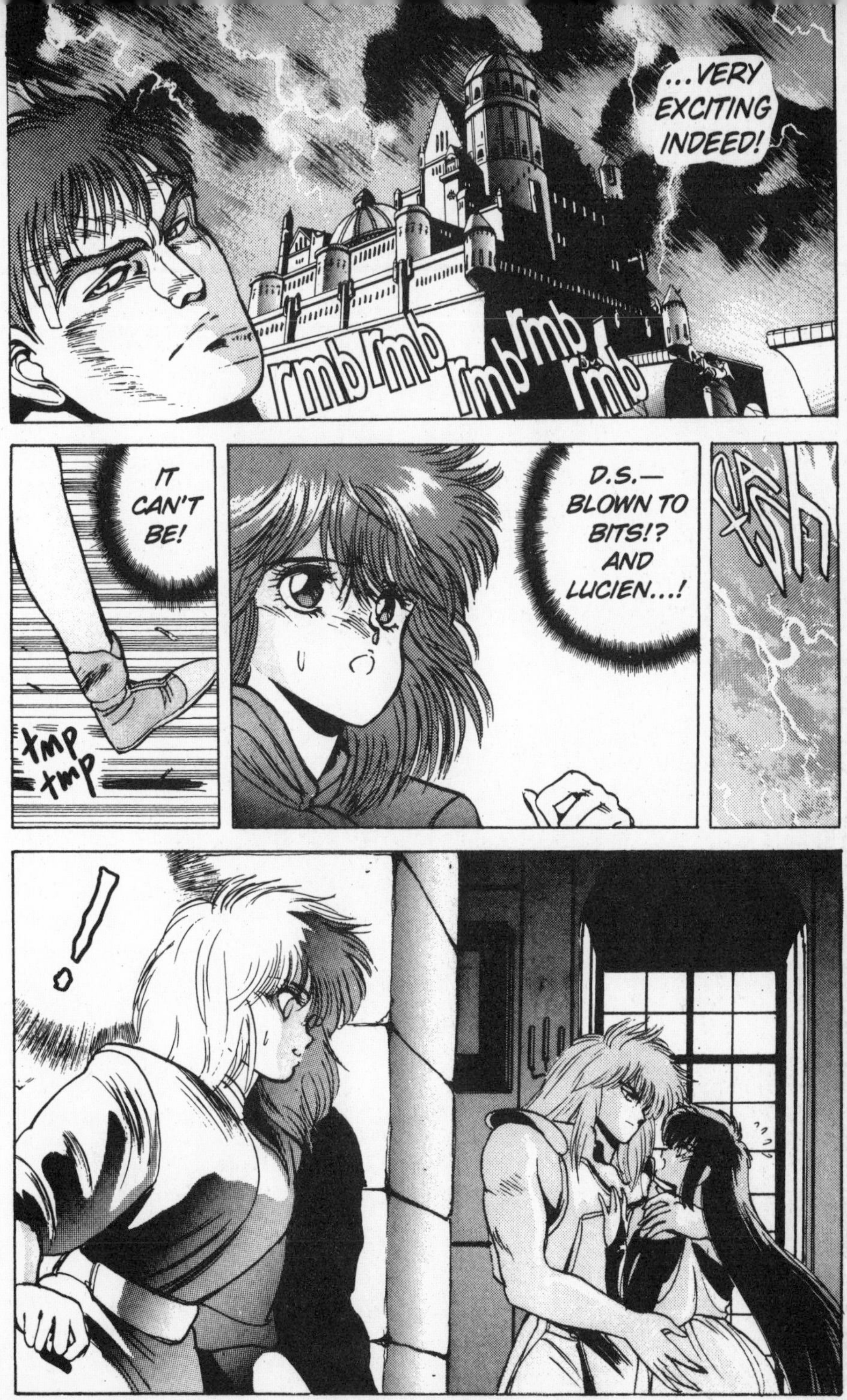
...VERY EXCITING INDEED!
rmb rmb rmb rmb rmb
IT CAN'T BE!
tmp tmp
D.S.— BLOWN TO BITS!? AND LUCIEN...!
!

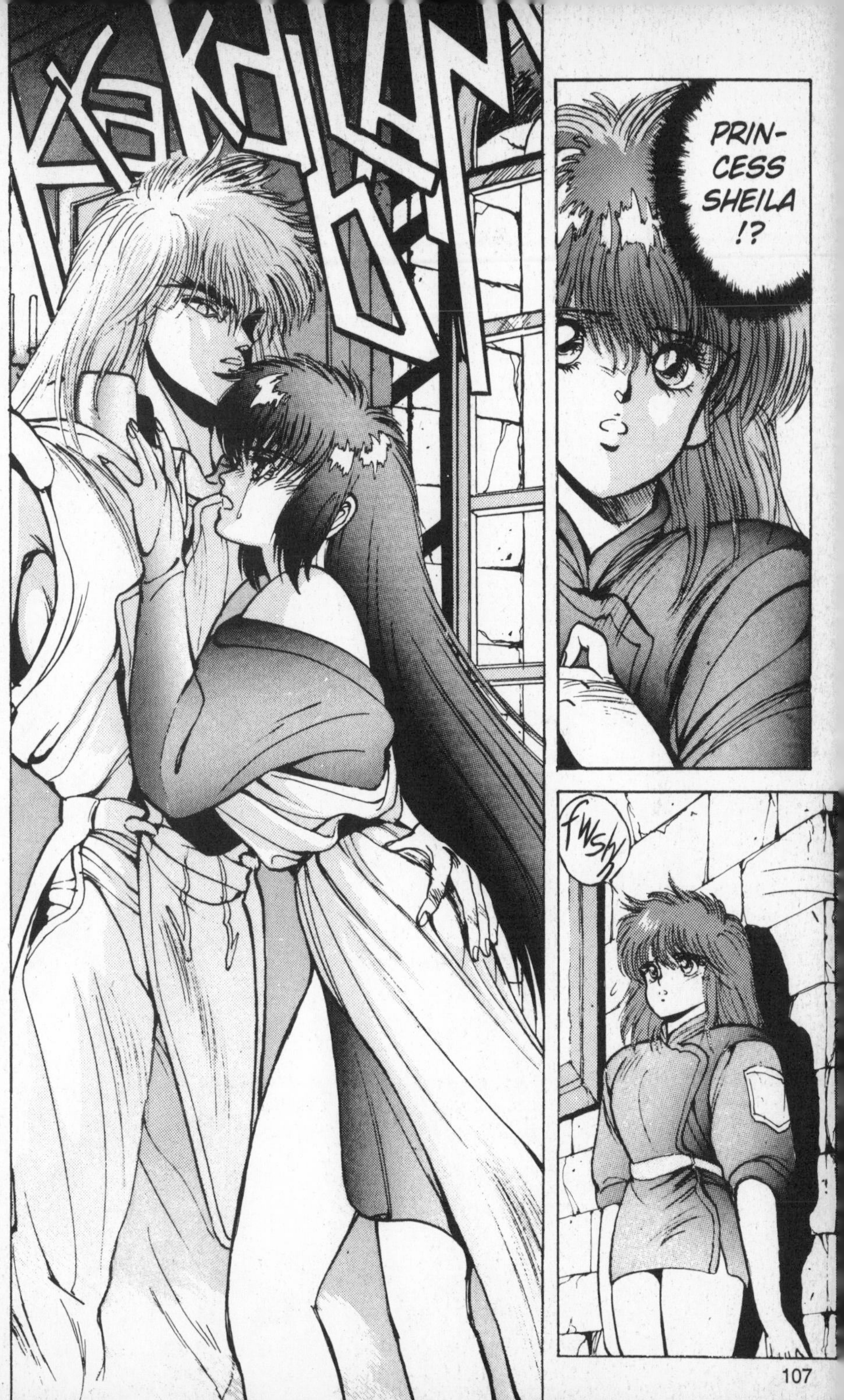
PRIN-
CESS
SHEILA
!?
fwsh

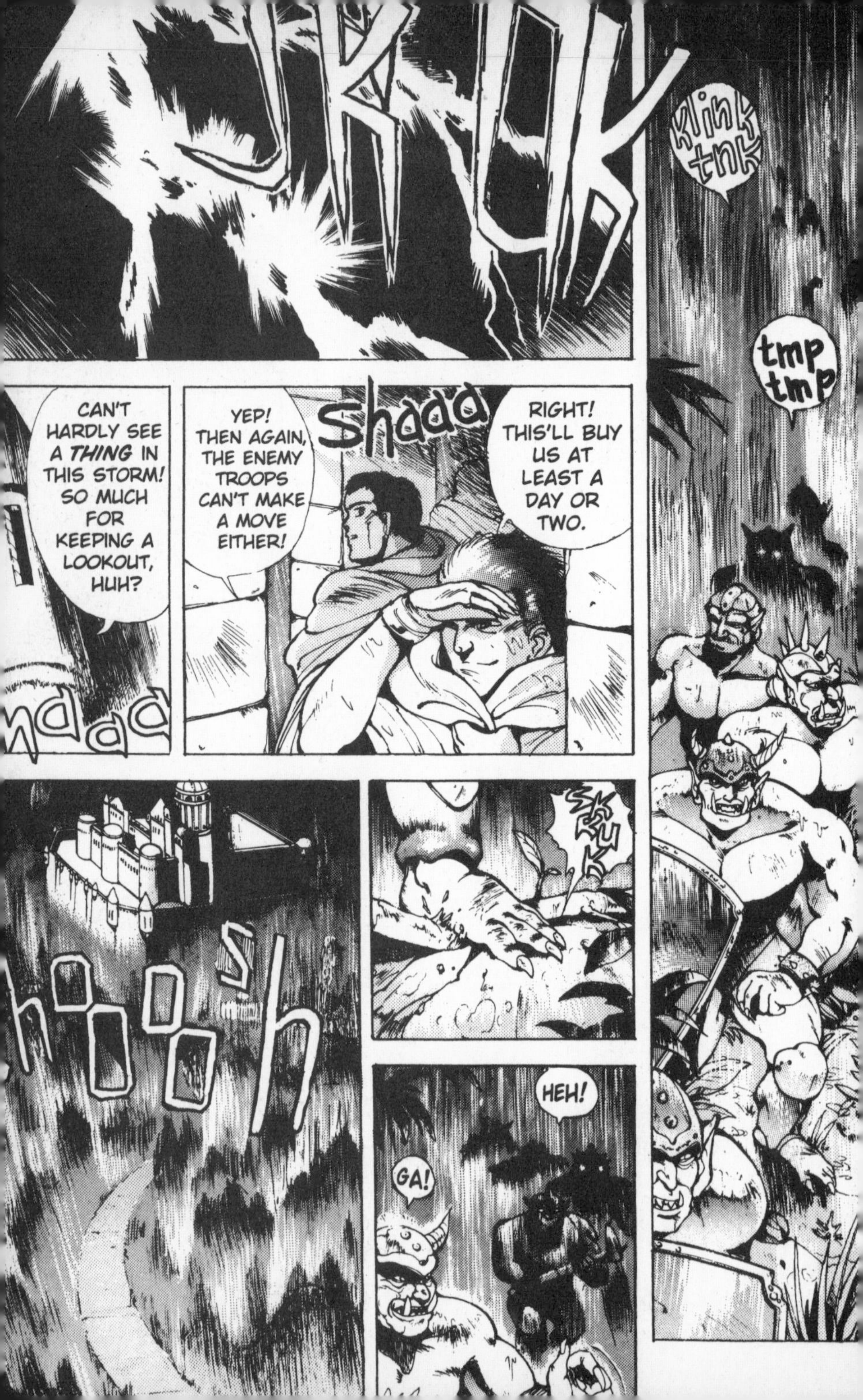
CAN'T HARDLY SEE A *THING* IN THIS STORM! SO MUCH FOR KEEPING A LOOKOUT, HUH?
Shaaa
YEP! THEN AGAIN, THE ENEMY TROOPS CAN'T MAKE A MOVE EITHER!
RIGHT! THIS'LL BUY US AT LEAST A DAY OR TWO.
HEH!
GA!
klink tnk
tmp tmp

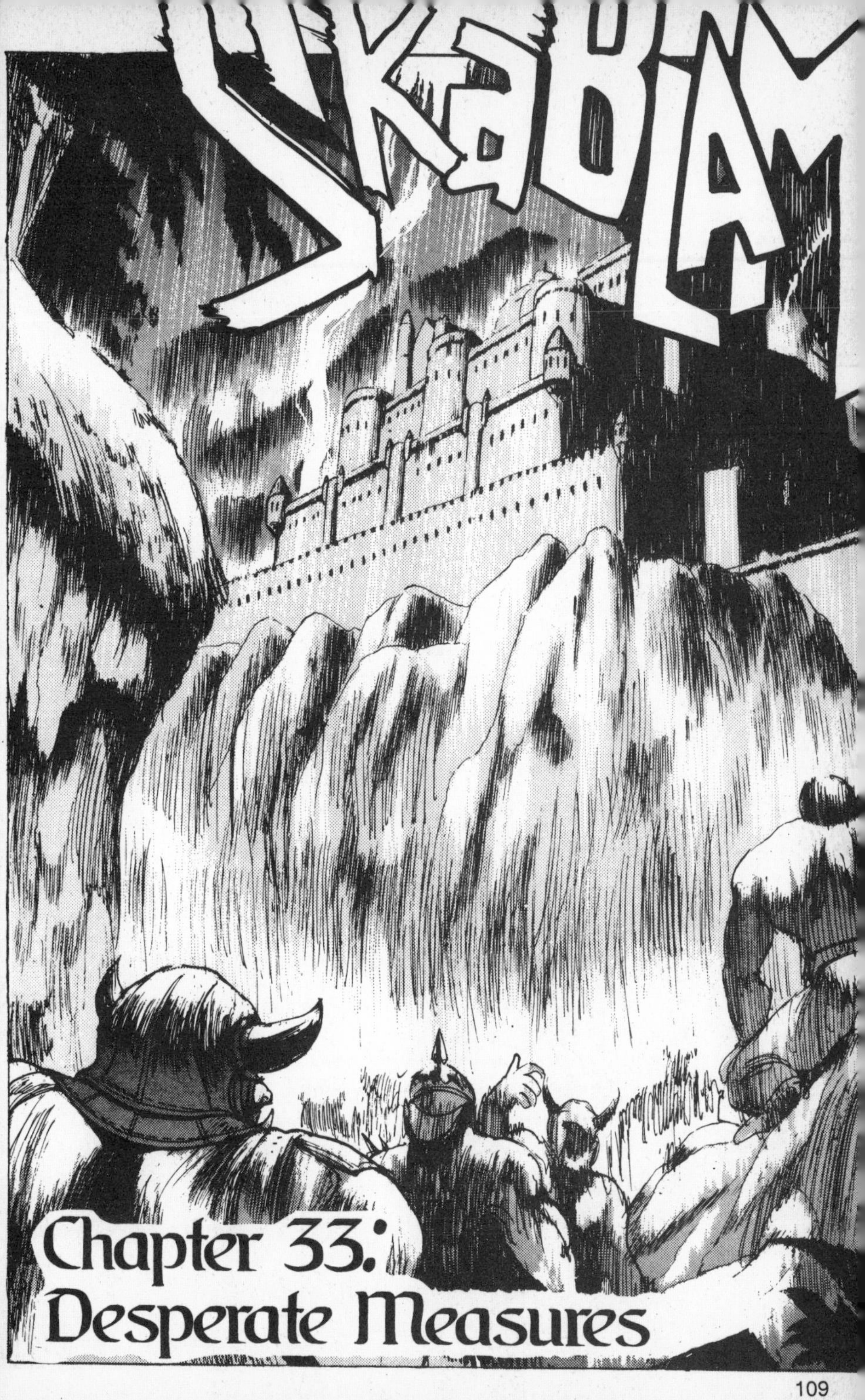

Chapter 33: Desperate Measures

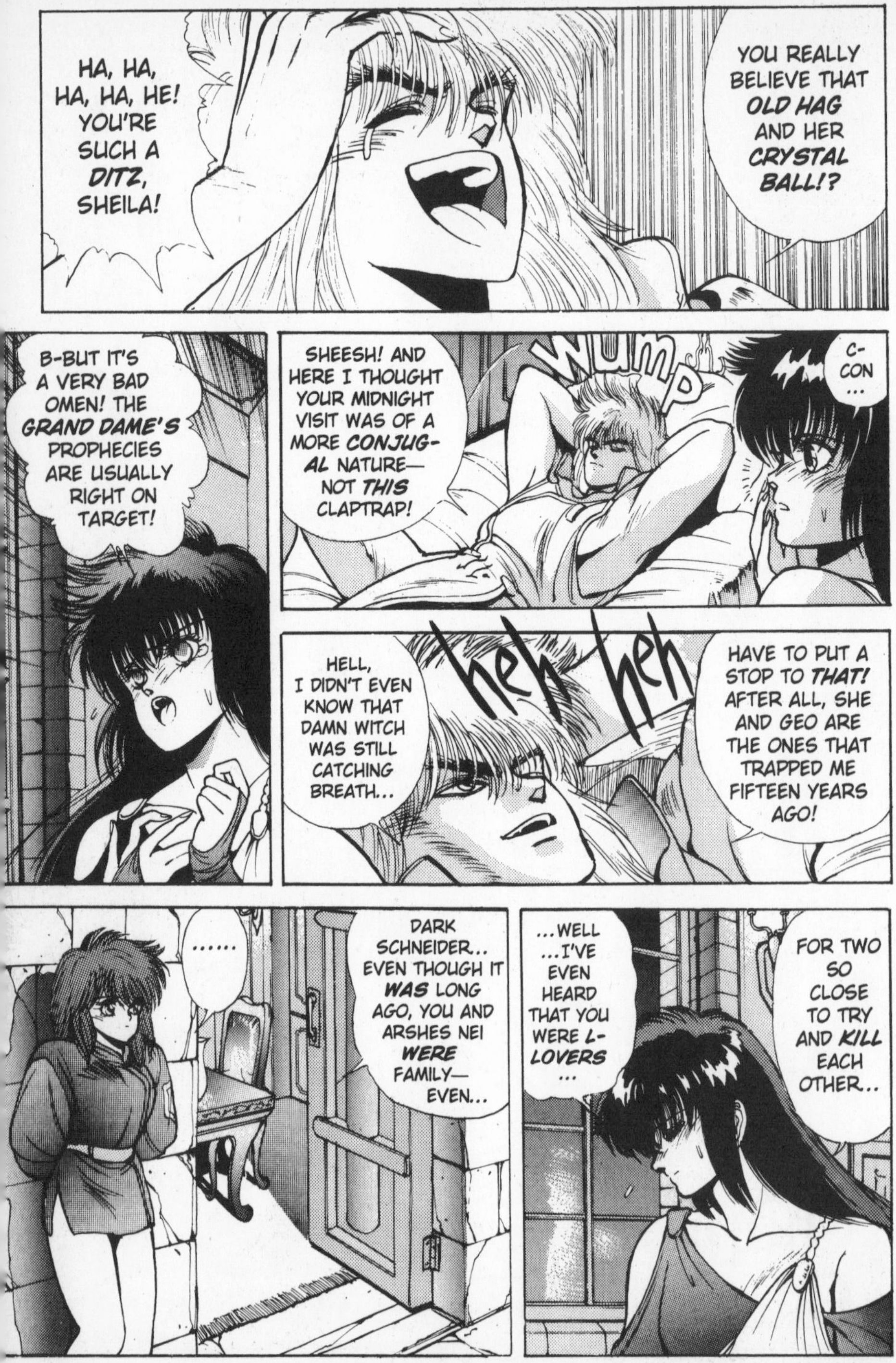
HA, HA, HA, HA, HE! YOU'RE SUCH A DITZ, SHEILA!
YOU REALLY BELIEVE THAT OLD HAG AND HER CRYSTAL BALL!?
B-BUT IT'S A VERY BAD OMEN! THE GRAND DAME'S PROPHECIES ARE USUALLY RIGHT ON TARGET!
SHEESH! AND HERE I THOUGHT YOUR MIDNIGHT VISIT WAS OF A MORE CONJUG-AL NATURE— NOT THIS CLAPTRAP!
WUMP
C- CON ...
HELL, I DIDN'T EVEN KNOW THAT DAMN WITCH WAS STILL CATCHING BREATH...
heh heh
HAVE TO PUT A STOP TO THAT! AFTER ALL, SHE AND GEO ARE THE ONES THAT TRAPPED ME FIFTEEN YEARS AGO!
......
DARK SCHNEIDER... EVEN THOUGH IT WAS LONG AGO, YOU AND ARSHES NEI WERE FAMILY— EVEN...
...WELL ...I'VE EVEN HEARD THAT YOU WERE L-LOVERS ...
FOR TWO SO CLOSE TO TRY AND KILL EACH OTHER...

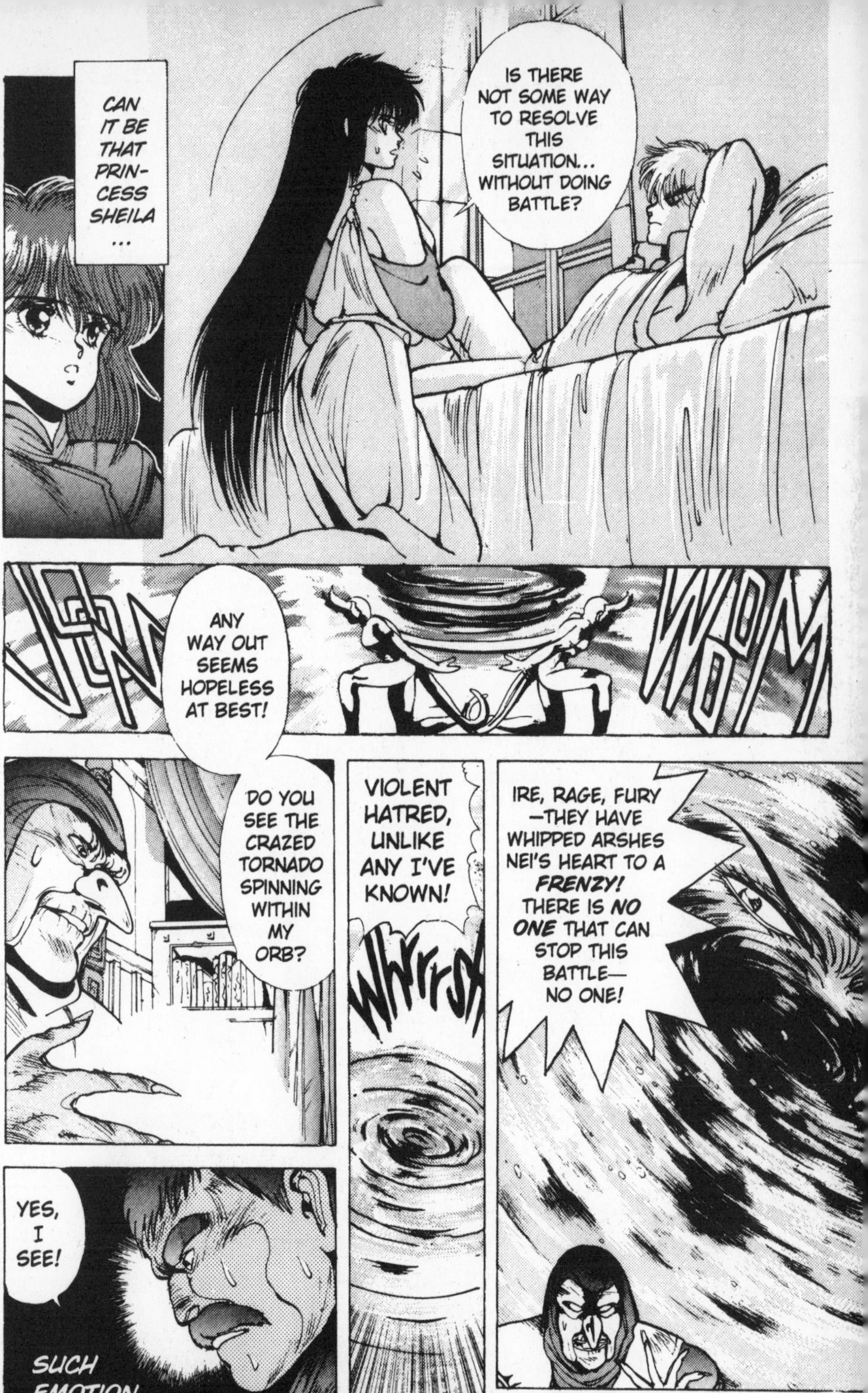
CAN IT BE THAT PRINCESS SHEILA ...
IS THERE NOT SOME WAY TO RESOLVE THIS SITUATION... WITHOUT DOING BATTLE?
ANY WAY OUT SEEMS HOPELESS AT BEST!
WOOM
DO YOU SEE THE CRAZED TORNADO SPINNING WITHIN MY ORB?
VIOLENT HATRED, UNLIKE ANY I'VE KNOWN!
WHRRRSH
IRE, RAGE, FURY —THEY HAVE WHIPPED ARSHES NEI'S HEART TO A *FRENZY!* THERE IS *NO ONE* THAT CAN STOP THIS BATTLE— NO ONE!
YES, I SEE!
SUCH EMOTION...

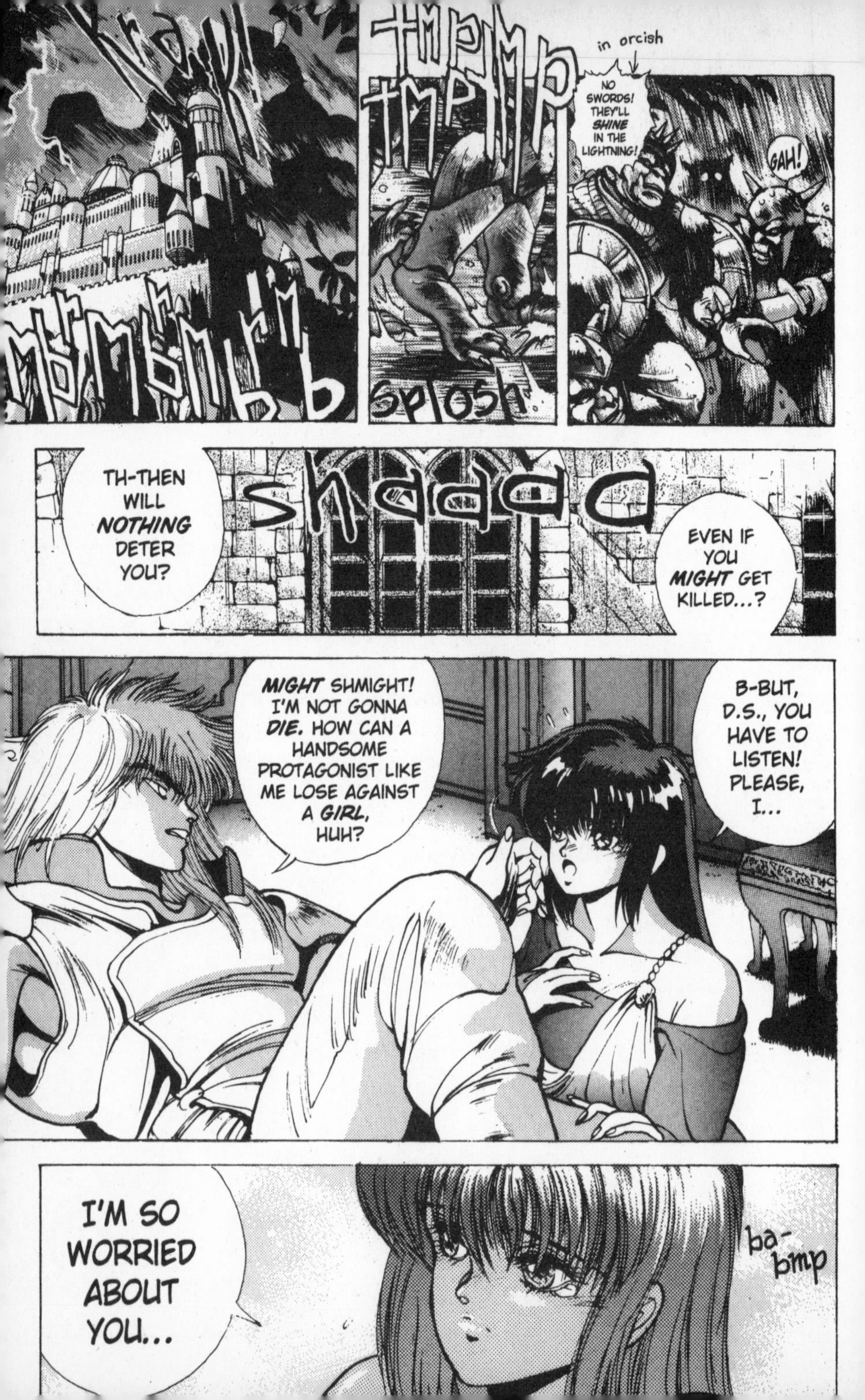

krakl
mbmbmbmbmbrmbrm
tmpmp tmpmp
splosh
in orcish
NO SWORDS! THEY'LL *SHINE* IN THE LIGHTNING!
GAH!
TH-THEN WILL *NOTHING* DETER YOU?
shaaaa
EVEN IF YOU *MIGHT* GET KILLED...?
MIGHT SHMIGHT! I'M NOT GONNA *DIE.* HOW CAN A HANDSOME PROTAGONIST LIKE ME LOSE AGAINST A *GIRL*, HUH?
B-BUT, D.S., YOU HAVE TO LISTEN! PLEASE, I...
I'M SO WORRIED ABOUT YOU...
ba-bmp

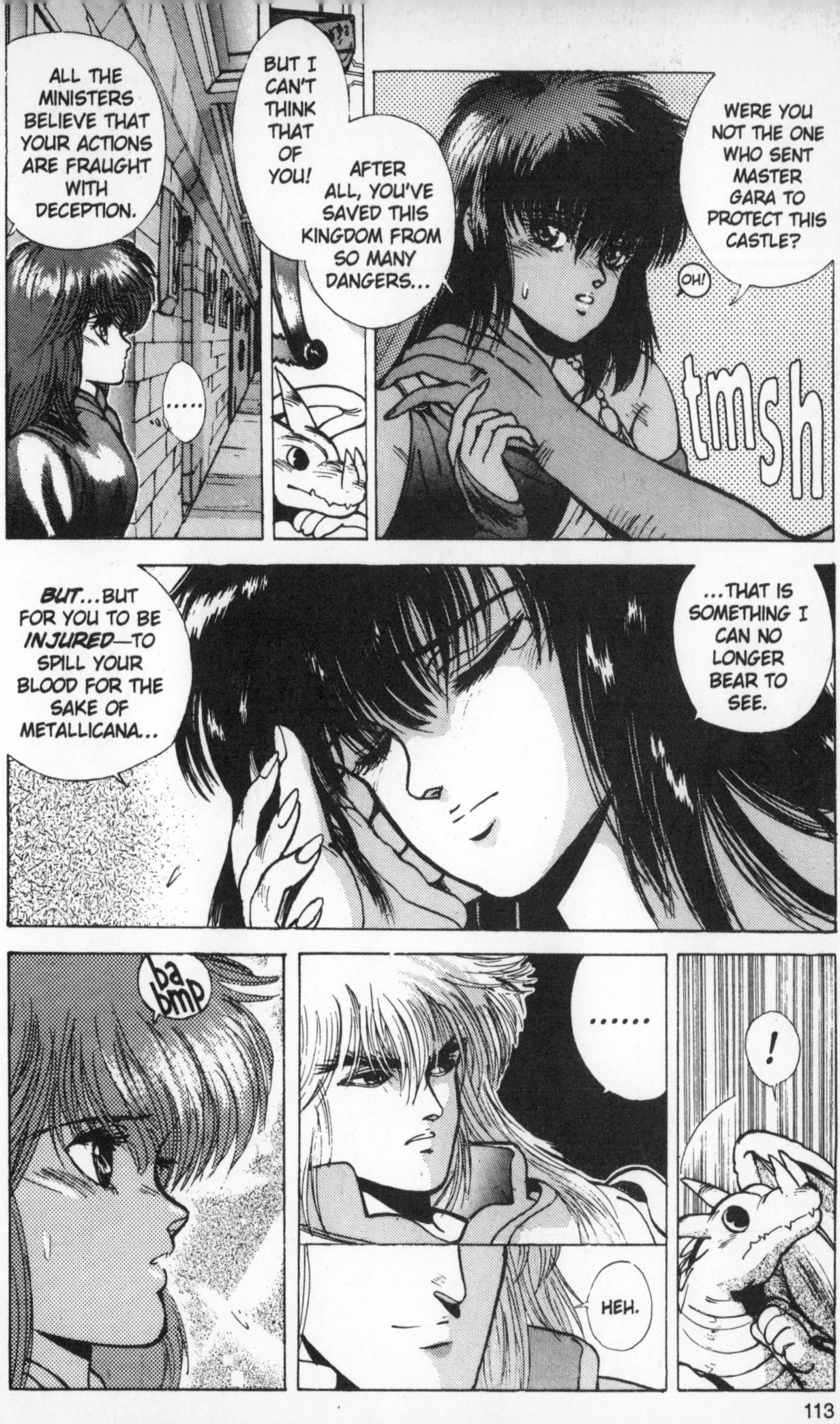
ALL THE MINISTERS BELIEVE THAT YOUR ACTIONS ARE FRAUGHT WITH DECEPTION.
......
BUT I CAN'T THINK THAT OF YOU!
AFTER ALL, YOU'VE SAVED THIS KINGDOM FROM SO MANY DANGERS...
WERE YOU NOT THE ONE WHO SENT MASTER GARA TO PROTECT THIS CASTLE?
OH!
tmsh
BUT...BUT FOR YOU TO BE *INJURED*—TO SPILL YOUR BLOOD FOR THE SAKE OF METALLICANA...
...THAT IS SOMETHING I CAN NO LONGER BEAR TO SEE.
ba bmp
......
HEH.
!

"FOR THE SAKE OF METALLI-CANA"!? HA, HA, HA, HA!

I'VE NEVER *HEARD* SUCH SHIT! WERE YOU REALLY THINKING *THAT*!?

WHAT?

......

?

HATE TO BREAK IT TO YOU, SHEILA...

...BUT ALL I WANT IS TO BE THE *ULTIMATE RULER* THROUGH *WORLD DOMINATION!* THAT'S IT...AND I'VE *NEVER* MADE IT ANY SECRET!

THESE LITTLE SKIRMISHES? I'M NOT DOING IT FOR *YOU LOSERS!* MY GOAL IS TO *GET BACK* MY ARMY OF DARKNESS!

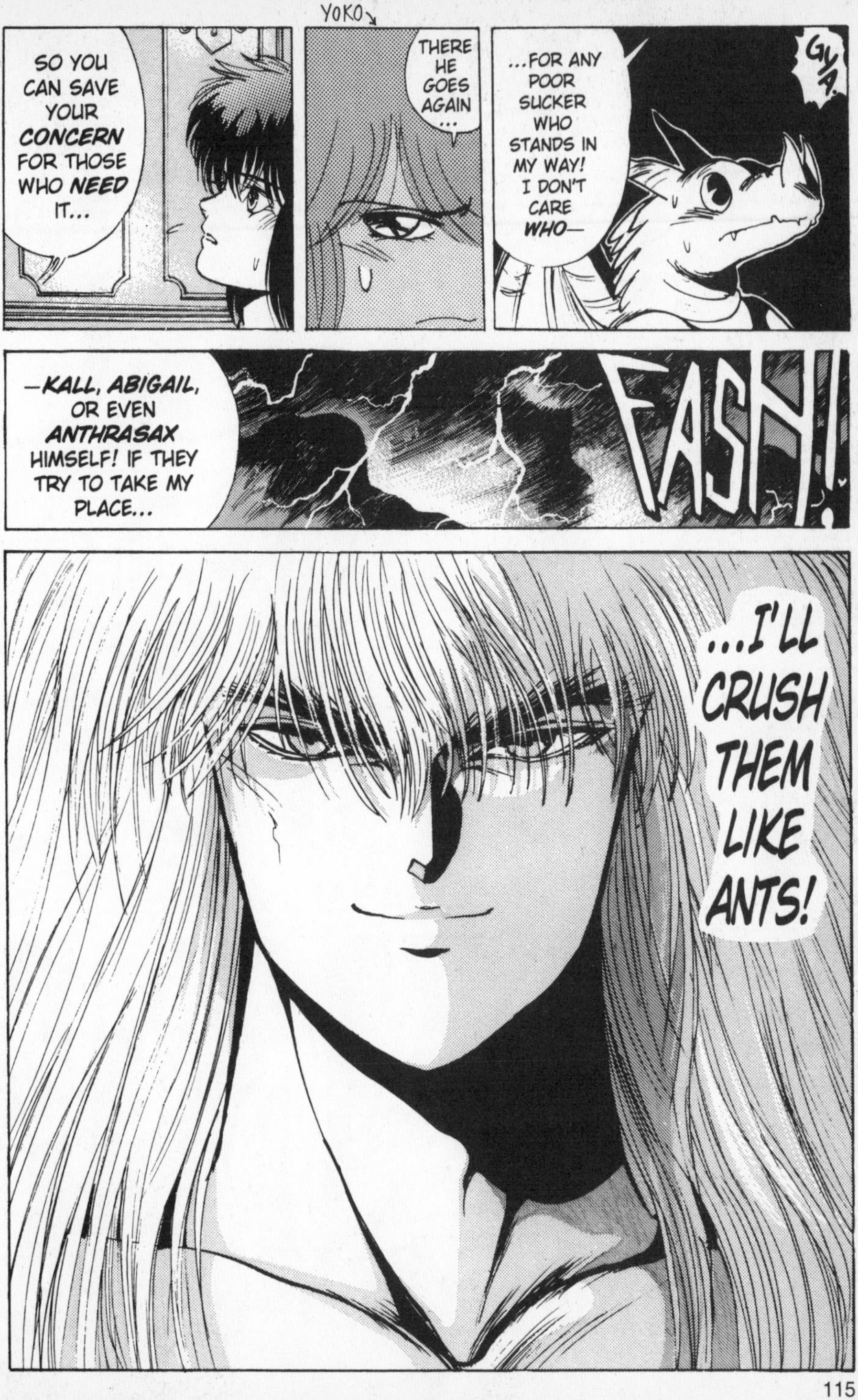
SO YOU CAN SAVE YOUR CONCERN FOR THOSE WHO NEED IT...
YOKO
THERE HE GOES AGAIN ...
...FOR ANY POOR SUCKER WHO STANDS IN MY WAY! I DON'T CARE WHO—
GYA.
—KALL, ABIGAIL, OR EVEN ANTHRASAX HIMSELF! IF THEY TRY TO TAKE MY PLACE...
FASH!!
...I'LL CRUSH THEM LIKE ANTS!

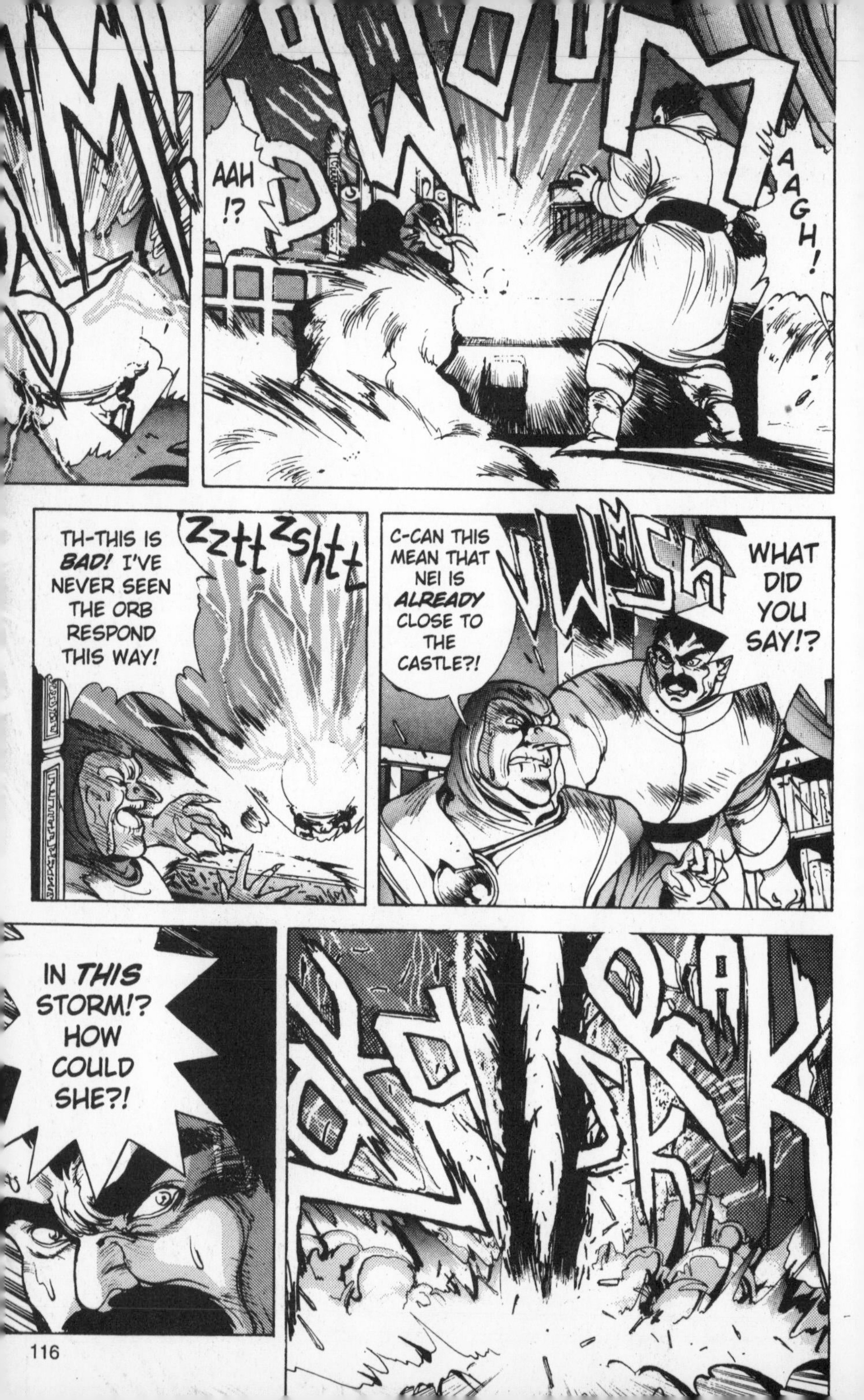
AAH!?
AAGH!
TH-THIS IS BAD! I'VE NEVER SEEN THE ORB RESPOND THIS WAY!
zztt zshtt
C-CAN THIS MEAN THAT NEI IS ALREADY CLOSE TO THE CASTLE?!
WHAT DID YOU SAY!?
IN THIS STORM!? HOW COULD SHE?!

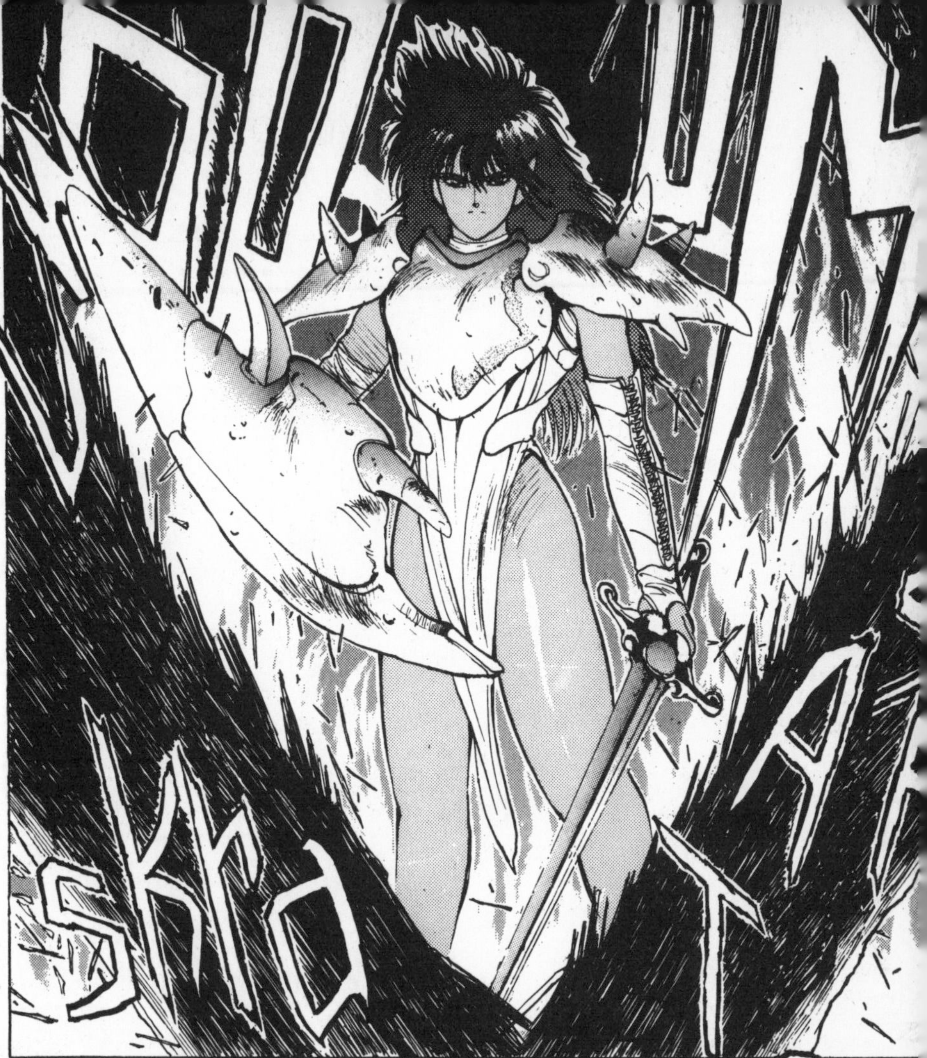

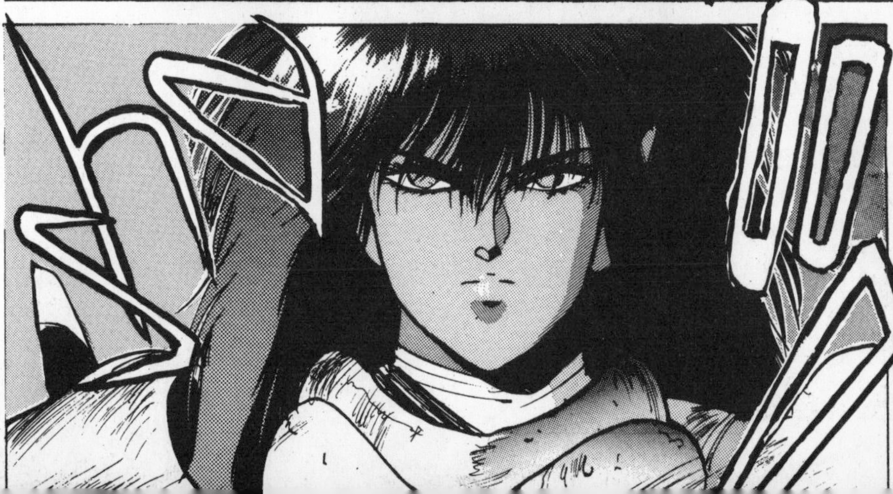

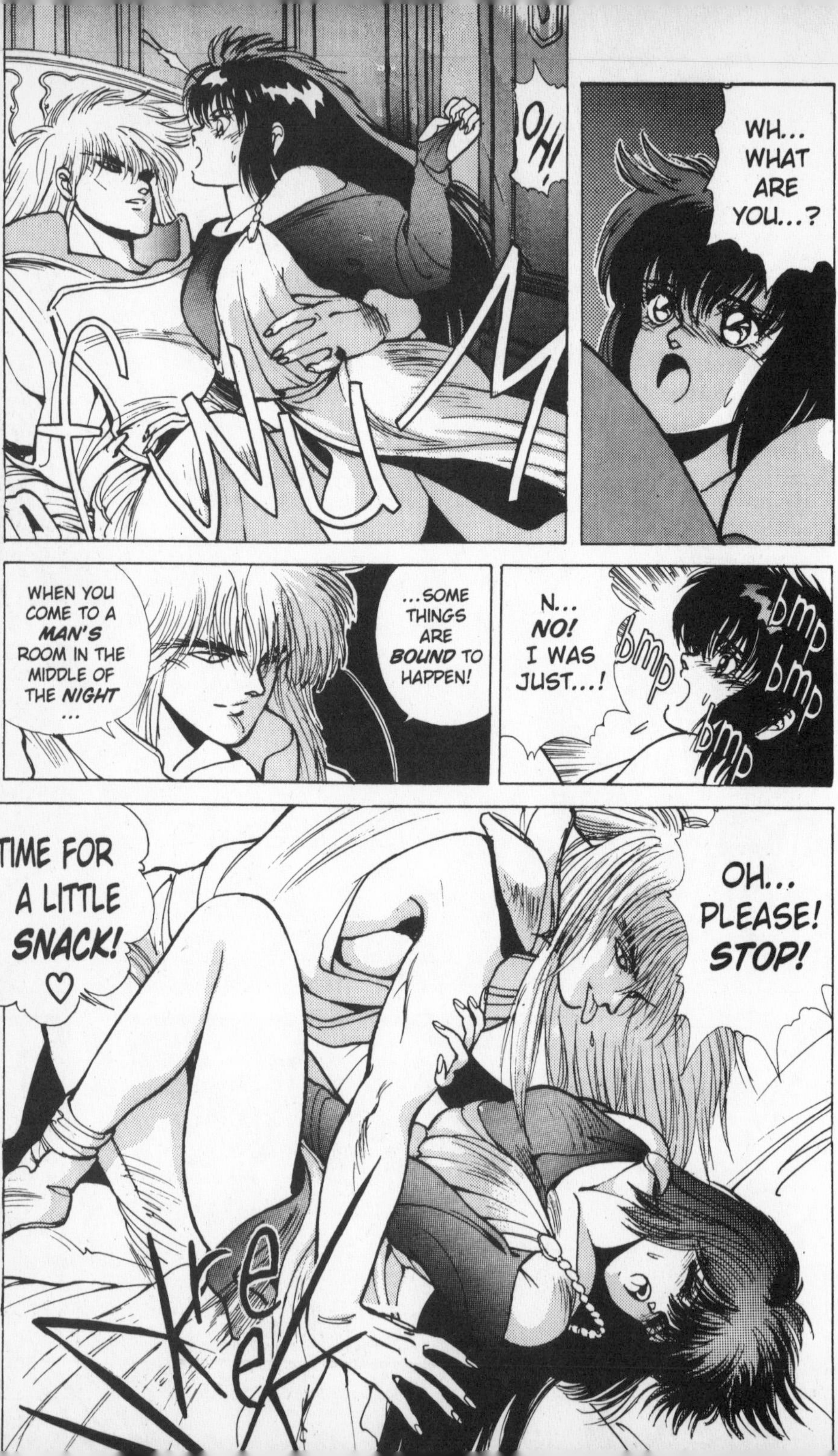
OH!
FWUM
WH... WHAT ARE YOU...?
WHEN YOU COME TO A ***MAN'S*** ROOM IN THE MIDDLE OF THE ***NIGHT*** ...
...SOME THINGS ARE ***BOUND*** TO HAPPEN!
N... ***NO!*** I WAS JUST...!
bmp bmp bmp bmp
TIME FOR A LITTLE ***SNACK!*** ♡
OH... PLEASE! ***STOP!***
KREEK

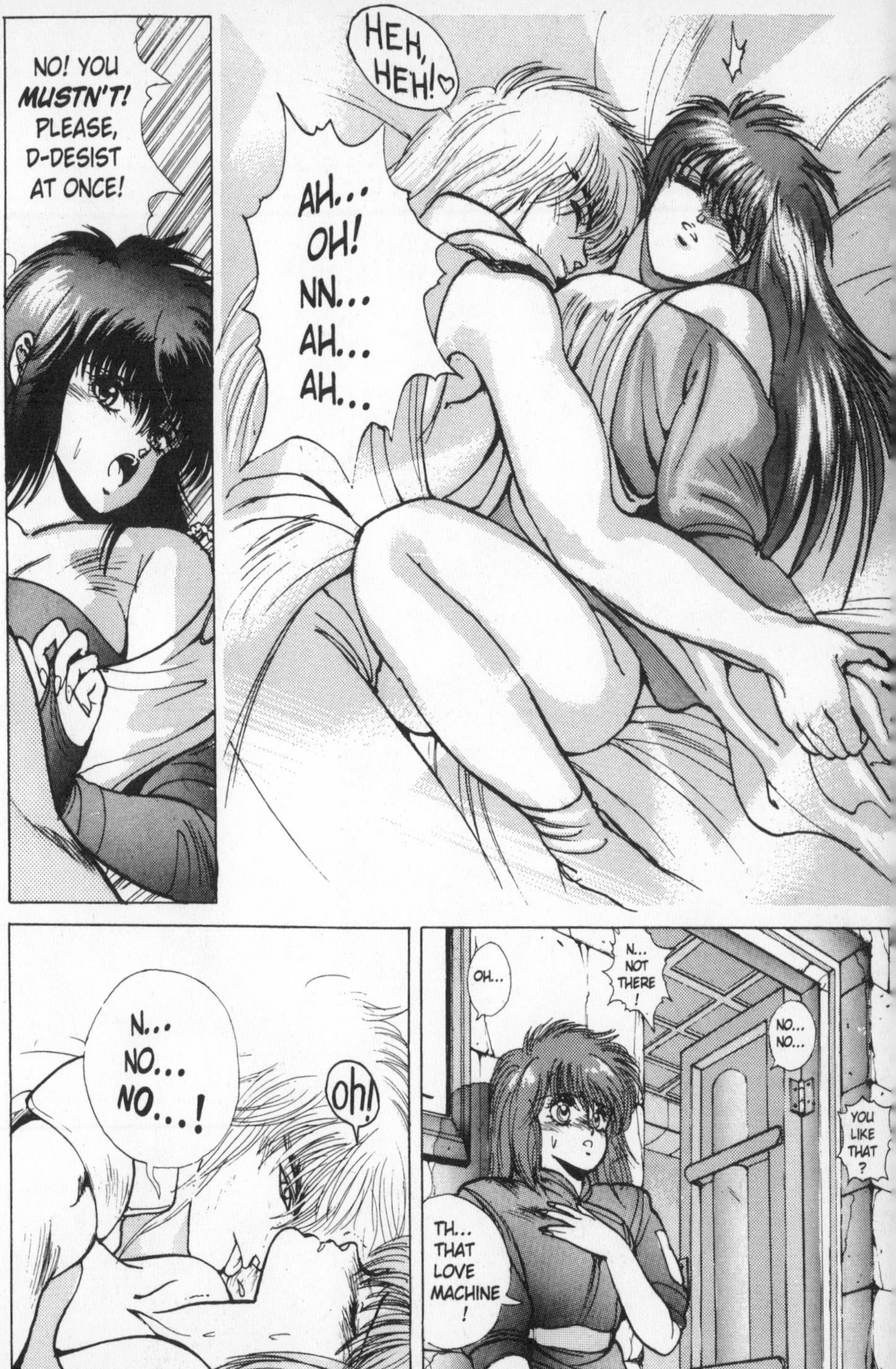
NO! YOU **MUSTN'T!** PLEASE, D-DESIST AT ONCE!
HEH, HEH!♡
AH... OH! NN... AH... AH...
N... NO... NO...!
oh!
OH...
N... NOT THERE!
NO... NO...
YOU LIKE THAT?
TH... THAT LOVE MACHINE!

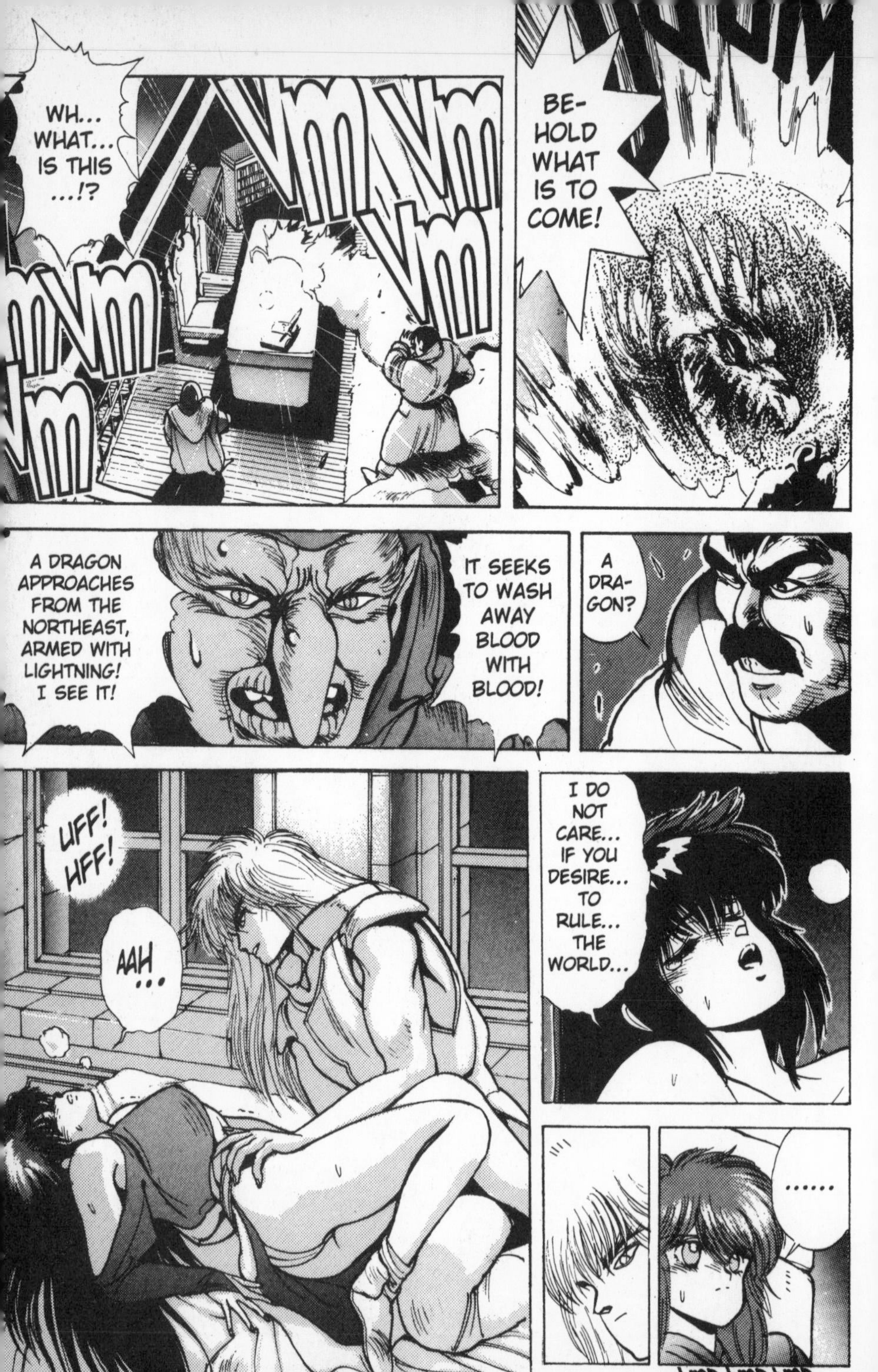
WH... WHAT... IS THIS ...!?
BE-HOLD WHAT IS TO COME!
A DRAGON APPROACHES FROM THE NORTHEAST, ARMED WITH LIGHTNING! I SEE IT!
IT SEEKS TO WASH AWAY BLOOD WITH BLOOD!
A DRA-GON?
UFF! HFF!
AAH ...
I DO NOT CARE... IF YOU DESIRE... TO RULE... THE WORLD...
......
bmp bmp bmp

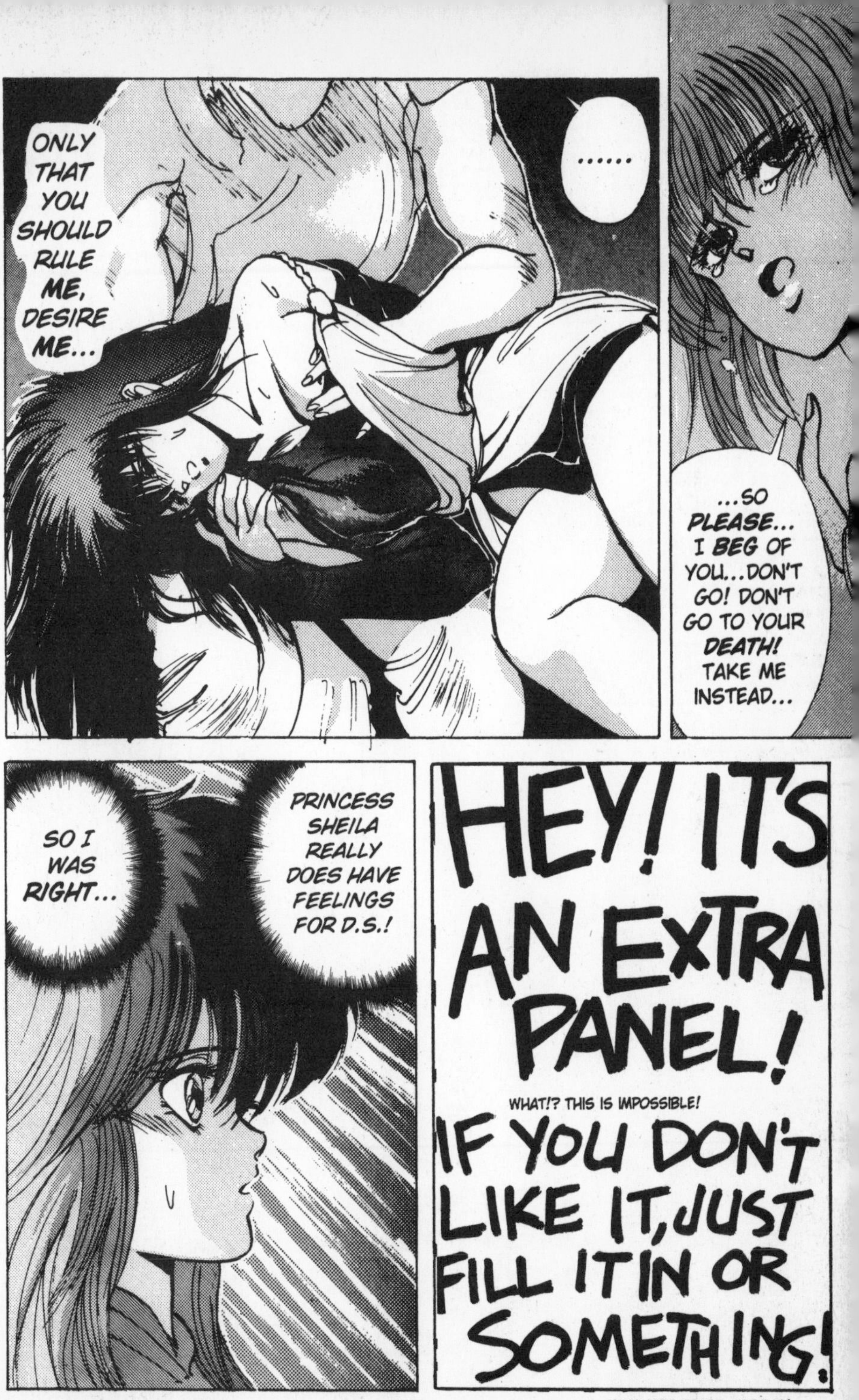

ONLY THAT YOU SHOULD RULE ME, DESIRE ME...
......
...SO PLEASE... I BEG OF YOU...DON'T GO! DON'T GO TO YOUR DEATH! TAKE ME INSTEAD...
SO I WAS RIGHT...
PRINCESS SHEILA REALLY DOES HAVE FEELINGS FOR D.S.!
HEY! IT'S AN EXTRA PANEL!
WHAT!? THIS IS IMPOSSIBLE!
IF YOU DON'T LIKE IT, JUST FILL IT IN OR SOMETHING!

HAGIWARA FEARS NOTHING!

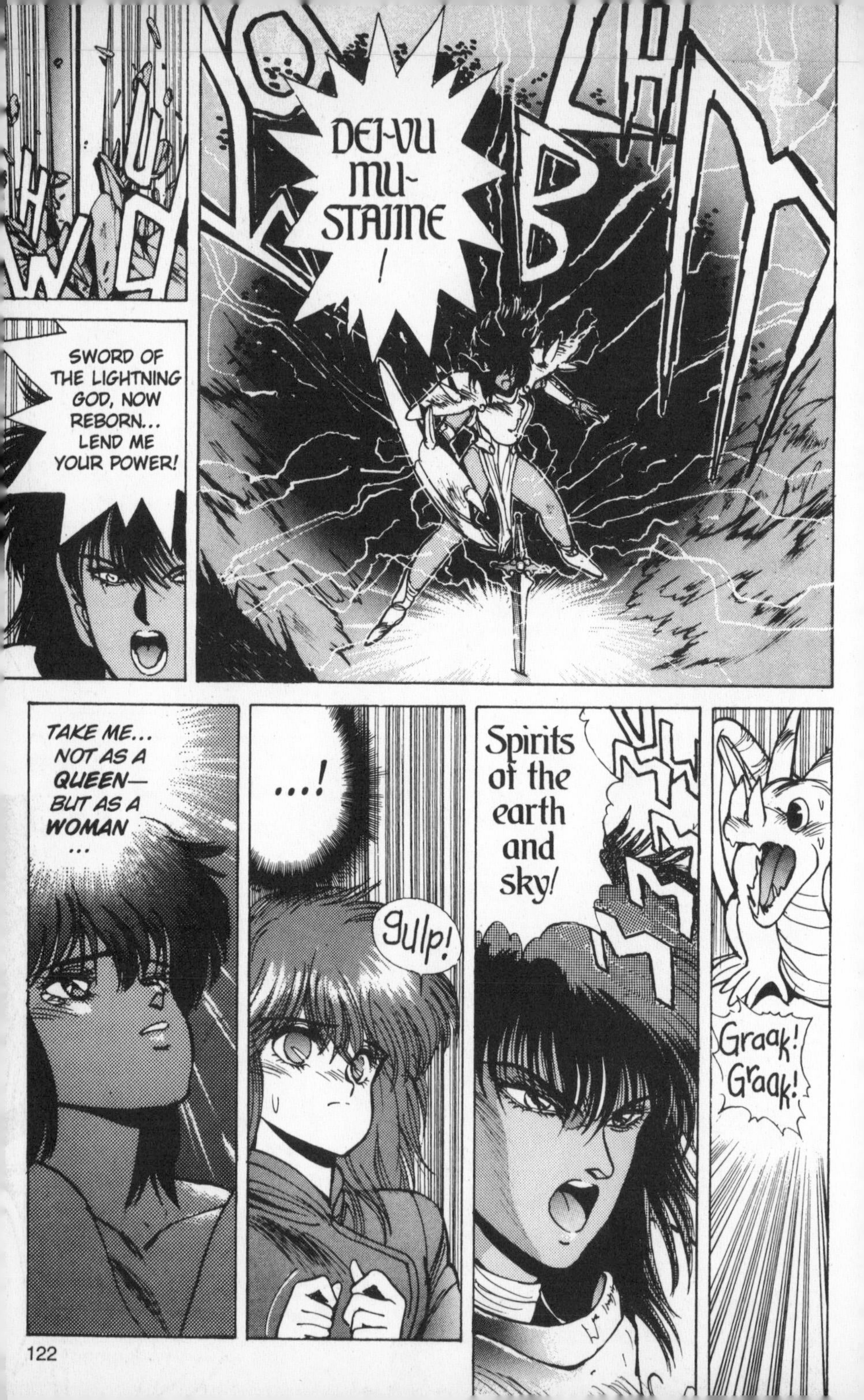
SWORD OF THE LIGHTNING GOD, NOW REBORN... LEND ME YOUR POWER!
DEI-VU MU-STAIINE!
TAKE ME... NOT AS A QUEEN— BUT AS A **WOMAN**...
...!
gulp!
Spirits of the earth and sky!
Graak! Graak!

...FOR HOW CAN I LET THE MAN I LOVE GO INTO BATTLE, KNOWING THAT CERTAIN DEATH AWAITS!

H-HEY, YOU TWO!

STOP IT RIGHT THERE!

CHOMP

YEEOOW!

In accordance with the pact of ancient times, fulfill your duties!

HMM!? THE ELEMENTALS GROW RESTLESS!

FMMSH

NO!

DAMN! WOULD SHE...?!

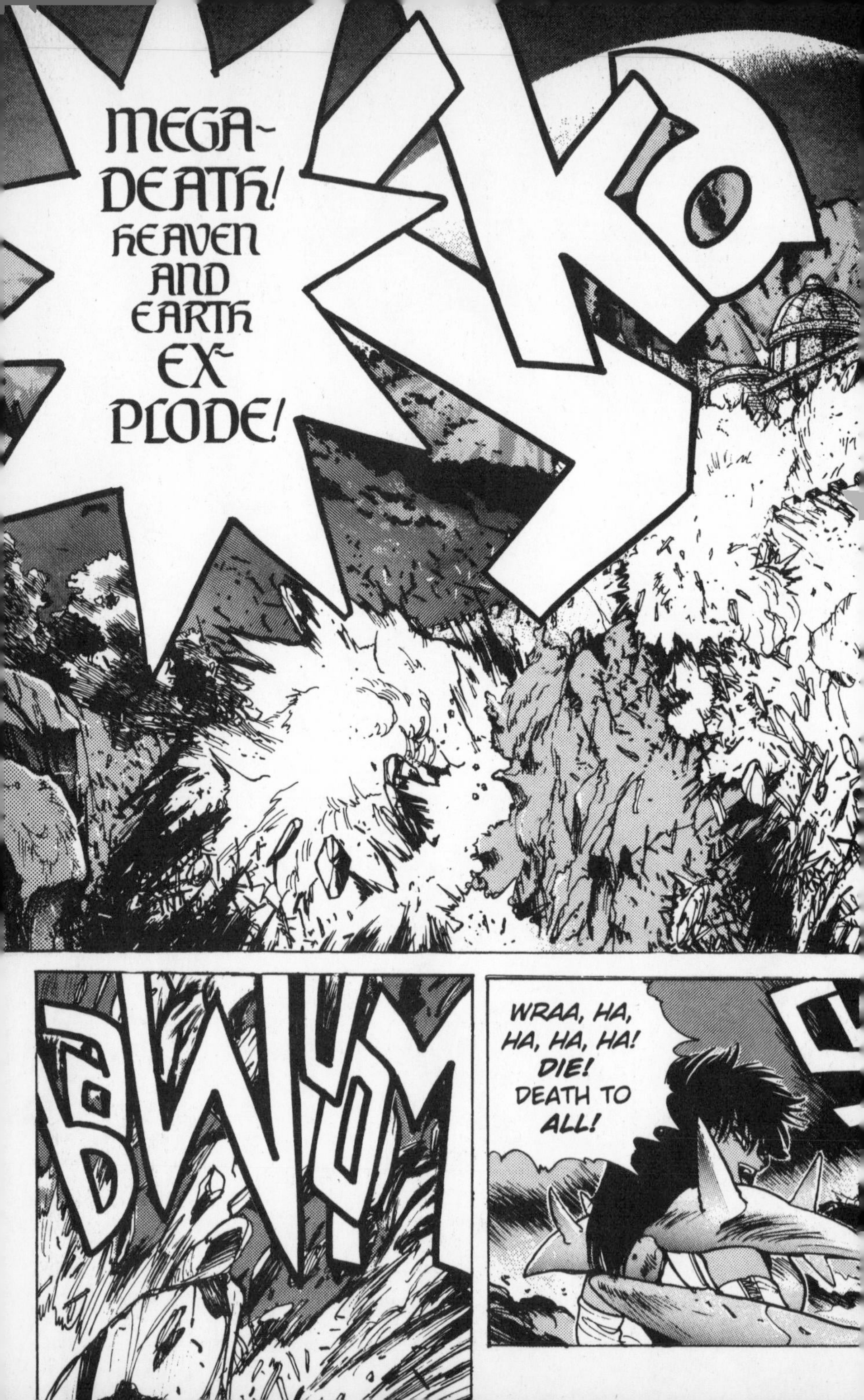
MEGA-DEATH! HEAVEN AND EARTH EX-PLODE!
WRAA, HA, HA, HA, HA! DIE! DEATH TO ALL!

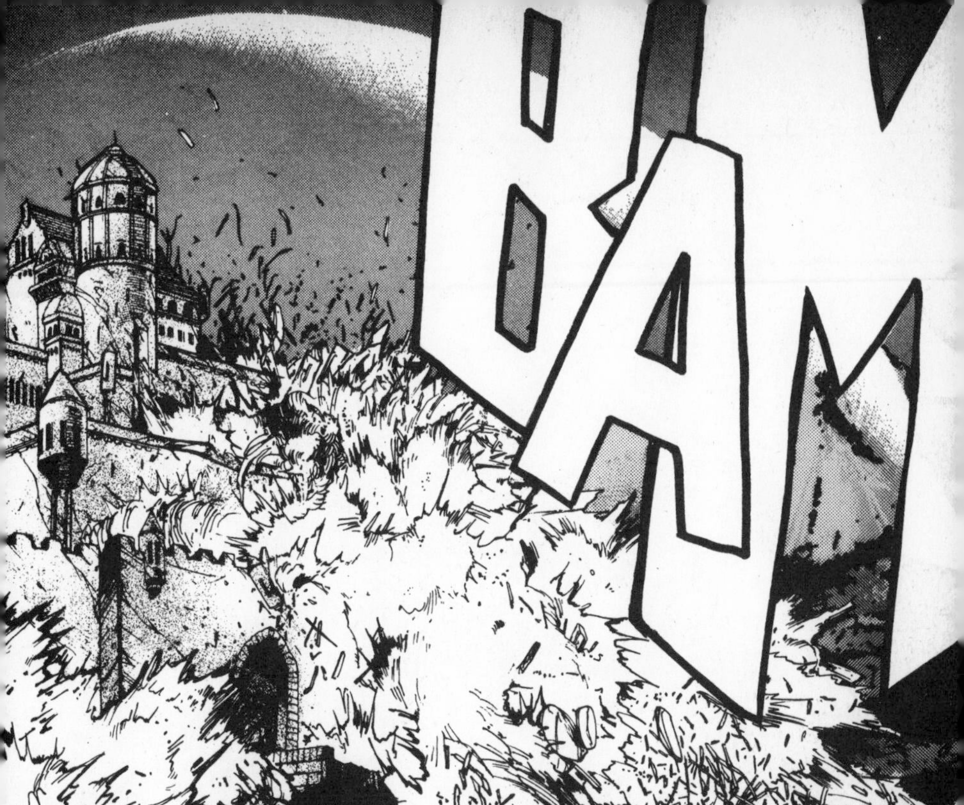
BAM

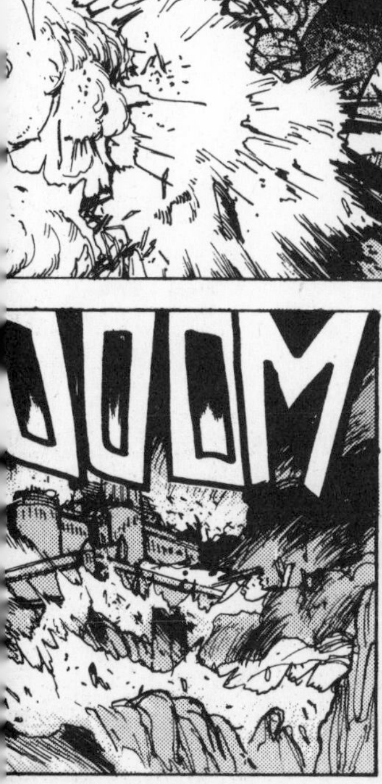
OOOM

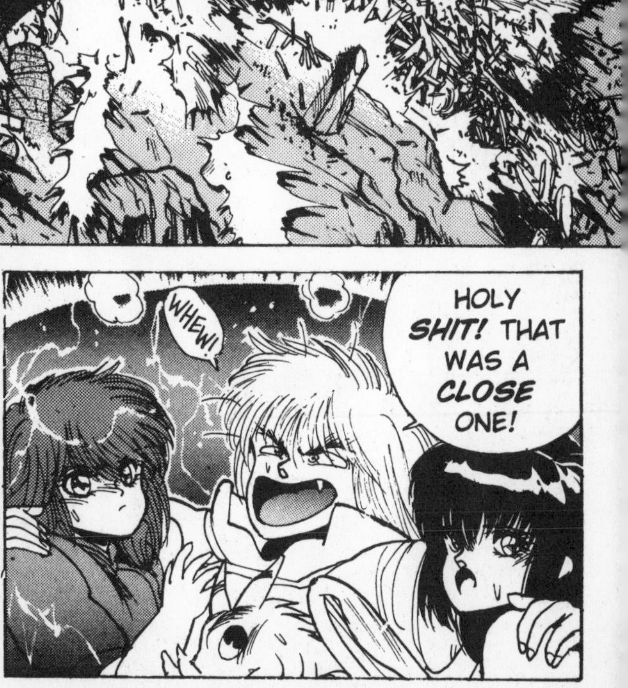
WHEW!
HOLY SHIT! THAT WAS A CLOSE ONE!

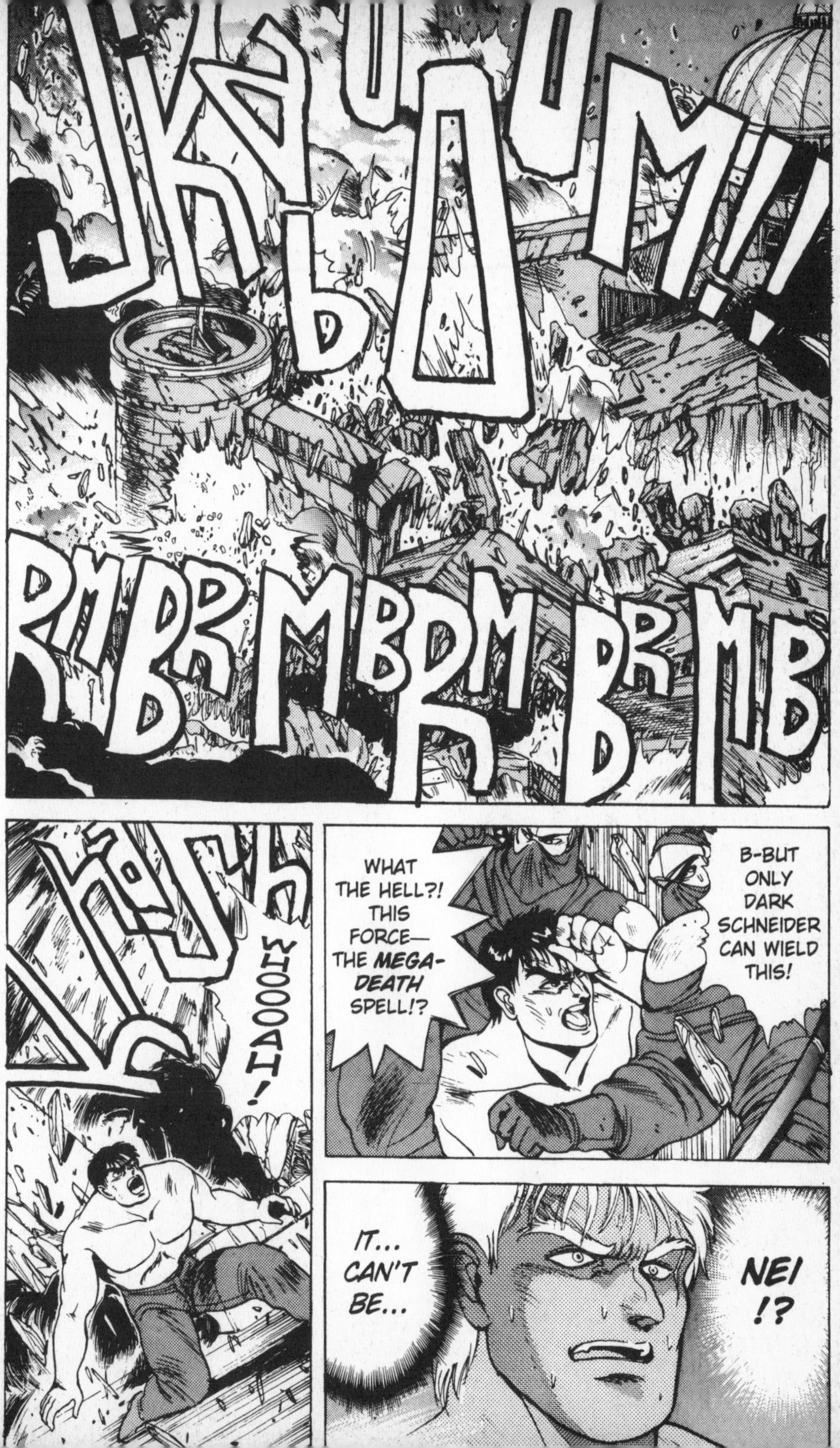
KABOOM!!
DRMB DRMB DRMB DRMB
WHOOOAH!
WHAT THE HELL?! THIS FORCE— THE *MEGA-DEATH* SPELL!?
B-BUT ONLY DARK SCHNEIDER CAN WIELD THIS!
IT... CAN'T BE...
NEI !?

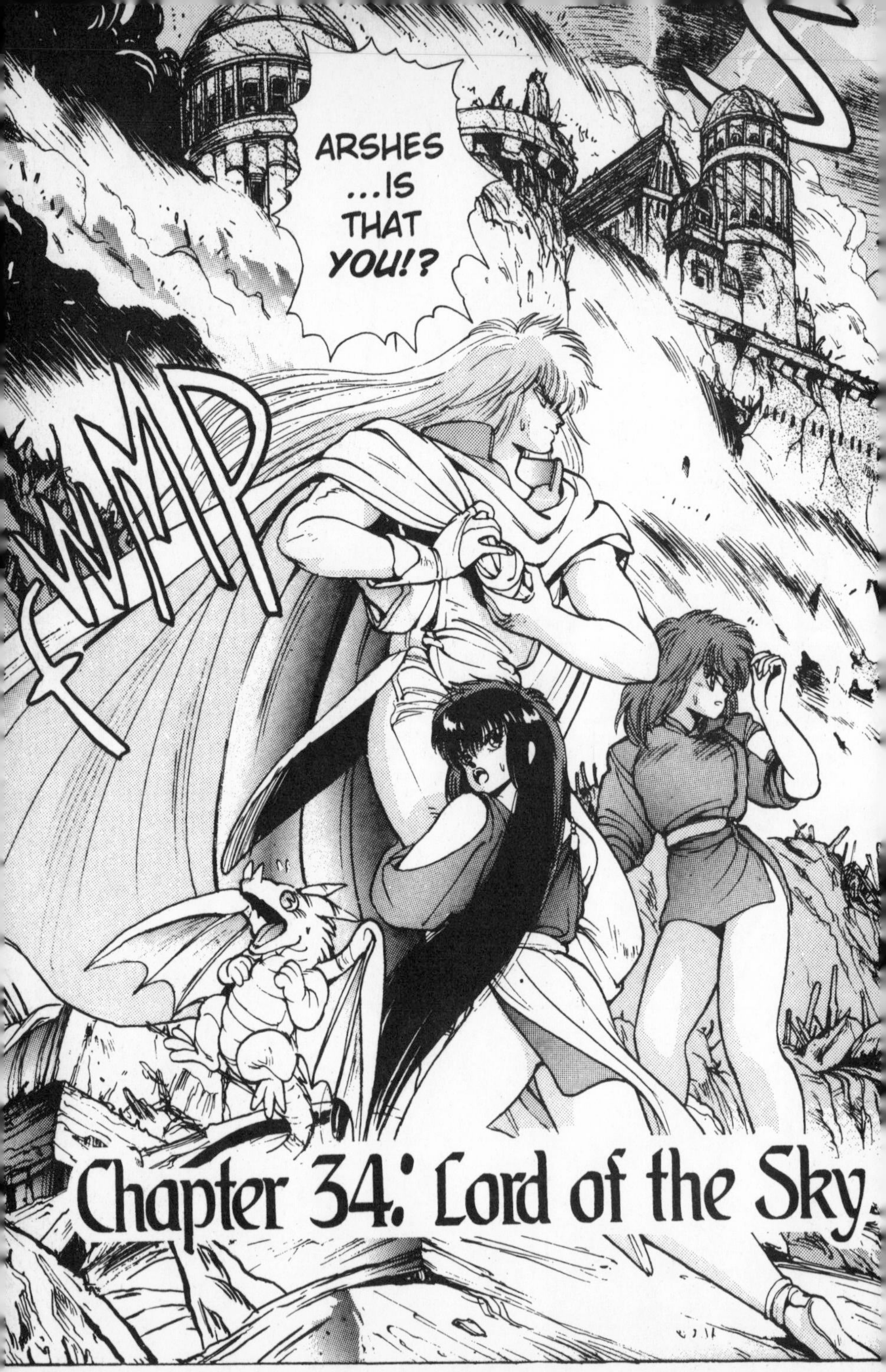
ARSHES ...IS THAT YOU!?
WMP
Chapter 34: Lord of the Sky

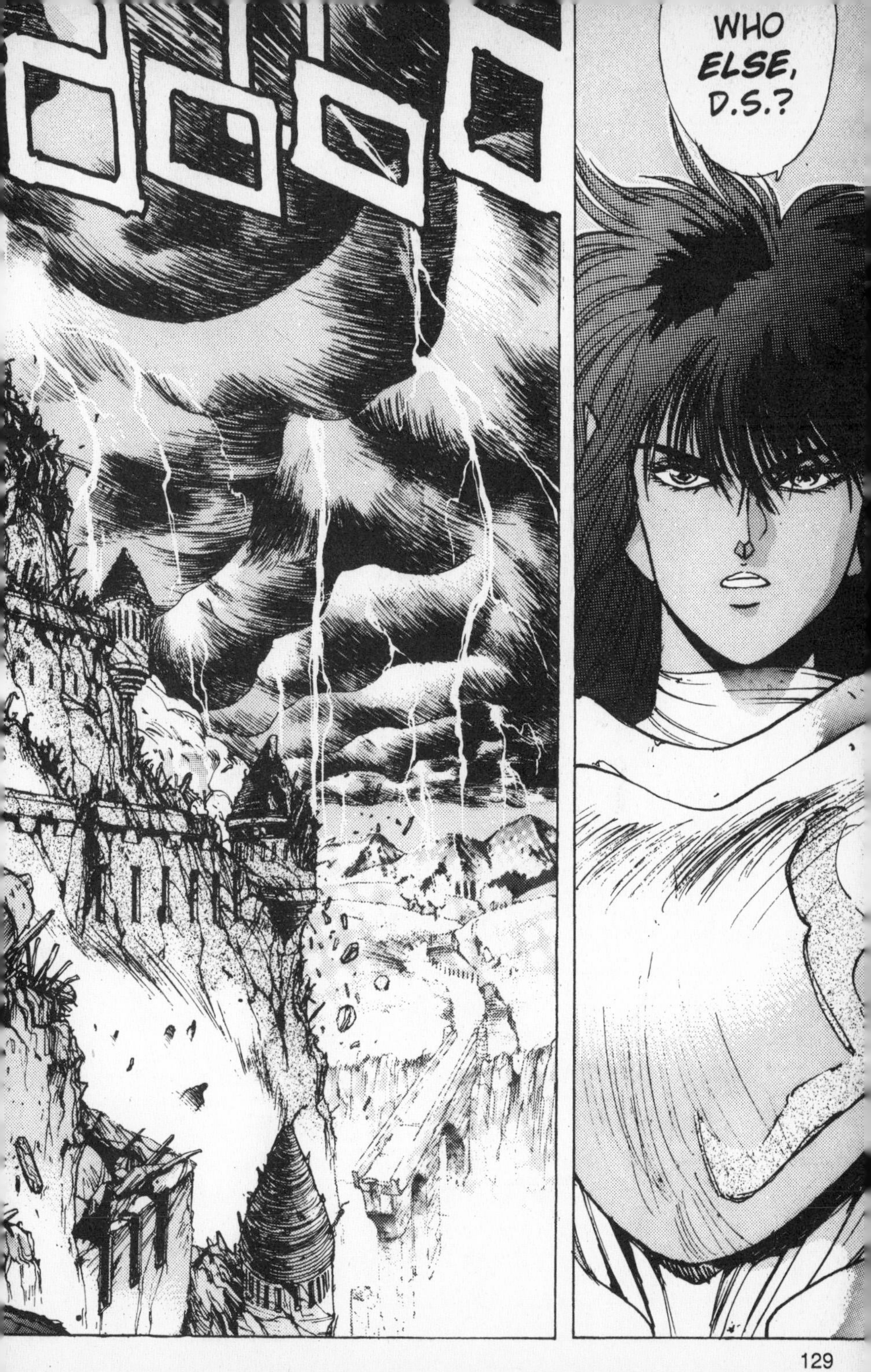
WHO ELSE, D.S.?

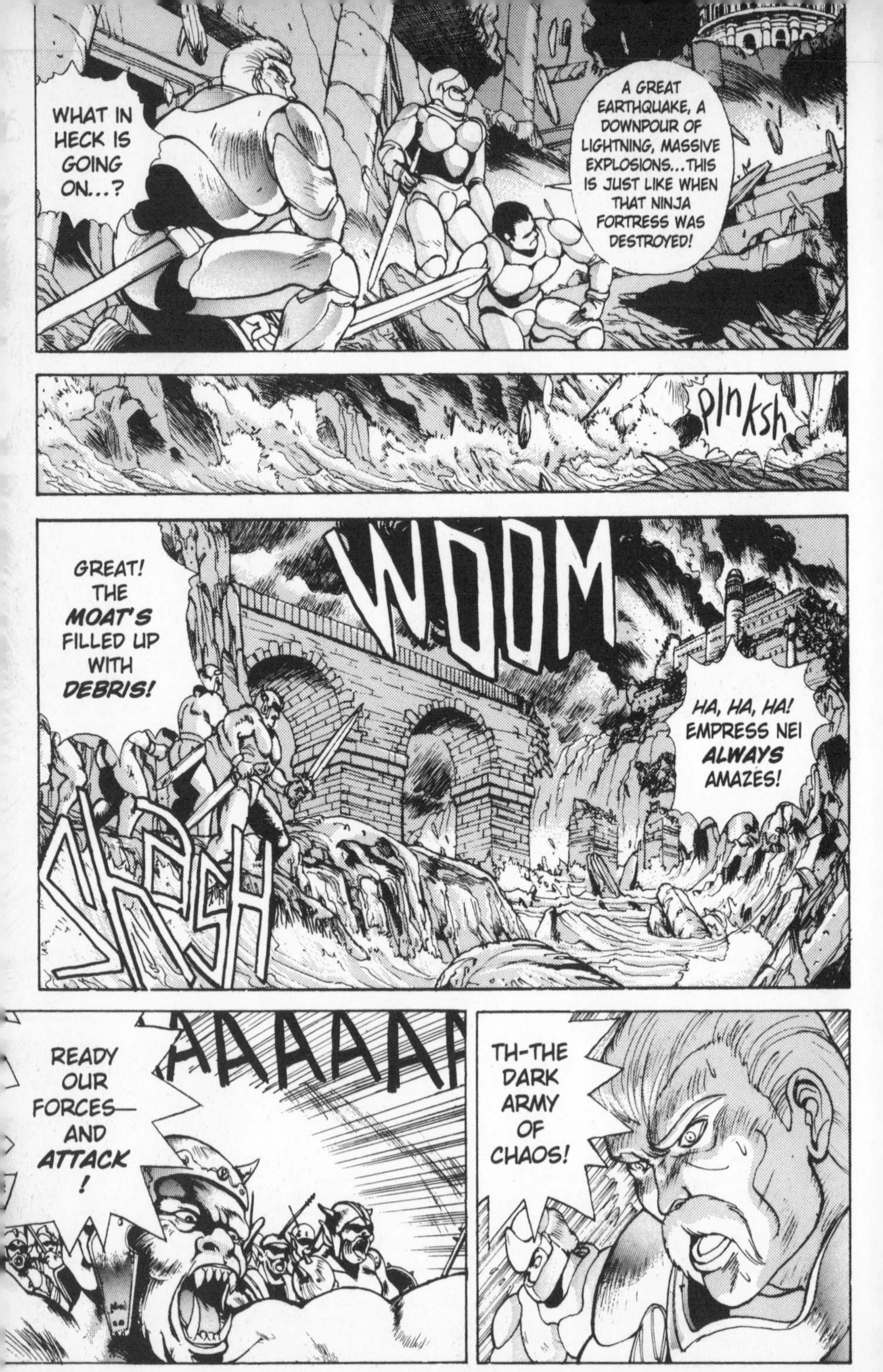
WHAT IN HECK IS GOING ON...?
A GREAT EARTHQUAKE, A DOWNPOUR OF LIGHTNING, MASSIVE EXPLOSIONS...THIS IS JUST LIKE WHEN THAT NINJA FORTRESS WAS DESTROYED!
plnksh
GREAT! THE ***MOAT'S*** FILLED UP WITH ***DEBRIS!***
WOOM
HA, HA, HA! EMPRESS NEI ***ALWAYS*** AMAZES!
SKRSH
READY OUR FORCES— AND ***ATTACK***!
AAAAAAA
TH-THE DARK ARMY OF CHAOS!

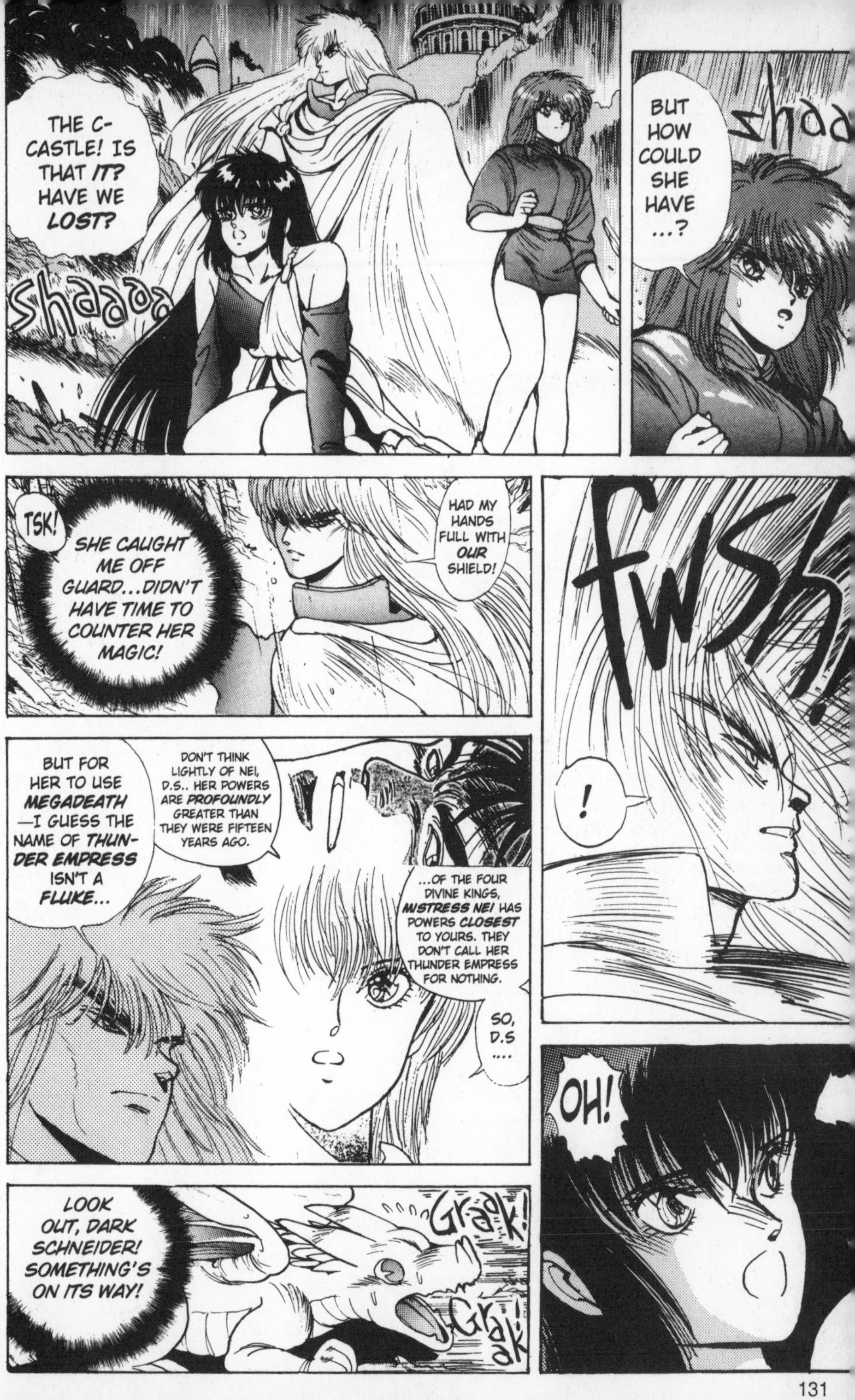

THE C-CASTLE! IS THAT *IT?* HAVE WE *LOST?*
SHAAAA
BUT HOW COULD SHE HAVE ...?
SHAA
TSK!
SHE CAUGHT ME OFF GUARD...DIDN'T HAVE TIME TO COUNTER HER MAGIC!
HAD MY HANDS FULL WITH *OUR* SHIELD!
BUT FOR HER TO USE *MEGADEATH* —I GUESS THE NAME OF *THUNDER EMPRESS* ISN'T A *FLUKE...*
DON'T THINK LIGHTLY OF NEI, D.S.. HER POWERS ARE *PROFOUNDLY* GREATER THAN THEY WERE FIFTEEN YEARS AGO.
...OF THE FOUR DIVINE KINGS, *MISTRESS NEI* HAS POWERS *CLOSEST* TO YOURS. THEY DON'T CALL HER THUNDER EMPRESS FOR NOTHING.
SO, D.S ....
FWSH!
!
LOOK OUT, DARK SCHNEIDER! SOMETHING'S ON ITS WAY!
GRAK!
GRAK!
OH!

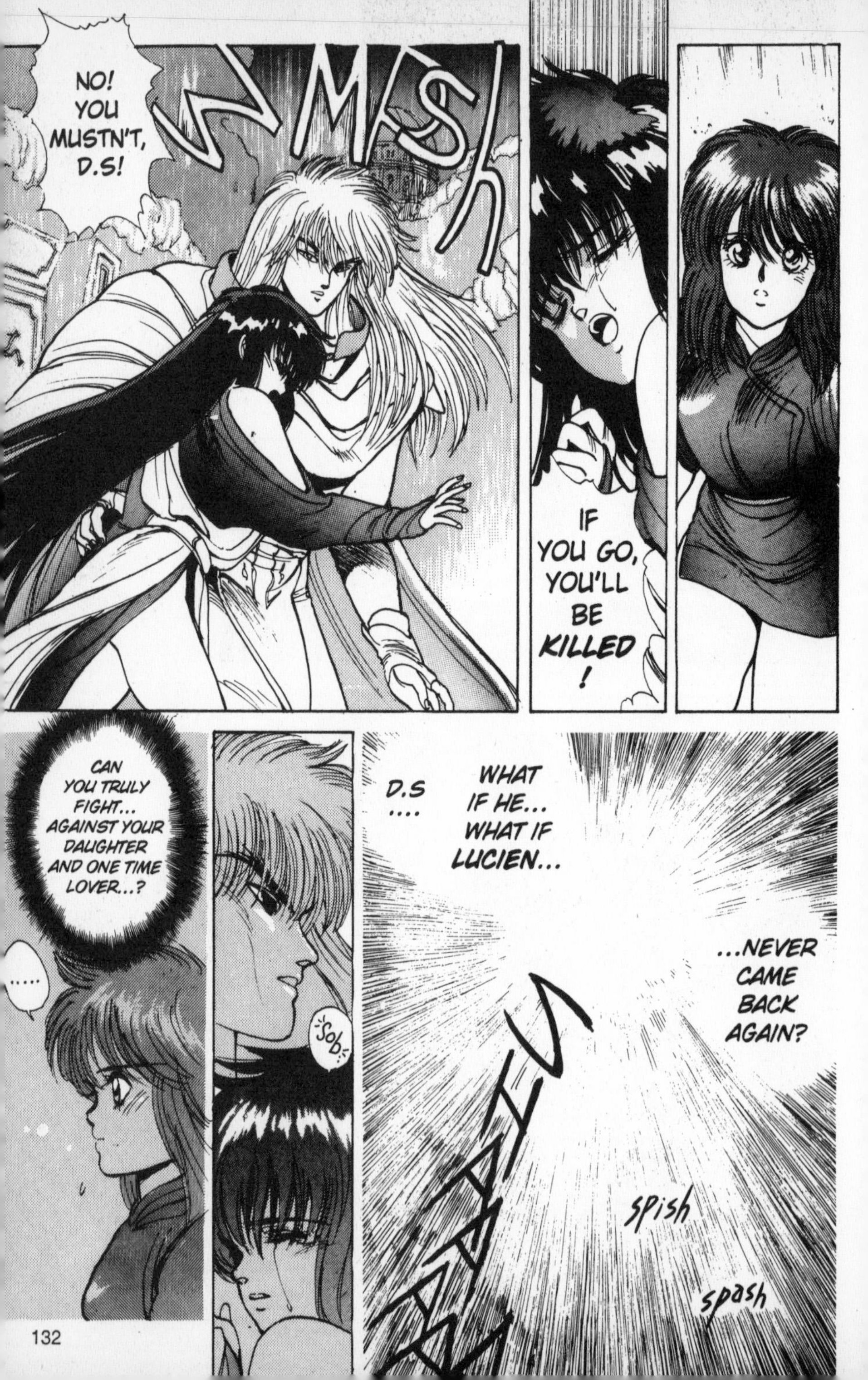
NO! YOU MUSTN'T, D.S!
IF YOU GO, YOU'LL BE KILLED!
CAN YOU TRULY FIGHT... AGAINST YOUR DAUGHTER AND ONE TIME LOVER...?
......
Sob
D.S....
WHAT IF HE... WHAT IF LUCIEN...
...NEVER CAME BACK AGAIN?
spish
spash

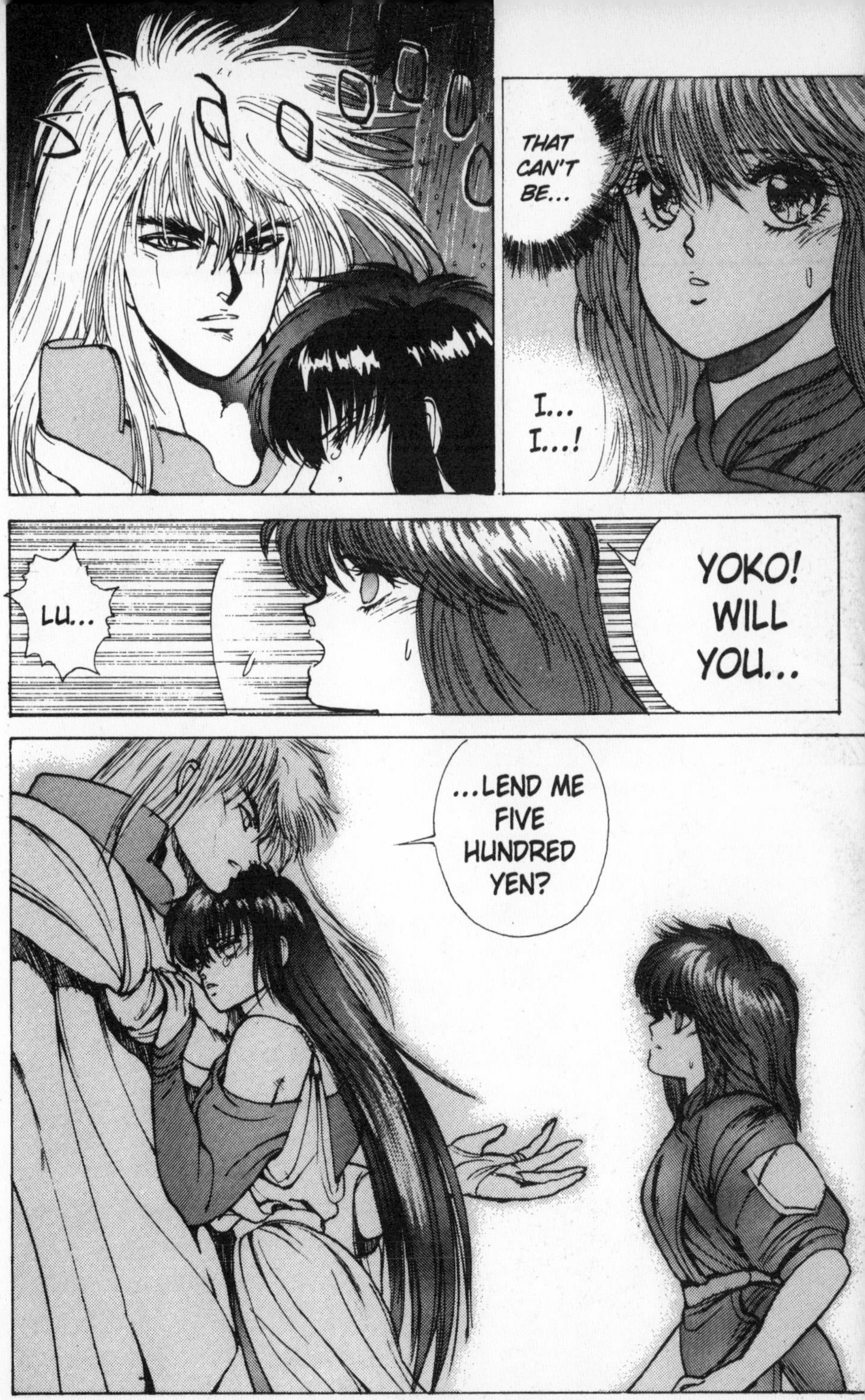
shaoooo
THAT CAN'T BE...
I... I...!
LU...
YOKO! WILL YOU...
...LEND ME FIVE HUNDRED YEN?

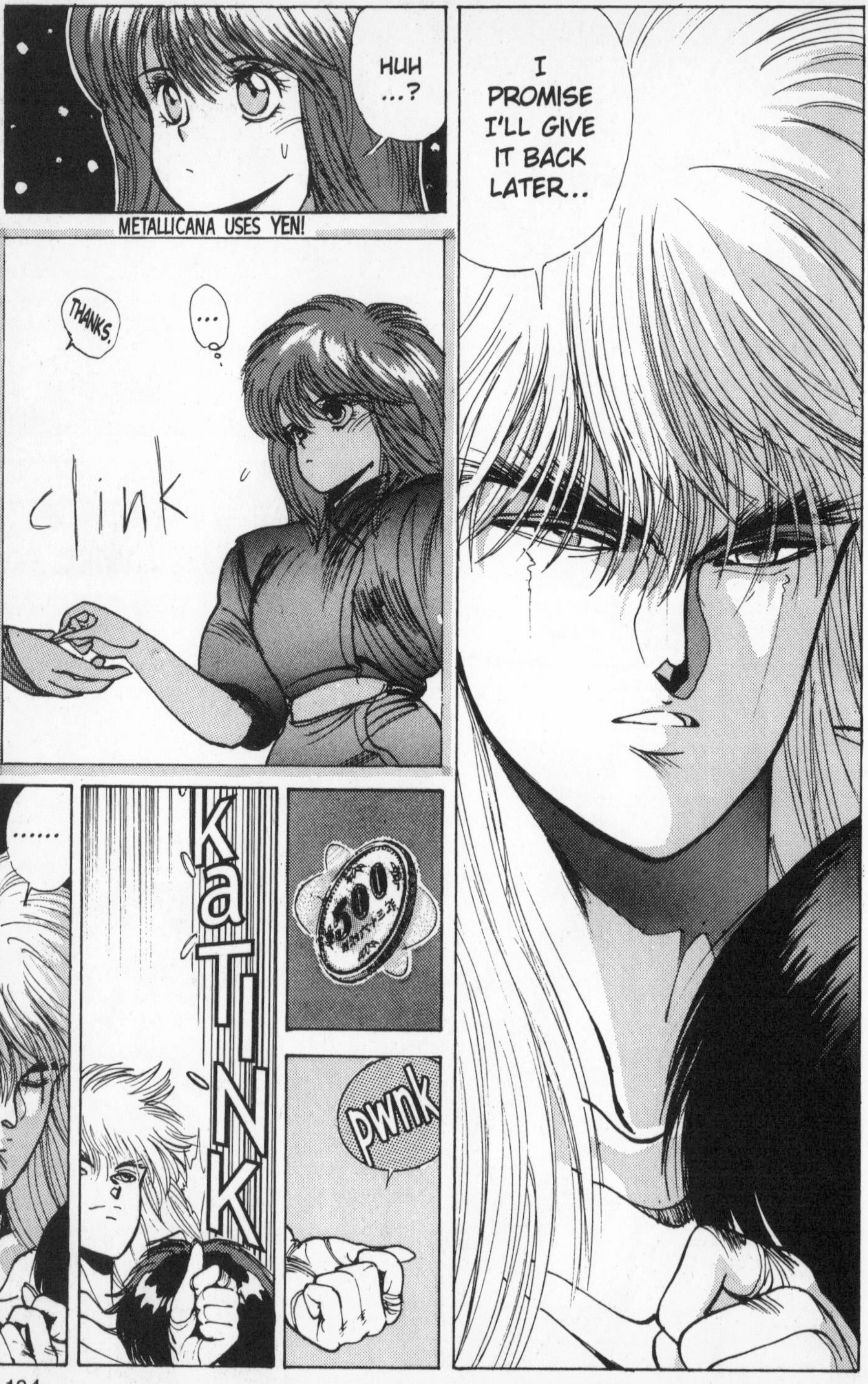
HUH ...?
METALLICANA USES YEN!
THANKS.
...
clink
......
KaTINK
pwnk
I PROMISE I'LL GIVE IT BACK LATER...

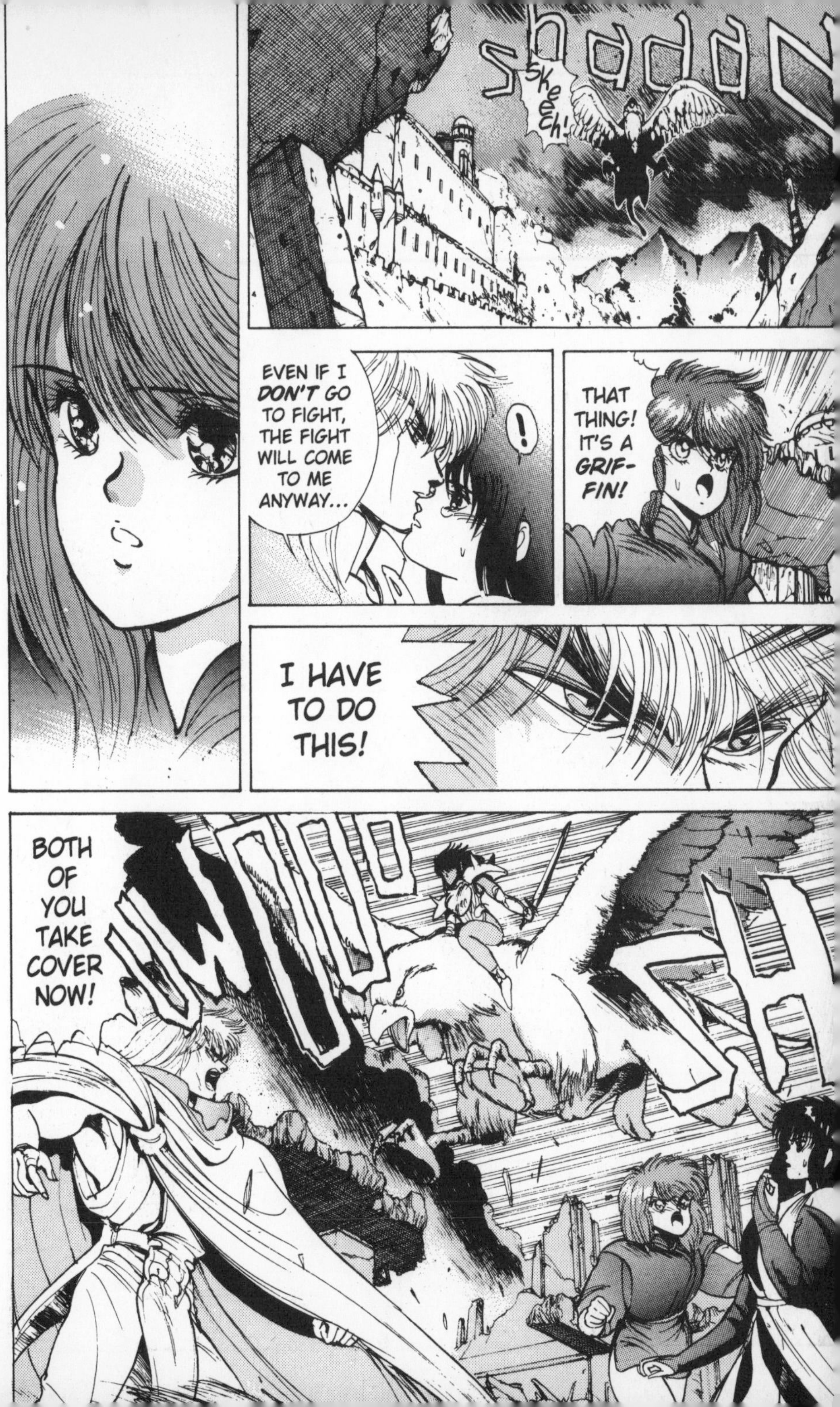
skeech!
EVEN IF I *DON'T* GO TO FIGHT, THE FIGHT WILL COME TO ME ANYWAY...
!
THAT THING! IT'S A *GRIF-FIN!*
I HAVE TO DO THIS!
BOTH OF YOU TAKE COVER NOW!

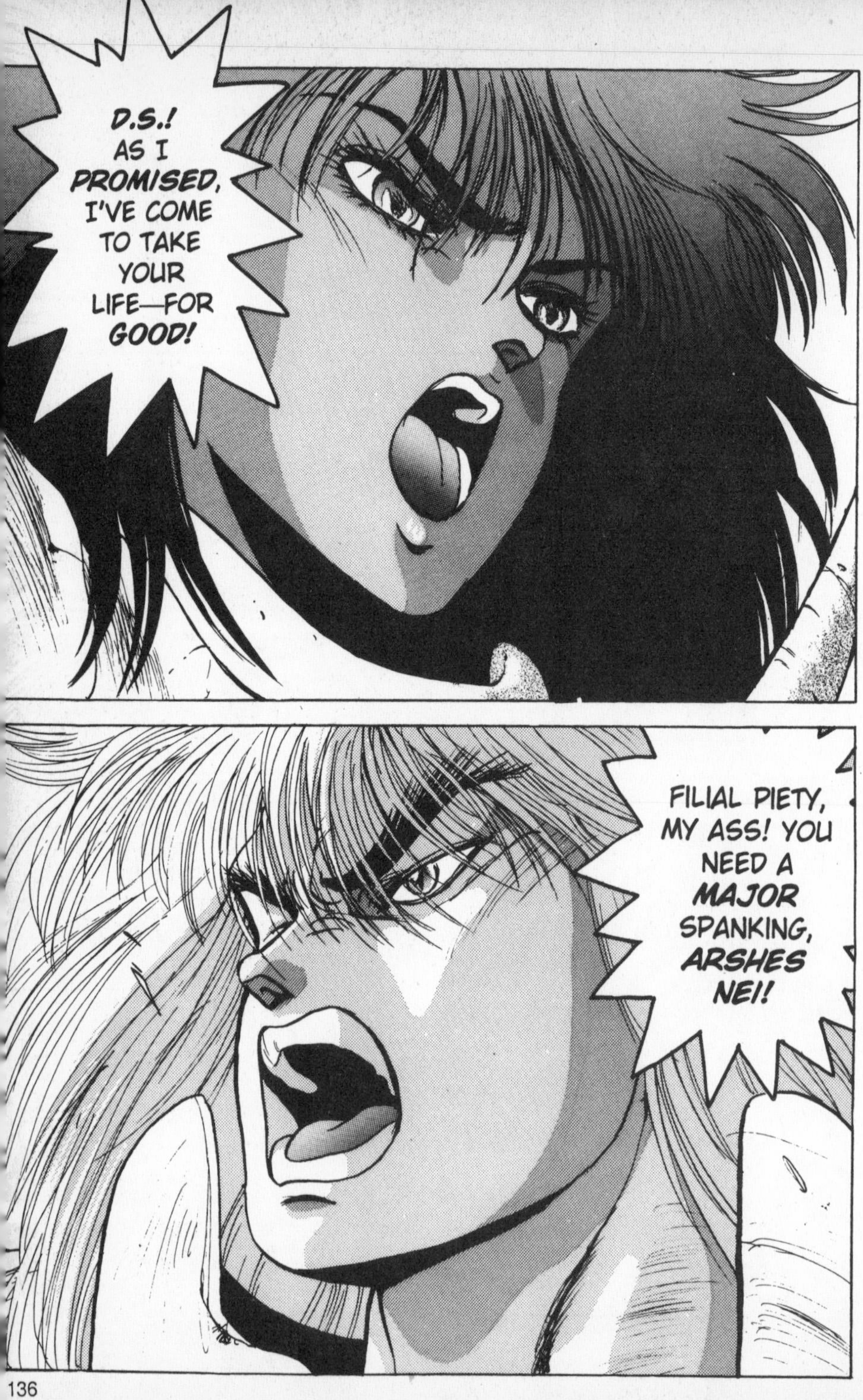
D.S.! AS I PROMISED, I'VE COME TO TAKE YOUR LIFE—FOR GOOD!
FILIAL PIETY, MY ASS! YOU NEED A MAJOR SPANKING, ARSHES NEI!

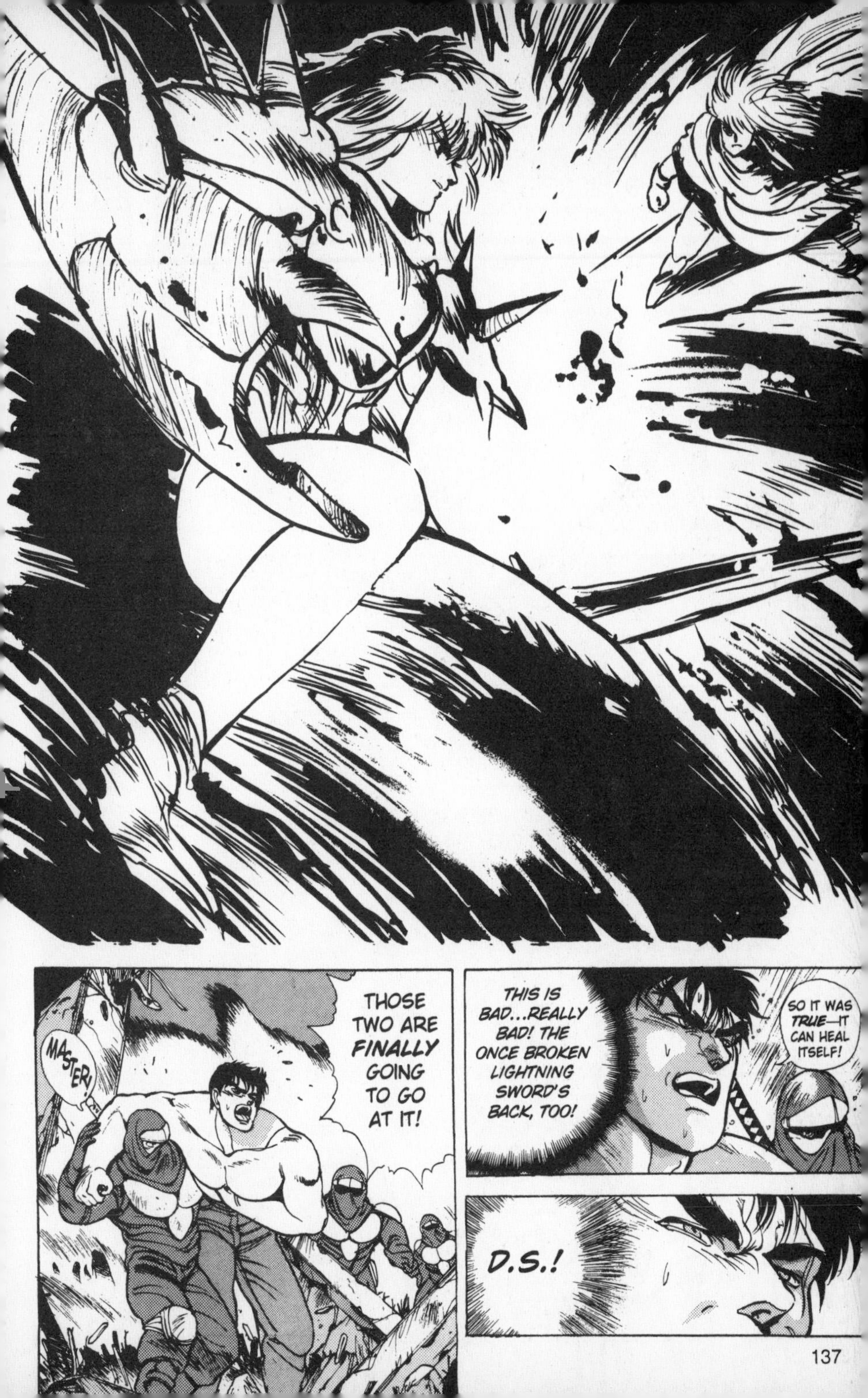
MASTER!
THOSE TWO ARE FINALLY GOING TO GO AT IT!
THIS IS BAD...REALLY BAD! THE ONCE BROKEN LIGHTNING SWORD'S BACK, TOO!
SO IT WAS TRUE—IT CAN HEAL ITSELF!
D.S.!

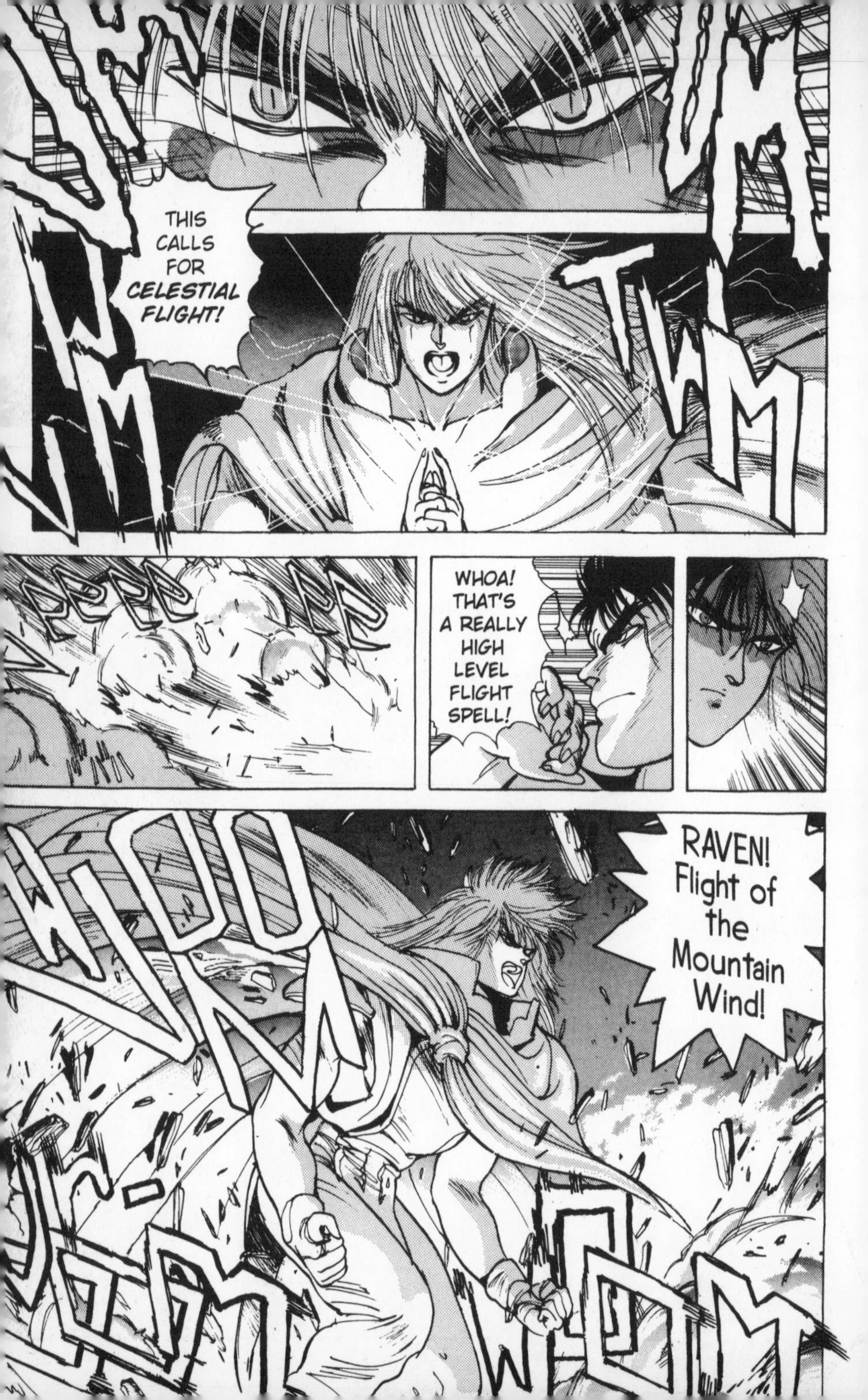
THIS CALLS FOR CELESTIAL FLIGHT!
WHOA! THAT'S A REALLY HIGH LEVEL FLIGHT SPELL!
RAVEN! Flight of the Mountain Wind!

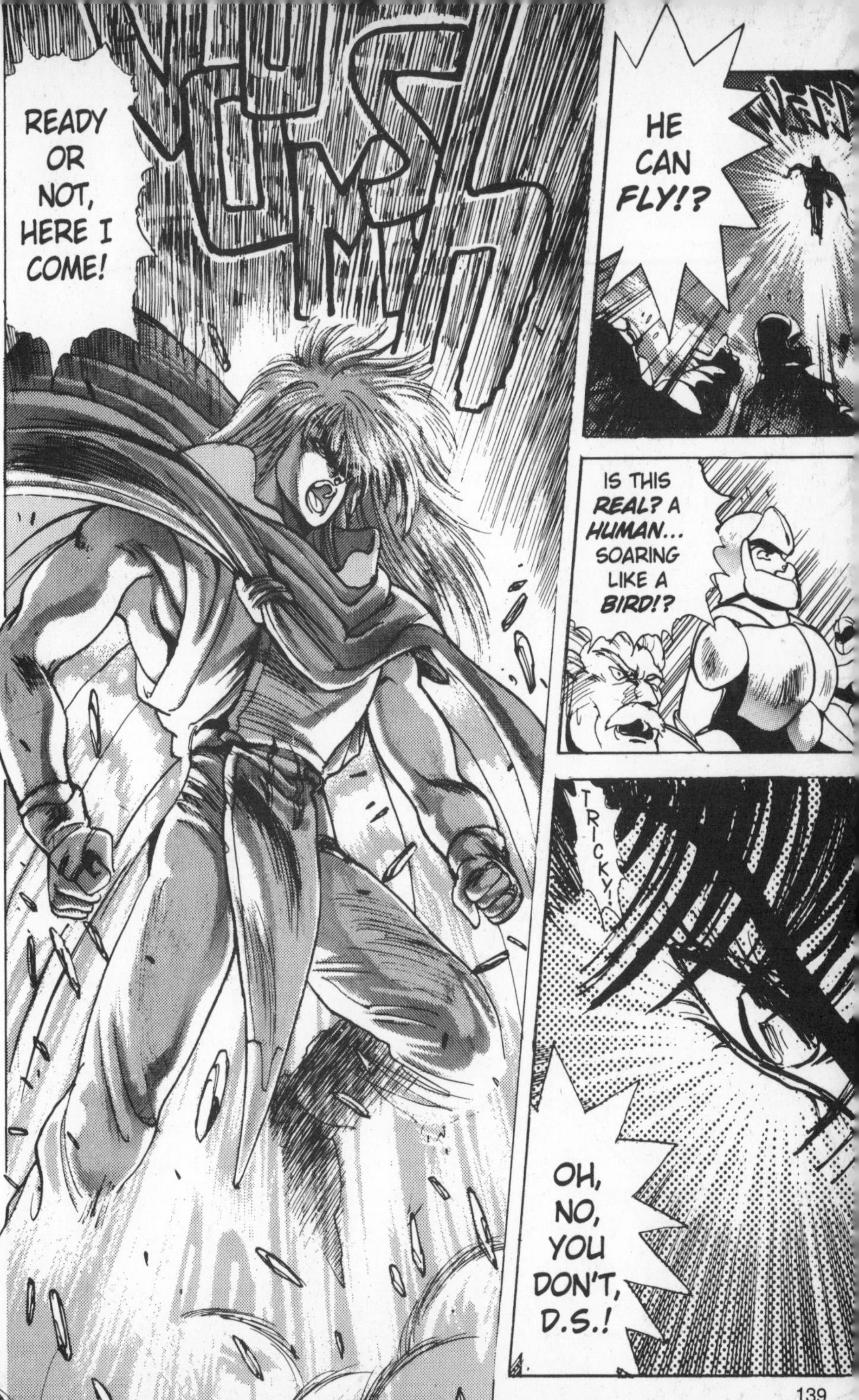
READY OR NOT, HERE I COME!
HE CAN FLY!?
IS THIS REAL? A HUMAN... SOARING LIKE A BIRD!?
TRICKY!
OH, NO, YOU DON'T, D.S.!

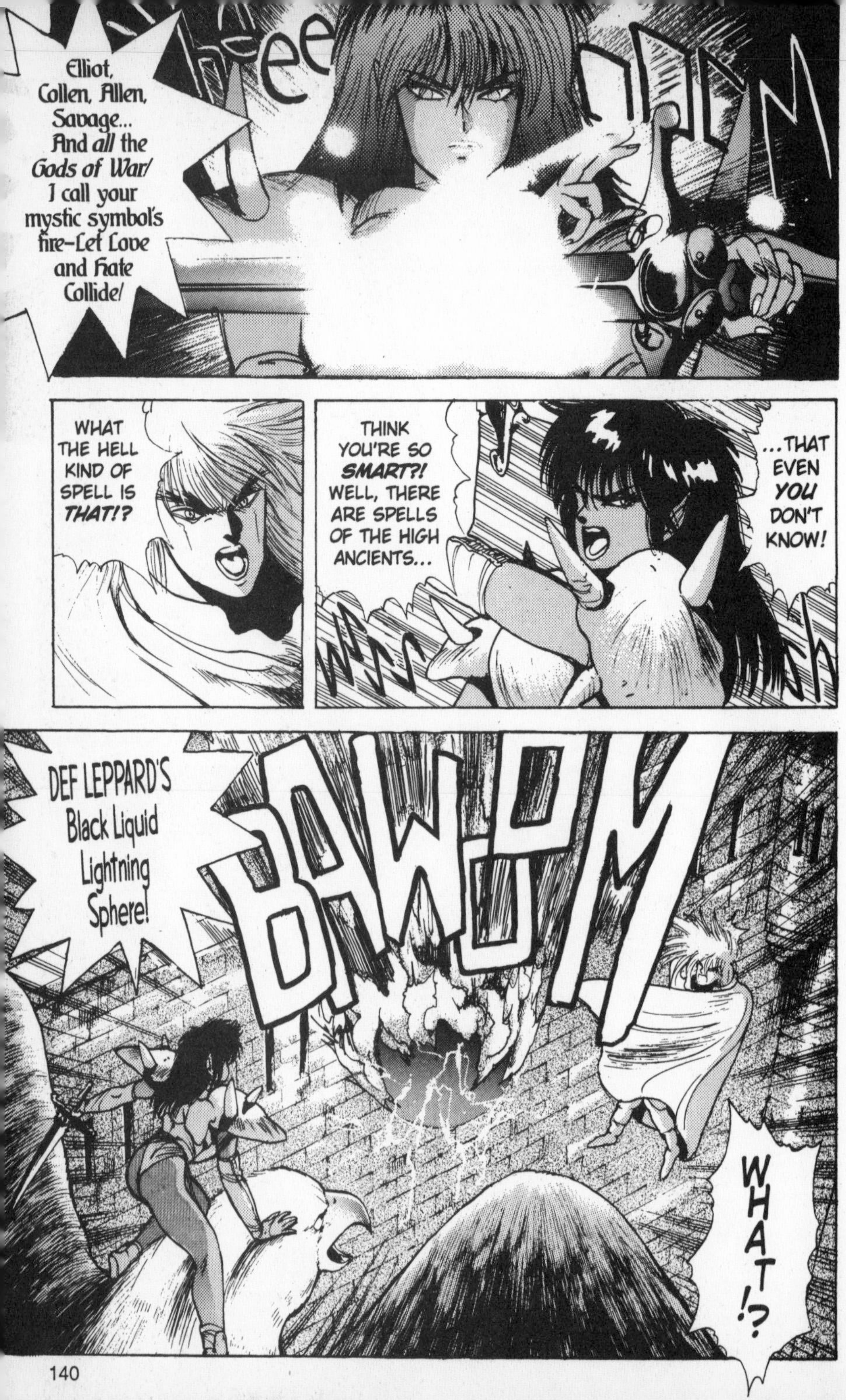
Elliot, Collen, Allen, Savage... And *all* the *Gods of War!* I call your mystic symbol's fire–Let Love and Hate Collide!
WHAT THE HELL KIND OF SPELL IS ***THAT!?***
THINK YOU'RE SO ***SMART?!*** WELL, THERE ARE SPELLS OF THE HIGH ANCIENTS...
...THAT EVEN ***YOU*** DON'T KNOW!
DEF LEPPARD'S Black Liquid Lightning Sphere!
WHAT!?

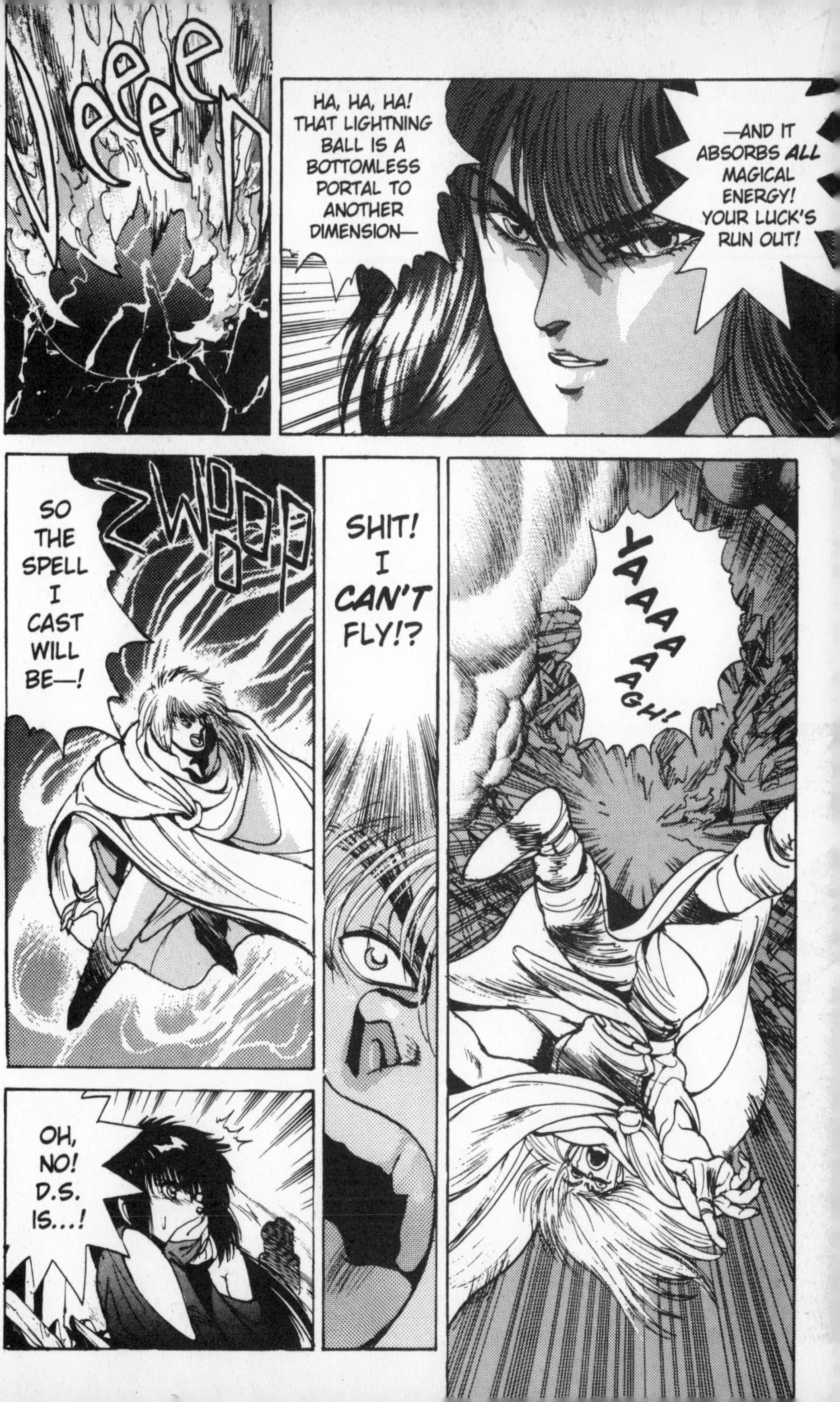
Veeeen
HA, HA, HA! THAT LIGHTNING BALL IS A BOTTOMLESS PORTAL TO ANOTHER DIMENSION—
—AND IT ABSORBS ALL MAGICAL ENERGY! YOUR LUCK'S RUN OUT!
ZWOOOP
SO THE SPELL I CAST WILL BE—!
SHIT! I CAN'T FLY!?
YAAAAAAAGH!
OH, NO! D.S. IS...!

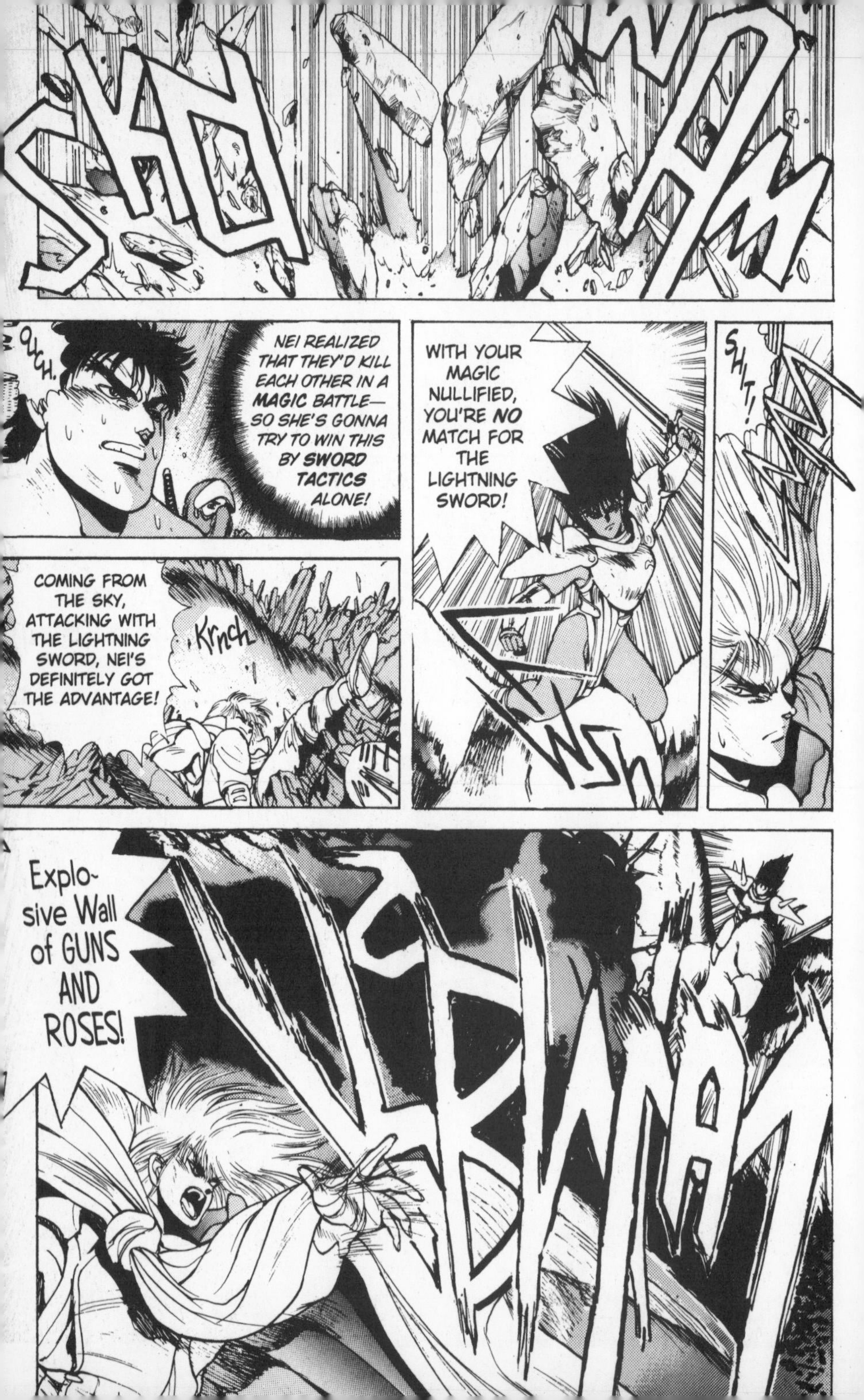
OUCH.
NEI REALIZED THAT THEY'D KILL EACH OTHER IN A MAGIC BATTLE— SO SHE'S GONNA TRY TO WIN THIS BY SWORD TACTICS ALONE!
COMING FROM THE SKY, ATTACKING WITH THE LIGHTNING SWORD, NEI'S DEFINITELY GOT THE ADVANTAGE!
Krnch
WITH YOUR MAGIC NULLIFIED, YOU'RE NO MATCH FOR THE LIGHTNING SWORD!
Wsh
SHIT!
Explo-sive Wall of GUNS AND ROSES!

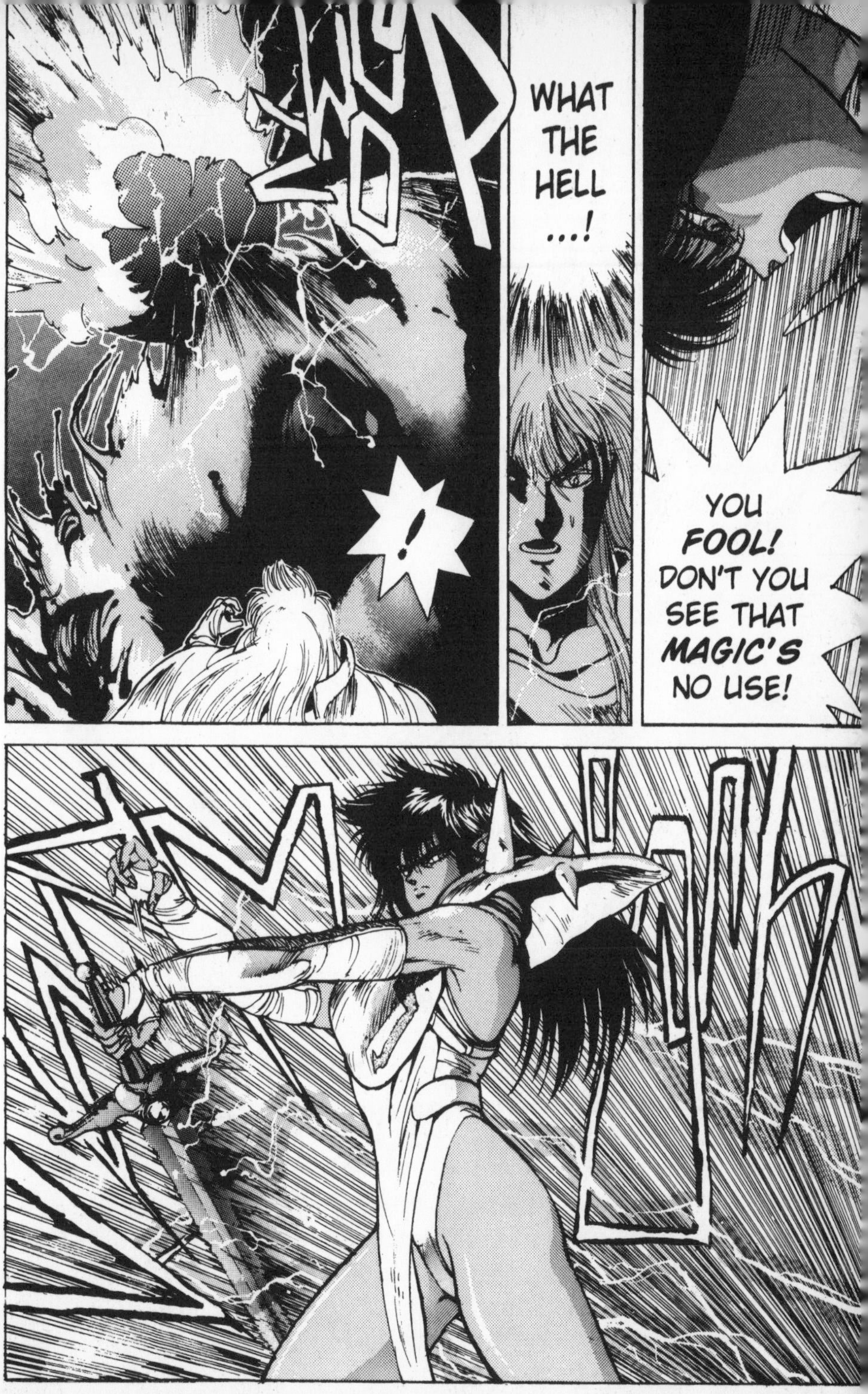
!
WHAT THE HELL ...!
YOU FOOL! DON'T YOU SEE THAT MAGIC'S NO USE!

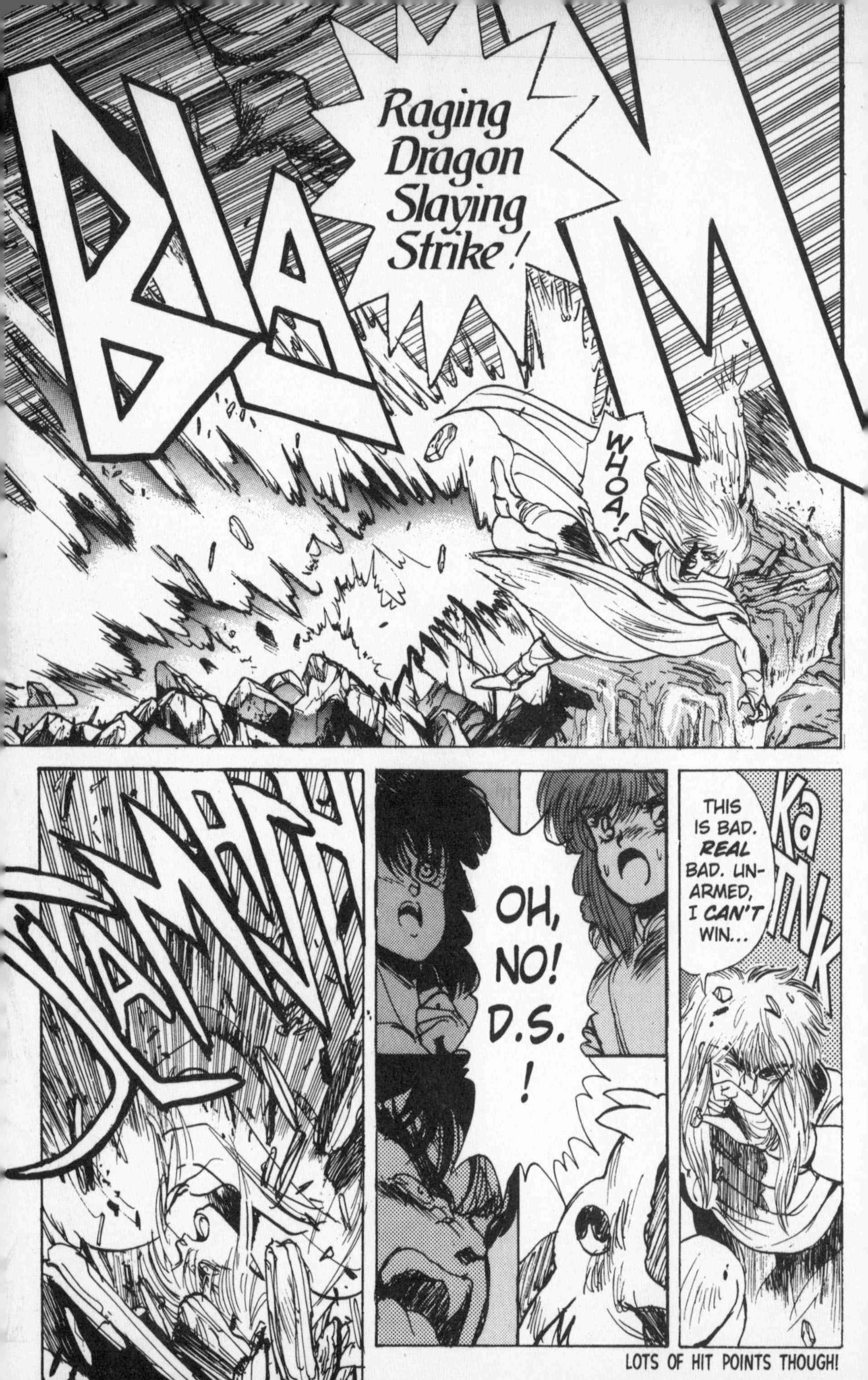
BLAM
Raging Dragon Slaying Strike!
WHOA!
WHAM
OH, NO! D.S.!
THIS IS BAD. REAL BAD. UNARMED, I CAN'T WIN...
KATINK
LOTS OF HIT POINTS THOUGH!

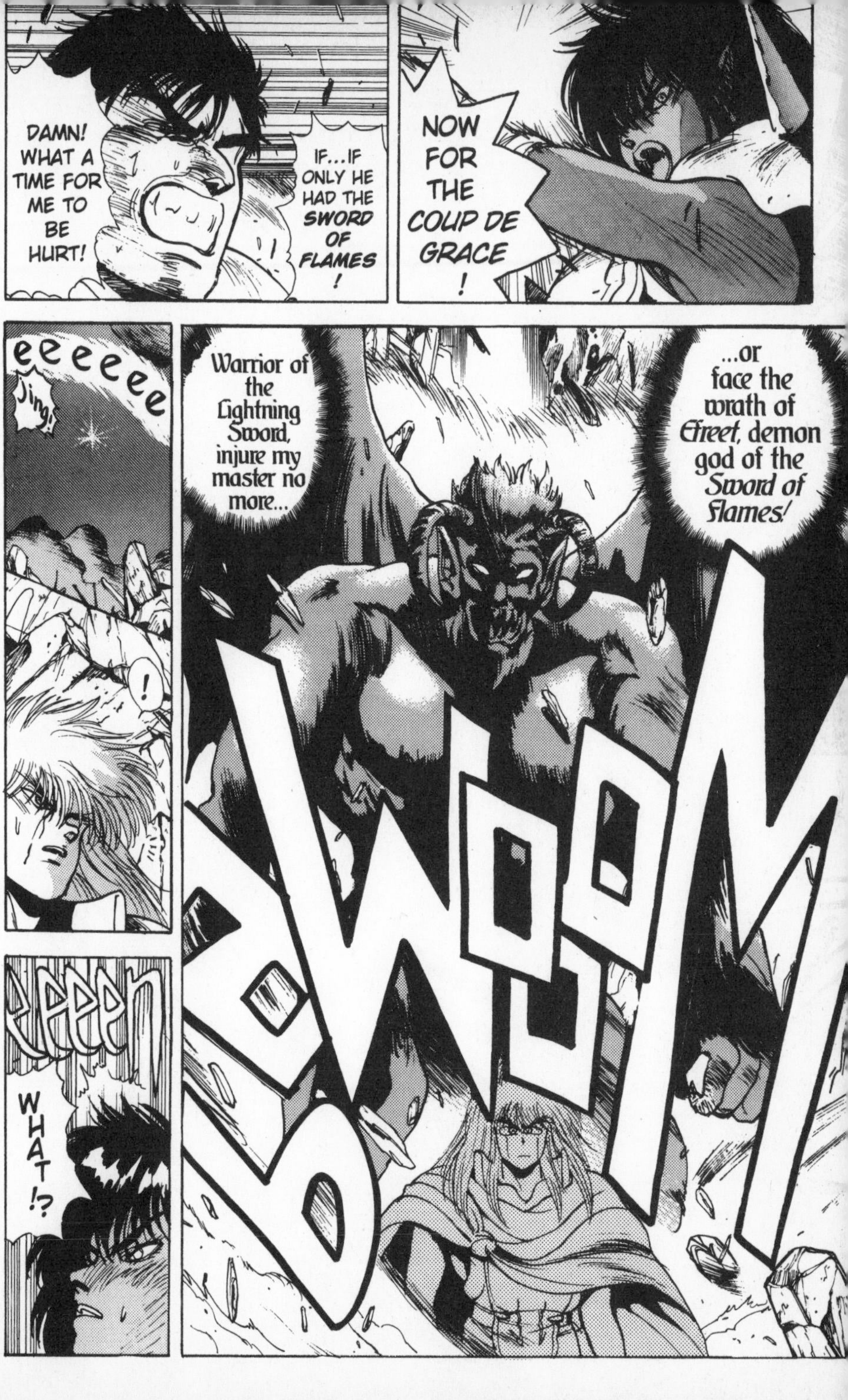
DAMN! WHAT A TIME FOR ME TO BE HURT!
IF...IF ONLY HE HAD THE SWORD OF FLAMES!
NOW FOR THE COUP DE GRACE!
eeeeeee
Jing!
!
Warrior of the Lightning Sword, injure my master no more...
...or face the wrath of Efreet, demon god of the Sword of Flames!
BOOM
eeeen
WHAT!?

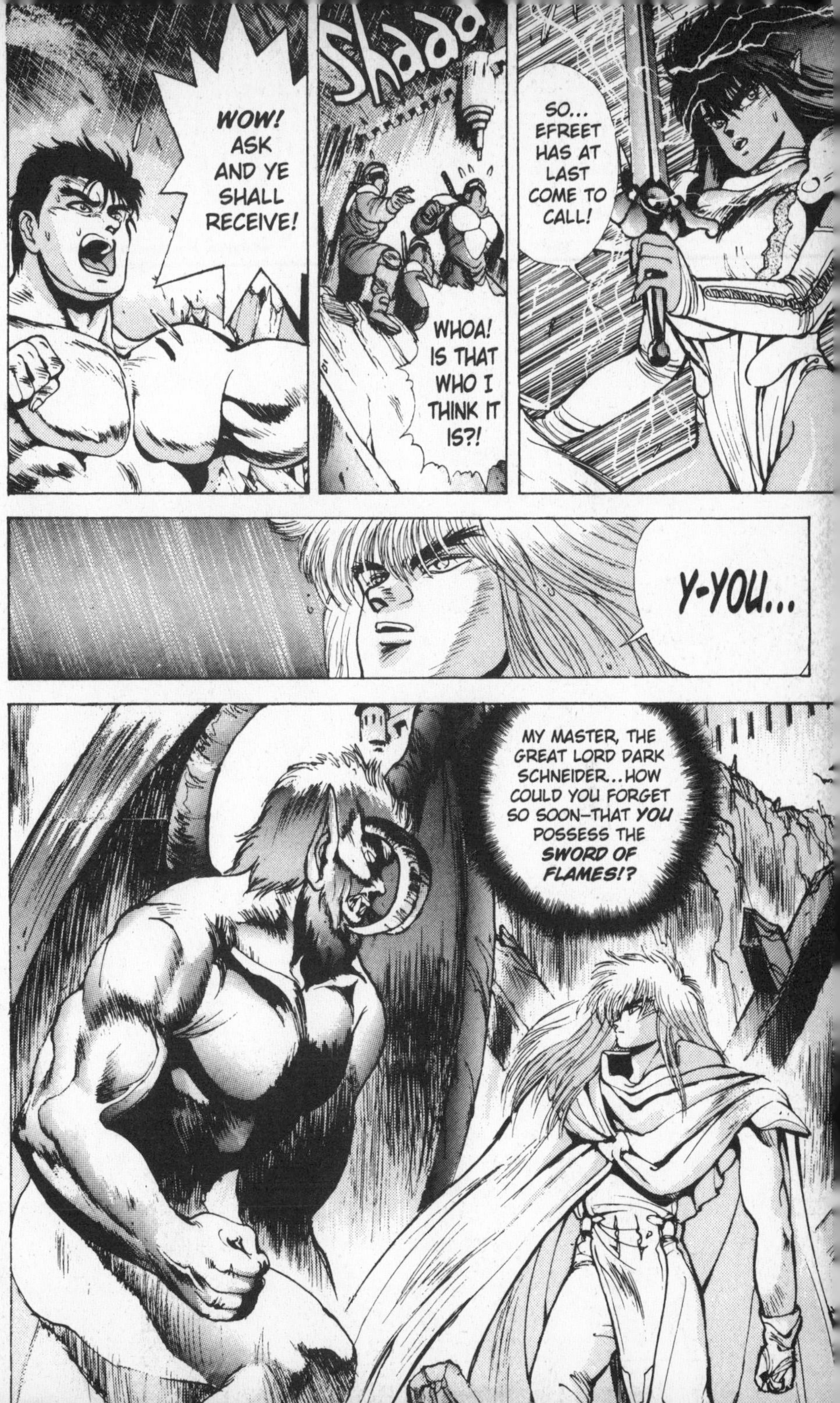

WOW! ASK AND YE SHALL RECEIVE!
SHADO
WHOA! IS THAT WHO I THINK IT IS?!
SO... EFREET HAS AT LAST COME TO CALL!
Y-YOU...
MY MASTER, THE GREAT LORD DARK SCHNEIDER...HOW COULD YOU FORGET SO SOON—THAT *YOU* POSSESS THE ***SWORD OF FLAMES!?***

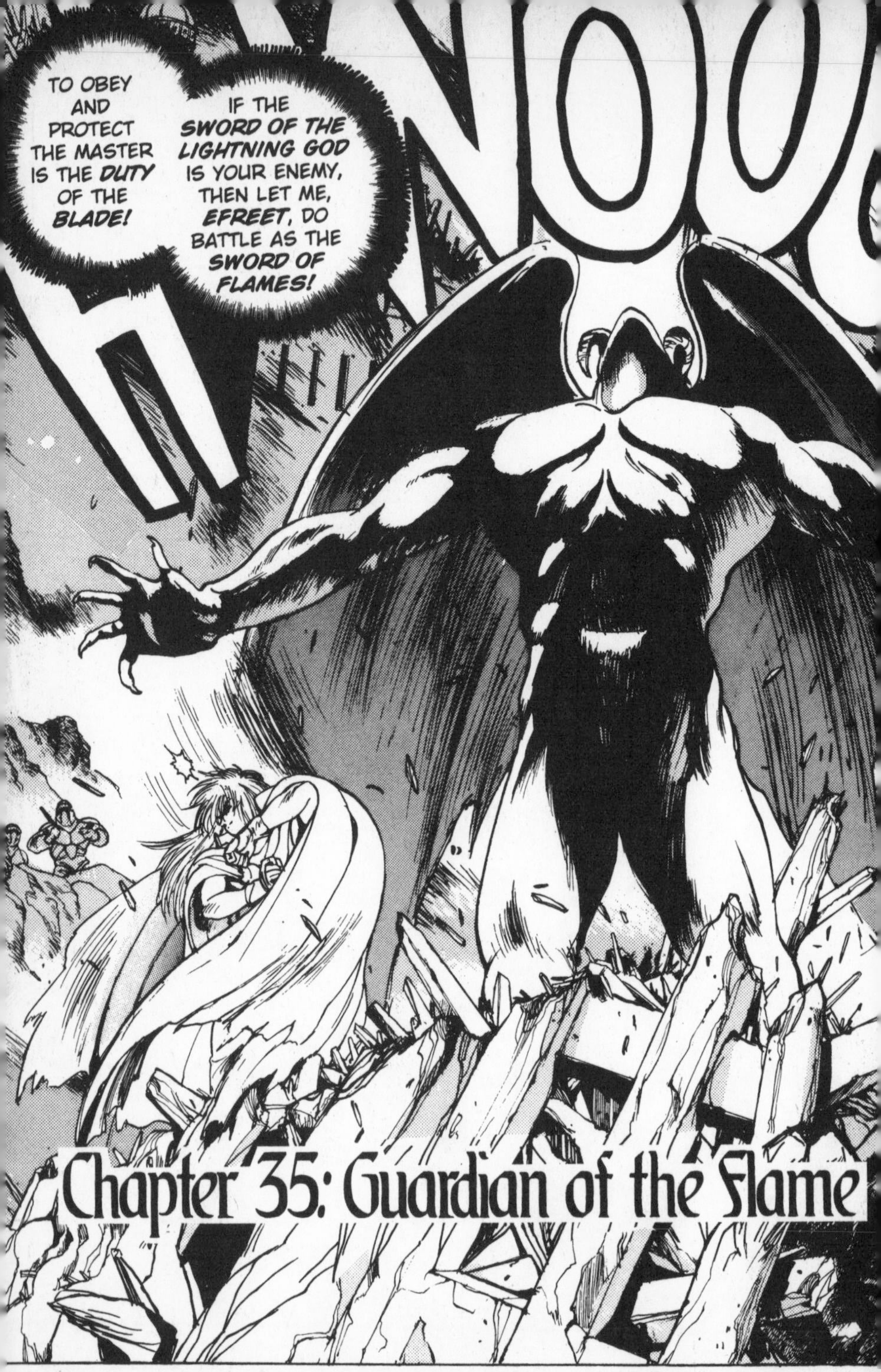
TO OBEY AND PROTECT THE MASTER IS THE DUTY OF THE BLADE!
IF THE SWORD OF THE LIGHTNING GOD IS YOUR ENEMY, THEN LET ME, EFREET, DO BATTLE AS THE SWORD OF FLAMES!
Chapter 35: Guardian of the Flame

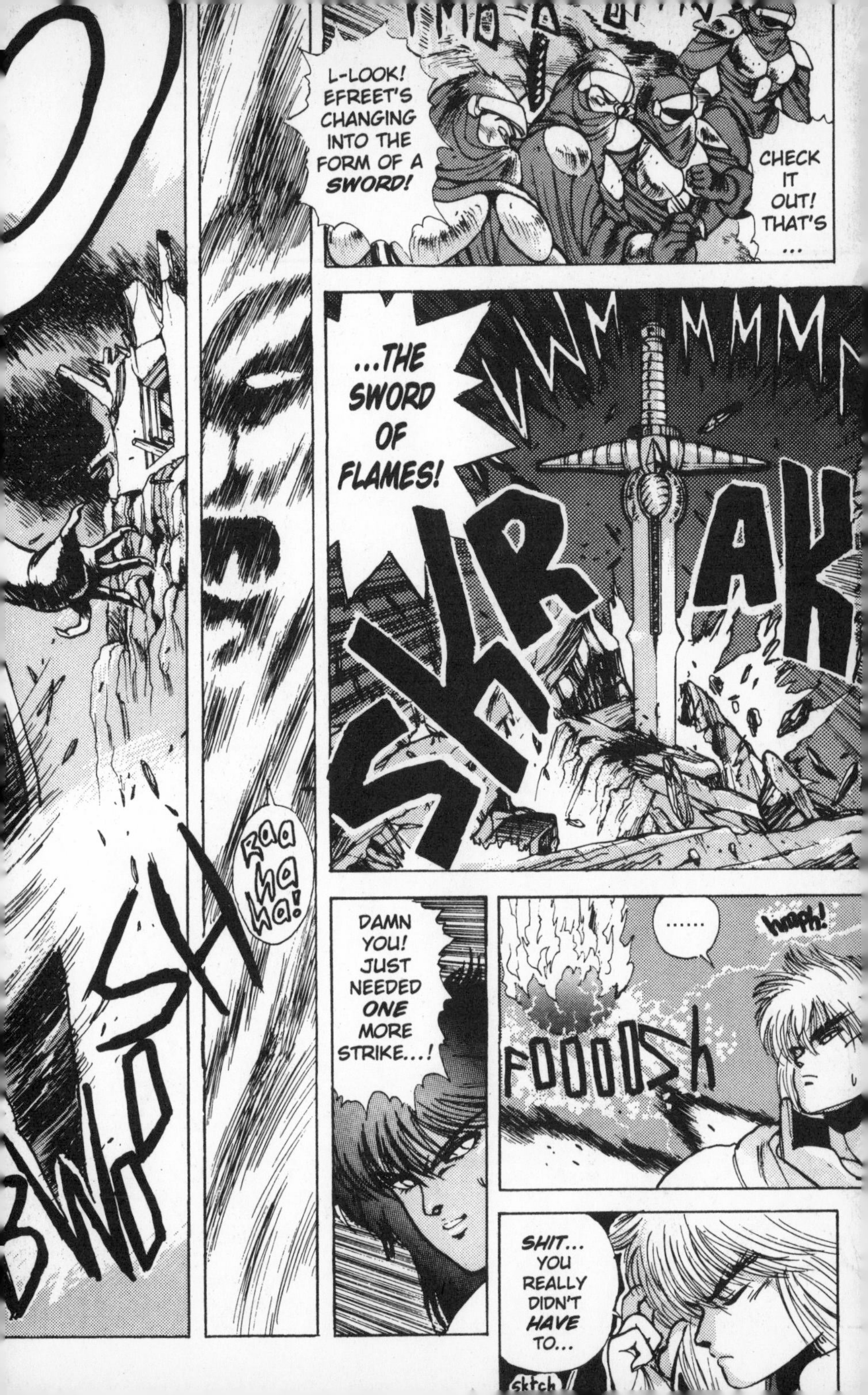
BWOOSH
Raa ha ha ha!
L-LOOK! EFREET'S CHANGING INTO THE FORM OF A **SWORD!**
CHECK IT OUT! THAT'S ...
...THE SWORD OF FLAMES!
SKRAK
DAMN YOU! JUST NEEDED **ONE** MORE STRIKE...!
......
hmph!
FOOOOSH
SHIT... YOU REALLY DIDN'T **HAVE** TO...
sktch

I CAN TAKE CARE OF *MYSELF*, EFREET! STILL...

GRRAH!

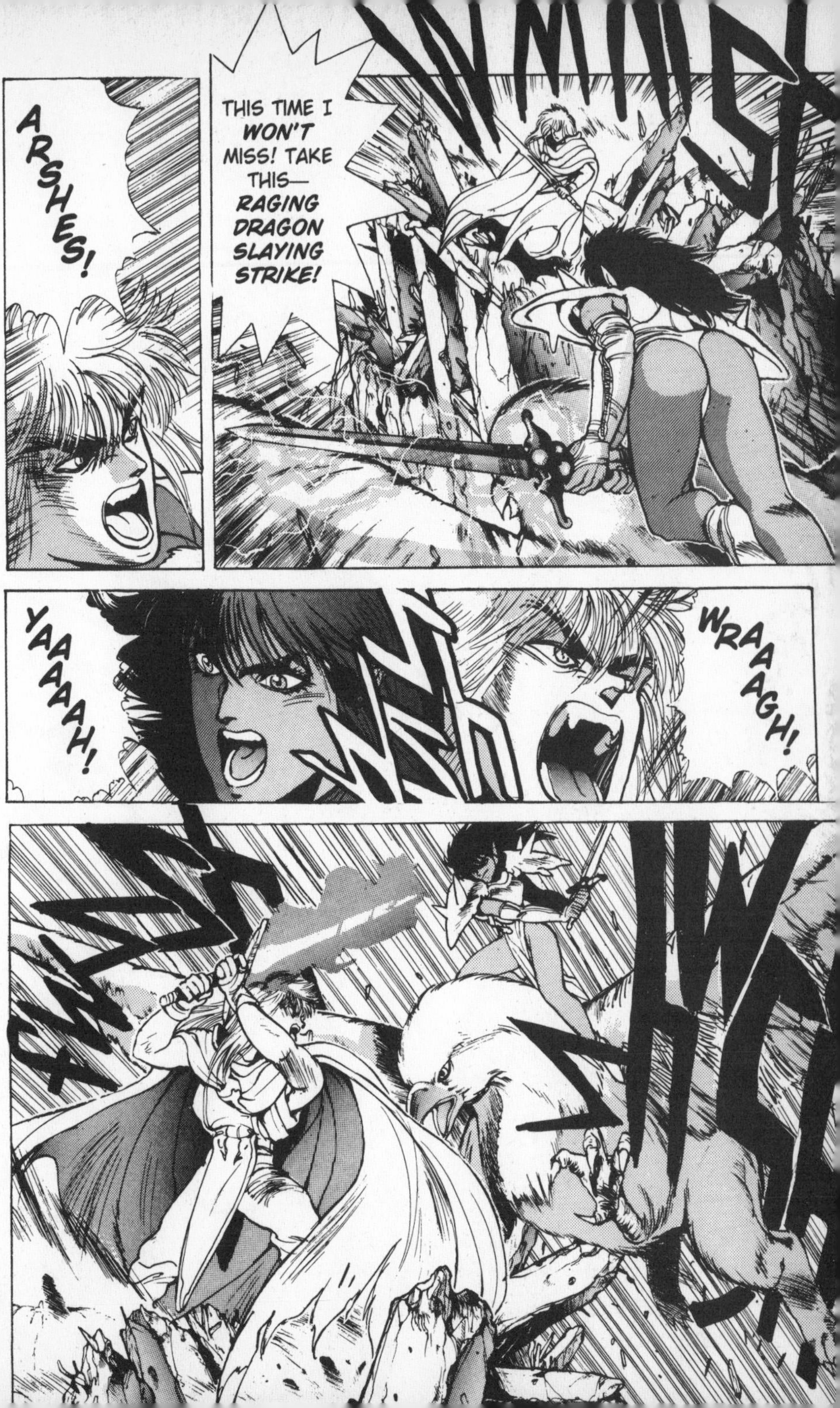
ARSHES!
THIS TIME I WON'T MISS! TAKE THIS— RAGING DRAGON SLAYING STRIKE!
YAAAAAH!
WRAAAGH!

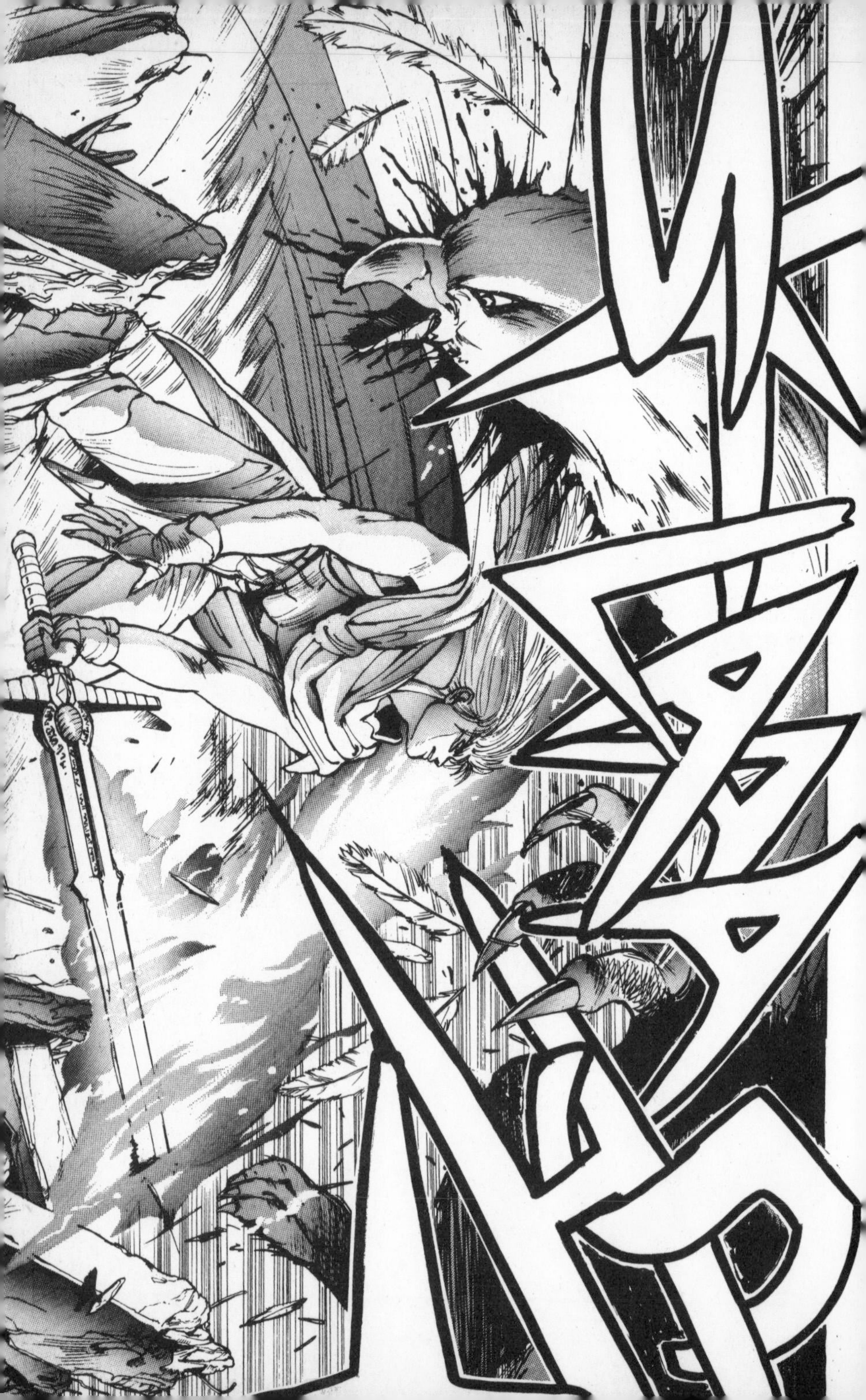

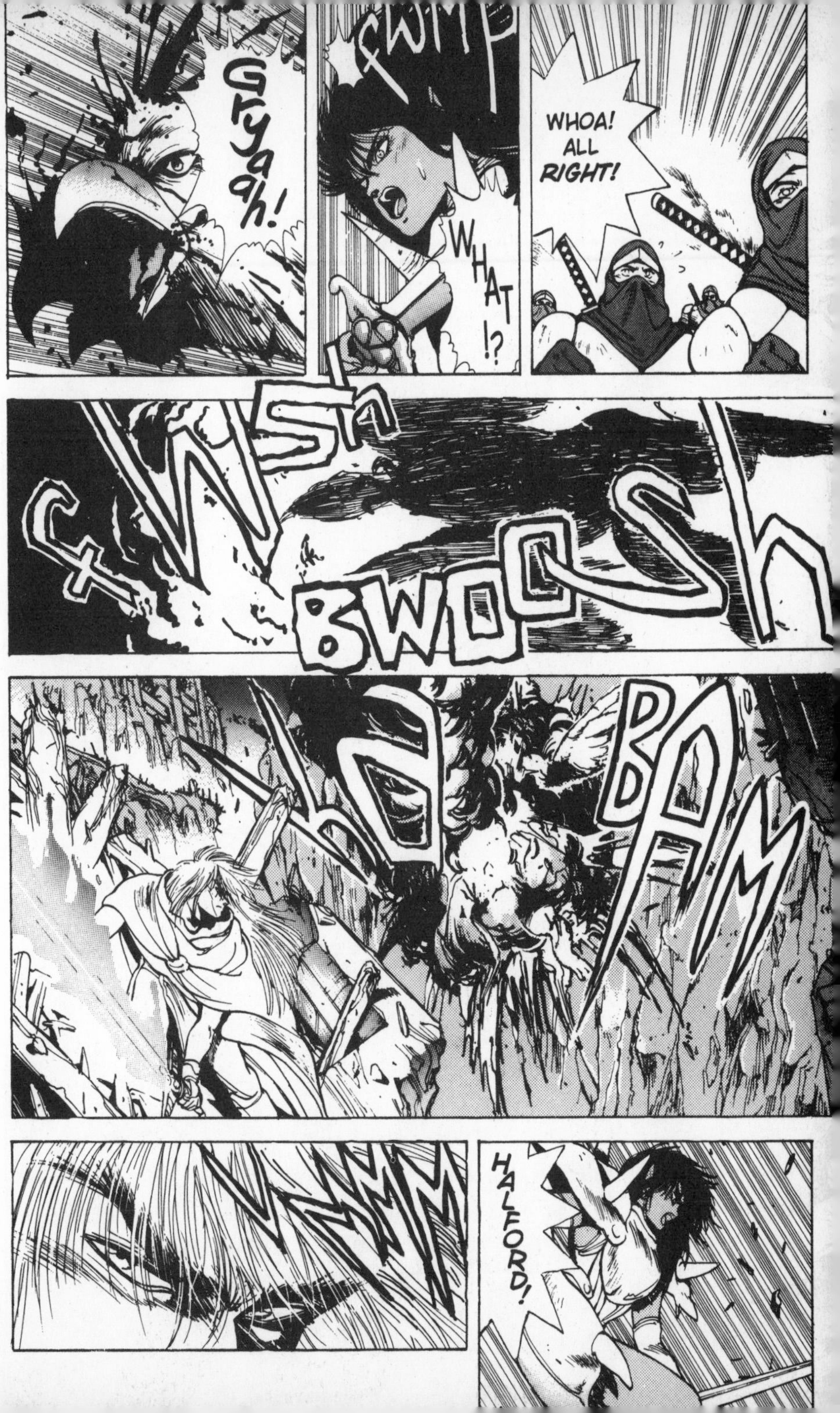
Gryaaah!
fwmp
WHAT!?
WHOA! ALL RIGHT!
BWOOSH
BAM
HALFORD!

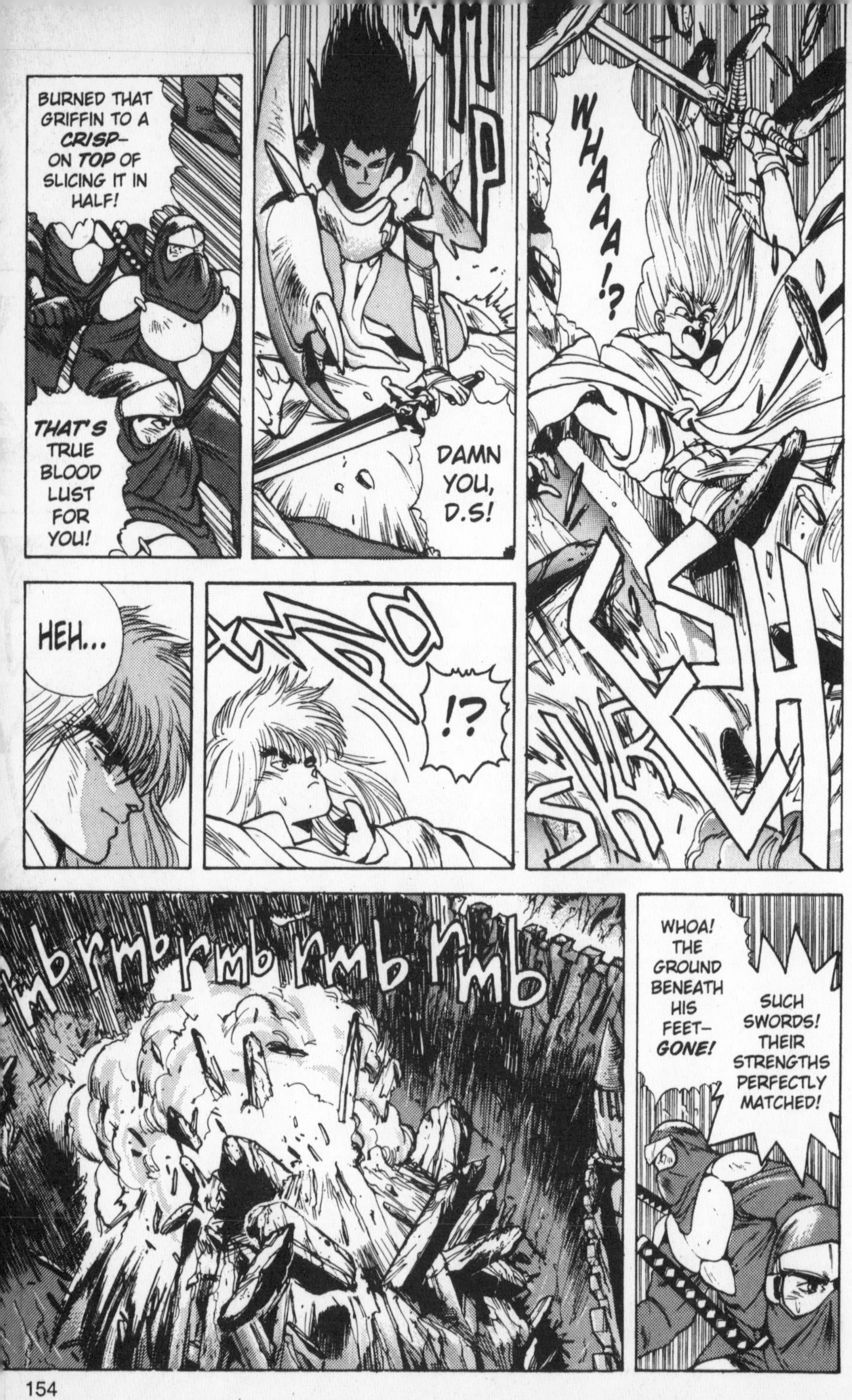
BURNED THAT GRIFFIN TO A *CRISP*— ON *TOP* OF SLICING IT IN HALF!
THAT'S TRUE BLOOD LUST FOR YOU!
DAMN YOU, D.S!
HEH...
!?
WHAAAA!?
rmb rmb rmb rmb
WHOA! THE GROUND BENEATH HIS FEET— *GONE!*
SUCH SWORDS! THEIR STRENGTHS PERFECTLY MATCHED!

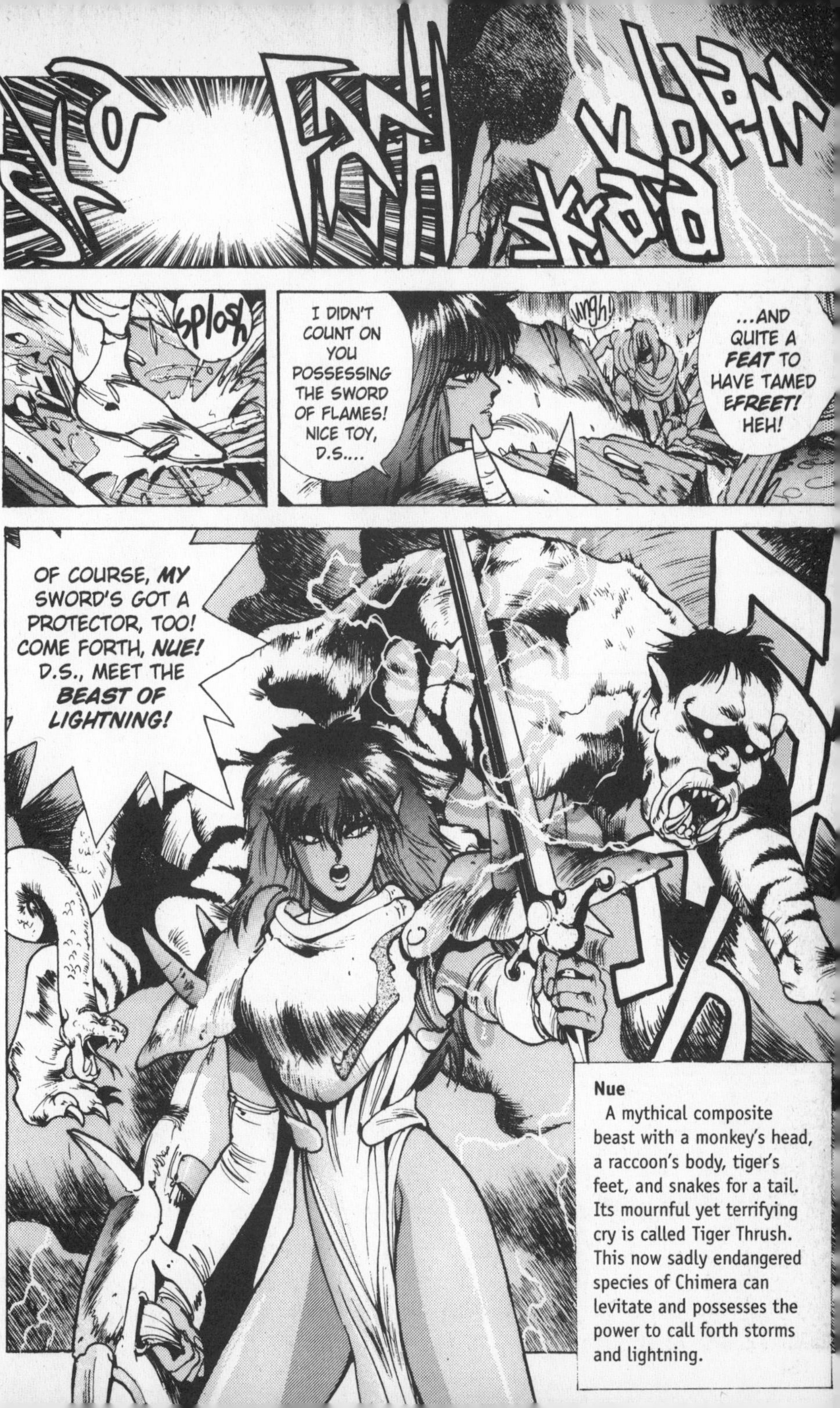
splosh
I DIDN'T COUNT ON YOU POSSESSING THE SWORD OF FLAMES! NICE TOY, D.S....
ungh!
...AND QUITE A ***FEAT*** TO HAVE TAMED ***EFREET!*** HEH!
OF COURSE, ***MY*** SWORD'S GOT A PROTECTOR, TOO! COME FORTH, ***NUE!*** D.S., MEET THE ***BEAST OF LIGHTNING!***
Nue
A mythical composite beast with a monkey's head, a raccoon's body, tiger's feet, and snakes for a tail. Its mournful yet terrifying cry is called Tiger Thrush. This now sadly endangered species of Chimera can levitate and possesses the power to call forth storms and lightning.

YEAH, YEAH— PLEASED TO MEETCHA! NOW LET'S GET ON WITH IT!

SHOK

MY DEAREST DARK SCHNEI- DER...

YOU CAN DO IT, LUCIEN...

AND I THOUGHT *EFREET* WAS AN *UGLY* SWORD GUARDIAN! UGH!

SPLOOSH

FIRE AND ELECTRICITY! THE TWO MAGICAL SWORDS ARE SPEWING FORTH POWER!

VMMMMMM

WHAT A TURN OF EVENTS! *TWO* DEMON SWORDS ABOUT TO DO BATTLE— AND WE WERE *HERE!*

LORD D.S. AND NEI ARE ON EQUAL GROUND, MASTER GARA!

WITH THE GRIFFIN OUT OF THE PICTURE, AND SWORDS OF SIMILAR STRENGTH—

DON'T BE AN IDIOT.

B-BUT CAN'T D.S. WIN NOW?

SURE, THE ODDS ARE BETTER, BUT AS LONG AS NEITHER OF THEM CAN USE THEIR MAGIC...

...D.S. IS AT A DISTINCT DISADVANTAGE IN THIS FIGHT!

ARE YOU SAYING THAT THE SWORD OF FLAMES CAN'T BEST THE LIGHTNING SWORD...?

NO! THAT'S NOT IT AT *ALL*...

ACTUALLY, THE SWORD OF FLAMES IS SLIGHTLY *MORE* POTENT THAN THE LIGHTNING SWORD...

OKAY. THEN WHAT—

IT'S SIMPLE, MORON! EVEN THOUGH D.S. POSSESSES SUPERHUMAN STRENGTH AND STAMINA, AT THE CORE, HE'S "JUST" A WIZARD!

IF THE BATTLE IS WITH A *SWORD*, THEN HE DOESN'T STAND A *CHANCE* AGAINST *NEI*—A *MASTER* OF THE SECRET HARIKEN SWORDSMANSHIP SCHOOL!

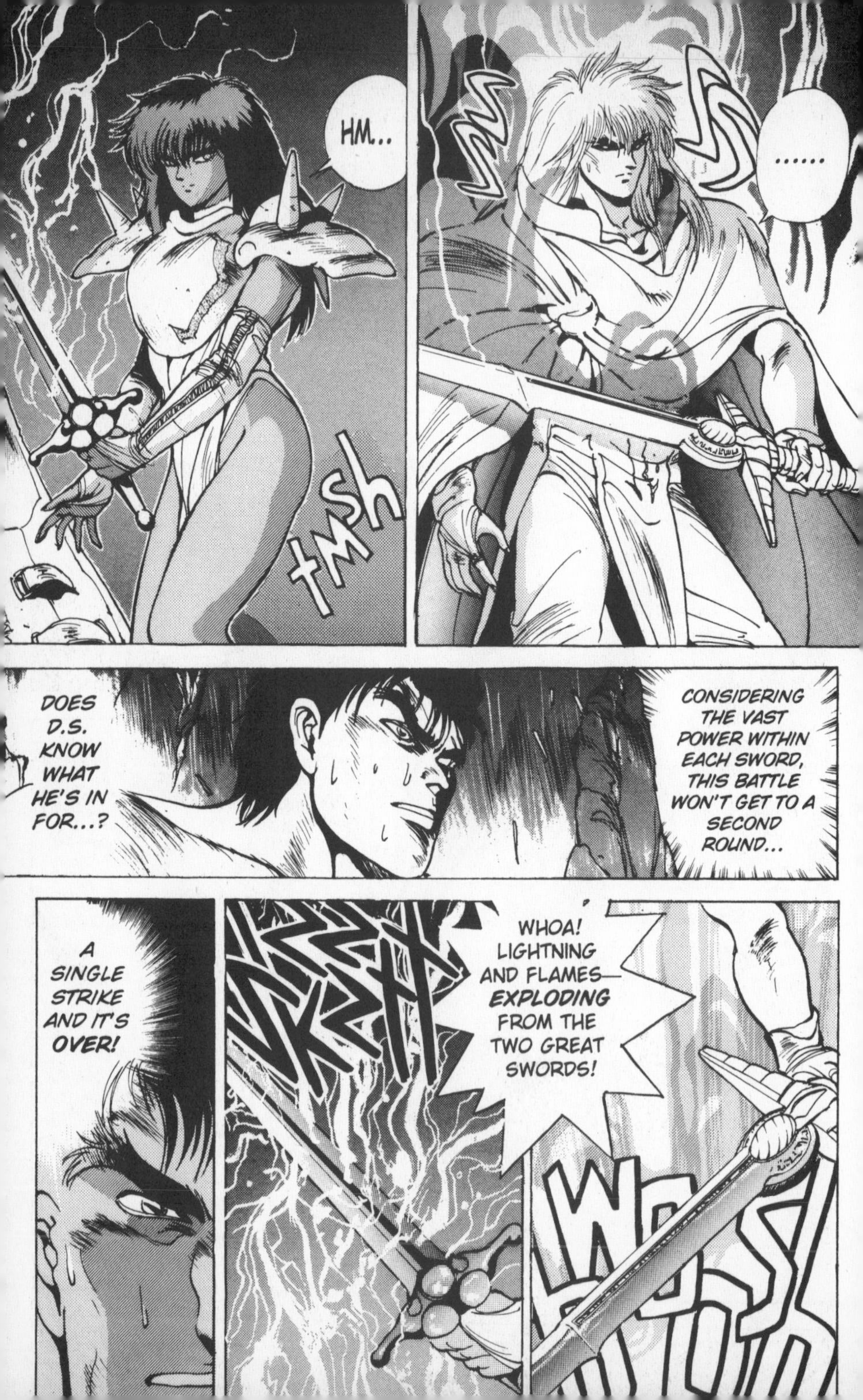
HM...
tmsh
......
DOES D.S. KNOW WHAT HE'S IN FOR...?
CONSIDERING THE VAST POWER WITHIN EACH SWORD, THIS BATTLE WON'T GET TO A SECOND ROUND...
A SINGLE STRIKE AND IT'S **OVER!**
WHOA! LIGHTNING AND FLAMES— **EXPLODING** FROM THE TWO GREAT SWORDS!

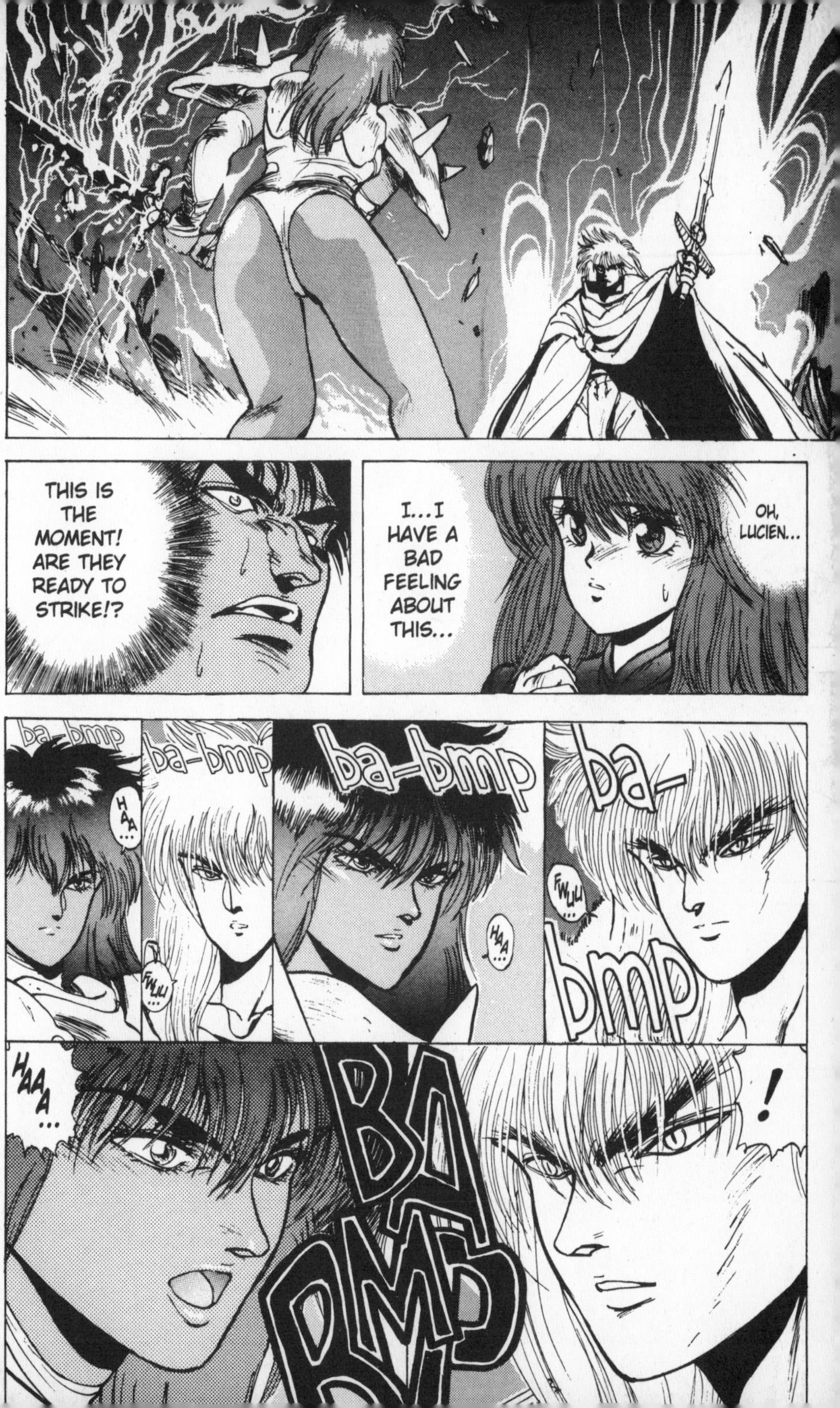
THIS IS THE MOMENT! ARE THEY READY TO STRIKE!?
I...I HAVE A BAD FEELING ABOUT THIS...
OH, LUCIEN...
ba-bmp
HAA...
ba-bmp
FWUU...
ba-bmp
HAA...
ba-
FWUU...
bmp
HAAA...
BA-DMP
!

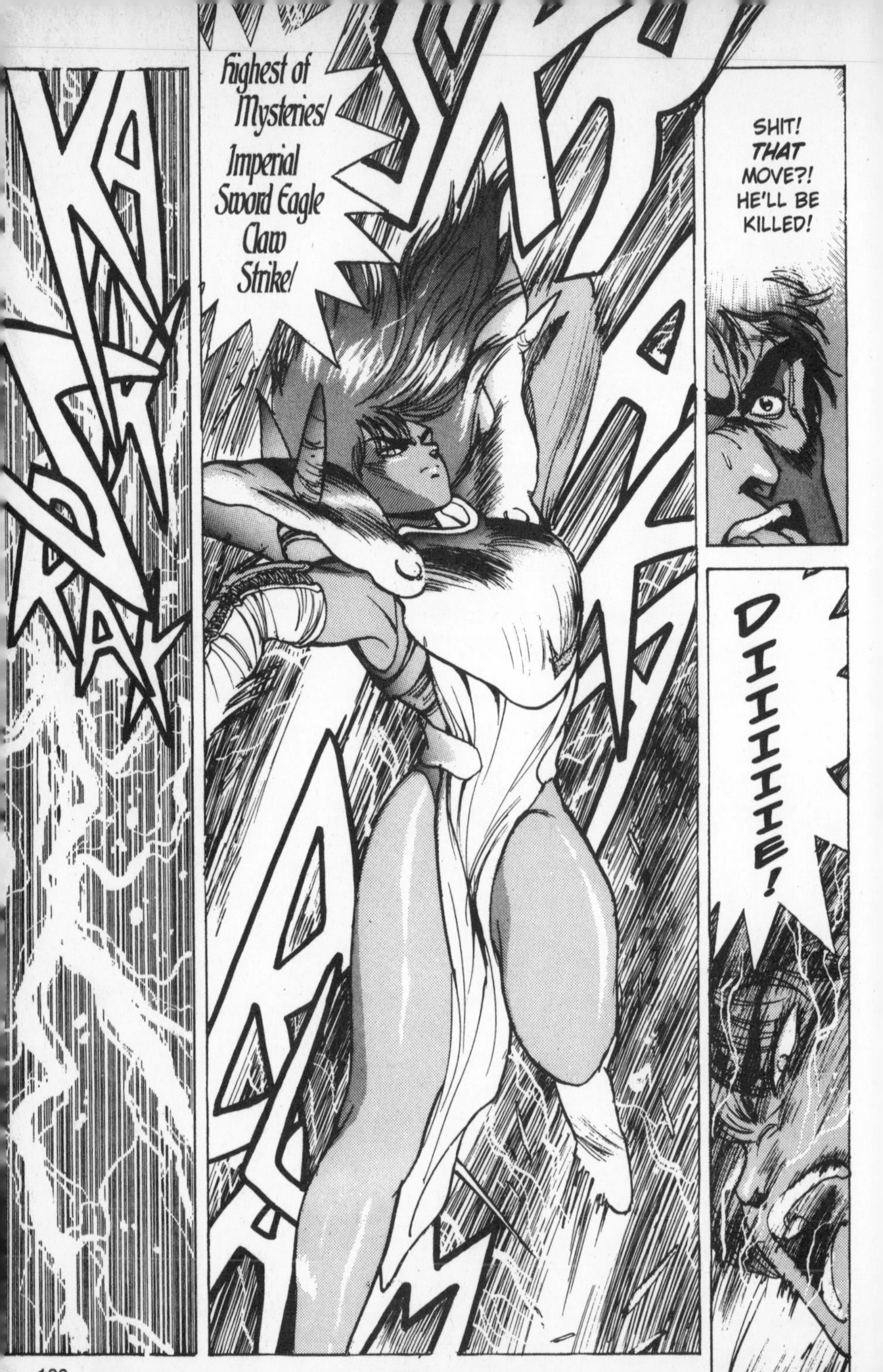
Highest of Mysteries!
Imperial Sword Eagle Claw Strike!
SHIT! THAT MOVE?! HE'LL BE KILLED!
DIIIIIE!

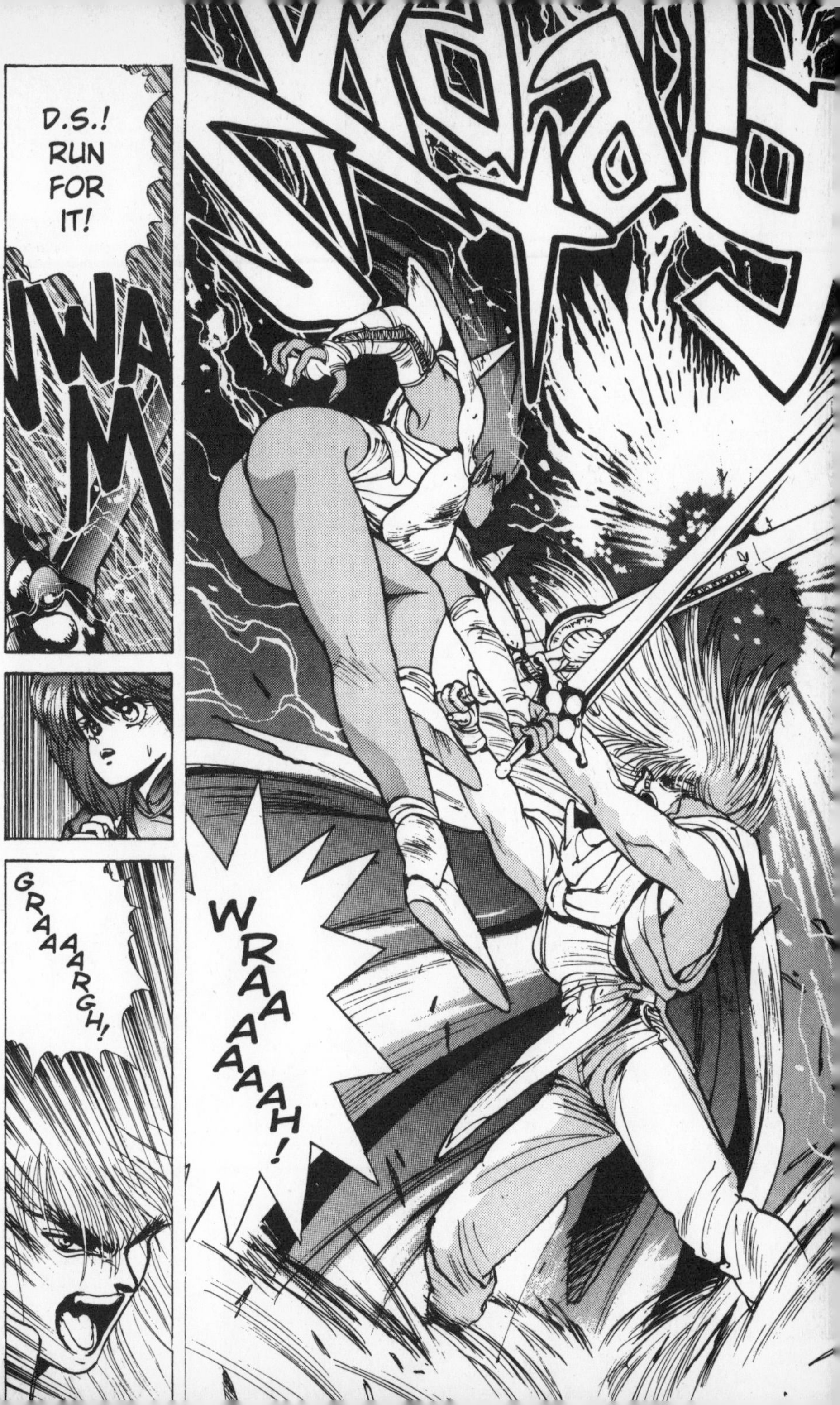
D.S.! RUN FOR IT!
GRAAAARGH!
WRAAAAAAH!

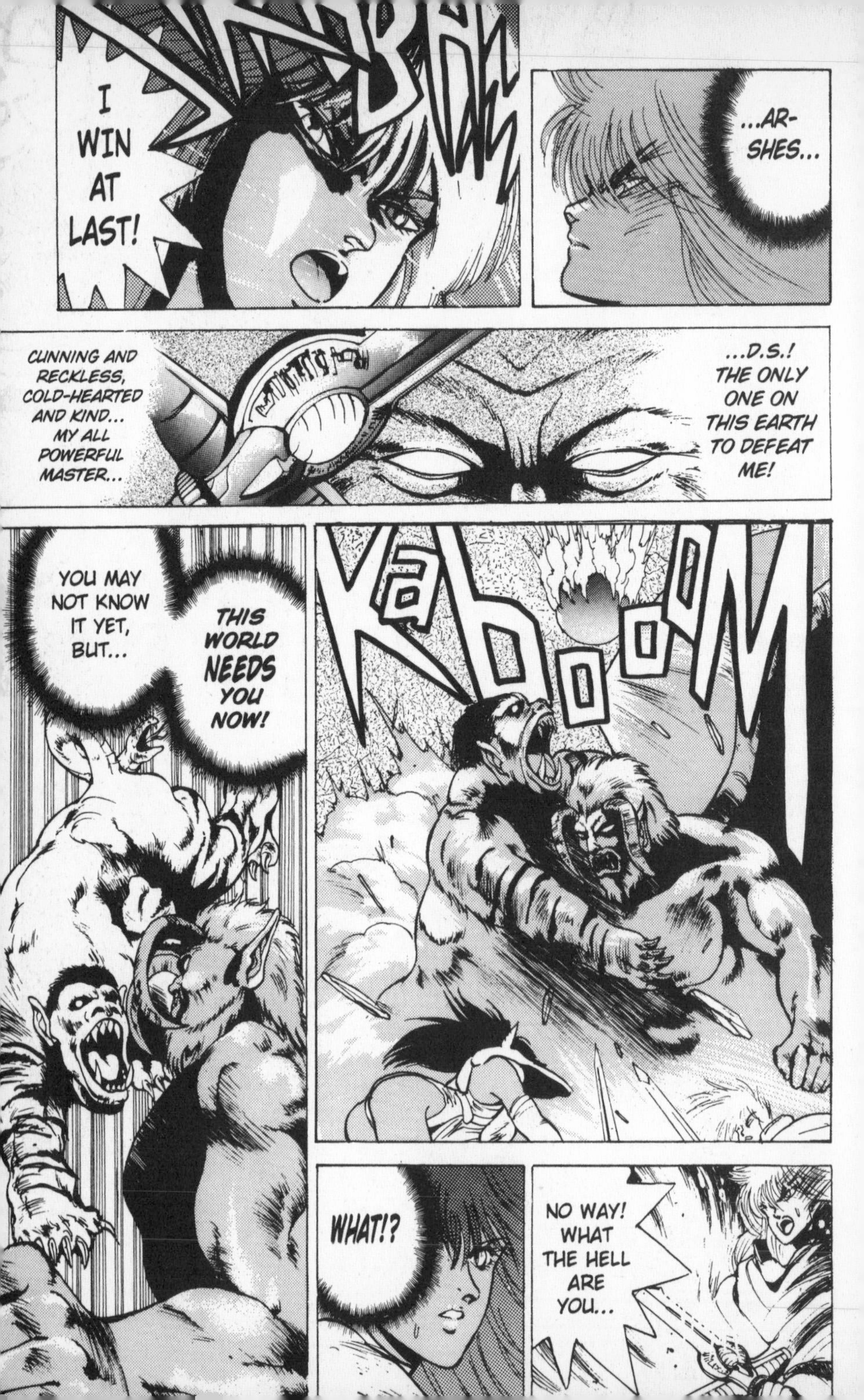
I WIN AT LAST!
...AR-SHES...
CUNNING AND RECKLESS, COLD-HEARTED AND KIND... MY ALL POWERFUL MASTER...
...D.S.! THE ONLY ONE ON THIS EARTH TO DEFEAT ME!
YOU MAY NOT KNOW IT YET, BUT...
THIS WORLD NEEDS YOU NOW!
KaBOOOOM
WHAT!?
NO WAY! WHAT THE HELL ARE YOU...

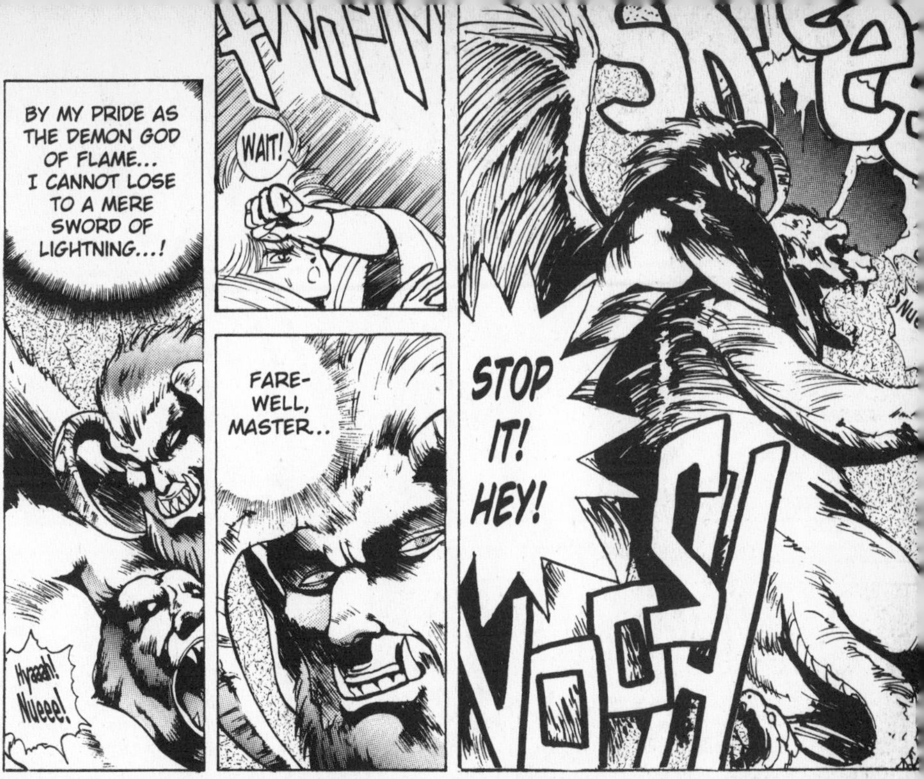
BY MY PRIDE AS THE DEMON GOD OF FLAME... I CANNOT LOSE TO A MERE SWORD OF LIGHTNING...!
Hyaaah! Nueee!
WAIT!
FARE-WELL, MASTER...
STOP IT! HEY!

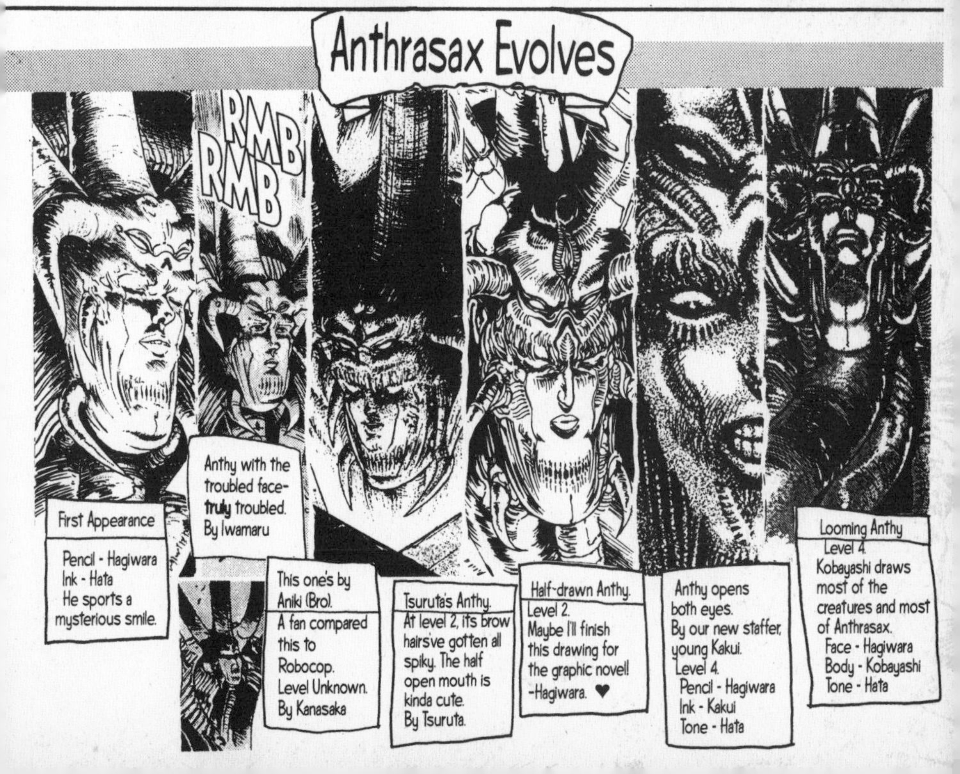
Anthrasax Evolves
RMB RMB
First Appearance
Pencil - Hagiwara
Ink - Hata
He sports a mysterious smile.
Anthy with the troubled face-truly troubled.
By Iwamaru
This one's by Aniki (Bro).
A fan compared this to Robocop.
Level Unknown.
By Kanasaka
Tsuruta's Anthy.
At level 2, its brow hairs've gotten all spiky. The half open mouth is kinda cute.
By Tsuruta.
Half-drawn Anthy.
Level 2.
Maybe I'll finish this drawing for the graphic novel!
-Hagiwara. ♥
Anthy opens both eyes.
By our new staffer, young Kakui.
Level 4.
Pencil - Hagiwara
Ink - Kakui
Tone - Hata
Looming Anthy
Level 4.
Kobayashi draws most of the creatures and most of Anthrasax.
Face - Hagiwara
Body - Kobayashi
Tone - Hata

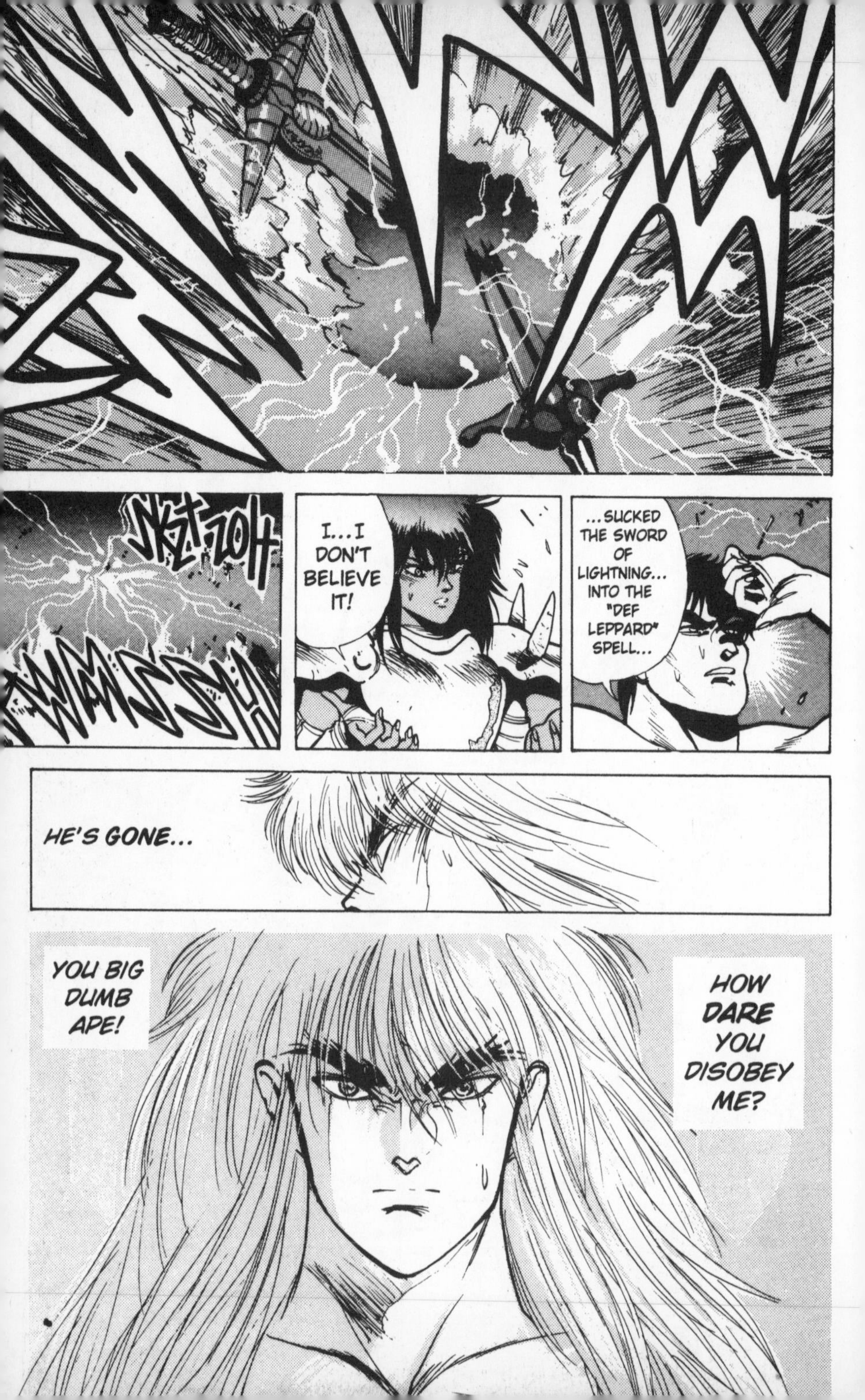
SKZT ZOH
I...I DON'T BELIEVE IT!
...SUCKED THE SWORD OF LIGHTNING... INTO THE "DEF LEPPARD" SPELL...
HE'S GONE...
YOU BIG DUMB APE!
HOW DARE YOU DISOBEY ME?

AHA!

SHIT, D.S.! FOCUS ON THE FIGHT!

THIS IS THE **LAST** TIME YOU'LL TURN YOUR BACK ON **ME!**

IT'S TIME YOU GAVE ME THE **ATTENTION** I DESERVE!

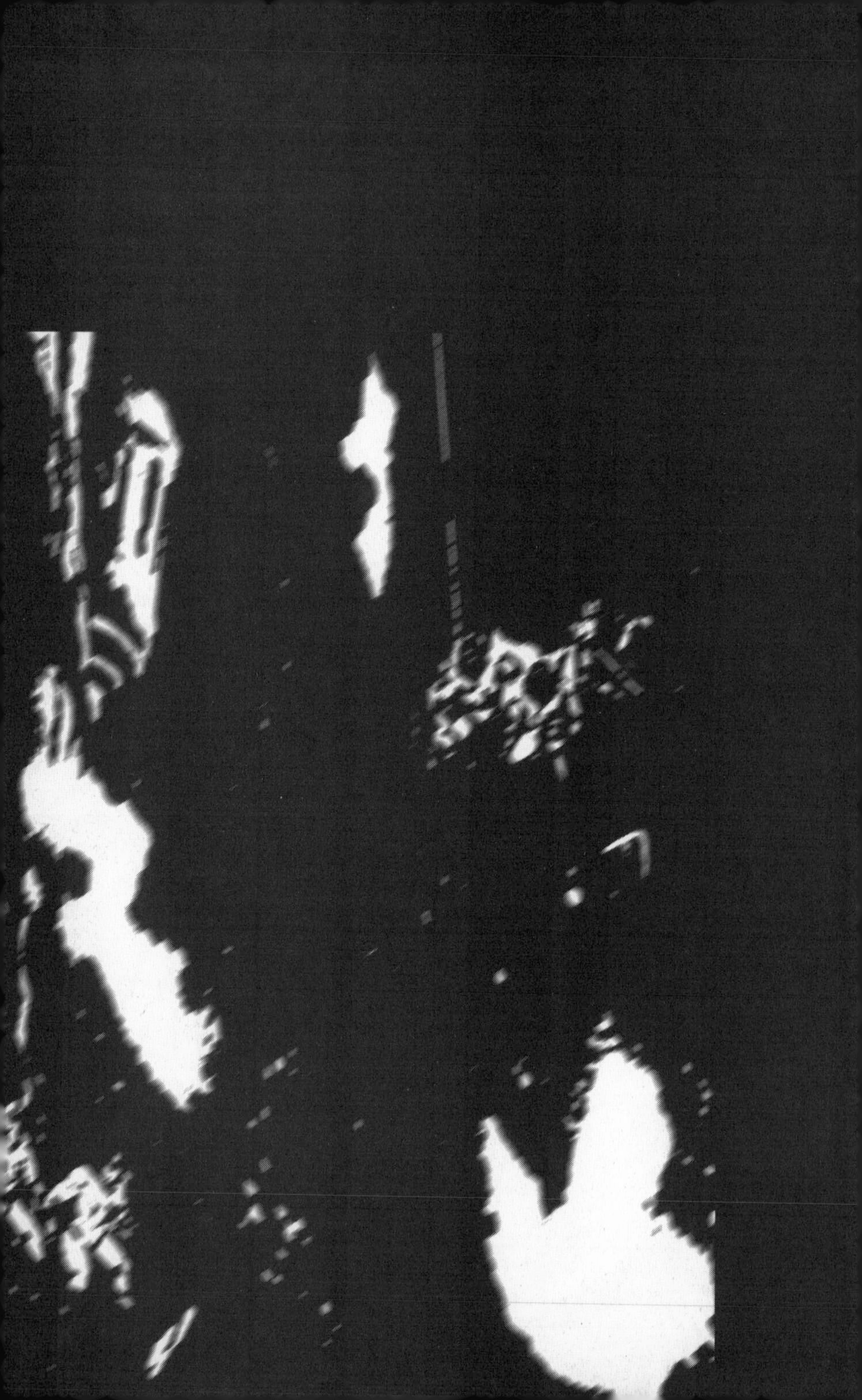

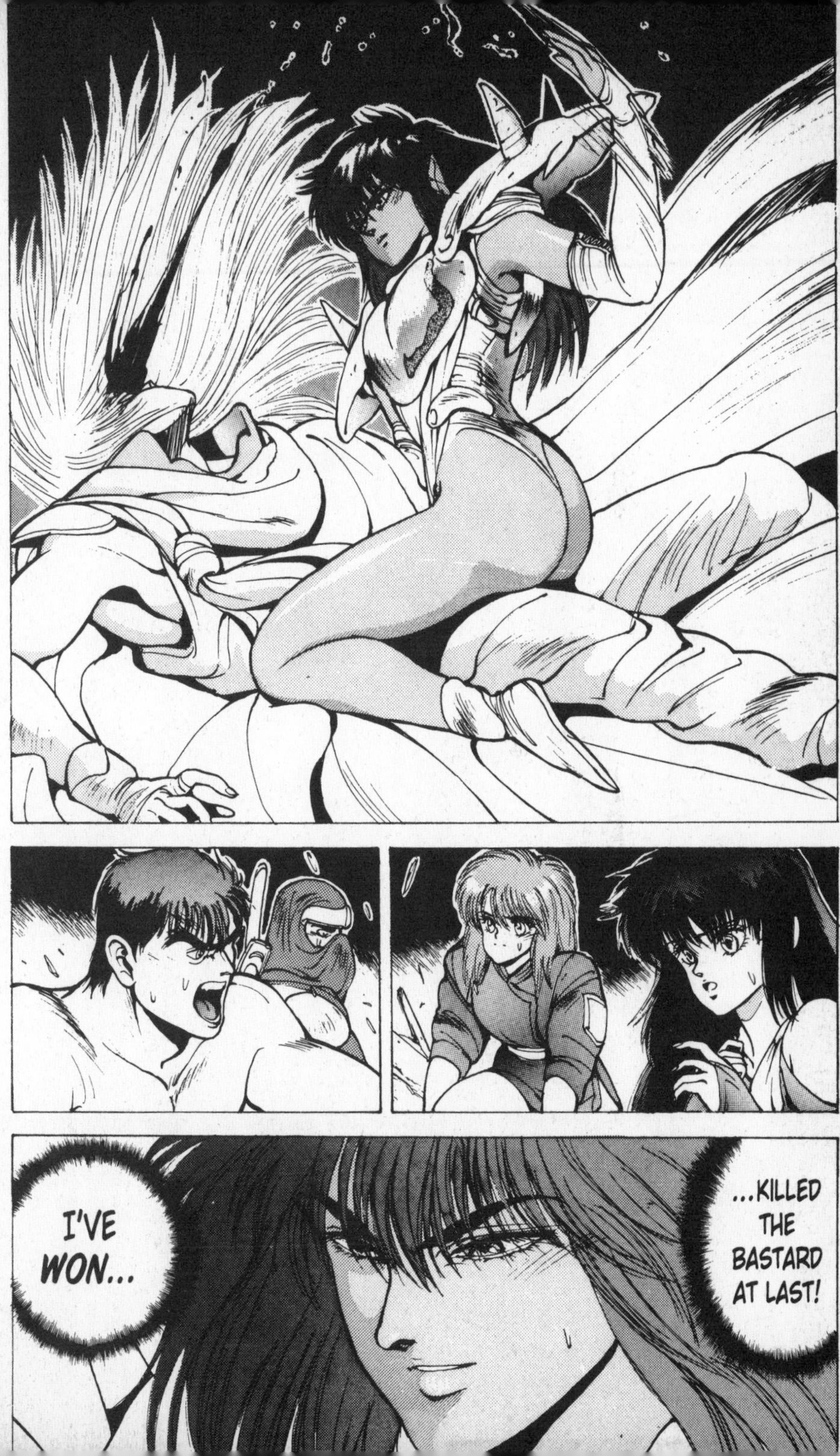
I'VE WON...
...KILLED THE BASTARD AT LAST!

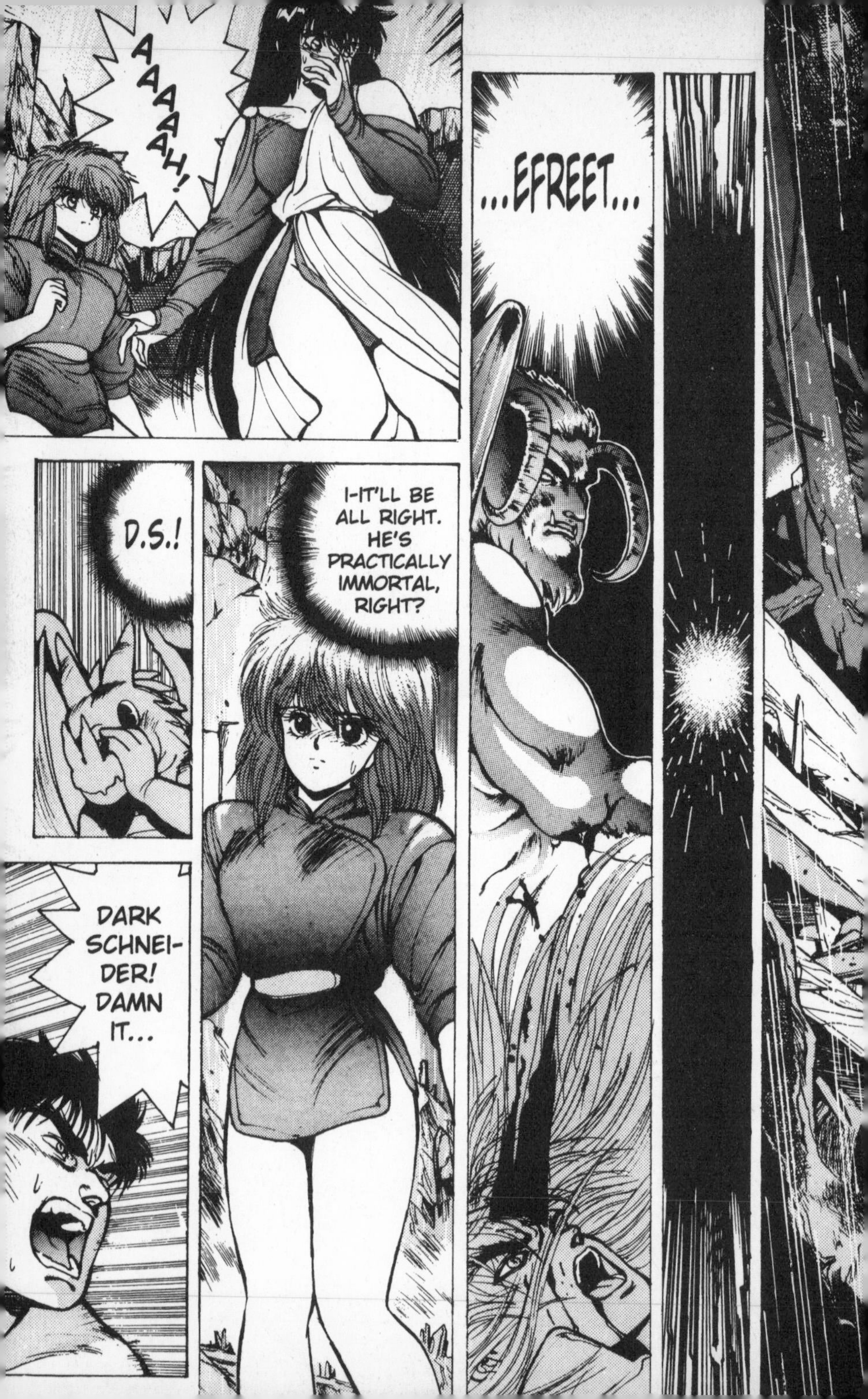
AAAAAH!
D.S.!
I-IT'LL BE ALL RIGHT. HE'S PRACTICALLY IMMORTAL, RIGHT?
DARK SCHNEI-DER! DAMN IT...
...EFREET...

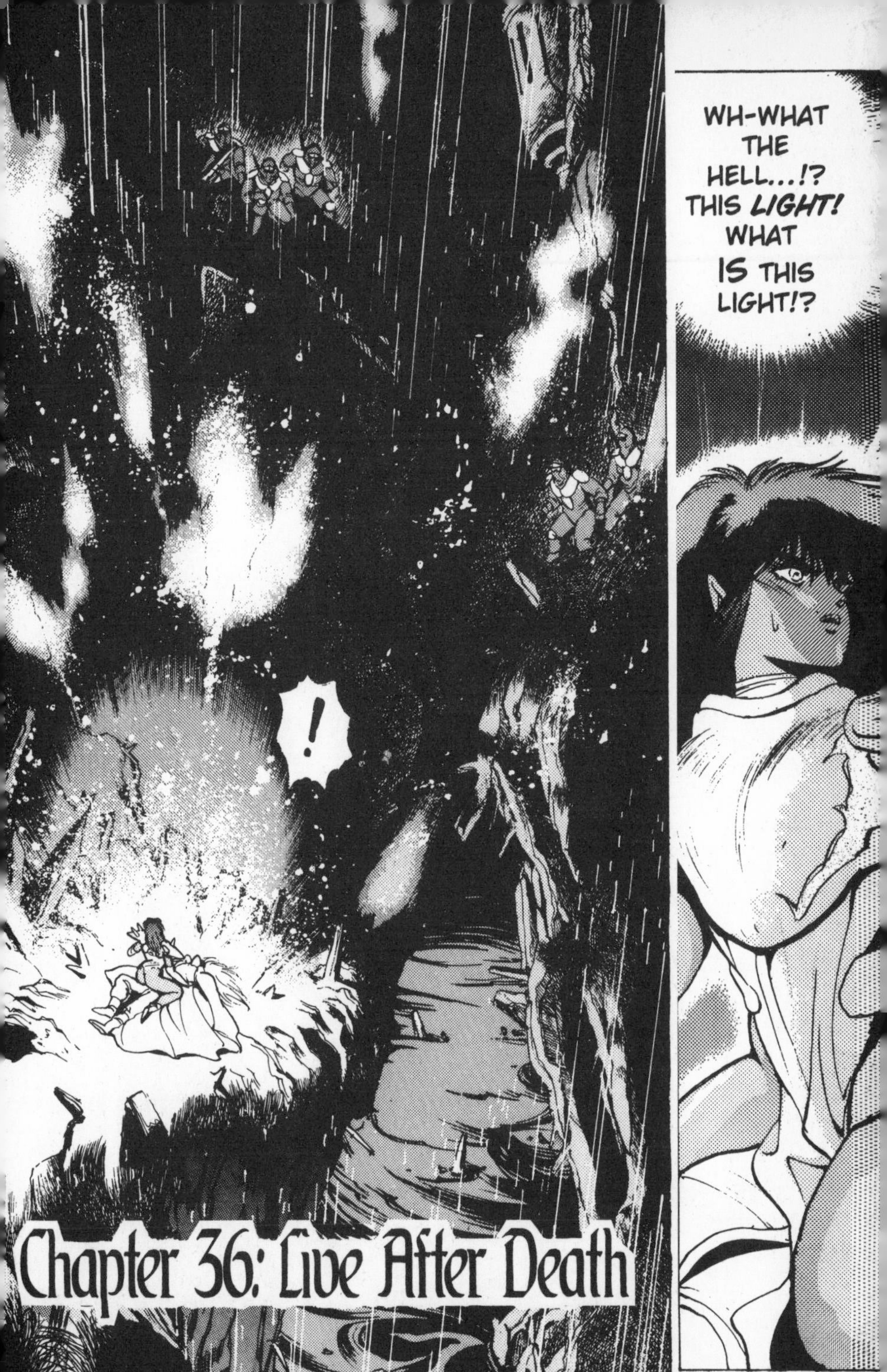
!
Chapter 36: Live After Death
WH-WHAT THE HELL...!? THIS *LIGHT!* WHAT IS THIS LIGHT!?

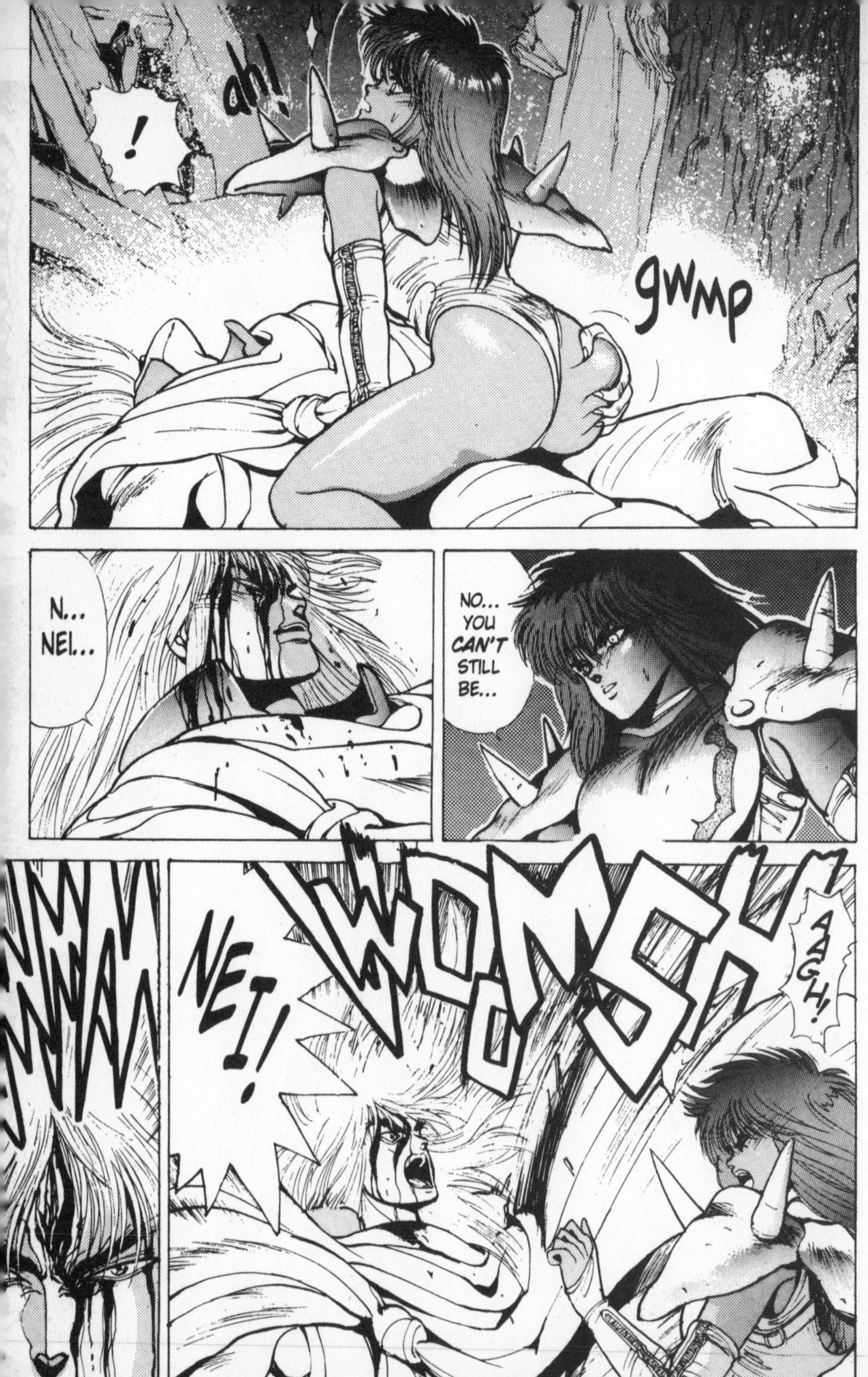
ah!
!
gwmp
N... NEI...
NO... YOU CAN'T STILL BE...
NEI!
WOMSH
AAGH!

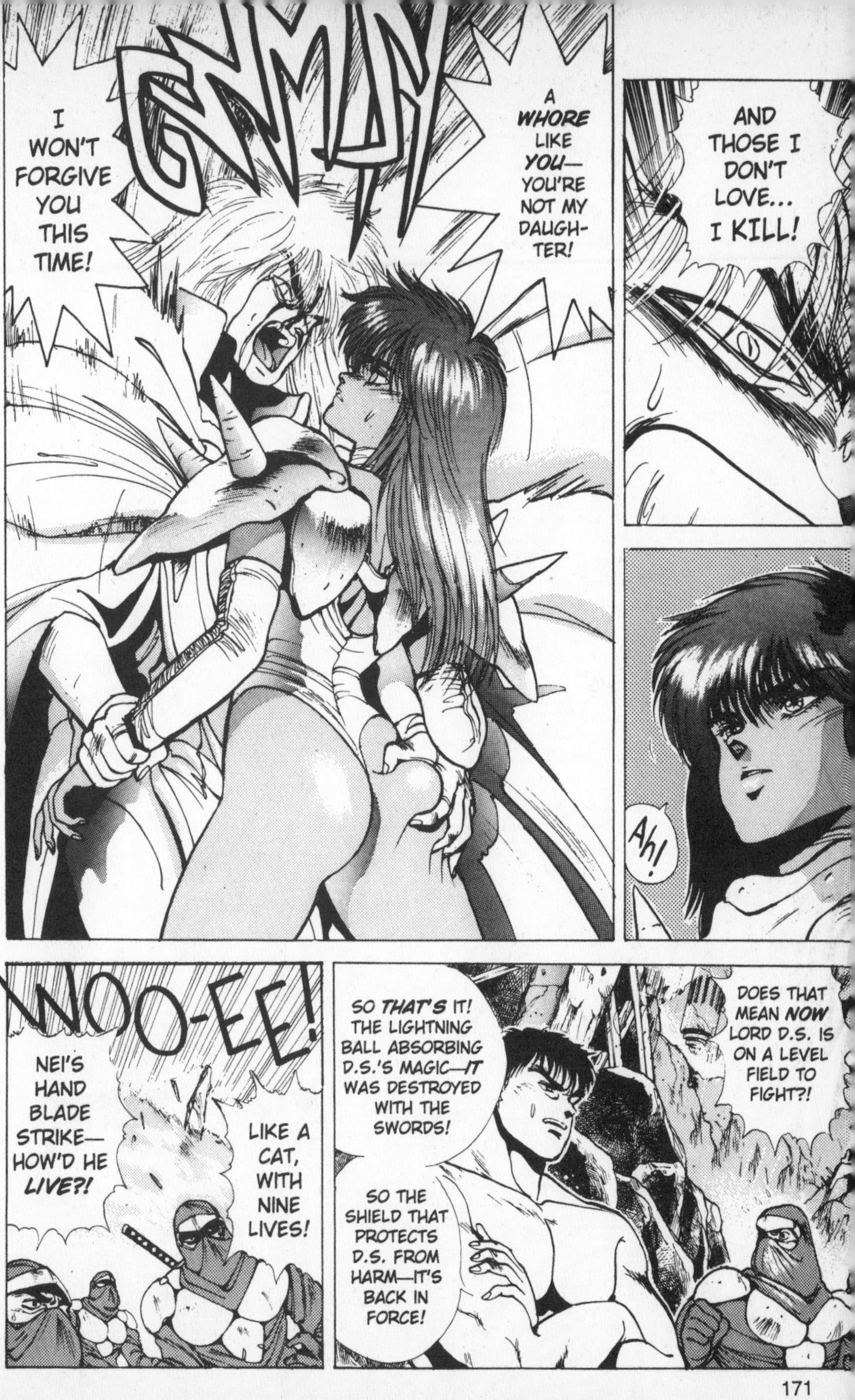
GMMM
I WON'T FORGIVE YOU THIS TIME!
A *WHORE* LIKE *YOU*— YOU'RE NOT MY DAUGHTER!
AND THOSE I DON'T LOVE... I KILL!
Ah!
WOO-EE!
NEI'S HAND BLADE STRIKE— HOW'D HE *LIVE?!*
LIKE A CAT, WITH NINE LIVES!
SO *THAT'S* IT! THE LIGHTNING BALL ABSORBING D.S.'S MAGIC—*IT* WAS DESTROYED WITH THE SWORDS!
SO THE SHIELD THAT PROTECTS D.S. FROM HARM—IT'S BACK IN FORCE!
DOES THAT MEAN *NOW* LORD D.S. IS ON A LEVEL FIELD TO FIGHT?!

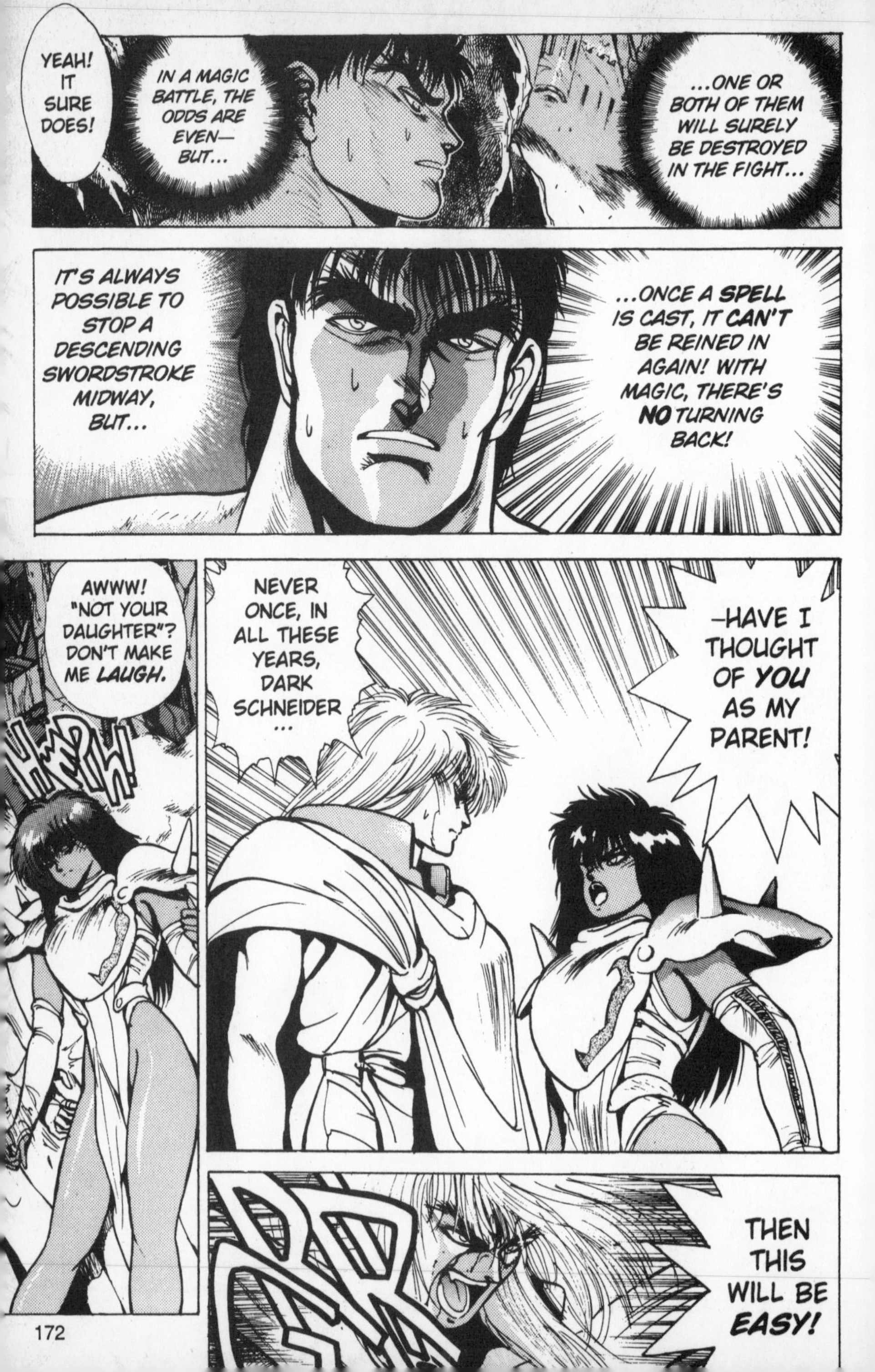

YEAH! IT SURE DOES!
IN A MAGIC BATTLE, THE ODDS ARE EVEN—BUT...
...ONE OR BOTH OF THEM WILL SURELY BE DESTROYED IN THE FIGHT...
IT'S ALWAYS POSSIBLE TO STOP A DESCENDING SWORDSTROKE MIDWAY, BUT...
...ONCE A **SPELL** IS CAST, IT **CAN'T** BE REINED IN AGAIN! WITH MAGIC, THERE'S **NO** TURNING BACK!
AWWW! "NOT YOUR DAUGHTER"? DON'T MAKE ME *LAUGH.*
HMPH!
NEVER ONCE, IN ALL THESE YEARS, DARK SCHNEIDER...
–HAVE I THOUGHT OF *YOU* AS MY PARENT!
THEN THIS WILL BE *EASY!*

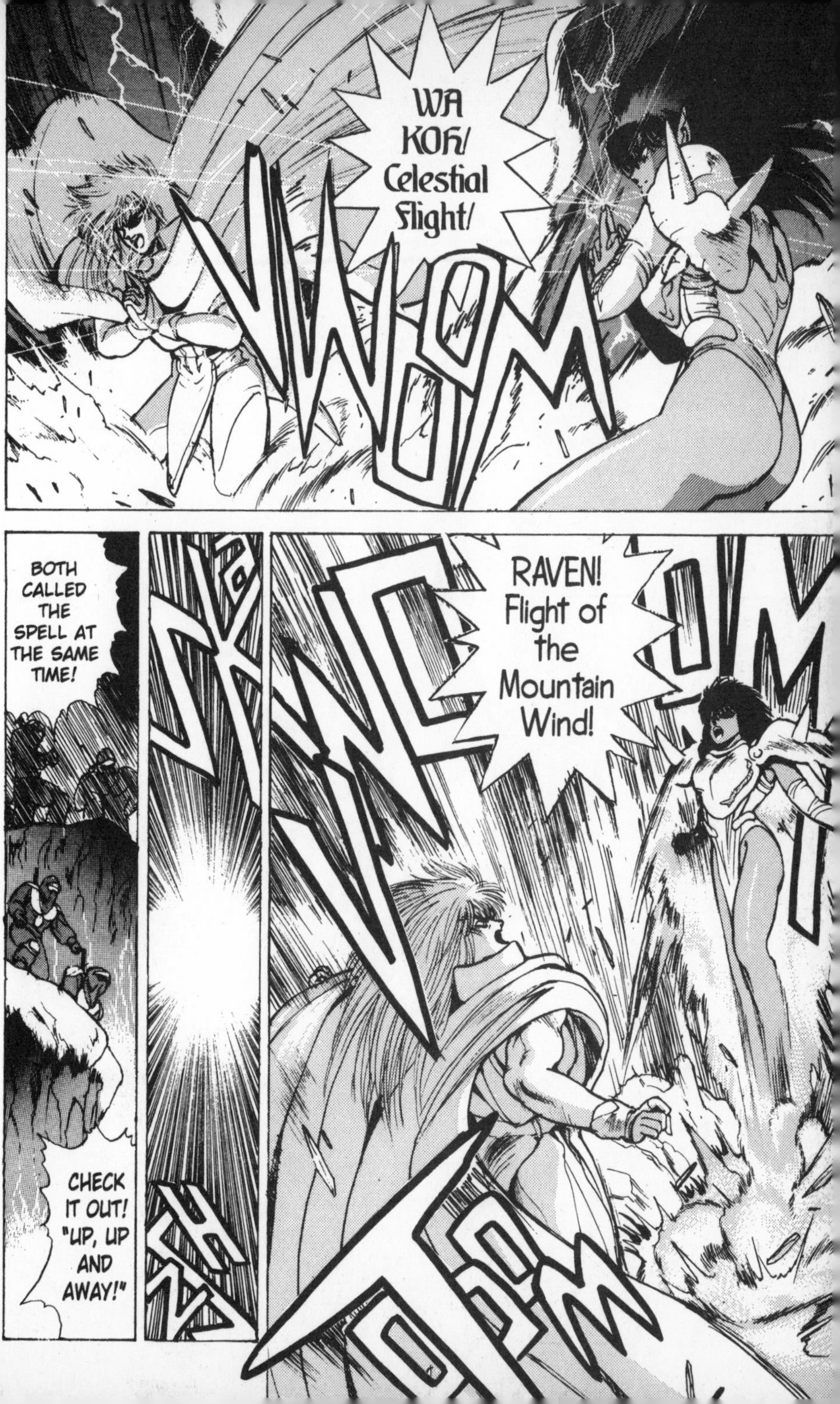
WA KOH! Celestial Flight!
BOTH CALLED THE SPELL AT THE SAME TIME!
CHECK IT OUT! "UP, UP AND AWAY!"
RAVEN! Flight of the Mountain Wind!

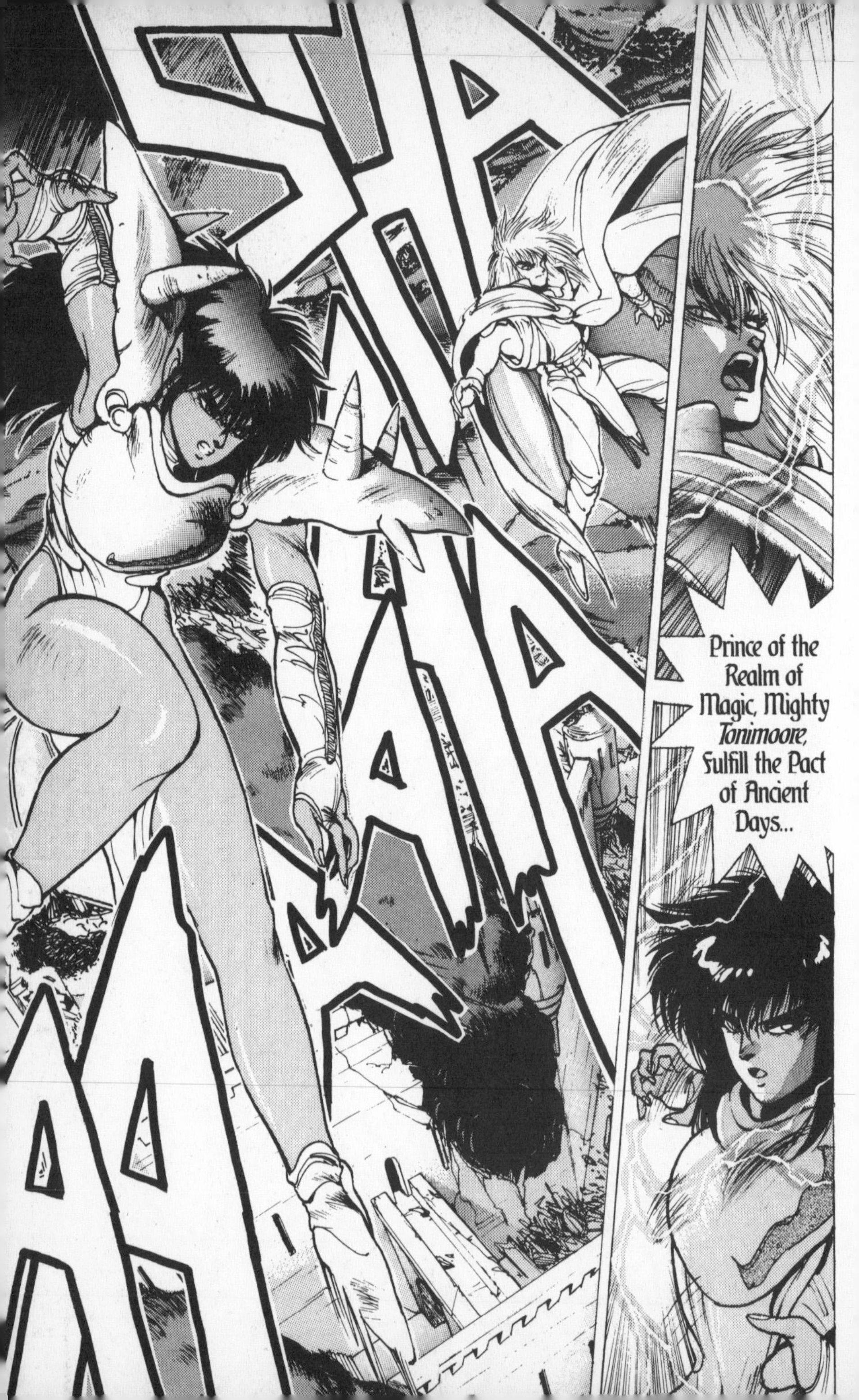
Prince of the Realm of Magic, Mighty *Tonimoore*, Fulfill the Pact of Ancient Days...

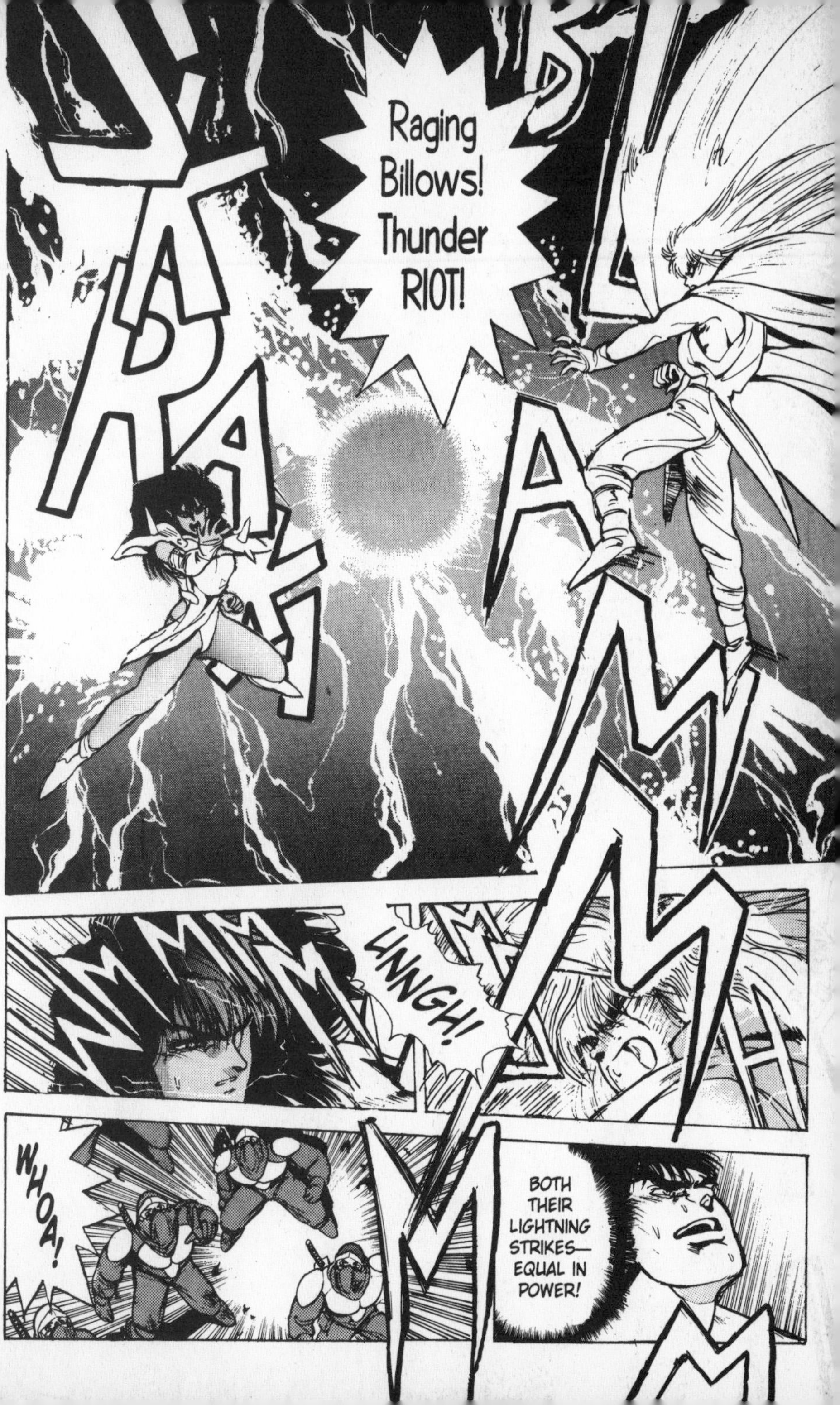
Raging Billows! Thunder RIOT!
UNNGH!
WHOA!
BOTH THEIR LIGHTNING STRIKES— EQUAL IN POWER!

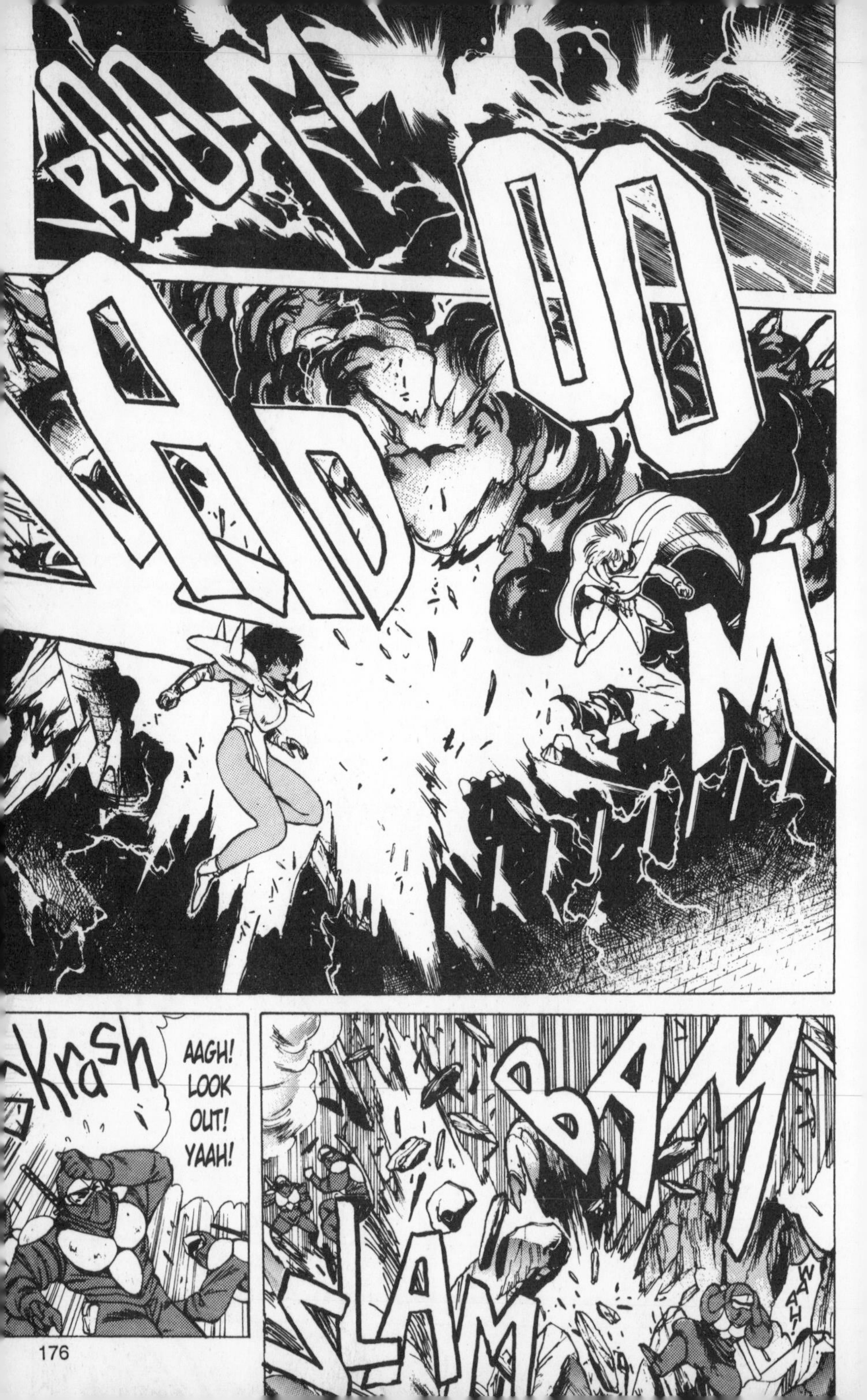
BOOM
BADOOOM
Krash
AAGH! LOOK OUT! YAAH!
BAM
SLAM
WAAH!

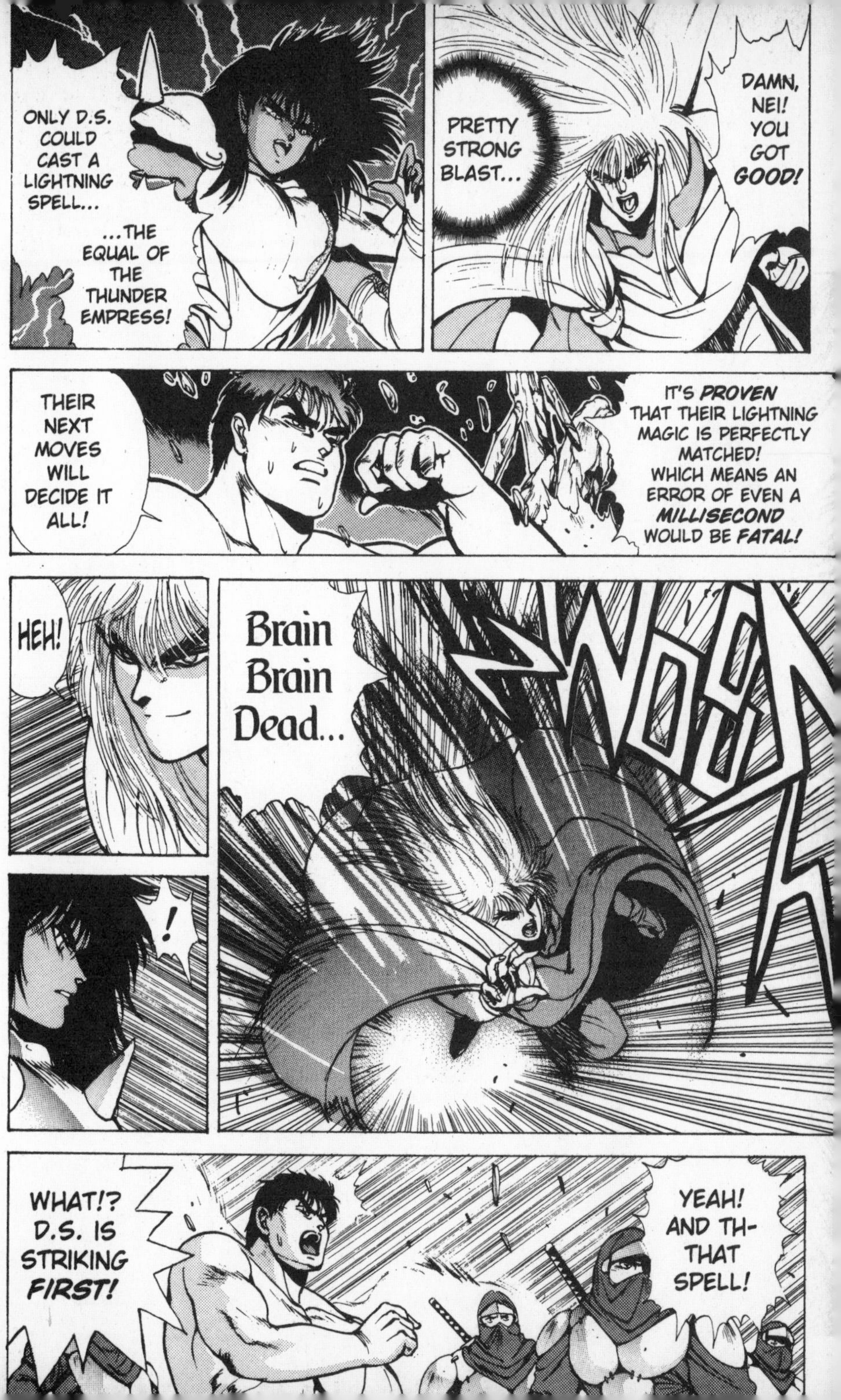
ONLY D.S. COULD CAST A LIGHTNING SPELL...
...THE EQUAL OF THE THUNDER EMPRESS!
PRETTY STRONG BLAST...
DAMN, NEI! YOU GOT GOOD!
THEIR NEXT MOVES WILL DECIDE IT ALL!
IT'S PROVEN THAT THEIR LIGHTNING MAGIC IS PERFECTLY MATCHED! WHICH MEANS AN ERROR OF EVEN A MILLISECOND WOULD BE FATAL!
HEH!
Brain Brain Dead...
!
WHAT!? D.S. IS STRIKING FIRST!
YEAH! AND TH-THAT SPELL!

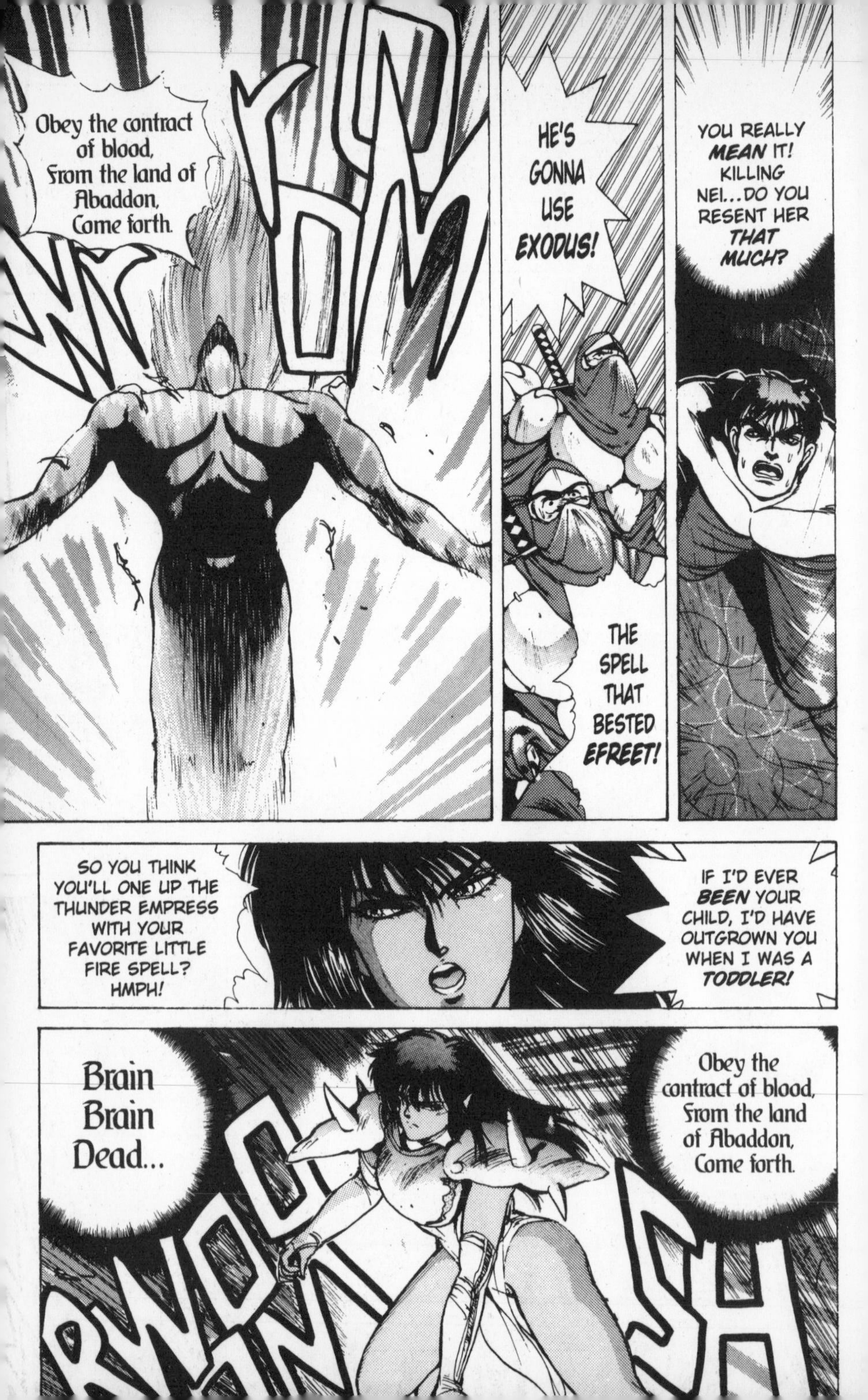
Obey the contract of blood, From the land of Abaddon, Come forth.
VWOM
HE'S GONNA USE EXODUS!
THE SPELL THAT BESTED EFREET!
YOU REALLY MEAN IT! KILLING NEI...DO YOU RESENT HER THAT MUCH?
SO YOU THINK YOU'LL ONE UP THE THUNDER EMPRESS WITH YOUR FAVORITE LITTLE FIRE SPELL? HMPH!
IF I'D EVER BEEN YOUR CHILD, I'D HAVE OUTGROWN YOU WHEN I WAS A TODDLER!
Brain Brain Dead...
Obey the contract of blood, From the land of Abaddon, Come forth.

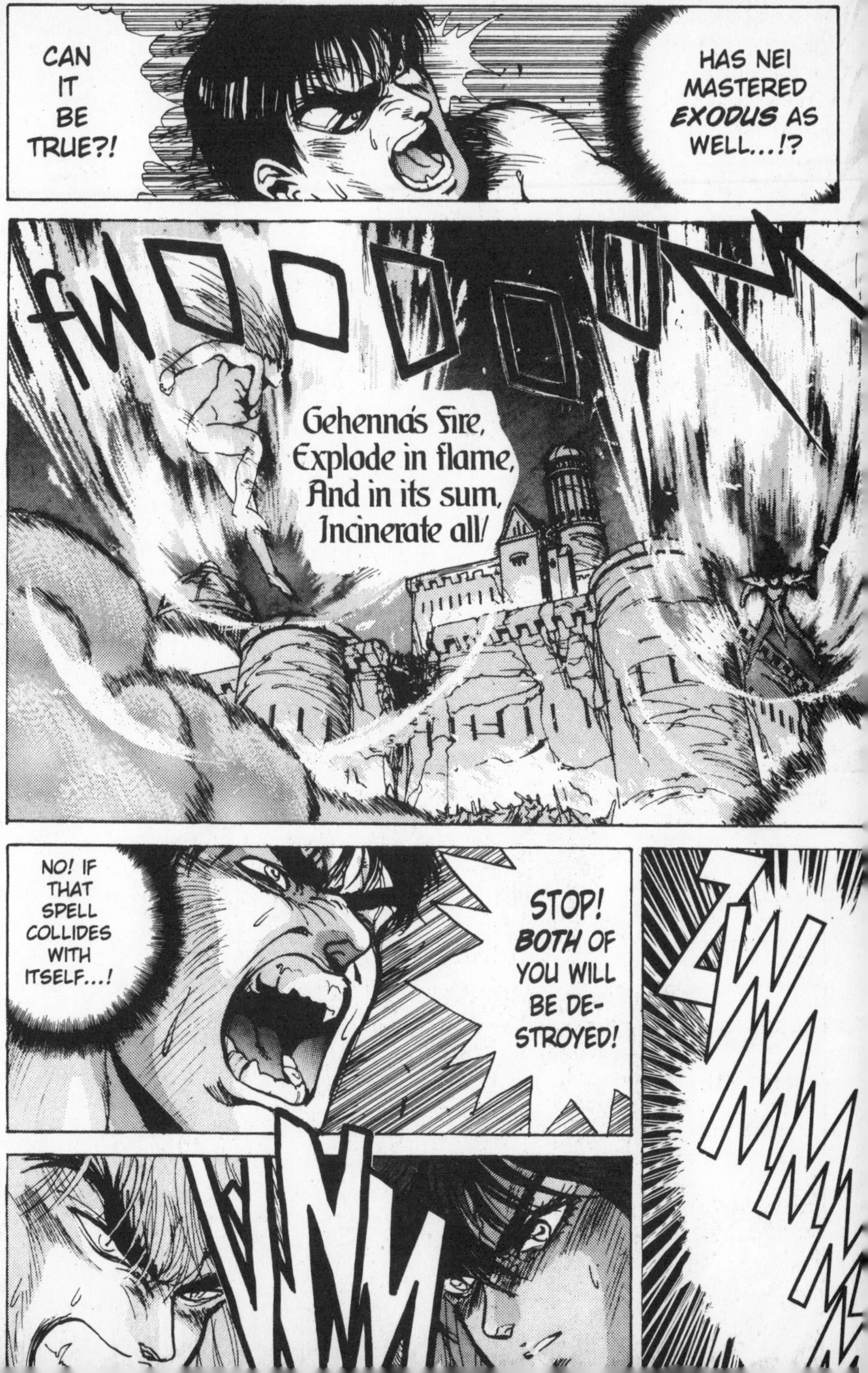
CAN IT BE TRUE?!
HAS NEI MASTERED EXODUS AS WELL...!?
Gehenna's Fire, Explode in flame, And in its sum, Incinerate all!
NO! IF THAT SPELL COLLIDES WITH ITSELF...!
STOP! BOTH OF YOU WILL BE DE-STROYED!

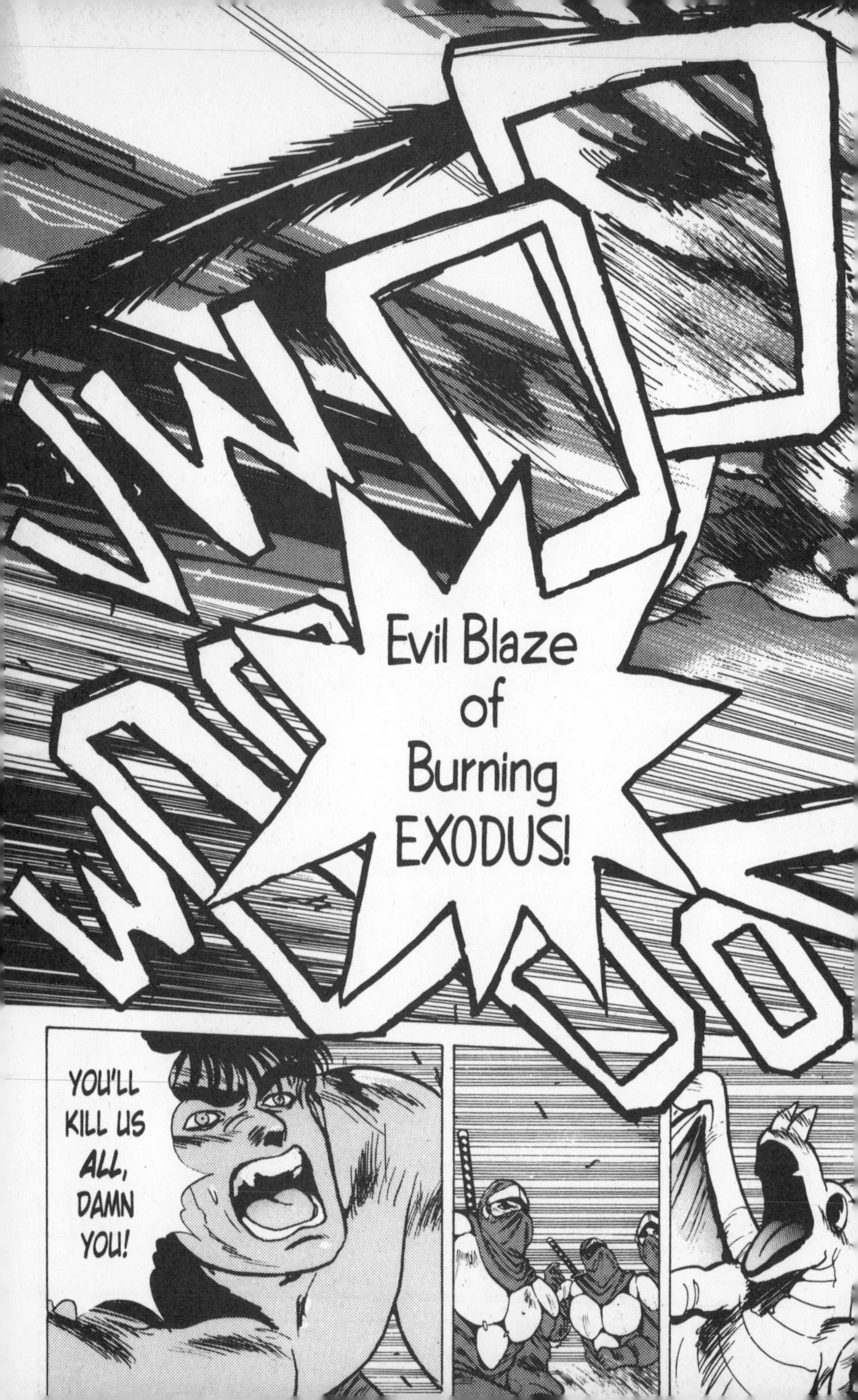
Evil Blaze of Burning EXODUS!
YOU'LL KILL US ALL, DAMN YOU!

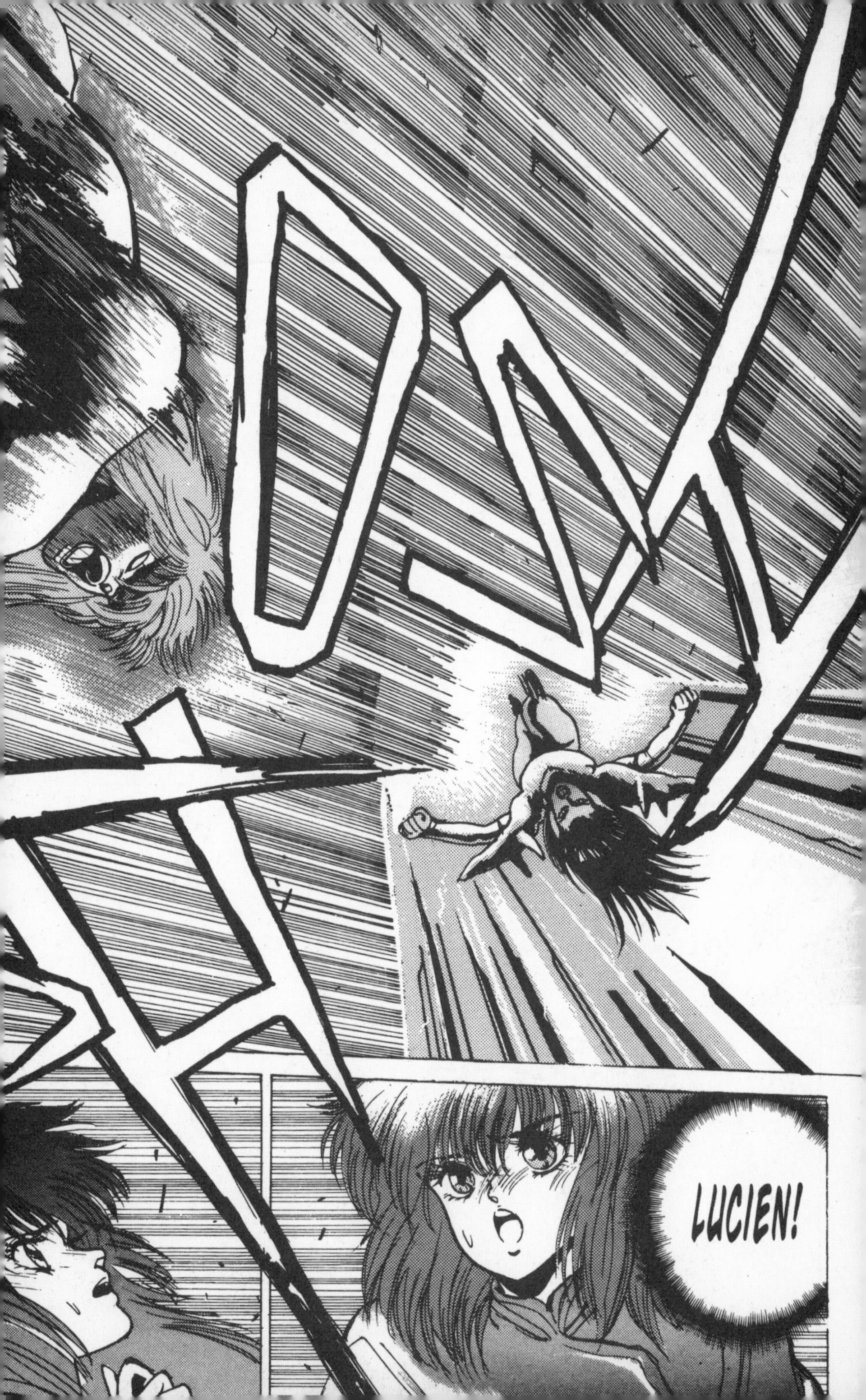
LUCIEN!

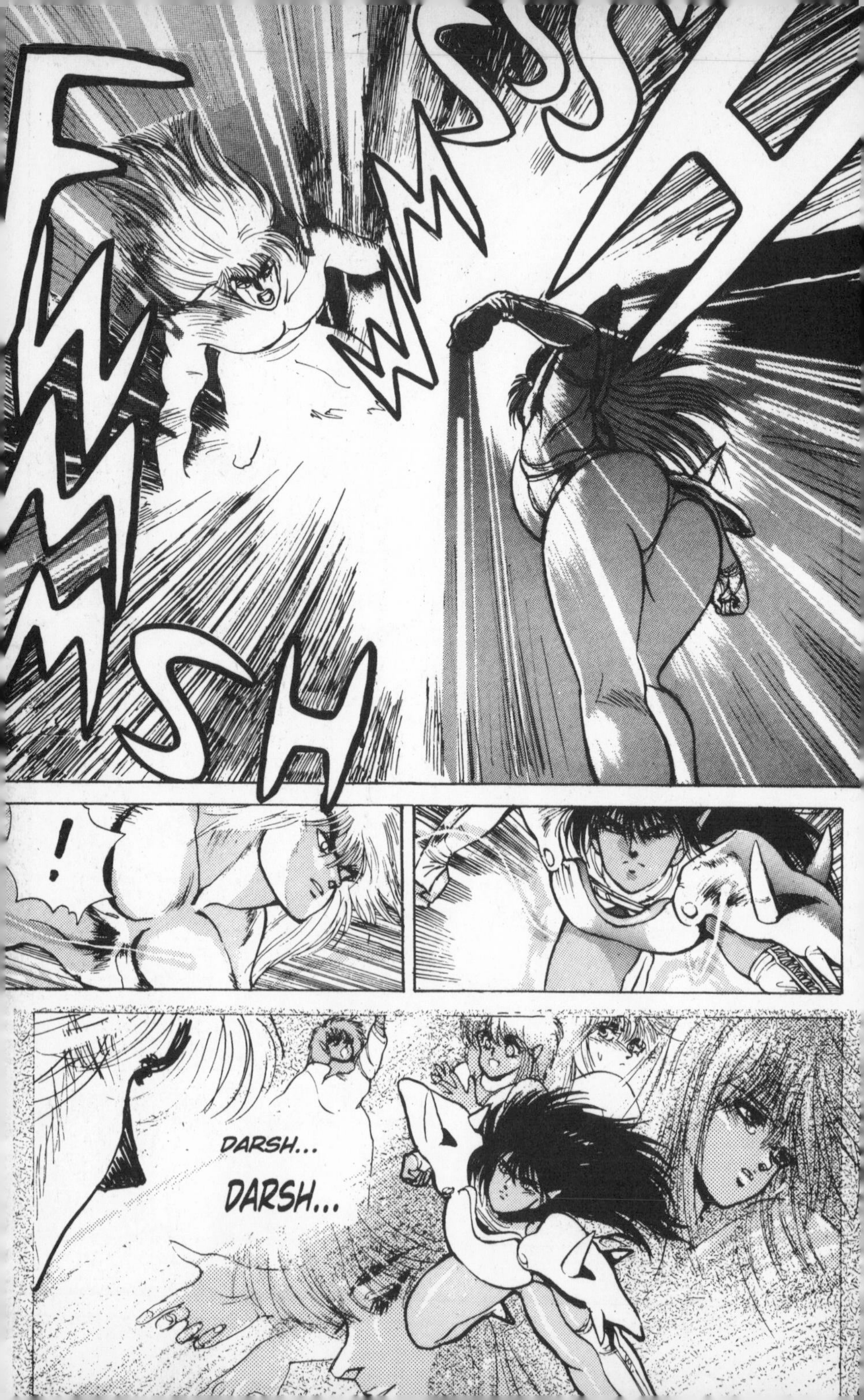
!
DARSH...
DARSH...

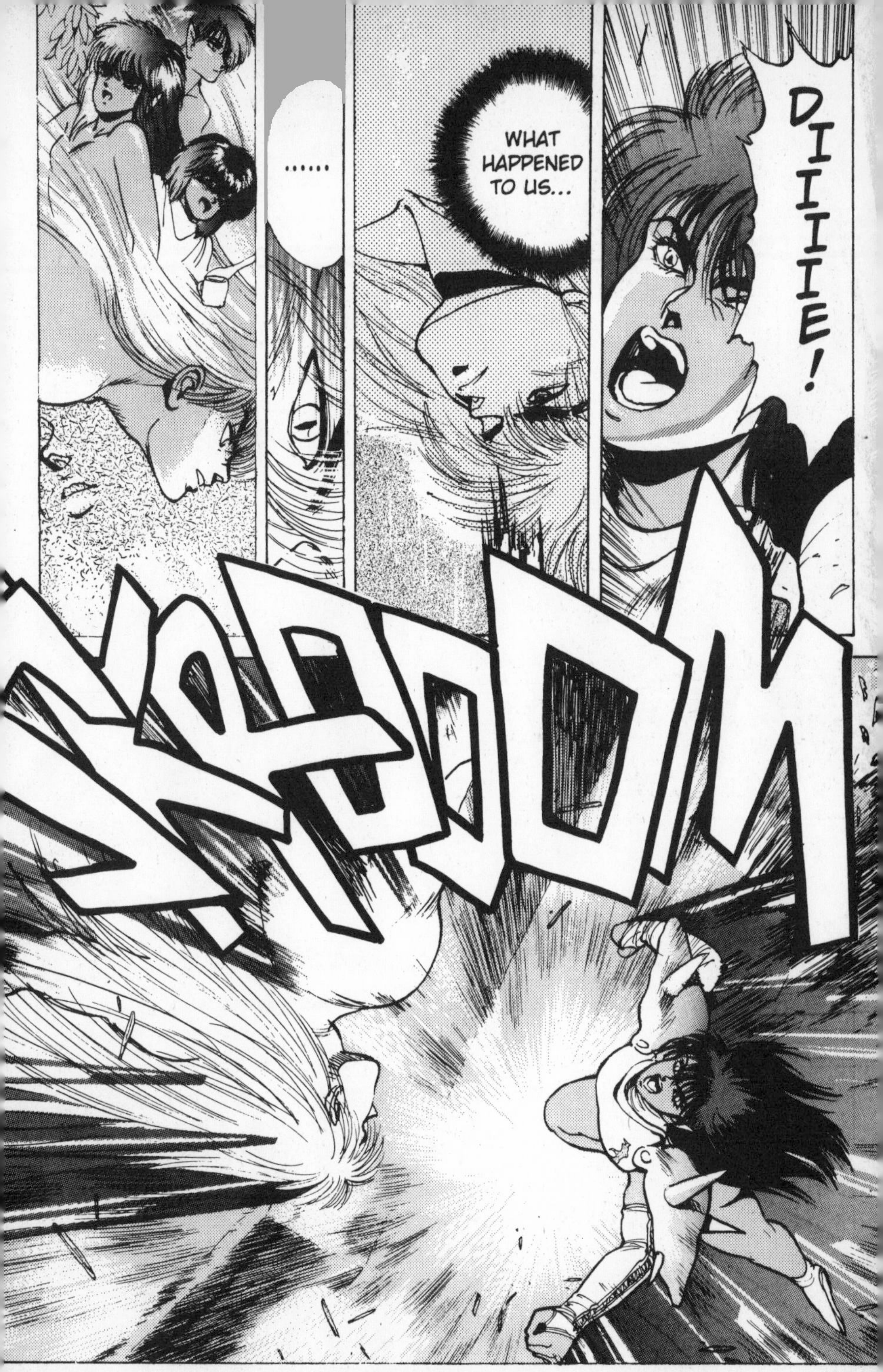
......
WHAT HAPPENED TO US...
DIIIIE!
KABOOM

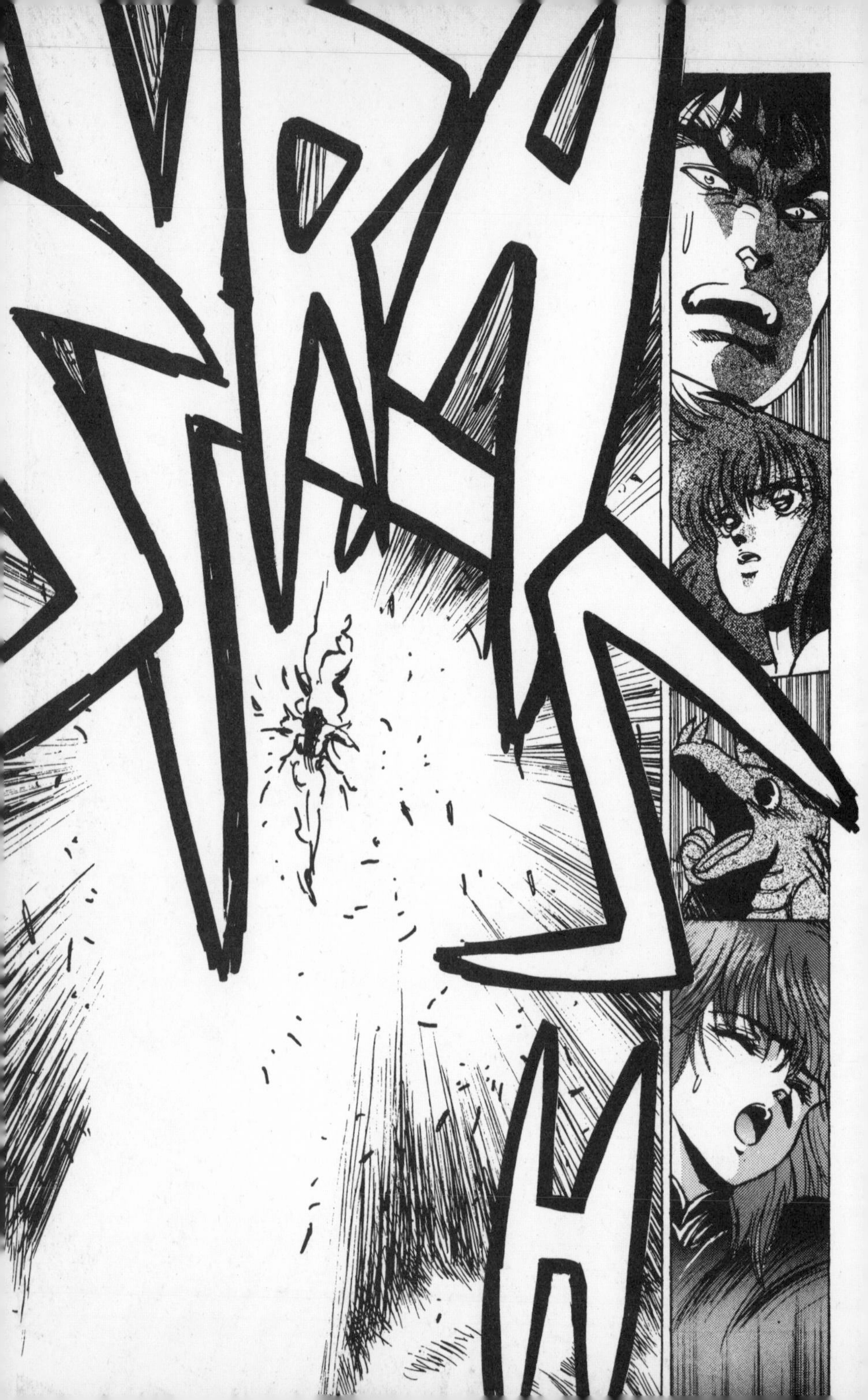

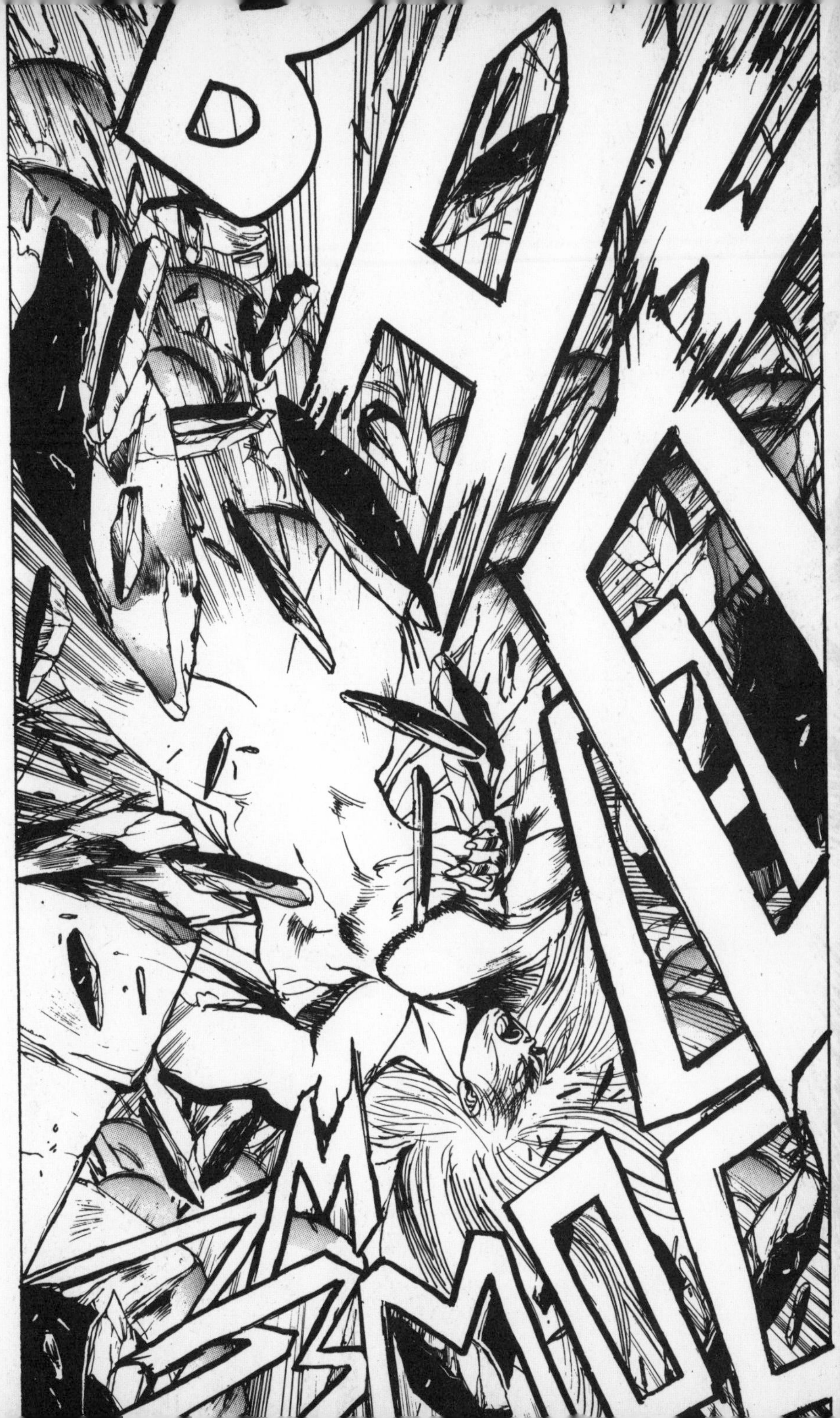

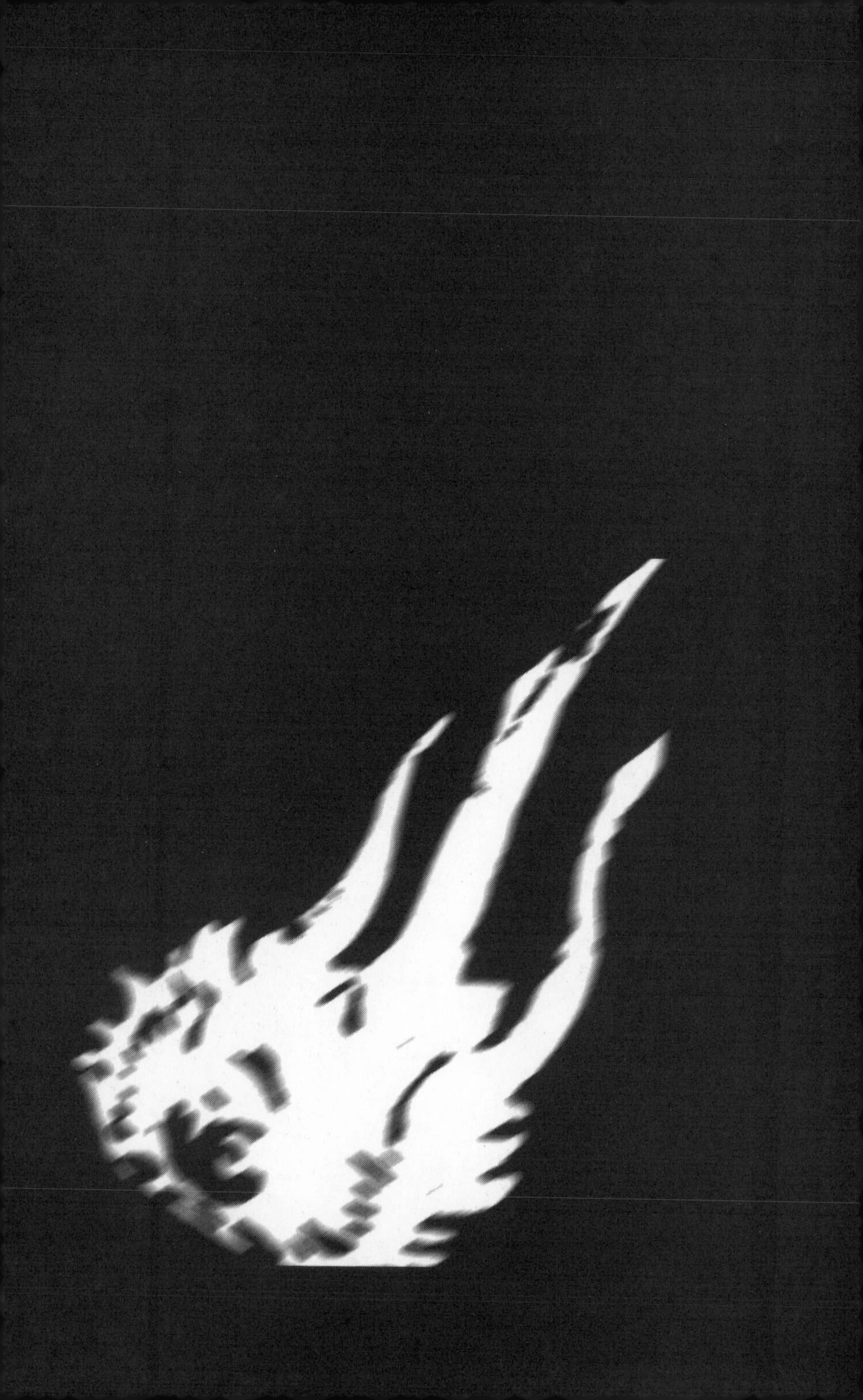

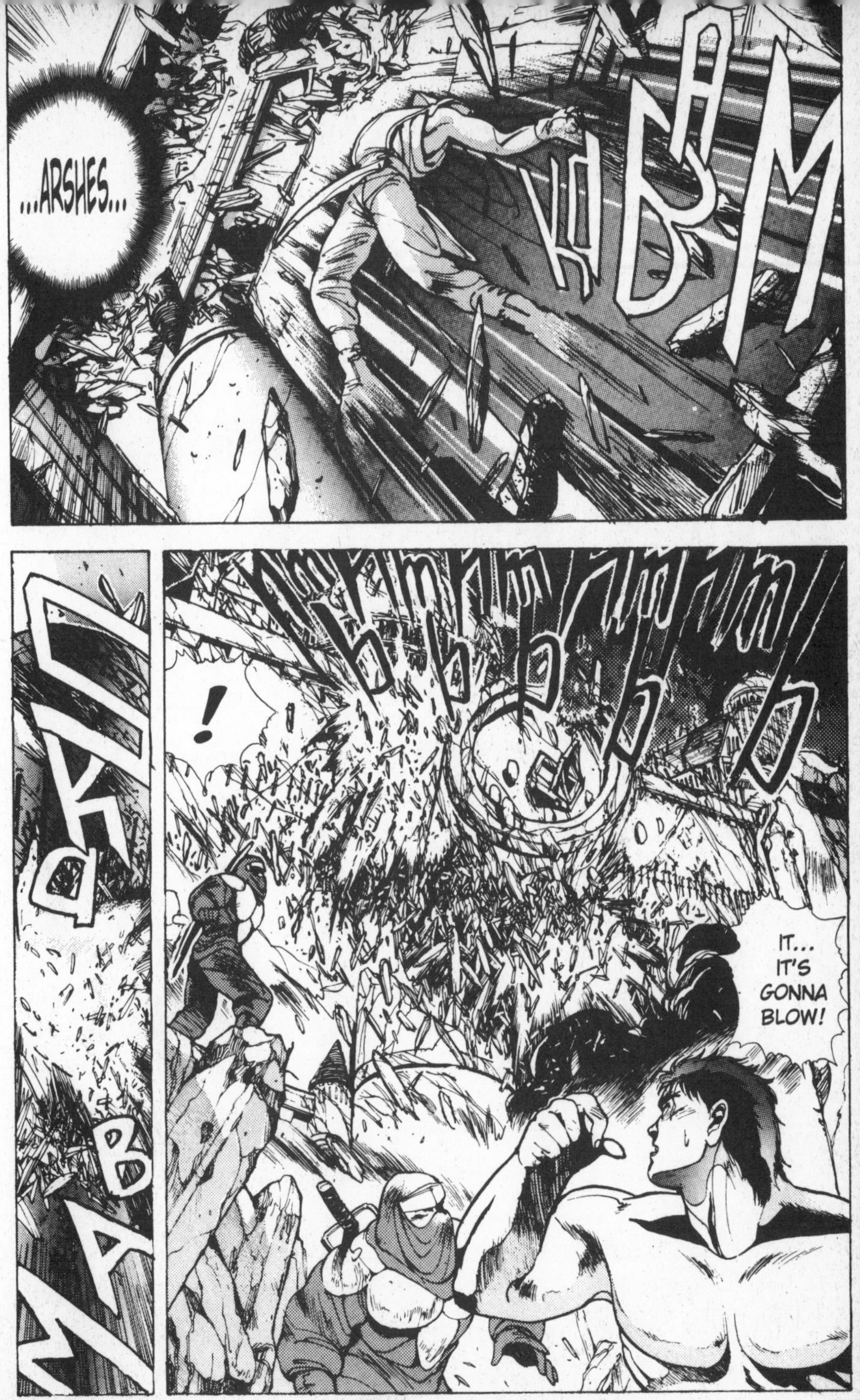
...ARSHES...
!
IT... IT'S GONNA BLOW!

LOOK OUT, D.S.!

!

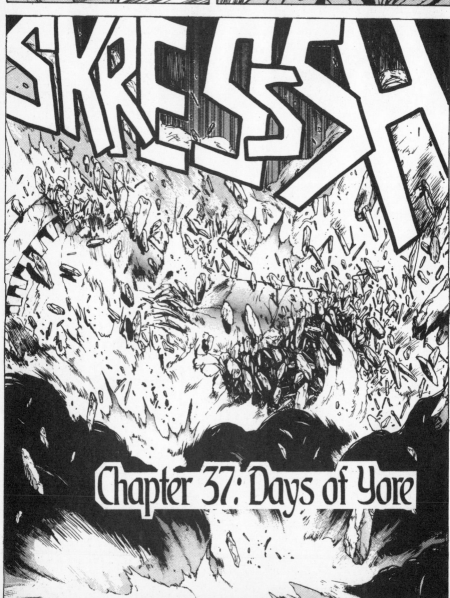

SKRESSSH

Chapter 37: Days of Yore

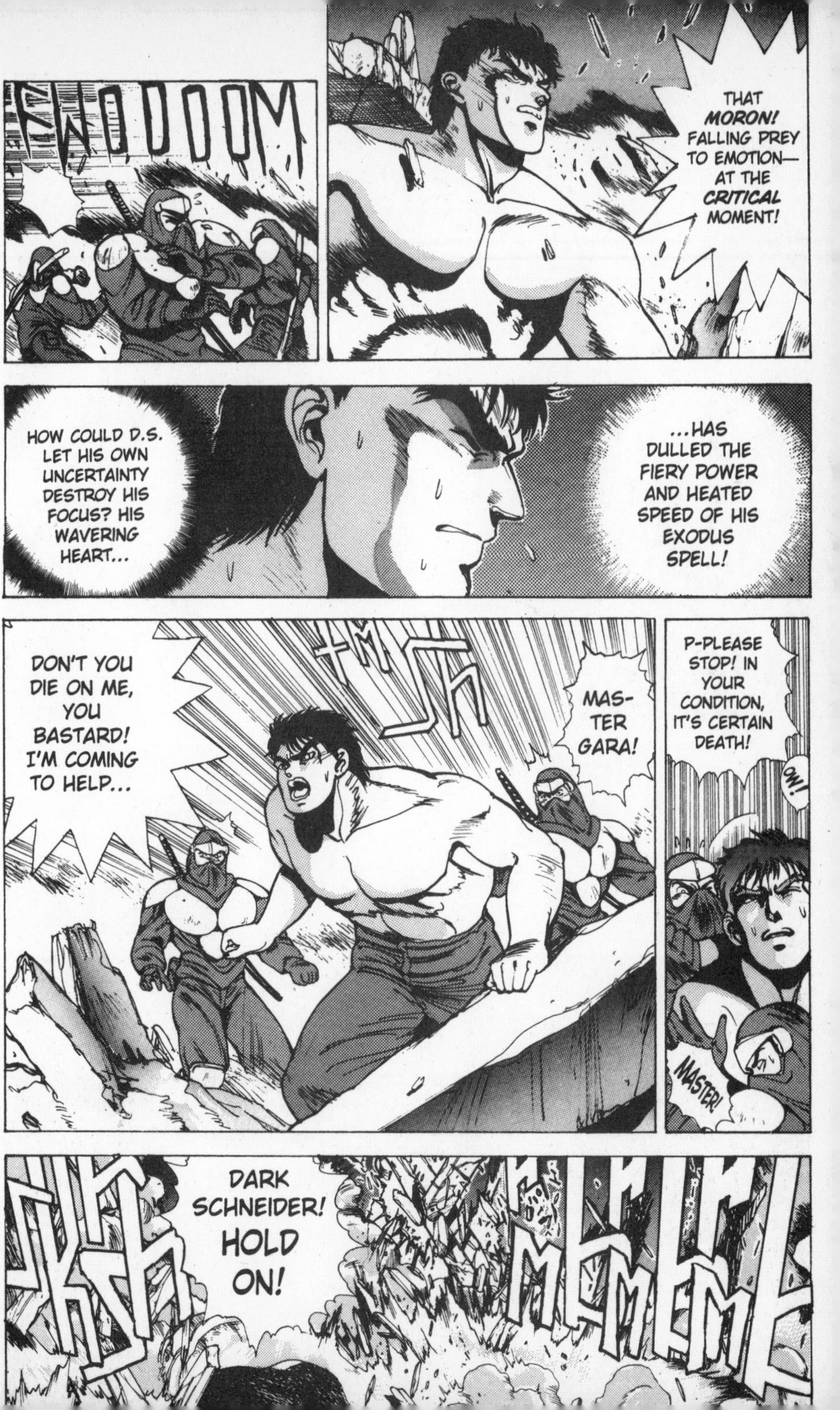
FWOOOOM
THAT MORON! FALLING PREY TO EMOTION— AT THE CRITICAL MOMENT!
HOW COULD D.S. LET HIS OWN UNCERTAINTY DESTROY HIS FOCUS? HIS WAVERING HEART...
...HAS DULLED THE FIERY POWER AND HEATED SPEED OF HIS EXODUS SPELL!
DON'T YOU DIE ON ME, YOU BASTARD! I'M COMING TO HELP...
MAS-TER GARA!
P-PLEASE STOP! IN YOUR CONDITION, IT'S CERTAIN DEATH!
OW!
MASTER!
DARK SCHNEIDER! HOLD ON!

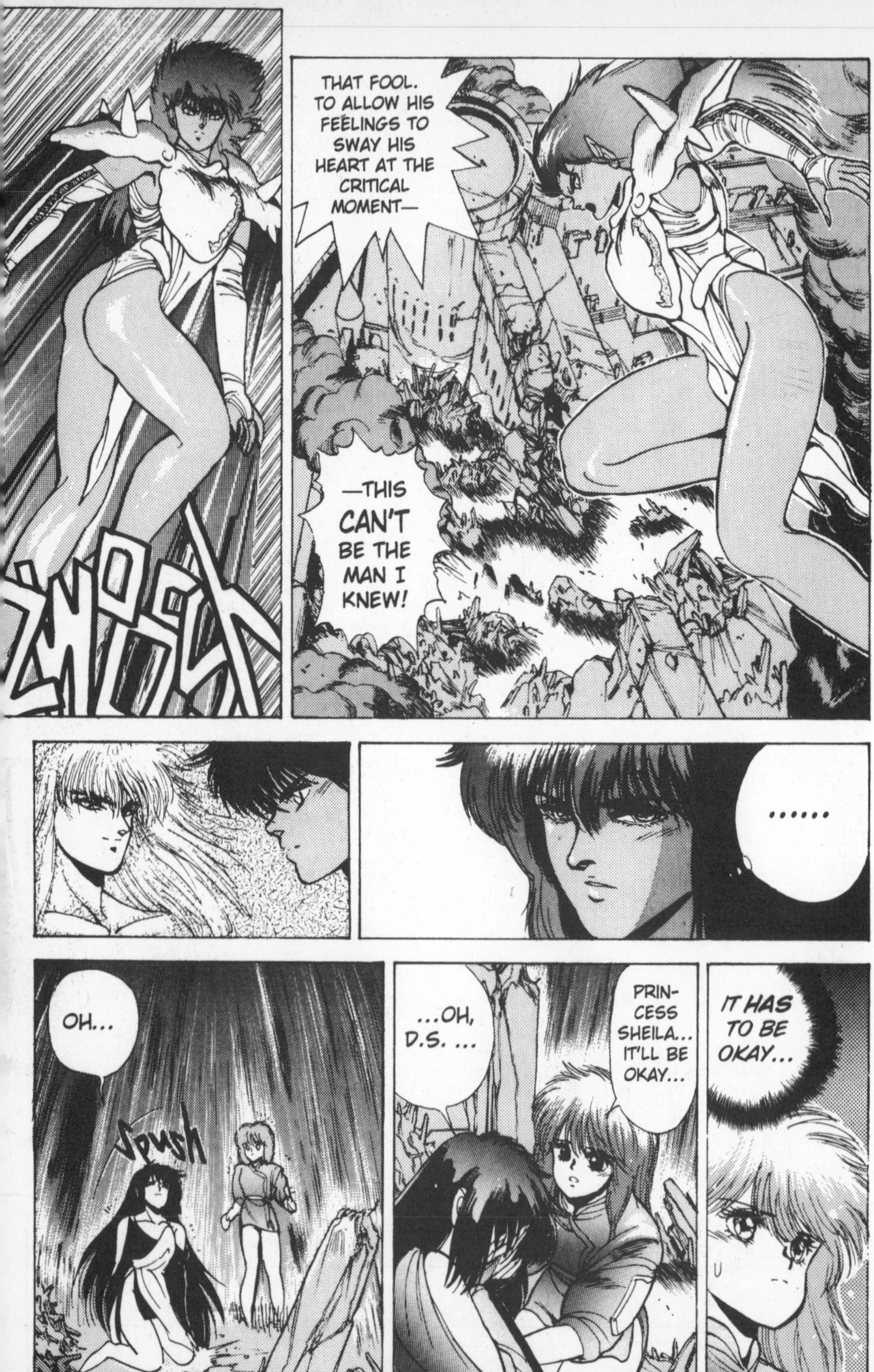
THAT FOOL. TO ALLOW HIS FEELINGS TO SWAY HIS HEART AT THE CRITICAL MOMENT—
—THIS CAN'T BE THE MAN I KNEW!
......
OH...
Spush
...OH, D.S. ...
PRIN-CESS SHEILA... IT'LL BE OKAY...
IT HAS TO BE OKAY...

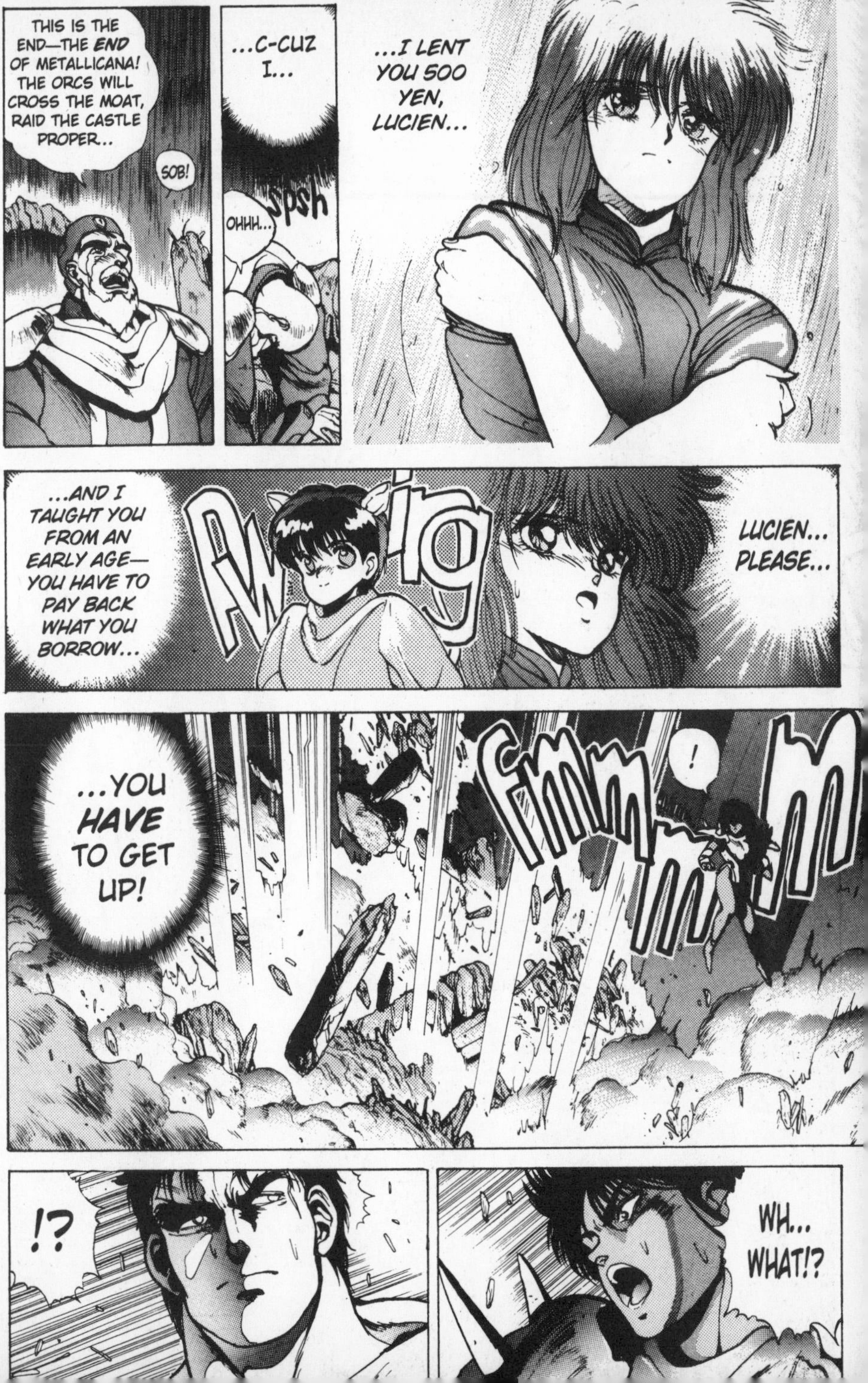
THIS IS THE END—THE END OF METALLICANA! THE ORCS WILL CROSS THE MOAT, RAID THE CASTLE PROPER...
SOB!
...C-CUZ I...
OHHH...
spsh
...I LENT YOU 500 YEN, LUCIEN...
...AND I TAUGHT YOU FROM AN EARLY AGE—YOU HAVE TO PAY BACK WHAT YOU BORROW...
LUCIEN... PLEASE...
...YOU HAVE TO GET UP!
!
!?
WH... WHAT!?

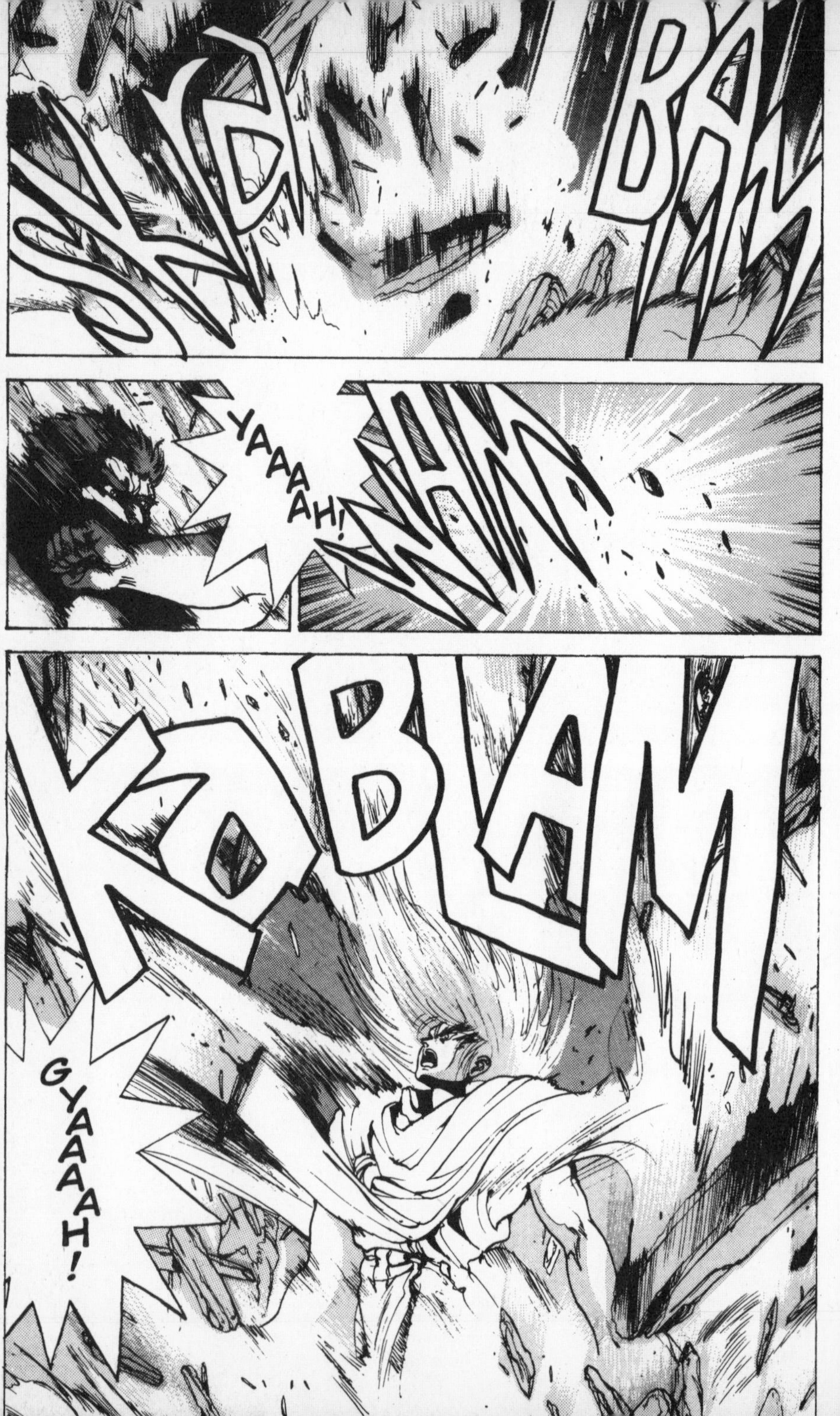
YAAAAAH!
KABLAM
GYAAAAAH!

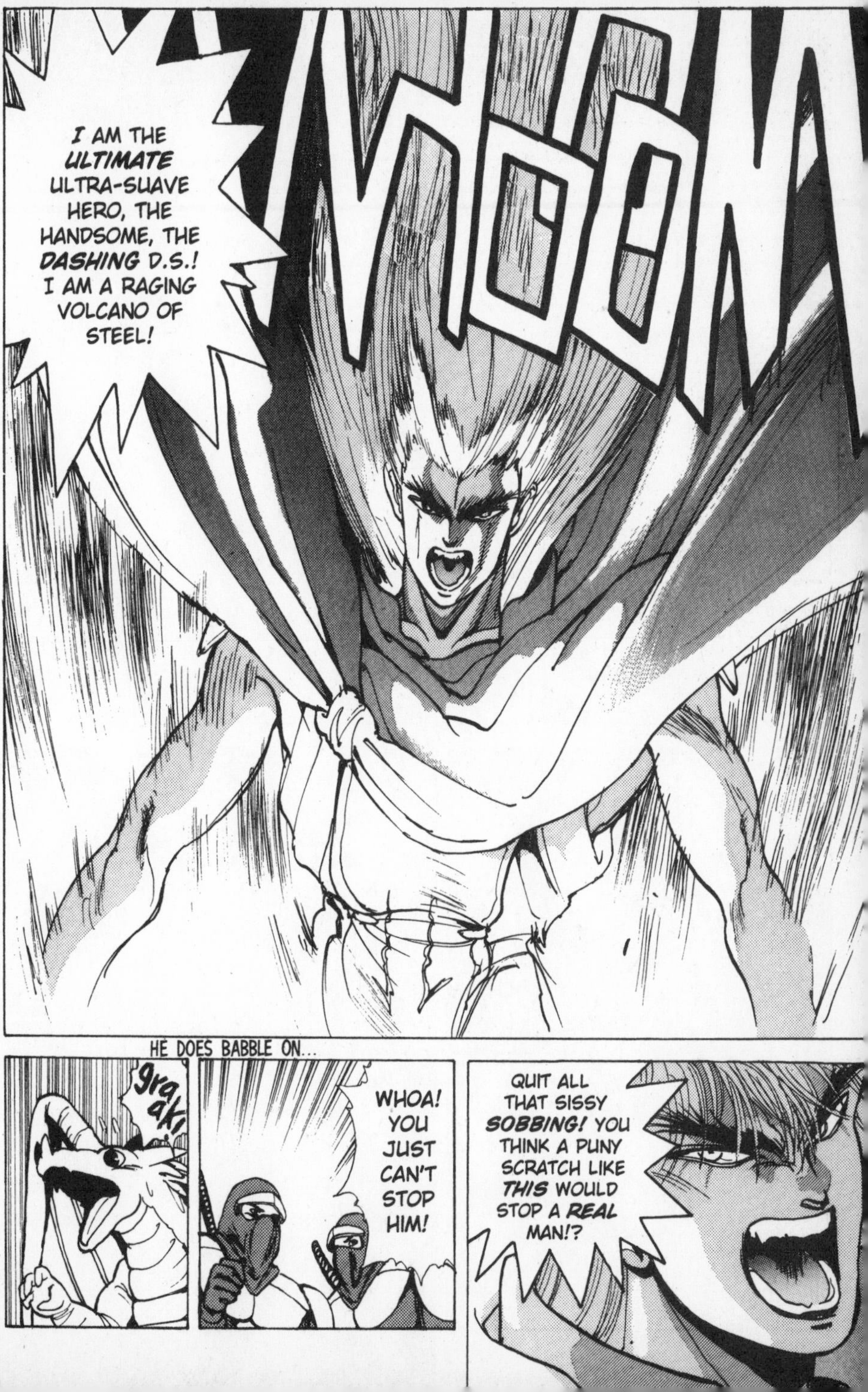
I AM THE ULTIMATE ULTRA-SUAVE HERO, THE HANDSOME, THE DASHING D.S.! I AM A RAGING VOLCANO OF STEEL!
VOOOM
HE DOES BABBLE ON...
gra aki
WHOA! YOU JUST CAN'T STOP HIM!
QUIT ALL THAT SISSY SOBBING! YOU THINK A PUNY SCRATCH LIKE THIS WOULD STOP A REAL MAN!?

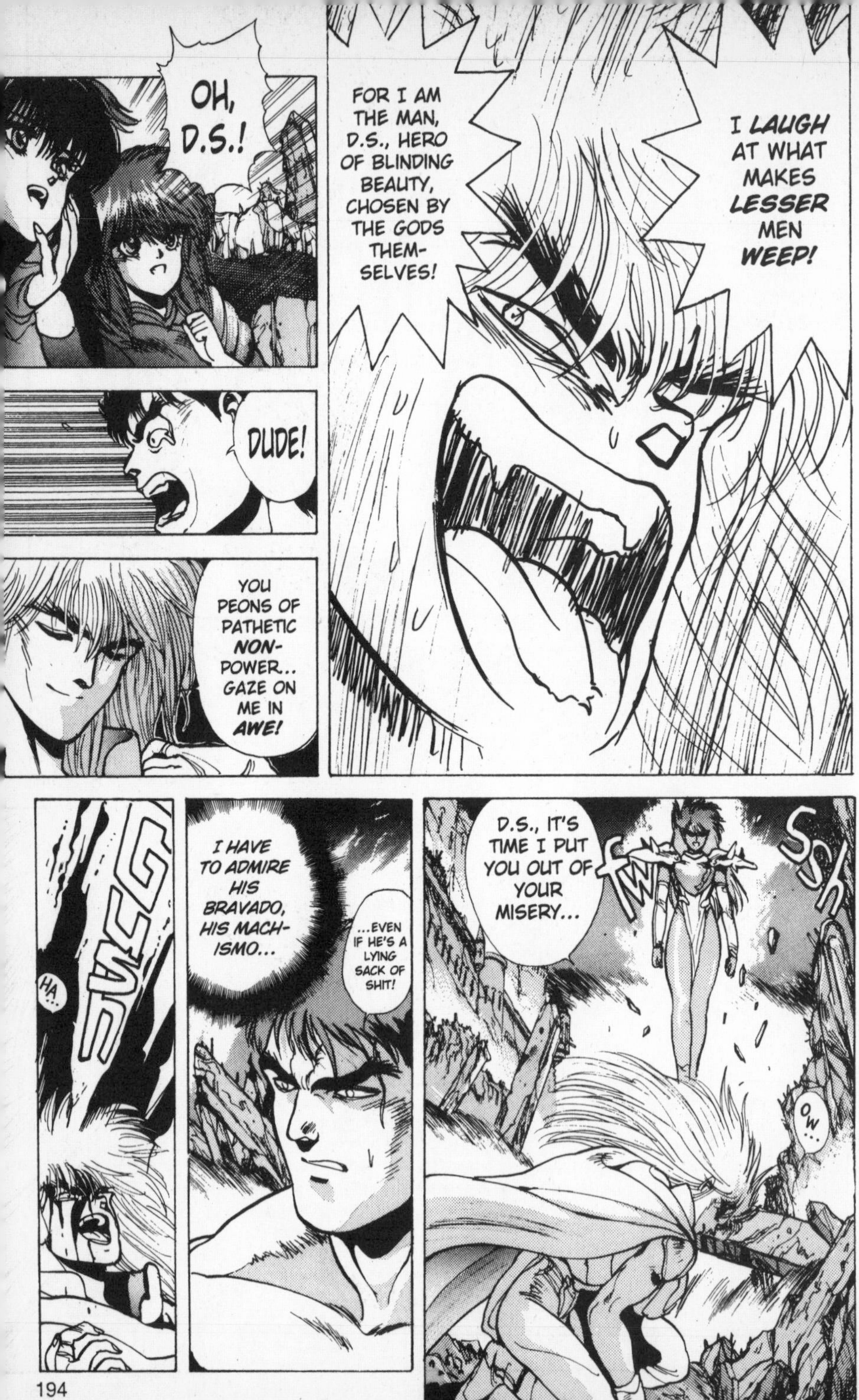
OH, D.S.!
DUDE!
YOU PEONS OF PATHETIC NON-POWER... GAZE ON ME IN AWE!
FOR I AM THE MAN, D.S., HERO OF BLINDING BEAUTY, CHOSEN BY THE GODS THEM-SELVES!
I LAUGH AT WHAT MAKES LESSER MEN WEEP!
GUSH
HA...
I HAVE TO ADMIRE HIS BRAVADO, HIS MACH-ISMO...
...EVEN IF HE'S A LYING SACK OF SHIT!
D.S., IT'S TIME I PUT YOU OUT OF YOUR MISERY...
fw
ssh
OW...

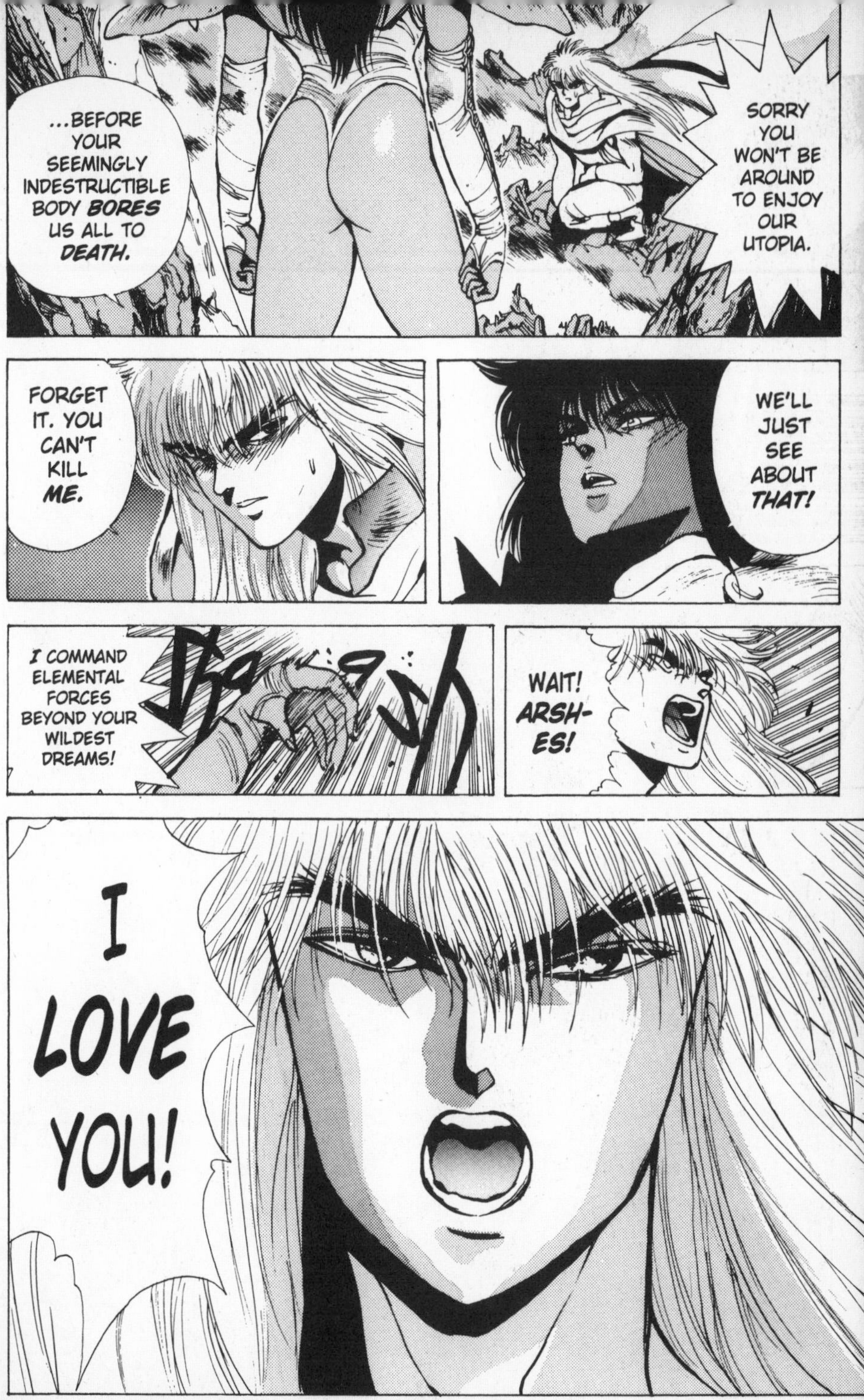
...BEFORE YOUR SEEMINGLY INDESTRUCTIBLE BODY BORES US ALL TO DEATH.
SORRY YOU WON'T BE AROUND TO ENJOY OUR UTOPIA.
FORGET IT. YOU CAN'T KILL ME.
WE'LL JUST SEE ABOUT THAT!
I COMMAND ELEMENTAL FORCES BEYOND YOUR WILDEST DREAMS!
WAIT! ARSH-ES!
I LOVE YOU!

BA-BUMP

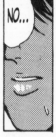

NO...

SH-SHUT UP! *YOU* LOVE EVERY DAMN THING THAT MOVES!

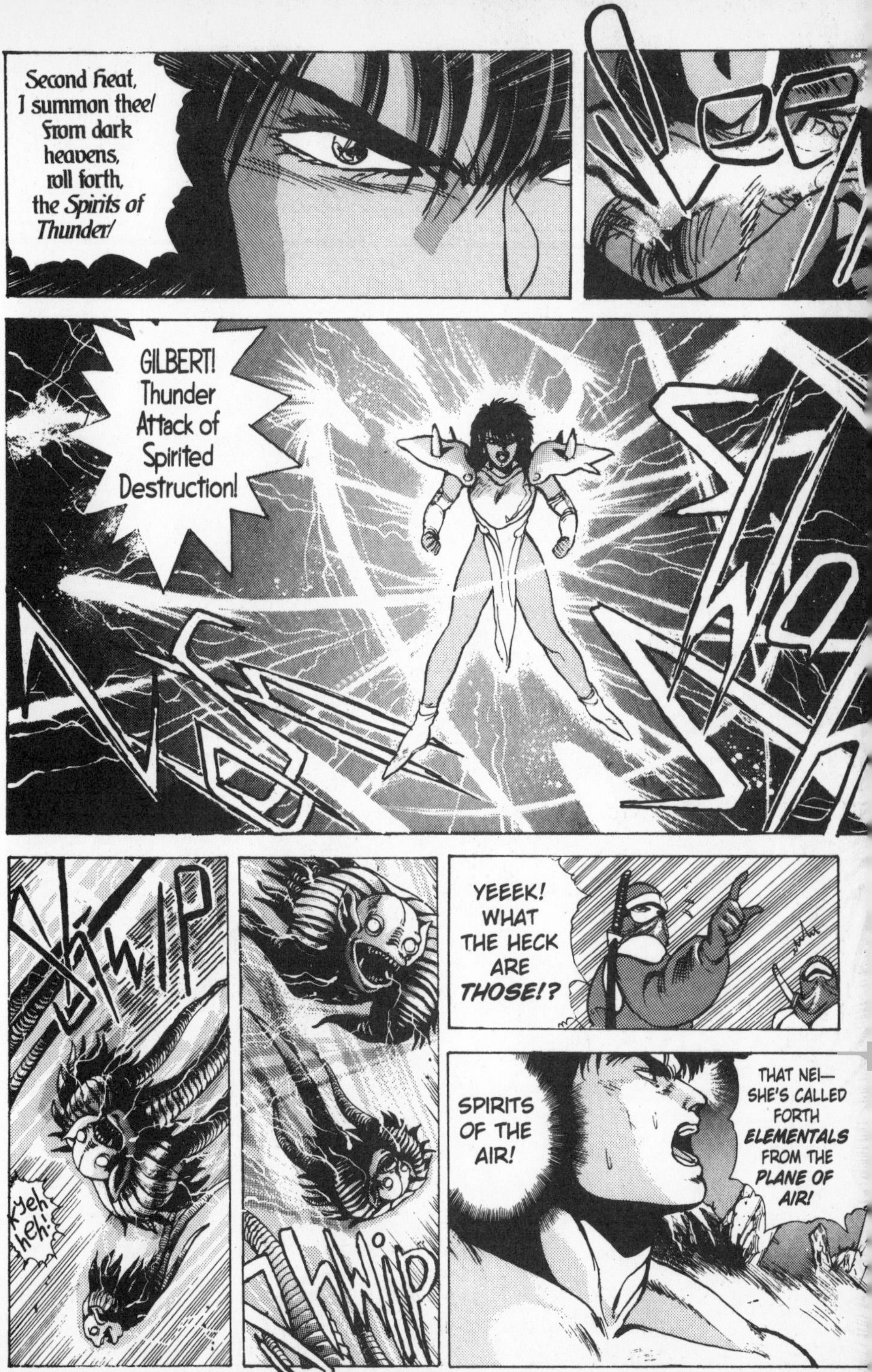
Second Heat, I summon thee! From dark heavens, roll forth, the *Spirits of Thunder!*
GILBERT! Thunder Attack of Spirited Destruction!
Kyeh heh!
YEEEK! WHAT THE HECK ARE *THOSE!?*
SPIRITS OF THE AIR!
THAT NEI— SHE'S CALLED FORTH *ELEMENTALS* FROM THE *PLANE OF AIR!*

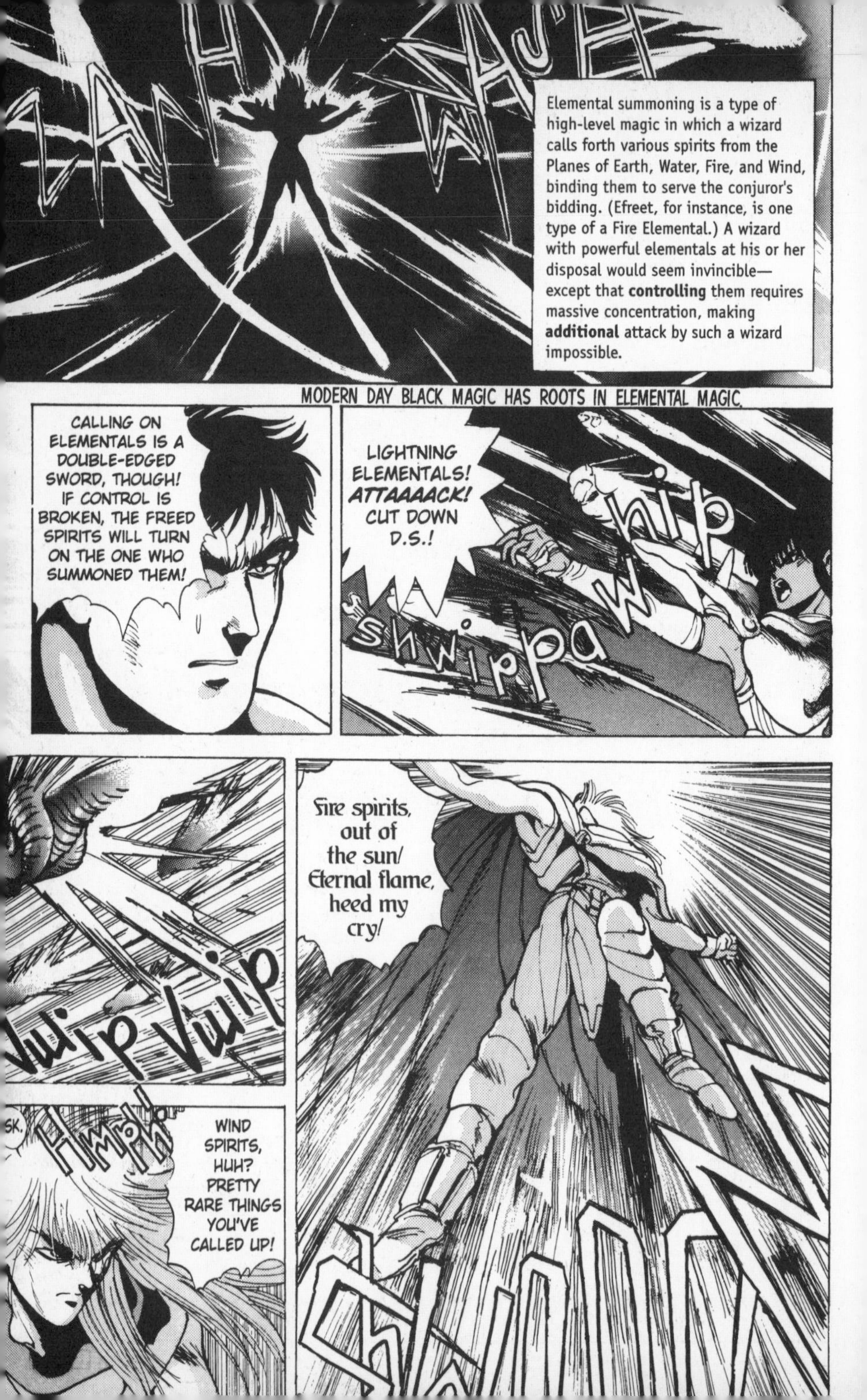
Elemental summoning is a type of high-level magic in which a wizard calls forth various spirits from the Planes of Earth, Water, Fire, and Wind, binding them to serve the conjuror's bidding. (Efreet, for instance, is one type of a Fire Elemental.) A wizard with powerful elementals at his or her disposal would seem invincible—except that **controlling** them requires massive concentration, making **additional** attack by such a wizard impossible.
MODERN DAY BLACK MAGIC HAS ROOTS IN ELEMENTAL MAGIC.
CALLING ON ELEMENTALS IS A DOUBLE-EDGED SWORD, THOUGH! IF CONTROL IS BROKEN, THE FREED SPIRITS WILL TURN ON THE ONE WHO SUMMONED THEM!
LIGHTNING ELEMENTALS! *ATTAAAACK!* CUT DOWN D.S.!
whip
shwippa
Vuip Vuip
Fire spirits, out of the sun! Eternal flame, heed my cry!
SK.
Hmph
WIND SPIRITS, HUH? PRETTY RARE THINGS YOU'VE CALLED UP!

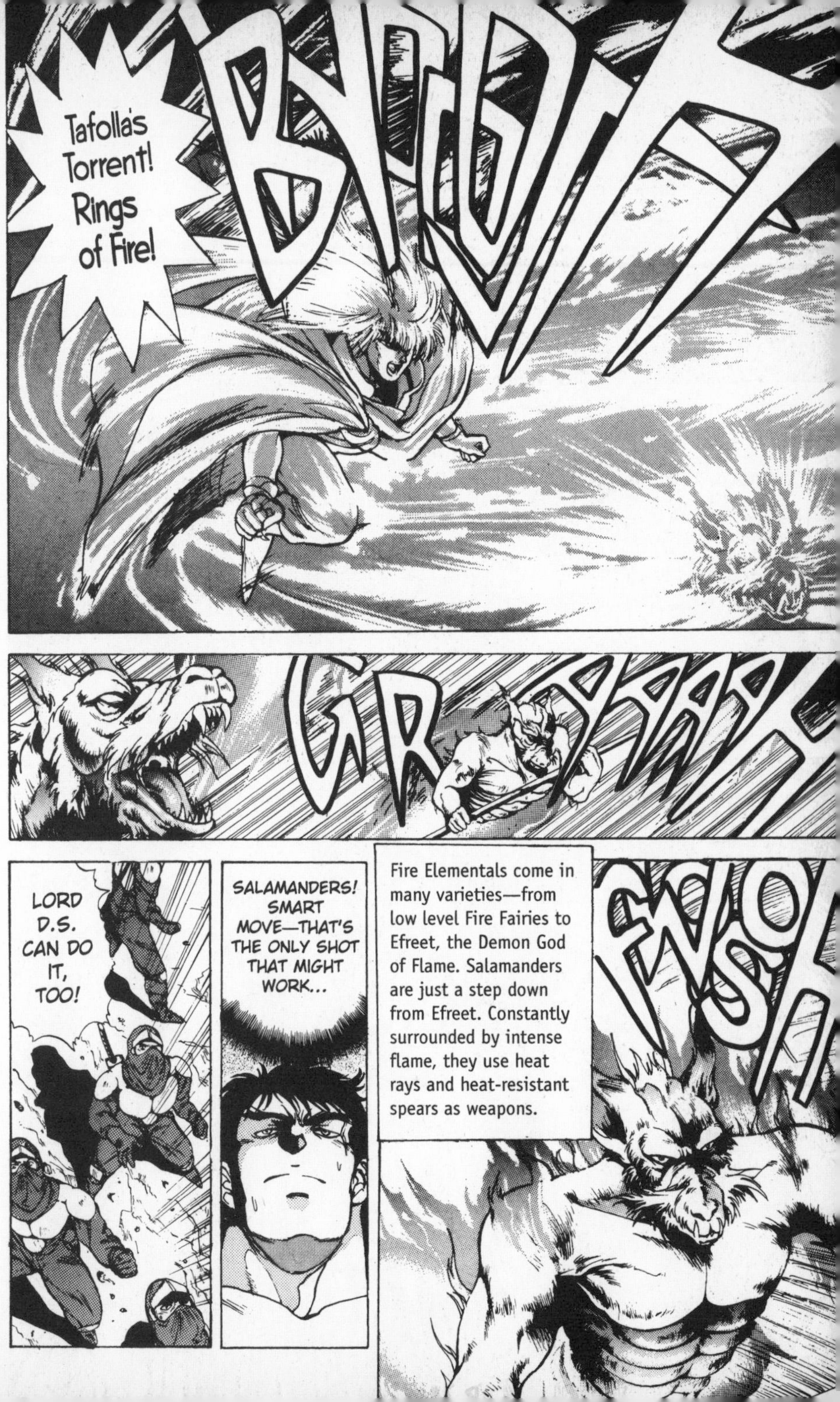
Tafolla's Torrent! Rings of Fire!
LORD D.S. CAN DO IT, TOO!
SALAMANDERS! SMART MOVE—THAT'S THE ONLY SHOT THAT MIGHT WORK...
Fire Elementals come in many varieties—from low level Fire Fairies to Efreet, the Demon God of Flame. Salamanders are just a step down from Efreet. Constantly surrounded by intense flame, they use heat rays and heat-resistant spears as weapons.

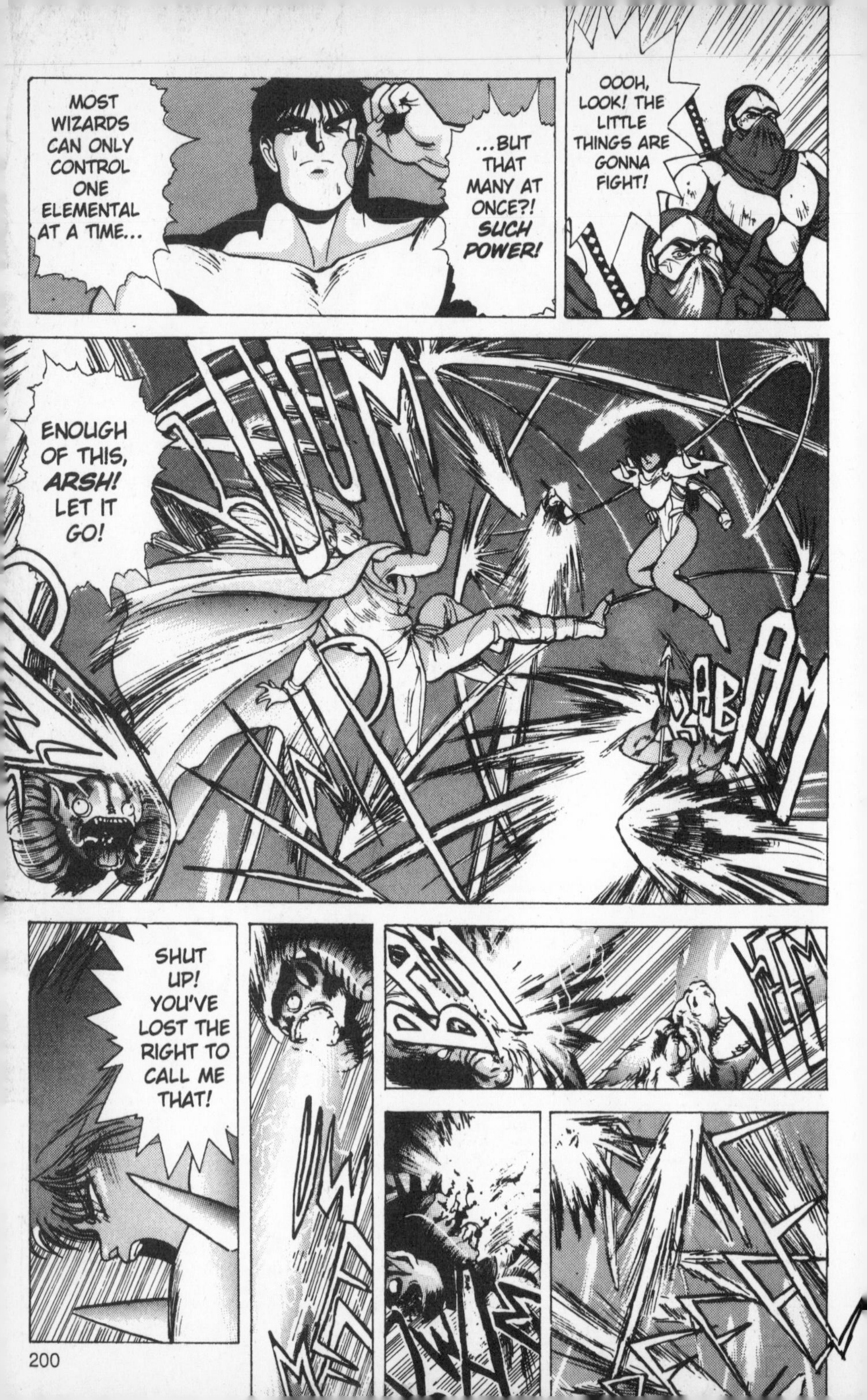
MOST WIZARDS CAN ONLY CONTROL ONE ELEMENTAL AT A TIME...
...BUT THAT MANY AT ONCE?! SUCH POWER!
OOOH, LOOK! THE LITTLE THINGS ARE GONNA FIGHT!
ENOUGH OF THIS, ARSH! LET IT GO!
KABAM
SHUT UP! YOU'VE LOST THE RIGHT TO CALL ME THAT!

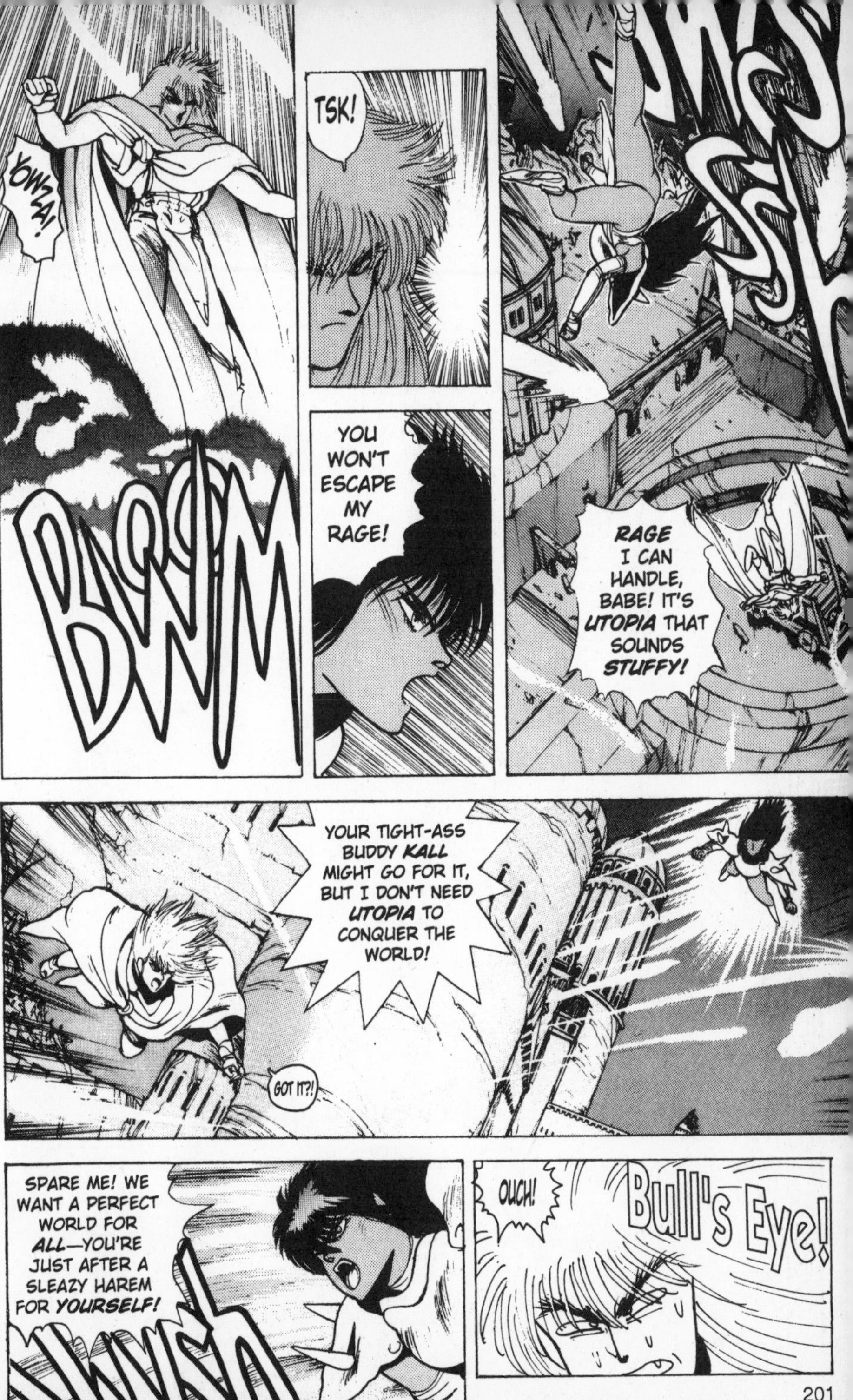
YOWZA!
BLOOM
TSK!
YOU WON'T ESCAPE MY RAGE!
RAGE I CAN HANDLE, BABE! IT'S UTOPIA THAT SOUNDS STUFFY!
YOUR TIGHT-ASS BUDDY KALL MIGHT GO FOR IT, BUT I DON'T NEED UTOPIA TO CONQUER THE WORLD!
GOT IT?!
SPARE ME! WE WANT A PERFECT WORLD FOR ALL—YOU'RE JUST AFTER A SLEAZY HAREM FOR YOURSELF!
OUCH!
Bull's Eye!

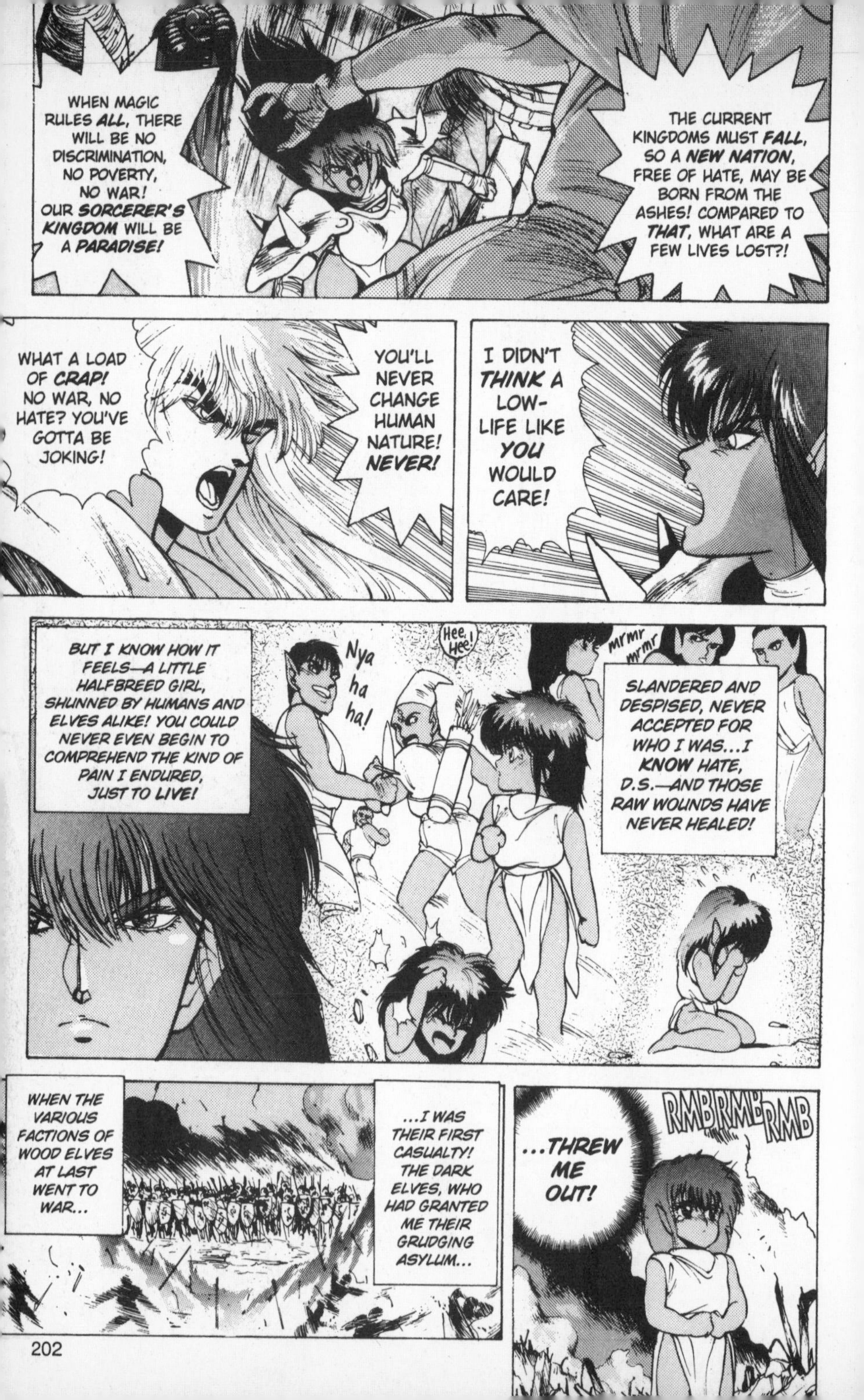

WHEN MAGIC RULES *ALL*, THERE WILL BE NO DISCRIMINATION, NO POVERTY, NO WAR! OUR *SORCERER'S KINGDOM* WILL BE A *PARADISE!*
THE CURRENT KINGDOMS MUST *FALL*, SO A *NEW NATION*, FREE OF HATE, MAY BE BORN FROM THE ASHES! COMPARED TO *THAT*, WHAT ARE A FEW LIVES LOST?!
WHAT A LOAD OF *CRAP!* NO WAR, NO HATE? YOU'VE GOTTA BE JOKING!
YOU'LL NEVER CHANGE HUMAN NATURE! *NEVER!*
I DIDN'T *THINK* A LOW-LIFE LIKE *YOU* WOULD CARE!
BUT I KNOW HOW IT FEELS—A LITTLE HALFBREED GIRL, SHUNNED BY HUMANS AND ELVES ALIKE! YOU COULD NEVER EVEN BEGIN TO COMPREHEND THE KIND OF PAIN I ENDURED, JUST TO *LIVE!*
Nya ha ha!
Hee, Hee!
mrmr mrmr
SLANDERED AND DESPISED, NEVER ACCEPTED FOR WHO I WAS...I *KNOW* HATE, D.S.—AND THOSE RAW WOUNDS HAVE NEVER HEALED!
WHEN THE VARIOUS FACTIONS OF WOOD ELVES AT LAST WENT TO WAR...
...I WAS THEIR FIRST CASUALTY! THE DARK ELVES, WHO HAD GRANTED ME THEIR GRUDGING ASYLUM...
RMBRMBRMB
...*THREW ME OUT!*

I COULDN'T UNDERSTAND... FOR DAYS I WANDERED THE BURNED FIELDS, LOOKING FOR MY TRIBE...

THEY FINALLY HAD THEIR EXCUSE—

MY POOR, SWEET GIRL...

tip tup

BUT THEY WERE LONG GONE. I WAS *ALONE*.

KWIP

KA-BLAM

Greaah!

BONAN

fsh

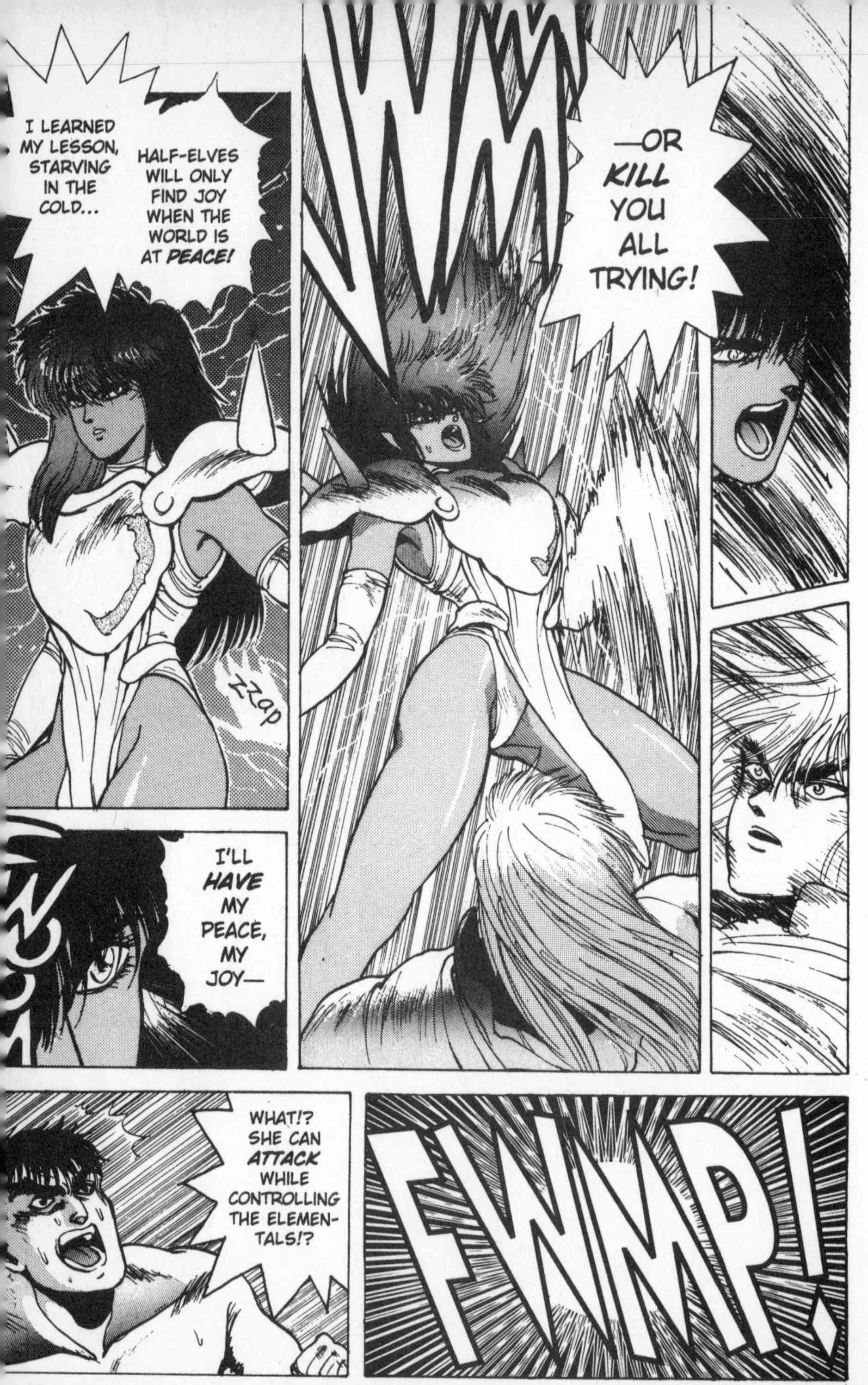
I LEARNED MY LESSON, STARVING IN THE COLD...
HALF-ELVES WILL ONLY FIND JOY WHEN THE WORLD IS AT *PEACE!*
zzap
I'LL *HAVE* MY PEACE, MY JOY—
—OR *KILL* YOU ALL TRYING!
WHAT!? SHE CAN *ATTACK* WHILE CONTROLLING THE ELEMENTALS!?
FWMP!

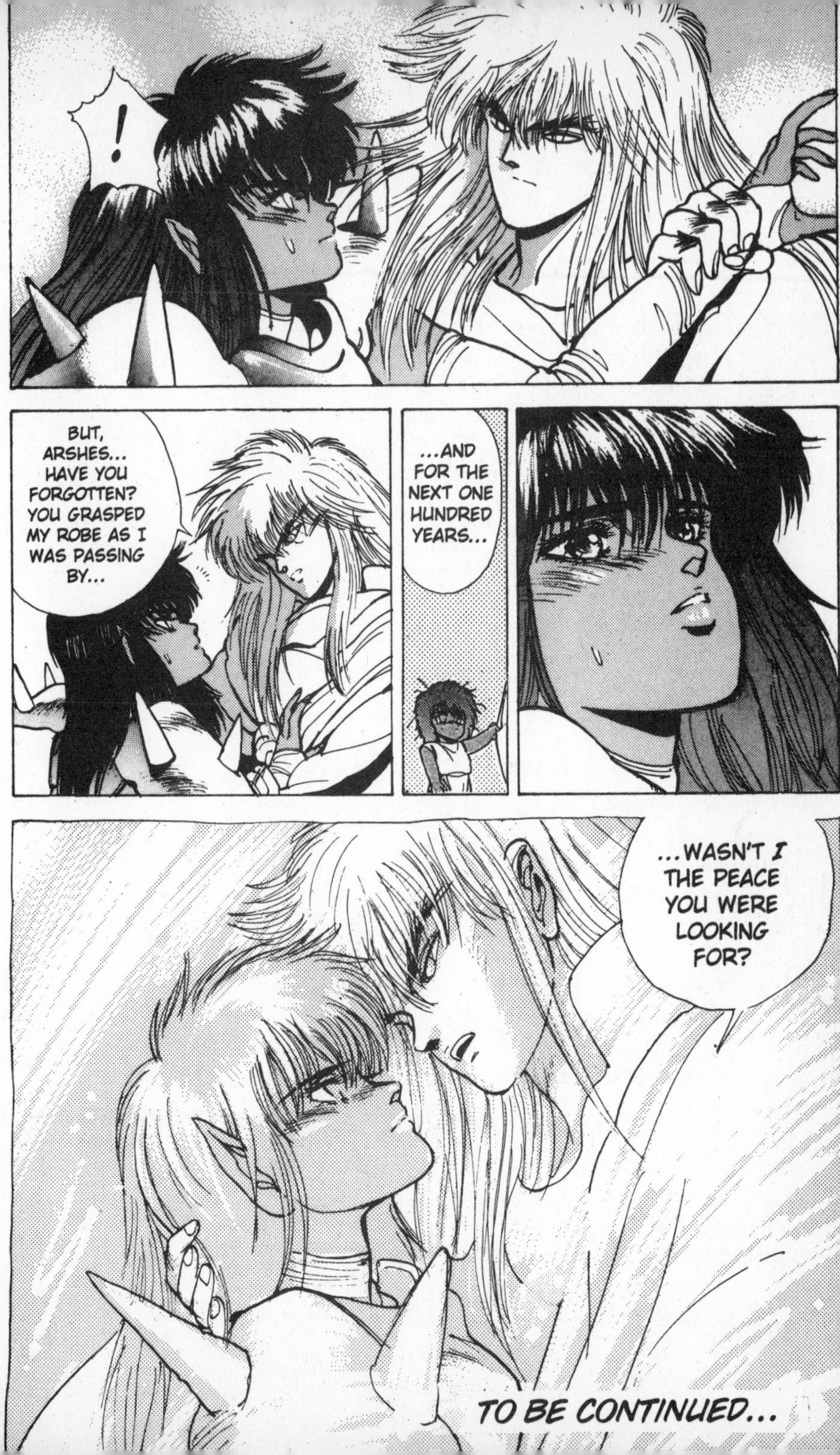
!
BUT, ARSHES... HAVE YOU FORGOTTEN? YOU GRASPED MY ROBE AS I WAS PASSING BY...
...AND FOR THE NEXT ONE HUNDRED YEARS...
...WASN'T *I* THE PEACE YOU WERE LOOKING FOR?
TO BE CONTINUED...

A NOTE FROM THE REWRITER

Is adapting **BASTARD!!** into English a guilty pleasure, a catharsis, or a tag team relay race? I'm never quite sure, truth to tell.

The mayhem level of the book is at an all-time high, mixing exuberantly innocent, in-your-face sexuality with malevolently vicious violence—a demonically potent brew, to be sure. Strangely, I don't mind.

Perhaps it's the challenge of giving Hagiwara's opus the page-turning glee it deserves. Tongue planted firmly in cheek, I mutter each snatch of dialogue and every sound effect aloud, striving for the most outrageous sense of fun I can find. It's not a book I can work on in a local café, that's for damn sure!

Each installment of **BASTARD!!** goes through four drafts to get it exactly right. From Kaori Kawakubo Inoue, our translator, the script heads to note-jotting Jason Thompson, editor extraordinaire, before reaching mild-mannered me. Jason's final gloss assures that I haven't totally lost my marbles somewhere along the way. In other words, **BASTARD!!** gets care and attention like nobody's business.

I'm not sure where on my resumé it says, "enjoys stringing Heavy Metal song titles into melodramatic incantations," but I'm glad someone finally put me to the test!

—Fred Burke

PRODUCTION NOTES

In the original Japanese edition of **BASTARD!!**, Kazushi Hagiwara often included messages to his friends and staff in the margin of the comics. We've kept some of these in the English version, but the others, which were removed, are listed here.

P.112
Ito Okahiko-*sensei*, I'd like to return the reference book that I borrowed from you, but...
P.118
Sheila's costume design by Miyo Ito [heart symbol]. Thanks!
P.137
Guess it didn't go as well as when Hataike-san did it [probably a reference to Hiroyuki Hataike, character and mecha designer for many anime, including "concept design" for the **BASTARD!!** anime.]
P.197
Qubeley [most likely a reference to the AMX-004 Qubeley from ZETA GUNDAM, which (1) has big shoulderpads like Arshes' armor, (2) has psychically controlled laser guns which circle around it like air elementals, and (3) is driven by a psychic pilot.]

COMPLETE OUR SURVEY AND LET US KNOW WHAT YOU THINK!

☐ Please check here if you DO NOT wish to receive information or future offers from VIZ

Name: _____

Address: _____

City: _____ **State:** _____ **Zip:** _____

E-mail: _____

☐ **Male**   ☐ **Female**   **Date of Birth** (mm/dd/yyyy): ___/___/_____ (Under 13? Parental consent required)

What race/ethnicity do you consider yourself? (please check one)

☐ Asian/Pacific Islander   ☐ Black/African American   ☐ Hispanic/Latino

☐ Native American/Alaskan Native   ☐ White/Caucasian   ☐ Other: _____

What VIZ product did you purchase? (check all that apply and indicate title purchased)

☐ DVD/VHS _____

☐ Graphic Novel _____

☐ Magazines _____

☐ Merchandise _____

Reason for purchase: (check all that apply)

☐ Special offer   ☐ Favorite title   ☐ Gift

☐ Recommendation   ☐ Other _____

Where did you make your purchase? (please check one)

☐ Comic store   ☐ Bookstore   ☐ Mass/Grocery Store

☐ Newsstand   ☐ Video/Video Game Store   ☐ Other: _____

☐ Online (site: _____)

What other VIZ properties have you purchased/own? _____

_____

How many anime and/or manga titles have you purchased in the last year? How many were VIZ titles? (please check one from each column)

ANIME
☐ None
☐ 1-4
☐ 5-10
☐ 11+

MANGA
☐ None
☐ 1-4
☐ 5-10
☐ 11+

VIZ
☐ None
☐ 1-4
☐ 5-10
☐ 11+

I find the pricing of VIZ products to be: (please check one)

☐ Cheap ☐ Reasonable ☐ Expensive

What genre of manga and anime would you like to see from VIZ? (please check two)

☐ Adventure ☐ Comic Strip ☐ Detective ☐ Fighting
☐ Horror ☐ Romance ☐ Sci-Fi/Fantasy ☐ Sports

What do you think of VIZ's new look?

☐ Love It ☐ It's OK ☐ Hate It ☐ Didn't Notice ☐ No Opinion

THANK YOU! Please send the completed form to:

NJW Research
42 Catharine St.
Poughkeepsie, NY 12601

All information provided will be used for internal purposes only. We promise not to sell or otherwise divulge your information.